ALMOST A GENTLEMAN

John Osborne is one of the most successful and respected British playwrights since the Second World War. His plays include *Look Back in Anger* and *The Entertainer*. *A Better Class of Person*, the first volume of his autobiography, was recently made into a television film.

John Osborne

ALMOST A GENTLEMAN

An Autobiography

VOLUME II
1955–1966

faber and faber

First published in 1991
by Faber and Faber Limited
3 Queen Square London WC1N 3AU
This paperback edition first published in 1992

Printed in Great Britain by Clays Ltd, St Ives plc

© John Osborne, 1991

John Osborne is hereby identified as author of this work
in accordance with Section 77 of the Copyright,
Designs and Patents Act 1988.

A CIP record for this book is
available from the British Library

ISBN 0-571-16635-0

2 4 6 8 10 9 7 5 3 1

To Lucy

Contents

Illustrations

OSBORNE, JOHN (JAMES): Actor, dramatist, Welsh-Fulham upstart; *b* 12 Dec. 1929; *s* of Thomas Godfrey Osborne of Newport, Mon. (*d* 1940), and Nellie Beatrice Grove of Fulham, Stoneleigh and Ewell; *educ* Ewell Boys' and Emsleigh Road schools, Belmont College, British Institute of Fiction Writing Science, Gaycroft School of Music, Dancing, Speech, Elocution and Drama; *engaged* 1947, Renee Shippard (eng't diss. 1948); *mistress* 1948, Stella Linden (diss. 1949); *m* 1951, Pamela Elizabeth Lane.

Career: Benn Bros reporter on *Gas World, Nursery World, The Miller* (ed. Arnold Running), 1947; ASM No. 2 tour *No Room at the Inn*; *Treasure Island*, Brighton (pirate), 1948; ASM Leicester; ASM tour *The Blue Angel*; Ilfracombe Rep; co-manager Victoria Theatre Hayling Island (title role *Hamlet*), 1950; Bridgwater Rep; Harry Hanson Company Camberwell, 1951; Frinton-on-Sea Rep; ASM tour *Rain*, 1952; Juv. Char. Kidderminster; Derby Rep, 1953; Arts Council Welsh tour *Pygmalion* (Freddy Eynsford Hill), 1954; *Seagulls over Sorrento*, Morecambe, 1955.

Plays: *The Devil Inside* (with Stella Linden), 1950, Theatre Royal Huddersfield; *Personal Enemy*, 1953 (unperf'd); *Epitaph for George Dillon* (with Anthony Creighton), 1954 (unperf'd); *Look Back in Anger*, 1955 (unperf'd).

I do not have the least pretension to 'appear before God, book in hand,' declaring myself the 'best of men', nor to write 'confessions'. I shall tell only what I wish to tell; and the reader who refuses me in his absolution must needs be harsh to the point of unorthodoxy for I will admit none but venial sins.

Hector Berlioz, *Memoirs*, 1848

A Stiff Prick hath no conscience.

St Augustine

Decidedly ours is a prosaic century.

Hector Berlioz, *Memoirs*, 1848

It is almost a definition of a gentleman to say he is one who never inflicts pain.

John Henry Newman, *The Idea of a University*, 1852

1. A Palpable Miss

M/Y *Egret*,
Cubitt's Yacht Basin,
London W12
12 August 1955

In that midsummer I felt oddly if unaccountably idling-over on some slow charge. It was an unfamiliar feeling, something like a rare intake of heart's ease. I was twenty-five and, for such an importunate soul as I certainly was then, the auguries were discouraging if not downright damning.

Trying to order the chaos of hindsight now, my spirit was partially disabled by diffidence but also fuelled by what was regarded as a reckless, untutored frenzy, a puzzling arrogance, destructive to others and to myself. That seemed to be the implicit impression I created among all those I encountered in my profession. Pamela Lane, my first wife, had confirmed this only a year before, refusing to keep faith with what she saw as a pursuit of distressful disorder. Anyway, I was easily and happily ignorable in those days, when I must have looked most certain to go away. And quite soon.

I didn't feel liberated from Pamela. The prospect of divorce never entered my sometimes wild projections of the future as I moped around the Welsh villages on an Arts Council tour of *Pygmalion*. I would simply resist any approximation to my feelings during those shocked, brooding months after we separated. Writing and finishing *Look Back in Anger* presented no purge or lasting comfort, no justification by either faith or works. I had addressed myself to events in some way. They were particular and personal, but they were not confined to the hulk of my marriage nor even to the wider constraints of general indifference, dislike or mere torpor.

For the first time I had written a play on my own. It had taken me something like seventeen days in all. It had been a sprint. I was apprehensive that anyone might pay attention to my solo dash. 'Don't expect anything. Then you won't be disappointed.' It was the battle-cry of misery of my mother, Nellie Beatrice, a little like the famous wartime catch-phrase, 'It's being so cheerful as keeps me going.' Nothing was so deadly as this sanctimonious, more-cheerful-than-thouness. I continued, then as now, to expect everything, disappointment most of all. It has been a useful mechanism.

I was beholden to no one. Pamela had told me that our three-year-old marriage and her career in the theatre were irreconcilable. She had taken up with a Jewish dentist in Derby. But I began to feel that her all-too-accountable desertion would resolve itself. I began to relish my celibacy. The acceptance of even temporary celibacy a few months before would have seemed like an Establishment heresy, handed down by magistrates, lady journalists, Tory MPs and BBC governors. At that time, the vows of poverty, chastity and obedience were abhorrent. Later, only obedience seemed unthinkable.

Pamela would come back. Our marriage could not be a closed incident, nor an open – or, worse, healed – wound. I felt oddly content to wait on events. Indecision can be a dangerous pawn, but not to those who are set to play an importunate game from the outset. I have seldom failed to rush in, to tread all over the place. But I check the time first very carefully. It is the one gift in which I have almost complete confidence.

Anyway, in that late summer of 1955 I had nowhere to rush in, let alone tread. Pamela was still working at Derby Rep. The telephone hadn't rung for weeks. The sun was shining on the creaky hull of M/Y *Egret* almost every working morning. Painting the length of the boat in nursery-like colours, listening to the Black Box record-player, reading Conrad while Anthony Creighton (my former fellow actor and 'collaborator') messed about with his primitive electronics, there seemed to be a summery, vibrant lull in the air which I hadn't felt much since days in the grass watching frogs and dragonflies as an eight-year-old.

My entitlement to forty-two shillings a week dole money had lapsed, but my expenses were minimal. My half contribution to the weekly mooring fee was ten shillings, Calor gas was cheap for the galley, and we used paraffin oil for the ancient heating-stove. Anthony and I were both vegetarian. I had converted him to a meatless diet not through evangelistic zeal but by practical appeal to our budget.

My own vegetarianism had been prompted by self-interest. I wanted to confound my pitted complexion, implacable daily headaches, throbbing glands, dish-cloth hair and dandruff. That my appearance had marginally improved (though not the headaches) was no doubt due a little to less toxic input. I still lived in some dread of the White Plague that had struck my sister and father and I felt I must be severe with myself at least in this matter of food. I had a superstition that if I could achieve my father's age of thirty-nine, and pass it, I would have managed a kind of pilgrimage into another, less chancy country. Meat could be equated with inner squalor. Vegetarianism might banish that, too.

Just as Pamela and I had consumed mounds of dull but decently cooked cabbage laced with the luxury of half a tin of baked beans, Anthony and I plucked the plentiful nettles from the river bank and stewed them lightly, congratulating ourselves on our homespun ingenuity. They tasted like sweeter spinach and, if you liked spinach, quite pleasant. Combined with the occasional Nuttolene health-shop fantasy like 'Risserole', or the lusty-sounding 'meatless steaks' and as much New Zealand cheddar as we could afford, we just managed to avoid actual hunger.

'If you don't eat it up, you'll grow up to look like Mr Attlee.' After 1945 my grandmother was still telling me that more than one bath a week was 'weakening', that I was outgrowing my strength and that Aneurin Bevin was a wicked man. The GIs, who had never bothered to count their change and left it on the bar counter for my mother to pick up, had gone. If one word applied to that post-war decade it was inertia. Enthusiasm there was not, in this climate of fatigue. Jimmy Porter was hurt because things had remained the same. Colonel Redfern grieved that everything had changed. They were both wrong, but that was hard to see at the time.

The country was tired, not merely from the sacrifice of two back-breaking wars but from the defeat and misery between them. The bits of red on the map were disappearing as the flags came down and the names we knew on mixed packets of postage stamps were erased. Like so much else, it all happened without people being very aware of it. The leaping hare of the Victorian imagination had begun to imitate the tortoise even before 1914, but in that summer of 1955 it was still easy enough to identify what we regarded as a permanent Establishment. The continued acceptance of hanging, the prosecution of homosexuals, and censorship in film and theatre made life easy for the liberal conscience. The Conservative Party could still be stigmatized as figures of fun on their grouse moors; Etonians dominated the Cabinet. The radical spirit would be unprepared for the new middle-class oligarchy when the old Establishment of Law, Church and Parliament was supplanted by neo-Tory grocers, PR men, trainee consultants and Gary and Tracey pink and greasy from a bargain-break on the Costa del Sol.

The physical excitement of writing *Look Back* turned the simplest negative pleasures into overpowering, self-imposed awards. The realization that one can change one's life as easily as shifting the furniture, rehanging a picture or discarding an ugly present has been a recurrent bonus. This has nothing to do with faithlessness or inconsistency; rather it is a natural versatility of spirit, a quality often suspect as frivolous. Perhaps Jimmy Porter did owe a glancing debt, though not much, to my first wife. For the moment, some pride, not altogether paltry, prevented me from contacting her. To be tentative was beyond me. It usually is. Later, after much dubious frenzy, I succeeded rather more with God than I ever did with Pamela.

3

Something, I felt, was going to turn up – if not God, something.

By early August, the wispy copies of the manuscript of *Look Back*, typed on Pamela's twenty-first birthday present from her parents, had been rejected, often with an exasperated or even gleeful parting cuff or kick, by every theatrical management and play agent I could find listed in the *Writers' and Artists' Yearbook*. The speed with which it had been returned was not surprising, but its aggressive dispatch did give me a kind of baffled relief. It was like being grasped at the upper arm by a testy policeman and told to move on. And not later, but at once. I might, as Kitty Black (then the doyenne of agents) had made clear, be put on a charge. Loitering with intent. Up to no good to anyone, and a particular nuisance to agents.

The play had been finished on 3 June, and only weeks later it was already ragged with over-active policing. The people responding to it in this way were not those to be incensed by mediocrity. Being purveyors of it, this was surely not the quality that had driven them to such quick offence. The implication was that I might have been guilty of an unintended breach of the peace rather than merely writing a dull and untheatrical work. There was a vehement, undisputed judgement: the play was a palpable miss.

The future loomed out of grasp but I had an apprehension of something and, for the moment, I was able and prepared for it to appear in some unforeseeable form. On 12 August it did. George Devine's weighty tread ended the lull undramatically on that summer day, but I knew I detected a difference. If it wasn't hope, which comes from within, it was the shadow of energy, which blessedly sometimes does come from without.

> Born with a contrite heart and a glimmering of sin, opposed to guilt, I came to realize that it is this opposition that divides the religious from the secular spirit.
>
> *Notebook*, 1963

Devine grappled aboard M/Y *Egret* from the rowing-boat he had commandeered. He had disregarded my instructions about how to reach me, avoiding the afternoon tide, and I was already timorously wishing I had persuaded him to let me visit him at his house in Hammersmith's Lower Mall. It was clear that he was determined to scrutinize his unknown author in his own cage. I clumsily hauled him on to the deck.

George was then forty-three, a heavy man, looking larger than he was, though not the huge bear-like figure he had been during his Young Vic days. All his old pupils insisted that some sea-change had taken place in him since then which had altered not only his girth but, more significantly, his personality.

4

I was not aware of this at the time, being confused by my remembrance of him as an endearing, innocent-seeming Tesman in *Hedda Gabler* and the harsh, terse voice I had heard over the telephone a few days earlier. I was still disconcerted by the way he had banged down the receiver with a peremptory grunt that made me feel I had already taxed his patience before we had even met. Seeing him appear through the trees with his blue open-neck shirt flapping over his trousers and his sandalled bare feet, I felt foolishly and inappropriately dressed in my give-away Loamshire blazer and flannels. I realized that I must look like some vapid juvenile in a Rank comedy about medical students breezing about on houseboats. It was too late to go below and change my absurd costume into some Left-Bank-ish outfit, stale with pastis and Gauloises.

'If I didn't have white hair and smoke a pipe, no one would listen to me,' he was to say later. On that day, he seemed younger and more foxy-nosed than I had expected. Far from being irritated by the delays of getting to the boat, he was amused as if bent on some unexpected scent. We went below while he asked questions and I tried to divest myself of Juv. Char. appearance, removing my clubby tie swiftly to look the more roughed-up serious before the initial image became indelible. The blue blazer, saved for and bought in Bridgwater for all-purpose use in Home Counties comedies, seemed to ring out like a leper's bell, begging radical scorn. It proclaimed my background of provincial hard-tat.

I anticipated a quick merciless viva and merciful dismissal. However little I knew of him, I was certain that George would not only refuse to suffer fools gladly but would make it quickly clear and row away, growling his irritation to the tides. What I had not anticipated was that he was driven by that most blessed of human virtues, abiding and open curiosity. That and unfeigned hope, in the face – most literally and finally – of cigar-wielding lackeys, vocational by-liners and even their voracious stringers.

George was to earn £2,000 a year as the first Artistic Director of the English Stage Company at the Royal Court Theatre. His assistant, Tony Richardson, was paid £14 a week. Neither time nor the imponderabilities of international financial trends in the following thirty years can conceal the fact that subsidy, patronage, loony licence and afraid-and-feigning fashion, disavowing elitism at every turn, have created a cultural system which is no more than democracy gone mad, where every Jack and Jill is better than their patron-person. 'I'm afraid that kind of idealism doesn't exist any longer,' the Chairman of the ESC said to me years later. The Sloane Square red hill-billies beamed.

George sat down on one of the shaky bunks in the main cabin and looked about him. Quickly, I decided that scrutiny was a natural part of his character, that it was not assumed and apparently not censorious. His censure seemed brutal, harsh and intent. His interest was patent and open. Perhaps this spirit led him so eagerly to buy women's magazines, like *Seventeen* and *Honey*, at railway terminals and read them in the pursuit of some small enlightenment on the way to provincial theatres, with more relish and sympathy than he read the playscripts brimming out of his briefcase.

George interrogated me closely, not only about my professional record but about my past and present personal life. It was probing but not prurient. Giving a half-way interesting account of myself had seemed unlikely enough a few hours ago, but his late arrival, and several whiskies burning a sore and acid inside, made me garrulous and even defiant.

It was strange to be examined in this encouraging manner. The Labour Exchange, the National Assistance man and my mother were the only ones who had expressed their cold interest in me during the preceding year. 'When do you think you will get a job?' 'Don't you think it's a funny profession you've chosen?' 'What makes you think you'll get on where all the others haven't?' Pride, for one thing. 'You can't go on like this for ever.' For the sake of forty shillings a week it was politic and fairly easy to agree. For the sake of a few tins of fruit and vegetables, it was neither too contemptible nor humiliating to bear Nellie Beatrice's company on her day off. 'You don't seem very lucky, do you? Poor kid. If only you could have been a barrister or a doctor.' Such Golders Green sentiments from my anti-Semitic mother had their horsefly charm.

Devine, of Wadham (like his associate, Richardson), Old and Young Vic, *gonfalonier* of Copeau, mask and mime, stern brother disciple of Saint-Denis, had come round to the tradesmen's entrance to chat to someone whose entire theatrical experience was below-stairs. Some sour euphoria lifted me up as I recited, like previous convictions, the reps I had managed to infiltrate: Kidderminster, Ilfracombe, Bridgwater, Sidmouth, Leicester, Dartford. Almost a Shakespearian sequence – Talbot, Gloucester, Hereford, Warwick, Northumberland. 'My Lords, ill news from the north. Kidderminster is dead and Bridgwater fled.' I asked for other convictions on number-three tours, twice-nightly and one-night stands to be taken into consideration. I felt much better. I offered George a drink, but the prospect of whisky at four o'clock in the afternoon clearly impressed him even less than the details of my career. Red wine was his day-long tipple, the bouquet of De Flores, as I found out later. He had a misty, underarm Beaujolais tang, not entirely unpleasant but a little forbidding, like the odour of black priestliness.

I ventured to smoke my pipe, but he had the pedantic pipe-smoker's cold eye for the novice, although I had been smoking one with some discrimination,

I thought, since I was fifteen. An old gentleman in a park in Aberdeen had even patted me gently on the shoulder, saying, 'It's good to see a young laddie enjoying the best companionship the world can offer. A pipe's your friend for life and ye canna say that for man nor woman.'

There is a fundamental antagonism between tobacco and women. One diminishes the other. This is so true that sooner or later men in love with women stop smoking because they feel or imagine that tobacco has a deadening effect on sexual desire and the sexual act. The fact is that love is gross and material compared with the spirituality of a pipe.

The Goncourt Journal, 18 July 1868

Years later, I gave George a pair of Dunhill pipes in a case for a Christmas present. He barely glanced at them and said, 'There's only one place to buy a pipe and that's Charatan's.' Thereafter I patronized them obediently until a few years ago I went into Dunhill's in Jermyn Street and bought the most enjoyable and reliable pipe I have ever owned (an ex-wife having smashed my previously prized one). I told the gentleman behind the counter of George's invocation to Charatan. He smiled. 'Oh, yes, sir. But it depends upon what you *want*.' When I bought my first car, I chose an Austin 110, a smartish, middle-priced model of the time. Parked confidently outside the stage door of the Royal Court, I showed it to George. He scarcely glanced at its creamy roominess and dashing crimson streak. 'Good God!' he growled. 'Why didn't you get an Alfa Giulietta? That's a *grocer's* car.'

That first August afternoon, he was particularly intrigued by my lunging performance as Hamlet in Hayling Island. 'We're interested in actors who are writers.' Or was it writers who were actors? He asked me what else I'd written. I mumbled about my 1950 Huddersfield World Première, luridly titled *The Devil Inside*, but not that I'd written it in collaboration with my mistress, nor that it had limped on for barely a week. Writing a play in tandem seemed a rather folksy enterprise. Anyway, George's somewhat vinegary puritanism was obvious even from the little I knew of his reputation.

Nor did I mention my two verse plays, so succinctly described by Pamela as 'dull and boring'. George's disapproval of Fry, Ustinov and John Whiting was almost startling in its bitterness: 'They're all absolute shit.' It was a little breathtaking. I was only accustomed to this kind of throw-away vehemence from myself.

I cautiously referred to *Epitaph for George Dillon*. Anthony had been characteristically over-excited about George's visit. If not *Look Back*, why not the play we had cobbled together barely nine months before? I hadn't thought of it. I wanted my own thoroughbred, as I saw it, to be paraded in the ring alone, not with a part-owned stable-companion.

From the garbled reports I'd received from Stratford-upon-Avon, then run by Anthony Quayle, I had the strong impression that returning officers and men who were palpably men were the order of the day. Knowing a little of George's war record and believing that men who had experienced killing with their bare hands would not tolerate epicene recruits, I had persuaded Anthony to stay in his cabin and wait for the all-clear invitation to join us. I feared that, fortified by gin, he would lurch in and, literally, queer my uneasy pitch.

George was obviously interested that I was living in this leaky old Rhine barge, only a mile downriver from his own pretty eighteenth-century house. Typically, he asked me closely about the economics of it, the cost of Calor gas, the mooring rental, the special telephone rate. I was forced to say that I was sharing it with another actor, not revealing that the boat actually belonged to him. It was acceptable enough that two young actors should live together in this way without any sexual implications, but I knew that I was dealing with someone of a rather particular generation. I had referred to my marriage to an actress and that we were living apart for the moment. I offered no confidence and none was sought, like the information that the telephone had been temporarily disconnected. It would either be repaired or not.

People often assumed that Anthony and I were lovers. This didn't bother me much but I didn't want this kind of absurdity to cloud my early encounter and cast new meanings upon the play (although they are meted out to this day in dumb textbooks imposed upon children for their A-levels). And my apprehensions were not entirely misguided. The Denville Players of Scarborough had made their conditions of employment brutally laconic: 'No fancy salaries and no queer folk.' It was as uncompromising as the cards then displayed in Hammersmith newsagents' windows: 'No Blacks. No Irish.' We at least knew where we stood.

I don't remember George's words, I doubt if there were any, but the implication was unmistakable. In the newly formed, middle-class-liberal English Stage Company, principles would be applied as rigorously as by the Denville Players. No fancy salaries and the nod that queer folk were not to be considered, certainly not as officer material.

2. Camp Following

The Carlyle,
New York

At last I can write about my particular sins without Lord Chamberlain-induced sex-change dishonesty, and even without fear of fussing Aunt Edna overmuch. But my own sins bore me terribly, which may be the lethargy of old age creeping over me, or just the disinclination to join in the chorus of voices endlessly *shouting* the love that once dared not speak its name, from every housetop in every country. Perhaps I should rewrite *Deep Blue Sea* as it really was meant to be, but after 20 years I just can't remember why I made all that fuss. 'Emotion recollected in tranquillity?' What balls! It's just another tranquil non-emotion, like T.S. Eliot.

Love,
Terry

Letter from Terence Rattigan to J.O., 1968

There was a bruised Forgotten Army side to George's antagonisms that was not always realistic. He was still sounding me out as the light was fading on the Thames, quizzing me about individual plays. I let slip that I had more or less admired *The Browning Version*. Realizing my error, I hedged that I had no high opinion of *Separate Tables*. Before I had time to compound my blunder on *The Deep Blue Sea*, he cut me short about the patent inadequacies of homosexual plays masquerading as plays about straight men and women.

Rattigan was later to write me long letters in the small hours from Bermuda and Paris, bitterly repudiating his deceptions, urging me against his own example and against becoming a tax exile. In both cases I was scarcely at risk. I have been upbraided constantly for a crude, almost animal, inability to dissemble. As for tax exile, not simple patriotism but hubris, middling xenophobia and dependence on the comforts of history and homeland make it seem as chilling as the prospect of the bang on the closing gates at the Scrubs.

Like many a lifetime radical of his generation, George was unaware of his own bigotry and sentimentality, which he saw as a harsh endorsement of plain honesty. But if ever an old dog unknowingly gave sanctuary to his fleas it was George Devine, however much he scratched in puzzlement.

As I was to discover, he was torn by so many conflicting instincts. A loveless childhood, abetted by a miserable legacy from his sharp-spined mother and an austere entry into a theatre he disliked, followed by seven bitterly resented years in the Royal Artillery, had left him as suspicious as he was responsive. His private life was dominated by a cold marriage and then by an affair with the designer Jocelyn Herbert (known as 'Brown' because of her addiction to dun-coloured sets) clouded by her self-sacrifice of 'waiting until the children have grown up'.

Perhaps his despondent years in Burma and then the harsh nursery world of the Young Vic had made him a blindfold victim of events, like enduring shell-shock or battle fatigue. He seemed to believe, in a simple-hearted way, that the blight of buggery, which then dominated the theatre in all its frivolity, could be kept down decently by a direct appeal to seriousness and good intentions from his own crack corps of heterosexual writers, directors and actors.

I was never properly privy to all aspects of Royal Court life and procedure. The abiding strength of homosexual strategy is to promote and encourage conspiracy. Only the players grasp the game, and one of its purposes is to make outsiders feel foolish. It was many months of walking in the late hours from George's house in Lower Mall back to the *Egret* before I realized the route was a kasbah for the cavortings of future Royal Court alumni. I did hear squeals and heavy rustling from the towpath but attributed them, rather enviously, to what were still known as 'courting couples'. Courting it was, Royal and male.

Working long into the night, George was equally unaware of this nocturnal scampering only yards from his desk. The love that dared not speak its name was not yet shrilling it from the roof-tops. I doubt if he knew, in those days of wine and Durex, of the supplies of penicillin rushed like plasma to the Dressing Station Upstairs at the Court for crusading veterans to staunch syphilitic wounds in mid-rehearsal. So sophisticated did this Dressing Station become in the mid-sixties that there was a map on the wall charting which swimming-pools and Turkish baths had been recently visited by certain of the theatre's directors. Flags dotted the metropolis for Royal Court strategic positions just as I had once plotted the course of Montgomery's stalemate and the Ardennes offensive.

George, who wanted at all times to have some idea where he was in a reeling universe, was repeatedly probing the overblown mysteries of camp. I tried without much success to lift one or two veils for him. He would ring me up earnestly: Was *I* camp? 'Now, I think we can take it that Mozart is camp. Or is he really? Then what about Beethoven? Byron, no. Kipling certainly not. What about Tennyson?' And so on.

However, we were not yet at that stage of confidence, if any. Getting there was to take a long time. I suppose we both did little more at that first meeting than throw down hints as if we were strange partners at a card game. But the Devine Grunt – more eloquent than his reluctant attempts at rhetoric – confirmed that I had been offered £25 from the English Stage Company for a year's option on *Look Back in Anger* with a £50 renewal clause. George was unapologetic about the sum but gave the weary impression that it was insufficient. I tried not to appear grateful.

Neither did I know then how deeply his contact with the unsmiling pieties of umbilical Francophilia had wounded and isolated his already lonely spirit. For as long as I could remember the literary and academic classes seemed to have been tyrannized by the French. The 'posh papers' every Sunday blubbered with self-abasement in the face of the bombast of the French language and its absurd posture as the torch-bearer of Logic, which apparently was something to which no one in these islands had access.

Certain writers gave the impression that it was downright indelicate to write in English at all, which is why the *Sunday Times* and the *Observer* were peppered with italics until they sometimes looked like linguistic lace curtains:

JIMMY: I've just read three whole columns on the English Novel. Half of
    it's in French. Do the Sunday papers make *you* feel ignorant?
CLIFF: Not 'arf.

Look Back in Anger

What we all needed was a short, sharp shock of clear-round-the-bend French logic: a dollop of the gynaecological metaphysic of Simone de Beauvoir, a trilogy from Sartre and a slice of melodrama from Camus, cigarette ever a-dangle at the café table, the existentialist Rick of *Casablanca*. Of all the gin joints in the world, Oxbridge men clamoured for a stool at this bar, and George was up there with them. Concepts like Being and Essence sound different with a tongue up your nose.

Concealed mystification of a very lofty sort seemed to prevail. Angus Wilson's stories, *The Wrong Set*, had been greeted like the tide of Elizabethan England, but Waugh and Greene were smirked at. Shaw was still regarded as a serious thinker, an adroit dramatist who had got a bit silly to himself in his dotage. T.S. Eliot was transferred from the then-revered closet of Edinburgh to a bewildered and respectful boulevard public in London. Christopher Fry was received with uneasy relief. Noël Coward was shown the door. He went against received Lit. Crit.

Chesham Place, sw1

I really am very grateful for your letter. It gave me a sharp and much deserved jolt. I absolutely agree that it is unnecessary and unkind to hand out my opinions of my colleagues to journalists. It is also pompous. I know by the grace and firmness of your letter that you will forgive me if I have inadvertently hurt you or even irritated you. I think far too highly of you to wish to do either of these things. I regret very much that since we first met we have known each other so little. This at least can be remedied if you are willing. There is so much that I would like to talk to you about even if our views on plays and playwrights may differ. Please come to lunch with me here either on Monday, Tuesday or Friday of next week or the Monday or Friday of the following week. You see I am pinning you down ruthlessly for the simple reason that I would truly like to see you. Please come. I shall not ask anyone else. What you said in your letter about admiration and respect is entirely mutual. You can telephone me here any morning.

Noël

Letter from Noël Coward to J.O., 1966

George was anxious for me to meet his associate director, Tony Richardson, and asked me along to 9 Lower Mall. Sophie Devine, George's wife, showed me up to his study. He was sitting at a drawing-board, a reassuring sight in itself. Perhaps play-making was an exercise to be worked out on a high stool with T-squares.

He called up the stairs and Richardson appeared. He had the authoritative stoop of a gangler who is born to mastery. In what was to become one of the most imitated voices in his profession he said, 'I think *Look Back in Anger* is the best play written since the war.' He announced himself as its director like a confiding toastmaster.

George sighed. 'You'll have to have an agent, I'm afraid.'

Agents have not changed much since I first became dependent upon them. To be dependent on an agent is like entrusting your most precious future to your mother-in-law or your bookmaker. Most of the female of the species even behave like mothers-in-law, dreaded by many a playwright's wife as she finds her weekends hounded by advice on her spouse's diet, work routine and sexual needs or deficiencies, patent to no one but the agent herself. Like shop stewards, flying pickets or the executive car salesmen of the new Conservative

Party, agents despise both innovation and tradition, protecting the laws of deceit, avarice and self-aggrandizement of those they 'represent'.

There were, and may be, exceptions. When I was once threatened with litigation by a Hollywood film producer, and in no position to bargain from any foreseeable strength, Robin Fox advised me: 'Tell him to go fuck himself, dear boy.' It may sound like little enough, but agents are unwilling to bite the hand of their most enduring source of 10 per cent, the manager or the producer.

Thirty years ago, in those days before television and video residuals, matters may have seemed more gentlemanly because the pickings were not so rich. A respectable agent with two or three stage stars and a brace of tried playwrights might earn a comfortable living without his secretary even having to call him to the telephone. Their main preoccupation was that they and their wives were given the best first-night stall seats, where they formed clear pools of indifference or grudging swank.

Even before Lindsay Anderson tried, to the terror of the English Stage Company and the even more craven Arts Council, to exclude critics from the Royal Court in a rather hilarious campaign against some nonentity, I made a similar effort to ban the presence of the bat-like predator-agent from first nights. This time the resistance came, predictably, from the actors. They were appalled at being deprived of what they inexplicably regarded as their 'support'. Fighting cocks may have felt some comfort from their 'supporters'. A dead cock has no supporters.

'They're none of them any good, any of them,' said George that day, 'but I'm afraid you're going to need one. It's a choice of two – Margery Vosper or Peggy Ramsay.' George looked doubtful. 'Ramsay's the best, there's no doubt. But I think you'd be better off with Margery. I can't see you and Peggy putting up with each other for long. Margery's a motherly old thing.'

This proved to be shrewd advice. In the event, Peggy Ramsay turned out to be the best agent I never had, extolling me with a generosity that she sometimes seemed to deny members of her own stable. Her sharpest reproof to me was when she demanded: 'Why do you keep *marrying* these women? I'm sure they can't possibly want to marry you! Oh, well, at least you seem to have given up marrying actresses and married a *real* woman this time. No one should marry an actress, least of all a writer.' It was the second, and last, piece of wisdom I received from an agent.

The following week I made an appointment with Margery, who, like most lady agents of the time, invariably wore a hat. She could be found every day at long lunch-time sessions with her colleagues over sausages and Guinness in the pub opposite the stage door of the Apollo Theatre. Again, George was right about her. She was motherly. She sat behind a desk in her office on Shaftesbury Avenue, three cramped, cheerful rooms like the staff quarters of a small, over-priced school for under-elevens. She rose from it like a welcoming headmistress, as if she were used to putting parents and new pupils at their ease.

In 1955 she was over forty, large-chested rather than breasted, with a flat porkpie-ish hat which, with the addition of a veil, would have done well for a modest wedding, like her navy-blue print frock with its comforting tucks and pleats. It was all reassuring if not stimulating. One of the comforts she could be relied on to dispense was an encouragement to modesty and, most welcome, not to take on too much – 'After all, you've done your bit for a while.'

'*Don't* think we should ask too much, dear. Mustn't look as if we're being greedy.' This homely caution meant being well-nigh supplicant to managers and producers. As Hugh 'Binkie' Beaumont, at the head of H.M. Tennant, and Rank and Associated Pictures would ride on indestructibly during her lifetime, this was perhaps a sensible conclusion. Her star prefects and source of income were the Welsh wizard Emlyn Williams and the husband-and-wife team of Hugh and Margaret Williams, purveyors of fragrant drawing-room comedies. They must have been her bread and butter for a good many years. Ronald Duncan, poet and playwright, was her prize-winner, but Margery was a firm believer in eating up your bread and butter and regarding the jam as a nice little treat to look forward to.

She was a kindly woman and I soon grew very fond of her. It was some twenty years before I was able to bring myself to leave her. When I made the decision she fought it fiercely, still believing that I would, as always, overreach myself. Although she must have been quite rich, she lived modestly in a dark but pleasant Edwardian flat off Tottenham Court Road. Her holidays were always spent in a pre-war bungalow in a suburban street in Worthing. She was an ace *Times* crossword-puzzler.

Having already turned the play down without explanation, Margery was a little lady-almonerish when she first met me. She was politely surprised by George's endorsement and baffled that the newly formed English Stage Company, with such board members as her own Ronald Duncan (dubbed 'the Black Dwarf' by Devine and Richardson, because of his diminutive height and poisonous spirit) and the Earl of Harewood, should have offered to advance me £25. 'Well dear,' she said. 'I don't think we're going to make much money out of this one, but it'll be very interesting to see what they say. Very interesting indeed.' It was Margery's verdict on everything I ever wrote.

3. May 8th

I am very much more interested in content than in form. I do not think
any play is really worth producing if it's not a play of ideas. Literally, the
play's the thing.

George Devine, 1956

Tony and George took a monkeyish delight in giving the manuscript of *Look
Back* to colleagues and acquaintances so that they could report their unfavour-
able reactions back to me. They used it as a litmus test of personality and
taste, enjoying my unease as much as the aversion of those who read the play.
One of the most revered of theatre dames loved it least of all. 'It should be
thrown into the river and washed out to sea so that it may never be seen
again.' Tony relished every syllable as he repeated her verdict.

During the months before Christmas I spent more and more evenings at
Lower Mall. I had never met anyone who could create the expectation of
excitement more openly and infectiously than Richardson, the unlikely son of
a bookish Yorkshire chemist. From standstill to breakfast time, visitors popped
in with a casualness that would have rocked those staid and silent suburban
streets of my boyhood in Stoneleigh – Michel Saint-Denis, Glen Byam Shaw,
Lindsay Anderson and Karel Reisz, or Bill Gaskill, pale with fatigue from
working at the all-night bakery down the road. Angus Wilson and Nigel
Dennis came and, later, Ionesco, Beckett, Helene Weigel. French was almost
obligatory and German encouraged.

The English Stage Company was to open at the Court in April the following
year. The first production would be *The Mulberry Bush* by Angus Wilson,
which had been received at the Bristol Old Vic with the unreliable enthusiasm
of London critics soothed by an expenses-paid night at a provincial hotel.
Nigel Dennis had been persuaded by George and Tony to dramatize his novel
Cards of Identity. Angus and Nigel were both novelists, both academic, one
gregarious, the other reclusive, and both discovered in middle age as the herald
voices of the time. George looked to The Novel as the fountainhead for his
dream of new theatrical vitality. Angus and Nigel were comic writers in a clear

tradition, and neither could be accused of frivolity. Could they and others, like Kingsley Amis and John Wain, be persuaded to bring their weight to bear and light up a theatre which had been intellectually disreputable for so long? Would it now be seriously regarded by the *New Statesman* and the *Observer*?

The original founders of the ESC – Ronald Duncan, Lord Harewood and C.E. Blacksell, a buffoon schoolteacher from Barnstaple – all regarded George's blacklist of writers (prosaic Priestley; clownish, commonplace Ustinov; lightweight Fry; frigid Whiting; middle-brow Mortimer) very seriously indeed. Their original intention had been to mount plays by all of them, a strategy George successfully resisted by a concerted campaign of devious manoeuvring over the next ten years.

He put on two of Duncan's plays (*Don Juan in Hell* and *The Death of Satan*) in the opening season with the unconcealed intention of killing them off as soon as possible. Bile was soon to spurt from the Black Dwarf of North Devon as his work was ruthlessly cut up by George and Tony and turned into a triumphantly unpresentable evening.

I was engaged to join the company as an actor after giving an audition for George at the Palace Theatre, where he was appearing in his own production of *King Lear* with John Gielgud. I gave the rabble-rousing speech by Jack Cade from *Henry VI* and, inexplicably, a piece from a particularly bad play by Sean O'Casey, *The Bishop's Bonfire*. George produced it later, and without me. The audition was soon over and never mentioned by either of us.

The Company Manager, Oscar Lewenstein, contracted me. I was to play as cast and understudy for £12 a week. Tony was directing a BBC crime series called *Tales from Soho* and was able to push a couple of one-liners my way. I became play-reader for £2 a week, taking home nightly some thirty or forty scripts. When I once complained of the burden to Tony, he said, his voice rising to its most imitable pitch, 'But you don't *read* them? Not all *through*?' I ventured some pious pretence about talent being missed through hasty scanning. He picked up a few scripts from my bag and went through half a dozen. Some took him twenty seconds, some half a minute, two minutes at most, a high-pitched, awesome Geiger counter. '*There*, that's how you read a play.'

The plays sent in at the time could be divided into a few recognizable categories. A number of them were written by clergymen's wives. Almost every post brought a play about Mary Queen of Scots, the Virgin Queen, Queen Victoria and Lady Jane Grey. These were all regular runners, but Mary Queen of Scots was Red Rum to them all. Then there were the plays about literary figures like D.H. Lawrence or Henry James; Loamshire plays; plays set in the past and plays set in the future where lone survivors of the Atomic Holocaust addressed themselves but not each other. Schoolteachers were almost as prolific as clergymen's wives. I read what was probably Robert Bolt's first play, *A Critic on the Hearth*, and recommended it. Tony made it clear that for someone who had written the best play since the war I had a lamentable critical intelligence.

Casting *Look Back* started early in the new year. Finding Jimmy Porter was certain to be difficult. We were seeking something instantly recognizable to us both. Fortunately we were unaware that we were casting what we were to be told weeks later was an unlikely freak and, later still, an archetype. The problem was the practical one of finding not a new archetype but an actor who could face the withdrawal of audience approval and, even, seem to incite it.

Casting is almost always achieved by default and sometimes by calculated compromise. I am not suggesting that selecting Kenneth Haigh was abject. It was a covert Richardson inspiration. The part claimed Kenneth like a stray dog. But then, there were no other takers. Kenneth took it and Tony nodded. Actors are launched by such nods before agents' demands make them unapproachable and reviewers claim to discover them. Tom Courtenay, Rita Tushingham, Albert Finney, Michael Caine, Sean Connery were all given this impeccable auction nod at exactly the right moment of risk by people like Tony, George and Harry Saltzman.

Casting Alison was almost as difficult. The known young stars were a vapid bunch. Actresses and their agents counted the number of Mrs Porter's lines, as well they might, and weighed them against a top salary of £40 a week. The part itself, among other things, was a study of the tyranny of negation. No doubt it was too much to expect anyone to realize that this was the source of its theatrical muscle. Alison's brutal power lay in the puny crackle of her iron. 'Why doesn't she throw the board at him?' The question is still asked by university students, their tutors and bushy-tailed young critics.

A film name, however untried, Rank or Pinewoody, might give some ballast to a cast of unknowns. Tony rang me excitedly to say that he thought he had found our Alison. She was appearing as Ophelia in Paul Scofield's *Hamlet*. She and the production were dreadful, but I must go and see her in a film called *Storm over the Nile*, an appalling remake of *The Four Feathers*, only watchable for the inclusion of the original's second-unit footage by Zoltán Korda.

As it happened I had heard of her. Her name was Mary Ure and I had seen her picture on the front page of *Picture Post* as she bought vegetables at Hammersmith market outside the Lyric Theatre, where she had scored a star-is-born kind of success in *Time Remembered* by Jean Anouilh, again with

Scofield. I went to see the film. Mary seemed only more wooden than the other players. 'She looks just like Elsa Lanchester,' I said. Tony had obviously made up his mind. 'I think you're *quite* wrong,' he said. 'I know she can be good. She's a tough little girl from Glasgow.' He made her sound like a sparky barmaid.

I stage-managed all the auditions for the company and received ten shillings for each one. One of the actors selected was Alan Bates and he was among those asked to give readings for Cliff. I favoured Nigel Davenport, but Tony dismissed him. 'Nigel's just like an old *horse*.' John Welsh seemed a fair choice for Colonel Redfern, in spite of his slight Irish accent. George would have been interesting casting, but it might have gone against his terse idea of himself. Glen Byam Shaw was cast almost to type in the film. Nothing seems to become a fierce soldier more than gentleness.

During the weeks of March the core of the company was assembled. Rehearsals for *The Mulberry Bush* took place in a church hall just behind Peter Jones. Those of us not appearing in Wilson's play were expected to go to classes conducted by Yat Malmgren. These consisted of lying on the floor and having your character analysed from your choice of movements. I can't pretend to describe it now as I didn't understand it at the time and found it difficult to take seriously. It was less arduous than PT and more tedious than morning assembly. At least it made you feel that term had started.

As an opening production, heralding the regime of a new company, *The Mulberry Bush* must have been a keen disappointment to George. The indulgent memories of provincial bedrooms often fade on reviewers returning to metropolitan responsibilities. The critics who had already seen the play in Bristol complained that a new company should begin with something untried. It was indeed a tentative start, and timidity, which usually pays such benefits in the theatre, was this time unrewarded. It was calculated caution, but unmistakable caution.

The follow-up, Arthur Miller's *The Crucible*, was more enthusiastically received. Even in Beaverbrook newspapers, McCarthyism could be acknowledged while holdings in South Africa went unmentioned. Besides, Miller was respected, already having saintliness thrust upon him. But the play was still an import, a known quantity, with a distinguished American imprint. No one could have known that my own play was almost consummately handicapped for the following race.

The atmosphere, if I remember it at all, seemed subdued and unspeculative. Rehearsals began in the church hall. Tony made it clear that I was to absent myself from them until I could be of practical help. I was a little surprised but soon grateful for his instinct. When I was permitted to be around, Kenneth was sullen and argumentative. Alan was agreeable and bent on pleasing. Mary was merry as a cockroach in a Kelvinside tea-room. She carped only once at a line about women being noisier than men. It wasn't her experience at all. I tried to point out that it was only the opinion of the character in the play, not mine. For once, I was dishonest in this respect.

Tony's technique of divide and rule was already adept. He kept insisting that I mustn't 'upset' the actors. He must have said the same to them about me. He controlled an iron conspiracy in which no one dared speak to anyone else out of his presence. George and I were mutually intimidated and isolated from each other by this simple ploy for months.

One day I was summoned to the scene of five glum actors. The third act sagged dangerously at the beginning. Tony peered at me bleakly. 'I mean . . . do you think you could *do* something about it? I mean why don't you write a *little song*, or something.' *A little song?* On the Number Nine bus on the way home I took out an envelope from my pocket and started to write my first song.

Now there's a certain little lady, and you all know who I mean,
She may have been to Roedean, but to me she's still a queen,
Some day I'm goin' to marry her,
When times are not so bad,
Her mother doesn't care for me,
So I'll 'ave to ask 'er dad.
We'll build a little home for two,
And have some quiet menage,
We'll send our kids to public school,
And live on bread and marge.
Don't be afraid to sleep with your sweetheart,
Just because she's better than you.
Those forgotten middle-classes may have fallen on their noses,
But a girl who's true blue,
Will still have something left for you,
The angels up above will know that you're in love,
So don't be afraid to sleep with your sweetheart,
Just because she's better than you . . .
                                    They call me Sidney . . .
Just because she's better than you.

By the time I got to Chiswick Bridge it was finished. When I took it in the following morning I had even improvised a tune. Tony seemed astonished that I had taken him at his word and invited me to sing it. Deeply embarrassed and in front of five sceptical actors, I sang my song to the tune in my head. After I had finished, Tony broke the silence and said, 'Yes, well, we'll *think* about it.' It was his way of saying that he'd made up his mind.

The English Stage Company now employs a full-time press officer and assistant. In 1956 this job was served part-time and just as ineffectively by a man called George Fearon. He was overpaid, but less so than his successors, at £10 a week. Mr Fearon was given a copy of the play and invited me for a drink at a pub in Great Newport Street. He equivocated shiftily, even for one in his trade, and then told me with some relish how much he disliked the play and how he had no idea how he could possibly publicize it successfully. The prospect began to puff him up with rare pleasure. He looked at me cheerfully as if he were Albert Pierrepoint guessing my weight. 'I suppose you're really – an angry young man . . . ' He was the first one to say it. A boon to headline-writers ever after. An Angry Young Man. ' . . . Aren't you?' I could see no help coming from that quarter.

We had one preview night, nearly unknown then when stars would be expected to clean up automatically for weeks in the provinces before descending on the West End. George and Tony were baffled by the persistent laughter. When the third act opened to discover Helena drooped over Alison's ironing-board, no one could ignore the cheers that applauded the ironing-board's performance. 'But why do you think they're laughing so much?' asked Tony, alarmed. 'Because it's supposed to be funny,' I replied. Neither of them was reassured.

The overnight stardom of the ironing-board was forgotten the following evening, 8 May. The occasion seems to have been confidently documented by the few who were there, but I remember little. I was sitting in the front row of the unfilled dress circle between Oscar Lewenstein and the writer Wolf Mankowitz. Wolf laughed loudly, and alone. Oscar glanced around him like a managing clerk anticipating a disastrous verdict from the jury foreman. Mary dispensed whatever spirit may have prevailed in wartime Kelvinside and pressed champagne on me in her dressing-room. Her unconcern for the play and herself was affecting as the night wore on. By the end of the evening I was very drunk as, for the first time, I went through the playwright's lap of dishonour round the dressing-rooms. This entails fawning upon an actor in front of his hostile and resentful relatives and agents while they look on with contempt for the ordeal you have inflicted on their idol. I was unaware that Binkie Beaumont, most powerful of the unacceptable faeces of theatrical capitalism, had been in the theatre and had walked out in the interval. Or that the critic T.C. Worsley had persuaded Terence Rattigan to stay.

Next morning, I woke in my cabin, still dressed, feeling cold and wondering whether anything had happened at all last evening, the anniversary of my father's birthday. I had a darkened recollection of my creaking bunk and kissing a very friendly plump girl rather older than myself. The taste of vinegary wine, whisky, Mary's champagne and too many Gauloises made me blush at the thought. I crept ashore, across to Mortlake, where there was a newsagent near Lady Hamilton's house. I bought all the dailies and walked back reading them.

There were five reviewers who made the dottle in the Devine pipe bubble with impatience. One was Philip Hope-Wallace, whose maidenly condescension seems to have been mysteriously revered by the less classy bibbers in El Vino. Whatever his possible charm in the bar, it was not on tap to those slogging at the rock-face. The others were Jack Lambert, who seemed to be able to draw off the actual blood of boredom from George, John Barber (whom he had known at Oxford) and Martin Esslin, the Hungarian opinion-maker and BBC mole, burrowing his way into the English air of London clubs. As for someone called Ossia Trilling, another Oxford poltergeist, whose copy flooded German-speaking newspapers and seeped back to chorus boys' magazines like *Plays and Players*, the dottle became positively volcanic.

When I arrived at the theatre, still nauseous from the early-hours drinking, George attempted to brace me up but his own disappointment seemed clearer and more stricken than my own. He told me there was quite a good notice in the *Financial Times*. Tony pretended to be astonished by both of us. 'But what on earth did you *expect*? You didn't expect them to *like* it did you?' His affected scorn was preferable to anyone's encouraging nod. Meanwhile, a gloomy rearguard action was being rehearsed in the foyer by Fearon. Coining 'Angry Young Man' still pleased him a little, although he could now see no usefulness in it. There was no advance at the box office. He had spoken to a psychiatrist who had seen *Look Back* and assured him that there were clinical examples of young men who behaved and talked like Jimmy Porter. Expert medical evidence might get us through the week.

In the afternoon, Tony held a short rehearsal. The actors were content. No one's performance had been put to any question and their courage in almost overwhelming their material had brought them solicitous attention. Mary was singled out among the victims. 'Mary Ure triumphs over undress.' She chattered on quite beguilingly.

Nellie Beatrice demanded to come to the second performance. I met her at Sloane Square station and she insisted in her usual semi-hysteria on making her way to Lyons for a coffee instead of the drink waiting for her at the theatre. 'I want to keep my head *clear* for the play. I read the *News* and the *Standard*,' she said. 'The write-ups weren't very good were they? I expect you're disap-

pointed, poor kid. Ah, well – perhaps you'll be in the limelights the next time.'
It was not unlike getting a girl in the family way, and for no explicable purpose.

During the first interval, people 'passing comments' forced her into the
upstairs bar for a drink 'to steady my nerves'. The barmaid confirmed her
disquiet. 'They don't like this one, do they dear? They don't like it at all.
Never mind, it won't be much longer. We're having Peggy Ashcroft soon.
They'll like that. But they don't like *this* one. Not a bit of it.'

There was no reproach or show of unease from George or Tony. There
was desultory talk of being 'saved by the Sundays', but if either one of them
nursed such hopes he concealed them from me. I watched the play for what
must surely be its last performance, and there were almost as many laughs as
there had been at the preview. The following day I walked over to the Mortlake
newsagent once again and bought the Sunday papers. I read the *Observer* and
the *Sunday Times* on a corporation bench in the bright May early morning
sunshine.

> *Look Back in Anger* presents post-war youth as it really is, with special
> emphasis on the non-U intelligentsia, who live in bed-sitters and divide
> the Sunday papers into two groups, 'posh' and 'wet'. To have done this
> at all would be a signal achievement; to have done it in a first play is a
> minor miracle. All the qualities are there, qualities one had despaired of
> ever seeing on the stage – the drift towards anarchy, the instinctive
> leftishness, the automatic rejection of 'official' attitudes, the surrealist
> sense of humour . . . the casual promiscuity, the sense of lacking a crusade
> worth fighting for and, underlying all these, the determination that no
> one who dies shall go unmourned . . . The Porters of our time deplore
> the tyranny of 'good taste' and refuse to accept 'emotional' as a term of
> abuse; they are classless, and they are also leaderless. Mr Osborne is
> their first spokesman . . . I doubt if I could love anyone who did not wish
> to see *Look Back in Anger*.
>
> Kenneth Tynan, *Observer*, 13 May 1956

> John Osborne is a writer of outstanding promise, and the English Stage
> Company is to be congratulated on discovering him.
>
> Harold Hobson, *Sunday Times*, 13 May 1956

I went back to the boat to ring Tony. At noon a dozen of us drank pints of
beer outside the pub in Lower Mall. George was grinning at me over his unlit
pipe.

The newspapers rang. Kenneth Tynan, then also a script-editor at Ealing, asked me to lunch within days to talk about writing a film. Another call came, this time from the Dorchester Hotel. Would I ring Mr Harry Saltzman – urgently? I was unused to American producers who leave messages for you to ring urgently about most unurgent matters. The call to breakfast with someone passing through the Dorchester or the Savoy was still a quaint myth. I had tea with Harry. He thought *Look Back in Anger* would be a big success in New York if handled properly. He had more flair than to suggest it be translated to Greenwich Village. Harry had just finished making a film called *The Paleface*, which he told me was the only loss-making movie ever made by Bob Hope. His own amusement at this was encouraging. An equally likeable staff writer on *Picture Post* interviewed me and then rushed me off by taxi to be photographed on the deck of M/Y *Egret*.

Mary made the inside of the magazine this time. She was living in Southwell Gardens in Kensington. A single bed in a cold basement suited her own frugal needs. Welsh-Fulham upstarts yearn for sybaritic necessities unknown to Scottish girls from the Clyde, whose cheerful response to a detumescent bedroom was to turn the gas fire up to half-pressure and put on a warm woolly. Spending a night with her meant an assault course of dressing in whispers, coping with the treacherous front-door latch, the landlady's ear ever-open for her returning cat, and then having to persuade a cab driver at 6.00 a.m. to take me outside the eight-mile limit for ten shillings. This was not what I had been used to in the provinces.

In spite of Kenneth Tynan and *Picture Post*, *Look Back* was only playing to moderate business. An effort was made to salvage something from the public confusion of those early weeks by somehow persuading the BBC to present a twenty-five minute extract on television, with an introduction by George Harewood. The response at the box office was immediate and takings went up from £900 to £1,700. A new production was presented at the Lyric, Hammersmith, to make way for the rest of the Court's repertoire.

Donald Albery had summoned me to his office at the New Theatre and offered to transfer the play. He demanded cuts from the passages which he said audiences found most offensive. The most indefensible were the bears and squirrels, which even Tynan had described as 'painful whimsy'. Everyone, said Albery, had been discomforted by them. Surprised by my own coolness, I pointed out that as by this time everyone had been warned against the ending they might feel deprived of it. I didn't try to justify the blackness of my play-making. We were both pleased not to budge, and *Look Back* waited nine years for its first West End presentation, at Albery's own theatre, the Criterion.

My pocket diary for 1956 is filled with the details of royalties. I took out my last £20 from the Post Office and opened a bank account. I was able to give Nellie Beatrice the largest tip she had seen since her GIs departed. I supplied Anthony Creighton with money and he gave up his agreeable social life at the telephone exchange. The entry for 21 December reads: 'Bank: In – £368. Out – £50. Self – £10.'

I was still earning £12 a week from the English Stage Company. Mary had been given some money by her father, bought herself a small house in Woodfall Street, off the King's Road, and we moved in. It was tiny, with one long narrow sitting-room, a kitchen, bedroom and bathroom and a space as big as a box-room which I could use as my study. She was working again for Binkie, in Arthur Miller's *A View from the Bridge*. We both felt we were doing rather well. Her director, Peter Brook, rehearsed long hours, often till nine or ten in the evening, so I saw little of her. The prospect of having all day to myself in Woodfall Street with a few hundred pounds in the bank was startling in its simplicity, and I had already tried to describe my next play to Tony.

But all these months, I knew that the matter of Pamela could not be left unresolved.

> Good nature, or what is often considered as such, is the most selfish of all the virtues: it is nine times out of ten mere indolence of disposition.
>
> William Hazlitt, *On the Knowledge of Character*, 1822

I still had a fugitive hope that Pamela might be the tenth exception, but I was more than fatigued by indolence of disposition and my present modest comfort changed nothing of that. It was clear that I would need the services of a lawyer. I knew nothing about such things, any more than I had about the mechanics of getting married to my twenty-one-year-old bride, having had to look it all up in *Whitaker's Almanack*.

I asked Oscar Lewenstein if he could recommend a solicitor. He knew someone he thought was just the man for me. 'You'll like him,' he said. 'He's rather like you, in fact he's rather like Jimmy Porter.' His office was in Ludgate Hill and his name was Oscar Beuselinck. His secretary and the switchboard girl were both sullen and looked like neglected evacuees, ignorant and ill-fed. The second thing he said to me was, 'You think I'm Jewish, don't you?' And then, grinning all over his face, 'Well, I'm not. You should look at my chopper.'

Oscar was not encouraging about my prospects of divorce, which must involve the risks of collusion. He leered conspiratorially and made it clear that my chances of wheedling any sympathy from a smart-minded judge were remote. I was not yet familiar with how happily lawyers deliver the unhappiest verdict on your life. It is like encountering the Oriental nod which means 'No.'

The whole enterprise seemed risky, seedy, indeed criminal. I wasn't intent on marrying Mary, and I was reluctant to go through the business of Pamela being pressed to unwilling action.

While he was rattling off my poor chances, the telephone rang. Cupping his hand over the receiver, he said, 'This is my bank manager. I'm screwing his cashier only he doesn't know that.' He assumed the voice he reserves for posh clients until he put the telephone down. He restored my theatrical faith within seconds. 'No, Johnco, if I don't get it three times a day I feel ill. If I don't get it once a day I feel *physically* ill. I really do. The other night I went home and fucked the wife. Got up, fucked her again. Delia gave me a gobble-job at lunch-time. Then I saw Jenny, that's the bank manager's cashier I was telling you about. Went back and fucked the wife again. *Not bad is it?*' You couldn't help liking him. Like Max Miller. No inner life to hinder. 'Have you ever had it on the kitchen table?' he asked as he saw me out.

Pamela was working in rep in York and I arranged to go up and see her on a Sunday. She met me on the station platform and we went into the buffet. I told her about Oscar and the technical complications of adultery. My train back to London was due in half an hour. I felt I could easily have persuaded her into an unresolving bed. She had heard that I was living with Mary and asked me if we intended to get married. I said, truthfully, that it was possible but not definite. She said nothing to this but told me that she had not been well lately, having had an abortion at a too-late stage, which only she could have contemplated. She saw me on to the train and absent-mindedly kissed me goodbye.

4. 'Take it Orfe'

> Despise the things of the world and be indifferent to all changes and events of Providence, but he that creates to himself thousands of little hopes, uncertain in the promise, fallible in the event, and depending upon ten thousand circumstances, shall often fail in his expectations, and be used to arguments of distrust in such hopes.
>
> Jeremy Taylor, *Holy Living*, 1650

During that spring and summer of 1956 I had been as much exhilarated by the prospect of being a company actor as anything else. The days of stage-managing, pushing wheelbarrows of borrowed furniture, calling surly actors and appeasing electricians and flymen seemed to be left behind.

I certainly enjoyed the rehearsals of *Don Juan* and *The Death of Satan*. It seemed like a cheery party in which no one, apart from the author, had any stake. I was aware that I was not any good in my small part (an American businessman in a silver wig) – like so many second-rate actors, I appeared to shine like pinchbeck in flashy roles – but no one else was much better. The Black Dwarf looked as if he was poised to spurt venom on to the stage from his perch in the stalls.

As the only other writer present, I felt some guilt in not sympathizing with his rage: his tiny form almost convulsed with frustration, his long, dark hair sprawled over his pale, papery face. The dress rehearsal took place four days after *Look Back* had opened. The euphoria of the two Sunday notices seemed to infect everyone. Duncan watched helplessly as his unactable double-bill, a rag-bag of Shaw, Eliot and St Augustine, was rolled back unceremoniously like a stack of dusty rugs in a department store. It was a small but cruel revenge on Verse Theatre and Higher Thought. I didn't know how he could have subjected himself to such mockery. Perhaps he still imagined that in performance it would somehow transcend indifferent presentation and reveal itself as a minor masterpiece. Even at my age, I would have been on the Number Nine bus home, demanding my name be ripped from Sloane Square.

After four performances it was taken off. Not a friend intervened, not even Harold Hobson with his bent for religious analogy.

Rehearsals then began for *Cards of Identity*. These were altogether different. So was Nigel Dennis. He attended more than Angus had done or poor Ronnie had been permitted. The script, a cobble-job, was sloshed together by Tony, George and Nigel. It was about a hundred pages too long. Sheets of paper were ripped from the actors, who were relieved to have less to say. Nigel wrinkled with pleasure when one of his jokes came off. He would come into the dressing-room and 'chortle' as Edwardian writers would have it. Chortling, like sauntering, was a rare spectacle. He had also struck up a close friendship with George, sadly to end in acrimony over the production of *August for the People*, leaving George with a breakdown, bitterly mourning the loss.

One half of the *Cards of Identity* cast never came across the other. The half I was in included Robert Stephens, Alan Bates and Ernest Milton, an actors' actor like Wilfred Lawson. From the outset it was clear that Ernest was unhappy. He said he was worried about his wife coping with a move to another house. But his part, Father Golden Orfe, was a drunken priest who had a long, self-reviling speech celebrating his loathsome condition which ended with the triumphant cry: 'I *stink* therefore I am!' Ernest, actor and fervent Catholic, had not understood its implications. His caution was correct. The passage caused more offence than any other in the play. When George took over as Orfe he delivered it in dashing fashion and collapsed in my arms before the unbelievers in the stalls started baying out their disbelief.

The first night seemed even more tight-arsed and jacketed than the ones I had already experienced at the Court. Before the long evening was half-way over it was clear that we were not simply playing to a hand-picked Jewish Charity audience but to a hard phalanx of dressed-up ill-wishers. During the last minutes a cloud of resentment and frustration was suspended over the auditorium. I don't think I was the only one to feel a tang of exhilaration wafting over us like cigar smoke at a smart boxing event.

Never having felt 'waves of love' over the footlights, I can only confirm that rollers of hate can be a most warming and stimulating dose of salts. Booing is a strange sound in the theatre, and I had never heard it in such pure form. It was a sound I was to come to know very well during the rest of my career. As my rebellious schoolfriend Mickey Wall used to say, 'If we could package it, it would be worth a guinea a box.'

... and who should turn up wearing false, sabre teeth and a hairless dome, but John Osborne ... ruthlessly funny as the Custodian of Ancient

Offices! The Royal Court's captive playwright stands out from an excellent supporting case.

Kenneth Tynan, *Observer*, June 1956

After a week or two the boos subsided and the audiences became smaller. The stage manager came round to tell me that Mr Devine wanted to see me in his dressing-room. When I got there, a startlingly familiar figure was standing beside him. It was Laurence Olivier with his agent, Cecil Tennant. It seemed that Olivier had been bellowing his strident displeasure about *Look Back* to Tennant, who persuaded him to see the play again. When the curtain rose, they found themselves watching *Cards of Identity*. 'You're my kind of actor,' Olivier told me. 'You like hiding behind make-up.' He said he was preparing a film of *Macbeth* and that I would be very good as the English doctor. I made a note to look it up when I got home. George winked at me.

Almost immediately we started rehearsals for Brecht's *Good Woman of Setzuan*. George had met Brecht during the continental tour of the Gielgud–Noguchi *King Lear* a year earlier. He had been very fired not only by Brecht's achievement but by his presence. The laconic, unmade-bed look, suggesting dark coffee-stained vests, the black and gold teeth, the cheap cigars, the pudding-basin haircut, possibly chopped off by his most official wife, Helene Weigel, with garden secateurs, and the black leather jackets soon to be adopted by another generation of Court directors – all these made an impression on George far removed from elegant theatre managers lunching at the Ivy.

It was a large cast with a lot of small parts, particularly for stoic peasantry. Three hours, fourteen scenes and thirty actors singing, dancing and speaking elliptical folk wisdom to demonstrate that the poor are often a greedy, ruthless and covetous lot. Joan Plowright was a motherly housewife, Nigel Davenport a Chinese policeman, Robert Stephens, Esmé Percy and John Moffatt were gods who descended, shakily. George was a Gradgrind tradesman, Peter Wyngarde an aviator, I was a peasant gardener and Peter Woodthorpe a waterseller. Nightly he goosed me with agonizingly accurate ferocity beneath my worker's rags as he made his entrance: 'I am Wang the Waterseller.' Peggy Ashcroft played a dual role as Shen Te and Shui Ta, one female, one male, adopting masks for the transition and giggling throughout.

The regard for Brecht was then ascendant because of Kenneth Tynan's enthusiasm and the recent visit of the Berliner Ensemble. None of us had any idea of how to begin to tackle him. It seemed to me as daunting as doing a Japanese Noh play in weekly rep. Language, custom, national temperament, training, or lack of it, even physical appearance seemed to doom the effort. The staccato theatrical method was helped tremendously by the German language itself. The new East German state looked like providing a rigour and political bite certainly lacking at home.

I felt like a contented conscript, prepared to do what I might be asked but aware that it wouldn't be much. I was just an underpaid squaddie with a free trip on tour to Brighton. In some vague gesture towards Stella Linden, my older woman, mistress and collaborator, with whom I had spent glorious and instructive months in a flat on the front in 1949, I booked into a bizarre vegetarian hotel. There was no alcohol, it was full of old ladies in half-light and huge portraits of biblical scenes. I soon realized my mistake and switched to the Royal Crescent, then the pros' hotel, where you could be waited on with whisky, wine and sandwiches all through the night.

One of the attractions of the Theatre Royal was its backstage bar which was, literally, on the stage. It was frequented by a more or less cheery collection of has-been bar-flies and Brighton bit-part players. One of these was Gilbert Harding, then at the height of his self-despised reputation as an early TV personality, a take-away Dr Johnson. I had met him once before, at the Savile Club, where he grabbed my knee in almost fatherly affection and demanded, in front of the company of floppy bow-tied waiters, I admit that Jimmy and Cliff were in love with each other and that was what *Look Back* was Really All About. 'Think they're buggers, do you Gilbert?' growled Compton Mackenzie. I hope I wasn't too priggish.

At the Sunday dress rehearsal of *Good Woman* Gilbert didn't recognize me, which was not surprising. He must have been in the stage bar for several hours and in the crusty mood for which he was so admired by a troglodyte television audience. I was sitting in the stalls. Presently, I became aware of old Gilbert slumped beside me and, after a few minutes, I felt a hand on my grey People's Republic knee. The costume was as impenetrable as it was unappealing. I froze, and hoped that the combination of Brecht and afternoon Brighton buzz would at least put the alienation effect to some useful purpose. After a few grumpy fumbles, he turned and growled in a voice immediately identifiable, 'Tell me – are you a boy or a girl?' 'Just a peasant. And I'm nearly on. Excuse me.'

I felt on holiday from events, not only from those of the past half-dozen years but from the persisting strictures of Stella and Pamela, the naked bullying, rabid caution and frozen hearts of Nellie Beatrice and Grandma Osborne who killed pleasure at interminable paces, and from everyone with a brief to diminish endeavour. Of course I was often to feel almost grievously threatened for years to come, but during those summer weeks I had a realization of sorts that I could at least go the full distance, and always would.

The following week in Oxford, Helene Weigel and Paul Dassau, Brecht's composer, came to see us at the New Theatre, and rehearsals began afresh. Aware of our bafflement and keenness to be instructed by visiting Marxist royalty, they were both friendly and encouraging. The interpretation of the songs was particularly difficult. One called 'Chang had Seven Elephants' involved a great deal of snorting, pachyderm stamping and earnest ear-flapping. Hopes were scuppered within minutes. All well-meant attempts to mime died under the Teutonic lash of Weigel and Dassau. To a couple of dozen willing but unequipped Anglo-Saxon actors, Brecht remained little more than the image of a bitten-off haircut and the sprout of a long cigar butt.

My abiding memory of the week is of dining with Peggy Ashcroft and Esmé Percy at an Indian restaurant by the Martyrs' Memorial. They talked entertainingly and Esmé's beloved dog farted incessantly under the table. Peggy grew impatient. 'Don't you think he needs a bit of a clean out?' 'Oh, but I only shampooed him this morning.' 'I meant clean *within*, not without.'

After we opened in London, there was a feeling of genial irresponsibility. It was a little like taking part in an event in some foreign country which hardly anyone understood. Everyone seemed in a good temper and under no pressure to shine. I was back in dressing-room Number Six with Nigel Davenport and Robert Stephens. Down in Number Three, the viper's hell-kitchen, we could eavesdrop on the shrieks of John Moffatt, Esmé and Peters Wyngarde and Woodthorpe. One evening, the peasant Woodthorpe, surrounded by Brecht's pantomime gods, was washing his feet, fresh from a blackened stage and a careless life. Exasperated after days of this thoughtlessness, Moffatt, a most fastidious and circumspect man, finally remonstrated: 'I do think, Peter, you might wait for the rest of us to wash our hands and faces before you put your filthy feet in the basin.' The reply drifted gamely up the stairs. 'Oh, come off it, little Miss Muffett. Get off your tuffet!' Like so much else, it was a relief from admired alienation.

Mary had opened in *A View from the Bridge*. We were snapped with Marilyn Monroe, we had supper with Richard and Sybil Burton at Emlyn Williams' house in Pelham Crescent (where we were announced by a butler). We were photographed in Cecil Beaton's dappled garden. He described me as an elegant camel. I had instruction from Wolf Mankowitz on how to write plays, the genius of F.R. Leavis, good butchering, and how to impregnate a girl and outwit the Inland Revenue. We went to Kenneth Tynan's Mount Street flat to meet Cyril Connolly and Peter Hall, with a gloriously pregnant Leslie Caron.

I was becoming aware that there was a concerted campaign to turn me into a plaything freak of what would now be deadeningly described as the 'media'. It was fairly clear, even to me, what they were up to. It continued quite unrelentingly until the end of the decade, when even Fleet Street could get no more juice from this oversqueezed fantasy. The sub-editors repeated late-night inspirations and looked forward in hope. What is modern society angry about? It seemed that no one could exorcise the whole invention. The inertia, defeatism and conformist suspicion of the despairing years of life in Britain since 1945 seemed to have been injected into some previously armoured nerve.

There was an almost tangible frisson from Lower Mall about the ludicrous attention that both the play and myself were receiving. George and Tony were both genuinely contemptuous of it. I can't pretend that, for me, the absurd spotlight and the feigned friendliness were not invigorating. The abuse, dislike and hell-bent discouragement were also hurtful. I could sense the danger, although none of us spoke of it. I was surely being set up for demolition at a not too late date. Instead of asking George or Tony for loyal advice, I gave interviews and wrote articles on crass subjects ('What's Wrong with Women Today'); I was offered ten times my weekly salary for 700 words which even I had the facility to turn out in an hour or so. Journalism intrigued me as a spur to my brooding, inhibited and ponderous method of working. Apart from the prize-like cheques, I felt an excitement at the carrot of a huge byline. I detected a streak of Wadham spinsterishness in George and Tony's unspoken distaste. It was flattering to be on one's own in this.

Within months of my ticking-off from every agent in London, I was reviewing the collected plays of Tennessee Williams for the *Observer* and writing film and television criticism for the *Evening Standard* and the odd few hundred words for anybody on almost anything from romantic love to favourite dishes. A magazine called *Lilliput*, famous as a beer-and-blazer publication, asked me to choose an item of clothing which they would have made for me if I posed in it. A harmless lark. Thinking of my grandfather's prophecies of becoming either prime minister or Bernard Shaw, I decided on a Norfolk jacket. I presented myself to a master and most traditional tailor in Holborn. Looking at my scuffed high-street sports jacket, he didn't bother to smother his scorn. 'What *kind* of Norfolk jacket?' What *kind*? I had assumed it was as identifiable as a hot-cross bun. 'There *are* thirty varieties, sir.'

I was gulled frequently. A journalist from the *Spectator* went through the letters on my mantelshelf while I was out of the room fixing him a drink. The magazine printed the details, including a note from the Inland Revenue. A few weeks later I found myself sitting next to Edith Sitwell. She brandished her great rings at me in welcome, saying that she had sent a protesting telegram from Hollywood to the editor: 'It was always a disgusting paper.' As Laurence Olivier said, 'No one ever won an interview.'

But I had also earned some money. Samuel French, the principal publishers of amateur editions, would offer only £25 for the rights of *Look Back*. I was intrigued to be in the market-place. The first amazing windfall was from Fischer Verlag – £300 for the German rights, more than my annual earnings for years. Unimaginable. I bought the *Encyclopaedia Britannica* with it.

Mary and I spent a week in Spain, south of Tarragona. It was my first trip beyond the Isle of Wight and I was apprehensive of flying and, most of all, being thwarted by language. The clerk at Thomas Cook's was not encouraging. The collapsed lip of the born official expanded into something like near-happiness. 'Oh, not married. Well, I can make the booking for you but I can't, of course, guarantee that you will get a room. Not together, at least. Still, it's up to you.'

Mary was as indignant as a housewife served a stale baptie with her morning coffee. The clerk was unimpressed by her show of Scots womanliness. 'I'm sorry. But there it is.' I almost wished we could go to Margate and Wonderland instead. 'After all, it *is* a Catholic country,' he said as he handed us our vouchers and luggage labels.

As it turned out Mary made the trip very enjoyable. She was fussy, bossy and implacably cheerful. The hotel was perched on stilts directly on the beach. There were a dozen rooms, bright tiles on the floors, a simple restaurant, seafood and champagne at a pound a bottle. It was run by a lady from Manchester who took our passports without a glance for immoral intentions. Mary was one of those unguarded souls who can make themselves understood by penguins or the wildest dervishes. Spanish was no problem. It would have taken a crabbed spirit not to be affected and plunge in with her almost literal carelessness. It was a good time. I was not in love. There was fondness and pleasure but no groping expectations, just a feeling of fleeting heart's ease. For the present we were both content enough.

> *What to do next?* There are too many books, too many plays, too much commentary and clamour. There is no progress only frenzy. There is too much decay of the heart.
>
> *Notebook*, 1976

As 1956 came to an end, my mood could hardly have been more different from what it was to be twenty years later. Christmas 1956 was the first since 1946 I had not spent working at Blythe Road post office. The year before I had grumpily refused Tony's offer to play a non-speaking sailor in his television production of *Othello*. Apart from pride, I pointed out that my BBC fee would be about half of what I would get by encouraged fiddling and overtime with the GPO. Mary and I spent Christmas quietly together in Woodfall Street.

Salisbury

Dear John,

Once again Xmas has been and gone. We have had a quiet time, nobody to see us but Bessie made it as festive as possible. Please forgive the type as eye operation was not too successful. We were very concerned because your card only arrived on Boxing Day and it worried us. Perhaps I will be more cheerful after I have been in hospital in January. Enjoy yourself John whilst you are young it does not last long believe me.

God bless.

Uncle Jack

Watford

Dear John,

Such lots of thanks for your Xmas parcel. Have put it away and shall drink your health and happiness at Christmas, say 12 o/c. We shall be thinking of you on Xmas Day. Guess you will have a lovely time. We shall just have my sister here and as my other Sister [who] passed away last Jan. had her birthday Christmas Day, we shall no doubt feel a little down.

Lots of love,

Uncle Sidney xxxx

Salisbury

My dear John,

I feel that I did not thank you sufficiently for your Xmas gift. We had a marvellous time. A capon, Xmas pudding, a drink and a piece of roast beef (reminded me of yours). You see with those Harrods hampers you have sent us in the past, you get trivial things, such as mustard, peppers, sauces, we have some 3 years old. We even had two items missing. Do not think I am ungrateful.

God bless.

Uncle Jack

Life in Woodfall Street was oddly settled, almost provincial. We might have been living in Leicester or Harrogate and far from the fiction that was generated about us both. Mary had been fêted by Binkie, fondled by Terry Rattigan, had played Ophelia to Paul Scofield in Moscow, been featured on magazine covers and appeared in two Arthur Miller plays. It was a fairly heady début for a girl who had only intended to be a drama teacher in Glasgow. She treated the whole crowded sequence as if it had hardly taken place.

She took scant interest in her surroundings and, despite her eloquence about her mother's oatcakes, kippers and jams, scarcely cooked at all. I didn't mind. I was quite happy to turn out my vegetarian dishes. The cupboards were bare. When she did cook, as for our first Christmas dinner, the kitchen was blackened. Fortunately, she never apologized. It didn't matter and there was always the Indian at the end of the alley. She would leave the house every day after instant coffee and a slice of toast and reappear in the late afternoon. She would go to her hairdresser (Phyllis Earle in Berkeley Square, grudgingly paid for by Binkie), meet a girlfriend for lunch and then 'go shopping at Harrods'. She rarely bought anything but a bagful of baubles from the make-up counter or a pair of stockings. But she always came back bubbling with happiness.

I was content that I was not making her unhappy in any way. I had no idea what pain I might have inflicted on Pamela and reflected on it daily. I hoped that despair or doubt would never blow on Mary's butterfly spirit. She was no sphinx and concealed no secrets apart from her forays into Harrods. But I still addressed myself to Pamela's motives: had she ever loved me at all; ungiven to gestures, had she married me so casually, withdrawing as quickly from my life and as imperceptibly as she had entered it?

The impression from Fleet Street was that Mary and I were a gilded couple who had won the football pools. She was asked her opinion on cooking, of all things, and the H-bomb. This cut no ice with Grandma Osborne. When I paid her a dutiful visit, she greeted me with as much warmth as she ever mustered and, as ever, asked me not a question. The thin smile was just as wintry and she told me with pride about cousin Tony's job as a probation officer in Macclesfield and cousin Jill's second or third baby. Fleet Street, the wireless and television had no dominion over the *South Wales Argus* and its Births and Deaths columns or the latest Warwick Deeping. I showed her a newspaper photograph of Mary, rising young star. She gazed at it briefly with her ever-painful eyes. 'She seems a pretty little thing.'

Mary, however, had powerful family support from her father and brothers. Her weekly telephone calls made clear how secure she was. The dialogue scarcely changed. 'And how are you?' 'Oh, we're all right. We've all had colds.' Always. 'Is that so? And how's the wee man?' (One of her brother's babies. He'd had a cold, too.) There were calls to her old nanny and reminiscences about sharing their 'sweetie coupons'. Perhaps she should never have set her sights on Dr Johnson's highway into England and the snares of Sassenach show-biz.

5. 'I Have a Go, Lady. I Do. I Have a Go'

Lowndes Cottage,
London SW1

Thankyou. Thankyou for the thrilling and lovely play which will no doubt be in the same Reps Theatre drawer as the Cherry Orchard and The School for Scandal before the century is out. Thankyou for the most deeply engaging part perhaps barring only Macbeth and Lear that I can remember – *certainly* the most enjoyable. I thank you for the play with all my heart, and for the pride it gives me to be in it, and for the joy of playing it. Hope I don't fuck it up for you tonight.

Letter from Laurence Olivier to J.O., 10 April 1957

Journalists insist that I wrote the part of Archie Rice in *The Entertainer* for Laurence Olivier, just as reference books have it that *Look Back in Anger* was originally titled *On the Pier at Morecambe*. These dumb speculations have a way of perpetuating themselves as fact. The true record may not be of much account but it is hard to justify tampering with it.

One evening, when Mary was rehearsing Arthur Miller, I went on my own to the Chelsea Palace. Max Miller was on the bill. Waiting for him to come on, I watched an act, the highlight of which was an impersonation of Charles Laughton playing Quasimodo. I had seen it before. A smoky green light swirled over the stage and an awesome banality prevailed for some theatrical seconds, the drama and poetry, the belt and braces of music hall holding up epic. This, the critics would later tell me, was the Brechtian influence on the play.

Music hall was on its last legs but there were still a few halls in and around London for me to visit, not yet quite defeated by grey, front-parlour television. I made notes for the play. I knew I was on to the problem – remembering George's dictum that all problems were technical ones – and I was even confident enough to give the play a title. I'd been listening to a record by a trumpet-player called Bunk Johnson. He was something of a legend, whose reputation had been revived by a few enthusiasts who had found him working in the Deep South as a truck driver, old and forgotten. They bought him a new set of teeth and he made a short comeback. One of the tunes he recorded was an old Scott Joplin number, 'The Entertainer'. It was graceful and touching and seemed apt for the play.

Sometime in early February 1957, George telephoned me. He was meticulous about not hectoring writers and so I was surprised when he asked, 'How's the play going, dear boy?' 'All right.' 'How far have you got?' This was most unlike him. He knew the powers of my evasion. 'Oh, I've finished the second act. Almost.' 'I see. I hate to ask, but something's just come up. I don't suppose you can tell me if there's a part in it for Laurence?' 'Laurence who?' 'Olivier.'

George persuaded me against all his practice. 'Would you mind awfully if I asked you to let me have the first two acts?' Believing us both wrong, I agreed. Olivier's response was immediate and astonishing. He wanted to play Billy Rice, Archie's father. Letting him read just two acts had confused everyone. A week later I rang Tony and told him I had finished. 'Read me the last page,' he said, and I mumbled Archie's last speech down the telephone to his final line, which Olivier found incomprehensible and made devastating. 'Let me know where you're working tomorrow night – and I'll come and see *YOU*.' It was to be Olivier's face but, I hoped, *my* voice – possibly my own epitaph.

Things moved quickly. Sir Laurence was suddenly 'available' and eager in the way of prized actors who come into season with occasional surprising suddenness and have to be accommodated while the bloodstock is raring. Tony and I were summoned to the Connaught Hotel where, for some domestic reason, the Oliviers were temporarily staying. It is hard to convey what a royal impression these two had made on the press and the public at the same time. In their different ways they had both promoted it.

Seeing Vivien Leigh for the first time, I could only remember watching *Gone with the Wind* as a twelve-year-old recovering from rheumatic fever, sitting in my wheelchair and fainting as she fled from the blood and cries of burning Atlanta. In the flesh, she was strangely robust in a pent-up way, like some threatened animal. Her voice seemed deeper and more rasping than the recollection of Scarlett's 'Great balls of fire' or, even more memorably, Blanche du Bois's 'I have always relied on the kindness of strangers.' I didn't feel she was overtrusting of these two odd-looking young men with their funny old play. Sir Laurence, long regarded by all (including himself) as a bequest to the nation, seemed to be speaking for both of them.

Tony was at his best adroit, northern, breathless-matter-of-factness, and put Larry at his ease a little. The necessity to cast quickly was paramount because of the great man's other commitments. He suggested George Relph to play Billy. It was an unexceptionable choice. There was a 'little actress you may have heard of – Dorothy Tutin'. Tony was keen and, although I wasn't, I felt it was too soon to carp. Then came the question of Phoebe, Archie's wife. Larry came up with a dull selection of H.M. Tennant and Elstree actresses. Suddenly, with dazzling Olivier craftiness, he said, 'Well, now, what about Vivien?'

Tony, machiavellian and master-technician though he might be, could dissemble no better than myself. The thought of the mouth that once purred through Tara's halls tackling such lines as, 'I don't want to end up in some dead and alive hole' was unthinkable. Before Tony had time to recover, Larry continued: 'I know she's all wrong in a way and far, far too beautiful, but I was talking to Edith the other day about that old woman she played in *Queen of Spades*. It took her five hours in the make-up chair but they put this rubber mask on her, do you see.'

I did see. I had seen the film and enjoyed it enormously, but Edith Evans was not only much older and plainer than one of the acknowledged beauties of stage and screen, she was also playing a woman who was supposed to be at least a hundred years old. *And* it was a film.

After a few minutes it was agreed, without any intervention as I remember from Vivien, that this was, after all, an impractical suggestion, that Vivien was of course far too beautiful and, most unfortunately, the British Public would never accept her as ageing, ugly and common. Larry discarded what was patently being imposed upon him and went on to other possibilities. Now that Vivien was out of the running, we all gratefully agreed to approach Brenda de Banzie, reputed to be trying but powerful, in a very different manner from Blanche du Bois.

When we got to the hotel lobby, Tony tripped out through the revolving door, his breath hitting the cold, late February air. 'What about that!' he whinnied. His gnashing laughter cracked out into Mount Street. 'Rubber masks! Oh, my dear God. Rubber masks!' It was funny enough, but the famous rubber mask was to shadow us for weeks to come, revealing pain, envy, suspicion and dislike.

At the beginning of 1957, the muddle of feeling about Suez and Hungary, implicit in *The Entertainer*, was so overheated that the involvement of Olivier in the play seemed as dangerous as exposing the Royal Family to politics. There was some relief that an international event could arouse such fierce, indeed theatrical responses, with lifetime readers cancelling the *Observer* and rallies and abuse everywhere. The Korean War had come and gone like a number two touring company: this one would run on well into foreseeable history. The season was open for hunting down deceivers and self-deceivers.

A special meeting of the English Stage Company was convened to make a decision about the production of *The Entertainer*. Left and Right became allies,

37

Lewenstein rooting with Blacksell. Olivier was an undisputed coup, but an embarrassment also. It was decided to drop the play.

Neville Blond, the Chairman of the ESC and its Council, was a Manchester textile magnate and sometime government adviser on transatlantic trade. His wife, Elaine, was a Marks & Spencer heiress. The pair of them promptly issued an invitation to council members for lunch at their flat in Orchard Court to discuss the matter. Over the next few years I attended a few parties at Orchard Court, a gloomy mausoleum block behind elaborate wrought iron-work near Selfridges. These were sumptuous spreads given in the manner of a Christmas party for servants and tenant farmers. Mrs Blond would itemize the value of the pictures on the walls and the price per yard of the upholstery. We were not expected to stay long. She was arguably the most charmless woman I ever met. A few years later she eyed me on the steps of the Royal Court, her cash-register eyes very cold indeed and said, 'Oh – *you're* still here, are you?'

On that first occasion, she told the Council, 'You'd be barmy not to do the play. With Olivier wanting to act in it!' 'You see,' said Neville, less stridently, 'we owe it to the boy.' In the event, George Harewood's casting vote carried the day. *The Entertainer* would go ahead.

I have no record of the cuts imposed on *Look Back in Anger*. The Lord Chamberlain's Office must have misjudged certain elements as for years television critics and provincial newspapers were to complain about the earthy, degrading or even filthy language. The only deletion I can remember was 'as tough as a night in a Bombay brothel and as rough as a matelot's arse'. 'Arm' was substituted for 'arse'.

Lord Chamberlain's Office,
St James's Palace, sw1
20th March, 1957

Sir,

The Entertainer

I am desired by the Lord Chamberlain to write to you regarding the above Play and to ask for an undertaking that the following alterations will be made:-

1) Act I, page 11, alter 'ass-upwards'.
2) Page 29, alter 'clappers'.
3) Act II, page 25, a photograph should be submitted of the nude in Britannia's helmet.
4) Page 27 alter 'pouf', (twice).
5) Page 30, alter 'shagged'.

6) Page 36, omit 'Right up to the flies. Right up.'
7) Page 43, omit 'rogered' (twice).
8) Page 44, omit 'I always needed a jump at the end of the day – and at the beginning too usually.'
9) Act III, page 3 alter 'wet your pants'.
10) Page 4, omit 'had Sylvia'.
11) Page 6, alter 'turds'.
12) Page 9, alter 'camp'.
13) A photograph of the nude tableau, page 20, should be submitted.
14) Page 21, omit 'balls'.
15) Scene 12, should be submitted in full.
16) The little song entitled, 'The old church bells won't ring tonight 'cos the Vicar's got the clappers'. Substitute: 'The Vicar's dropped a clanger.'

Any alterations or substitutions should be submitted for approval.

Yours faithfully,

Assistant Comptroller

The ESC, the Council and the Lord Chamberlain were contained and we were in business. It was too late for reservations or quibbling. Olivier had to fit Archie in during April for five weeks before his summer commitment to *Titus Andronicus*. The opening was announced and within a few days every seat for the short season had been sold. I was happy and unapprehensive. Whatever the pressures or ill-feeling that might occur during the next few weeks, there would be little room for manoeuvre, let alone going back.

I was anxious that Olivier should not be tempted into the snare of making Archie funny. It would have been an understandable mistake for an actor unused to little less than worship. As it was, people perpetuated the myth that the character was based on Max Miller. Archie was a man all right and one which most people, especially maidenly middle-class reviewers, found unfamiliar and despicable. If they had been baffled that an educated young man, even an ungrateful graduate of a white-tile university, should *choose* to work at a market sweet-stall, they were mystified by Archie. What could possibly be interesting to the civilized sensibility in the spectacle of a third-rate comic writhing in a dying profession?

Max Miller was a god, certainly to me, a saloon-bar Priapus. Archie never got away with anything. Life cost him dearly, always. When he came on, the audience was immediately suspicious or indifferent. Archie's cheek was less than ordinary. Max didn't have to be nauseatingly lovable like Chaplin. His humanity was in his sublime sauce, Archie's in his hollow desperation. Max got fined £5 for giving them one from the Blue Book and the rest of the world laughed with him. Archie would have got six months and no option.

Olivier took the point from the outset, although he did go and see Miller's fearsome widow. We all paid visits to the remaining London halls. The Chelsea Palace, the Met in Edgware Road and Collins' in Islington were all about to be swept away. When I wrote in the play's published edition that the music hall was dying, I hadn't been aware that the bulldozers and iron balls were poised quite so close to home.

I was especially keen that we should go a few times to Collins', where I had witnessed some of the worst acts imaginable, although the occasional star, like Albert Whelan whistling over his white gloves, Randolph ('On Mother Kelly's Doorstep') Sutton and Ella Shields failing to light her pipe on her sailor's uniform, tottered through their fifty-year-old routines with a kind of detached dignity to a supine audience.

We missed a Scots comedian called Jack Radcliffe who did a very eerie deathbed scene. I thought the spectacle of a 'dying' comic in a sketch about death performed to an almost comatose audience would help an actor who could hardly have witnessed such a farewell to hope and dignity, let alone taken part in it. We did see a more robust act by a Cockney, Scott Sanders, whose signature tune was 'Rolling round the world, waiting for the sunshine and hoping things will turn out right', which he played on a series of pots and pans hanging on a barrow. He was loud, brisk, seldom funny and looked as if he knew it, hurtling through his act hoarsely before retreating to the pub next door. 'Why have you got that lemon stuck in your ear?' 'You've heard of the man with the hearing aid? Well, I'm the one with the lemonade.'

I felt it was important to engage Vivien's support. The rejection of her rubber mask must have added to the rather icy feeling that became clearer during the next few weeks. Once, in Collins', a semen-filled handkerchief was hurled into my lap from somewhere in the dim auditorium. Such an incident would have delighted Lady Olivier. She took to it all, laughing at the dog acts filling the stage with flags, the ventriloquists whose lips flapped like Esther Rantzen on a bad night, the xylophone players with their 'popular melodies'. Unlike the slumped, morose audience around us, Vivien joined in.

One of Olivier's central problems was to persuade audiences that such poetic awfulness could be authentic. The pressure of time was no bad thing and we threw ourselves into what was a unique venture for everyone. Larry was enthusiastic. Tony was at his infectious best. George Relph was clearly going to be splendid as Billy: every flick of his hat or delicate buffing of his fingernails so like my grandfather – and much more agreeable. He had been shot through the throat during the First World War and, having been a successful juvenile, had been forced to become a character man. Brenda de Banzie would hiss in triumph at any old stage-hand or fireman as she came off, 'Look – real tears.' Dorothy Tutin seemed a modest, friendly girl who liked a glass of Guinness and I soon found myself assured that she would give a tougher performance than I had anticipated. Richard Pasco, fresh from playing the second Jimmy Porter, was already a friend.

Jock Addison, the composer, had come with us on our music-hall outings. On these visits he had seemed strangely cautious, but I was unfamiliar with his almost Ben Travers containment. When I suspected he might be bored he was merely worrying over whether to score for two trumpets or one trumpet and a trombone. I was uncertain that he approved of my lyrics. The problem had been to produce something that was identifiably atrocious but good enough to be enjoyable pastiche. Jock set my lyrics in his painstaking way, almost like someone undertaking a set exam piece. The result, with its grasp of the crummy pit orchestra, was not just an accompaniment but an insight into the heart of the play. 'Why should I care' went unnoticed at the time. When Olivier died, it was on every news bulletin.

Jock's wife, Pamela, was visibly shy and wary of theatrical folk, particularly divide-and-rule men like Tony. The nearest thing to a dramatic experience for her would be an accident in Fortnum and Mason's food hall. Two of the characters in *The Hotel in Amsterdam* are approximations to the Addisons, although I did them small justice. Jock was to score most of the early Woodfall movies, including *Tom Jones*, for which he won an Academy Award. During the next decade, our lives, along with a dozen or so others, spun in a kind of dizzying pattern around Tony and his circle. When Richardson finally said his unfond farewell to England and settled in Los Angeles for good, the centre didn't exactly fall apart, but the heavens moved to a different rhythm.

In rehearsal there were disturbing rumours about the Oliviers' domestic life. I was not privy to this, although I had the impression that George and Tony knew about the early-morning visits to girls on Thameside houseboats, recriminations and physical vengeance. I hoped that it was not true, for the selfish reason of safeguarding my play and protecting it from prurient interest in Britain's most famous and near-royal couple, which would surely divert attention from what was happening in the theatre itself.

Vivien's watchful presence was the most dangerous threat to the production's progress, and everyone from George to the ASMs was aware of it. She would drop in without warning and sit in the dress circle with Bernard, her chocolate-uniformed chauffeur, a row behind her. It was usually an unobtrusive entrance, but stardom has no use for tact. Her presence was as distracting as an underwear advertisement at a Lesbians for Peace meeting. She had only recently shouted in protest from the public gallery of the House of Lords about the demolition of the St James's Theatre. What if she should stand up and shout from the dress circle of the Royal Court?

In the event, she always sat quickly and quietly, occasionally asking the chauffeur for a light, intent on Olivier. It was, of course, impossible to know what she was feeling and I could only guess at the pain. It seemed complicated, to say the least, that she should be yearning for a rubber mask to turn her into a sort of Brenda – like Niobe, all real tears. Sad also. The clash of feeling made her want to take part in a gamble in which she could hardly have believed, merely to share an act of possible public folly. If Larry was out of his depth now and then, so were we all, but none more so than Vivien, which made her isolation increasingly obvious.

Olivier was relishing his front-of-cloth scenes, attaining an astonishing skill at throw-away business, like a spastic Jimmy Cagney. One Saturday run-through, about midday, he sprang his first realized version of the scene in which Archie sings the blues and crumples slowly down the side of the proscenium arch. The spring sunshine and the noise of the Sloane Square traffic poured through the open door. A dozen of us watched, astounded. Vivien turned her head towards me. She was weeping. I immediately thought of the chill inflection in Olivier's Archie voice: 'I wish women wouldn't cry. I wish they wouldn't . . . '

Before the dress rehearsal, Vivien made a final effort. To do what? I don't know. The production had perhaps become a vehicle containing all her sense of loss to come or already endured. When Tony, George and I were summoned to Number One dressing-room, Olivier was tired, he said little. Like a lioness protective of her energy, she was word-perfect in her complaints and criticisms. Her feverish fury erupted in the cramped room, with its view of the London Transport canteen and the corner of W.H. Smith. After weeks of frustration, watching rehearsals and fuelled by the reception of surely indignant reports back at Binkie's base camp, she lashed out at us all. Finally, edging her fur coat through the door, she said to George, pale but a-puff on his tobacco: 'I was always very fond of you, George. But I could never stand that fucking awful pipe. If you'd been married to me, you would have had to smoke it outside in the garden!'

6. Barwick's Suit

Reticence is called elitism and priggishness passes for compassion ... Is it all to do with hatred of the past?

Notebook, 1982

The Entertainer opened on 10 April. On the same day I was due to appear at the Law Courts in the Strand for my petition against Pamela. Months had elapsed since our last meeting, in the buffet on York station. I had gone on hoping I would hear from her. Some vagueness of purpose or even forgetfulness would surely delay the final resort to the court. Mary seemed happy enough in her chirrupy way but I was fairly certain that she would find an obstructive wife too much for her Calvinist morality to accommodate.

She was still largely unaffected by theatrical bohemianism. When I occasionally lapsed into what was then known as 'outrageous camp', she would plead with unsimulated disquiet. 'Oh, do stop it, John. You sound *just* like a queer.' The thought of me making mischief in front of her rugby-playing brothers from Watson's Academy (Scottish camp if ever there was) dismayed her. But, like so many actresses, she found this nonsense perfectly acceptable in crimpers and small-part players. Gordon, her favourite dresser from H.M. Tennant days, was already rather creaky: 'Binkie! Don't talk to me about him. Do you know what I call him? Binkie-Bonkie-Boo-Boo! I do! – Come with me to Woolworth's. I want to buy a lemon shampoo.'

Surely Pamela, sphinx, muddler and arch-procrastinator, could be relied upon to equivocate triumphantly at the last moment? Divorce in 1957 was as risky an adventure and as much a taint on the character as a number of indictable crimes. The concept of guilty and innocent parties was perfectly suited to the avarice and conformism of lawyers, enabling them to encourage their respective clients to go for each other's jugulars like fighting Staffordshires. The implication was that both parties were guilty for having got themselves into such an unthinking mess and, if both dogs died, everyone else got their bets paid.

Divorce, then as now, was concerned almost exclusively with the double-headed monster of sex and money. But worse than physical cruelty or moral indecency was the sin of collusion. The whole masquerade of 'proving' adultery had been lampooned for years by Evelyn Waugh and others. The law remained immune to ridicule. This muddled farce was compounded in my case by Pamela's near-terminal indecision and, more seriously, by the actor we had selected to play the part of co-respondent. I was not sure whether he was the *de facto* party, and tried not to brood about it. He was preferable to the Jewish dentist from Derby, whom I had suggested in some malevolence.

Oscar Beuselinck's clerk, Charlie Barwick, had taken over my case and was even more gloomy about my prospects of success than Oscar, who seemed to regard the whole lengthy business with no more distress than being refused renewal of a dog licence. 'Can't say I think much of your co-respondent, John. Very dodgy. Scruffy cove. Welsh. No collar and tie. We'll have to smarten him up a bit if it does come to it. You may have to buy him some decent clothes. They could go in with our fees.'

As there was no matter of alimony or custody of children, and I had been to all intents and purposes deserted by Pamela, all this dressing-up seemed infinitely frivolous. I had not owned a suit since I joined Harry Hanson's company in Camberwell six years earlier. ('Own Wardrobe and Dinner Jacket.') Bought from a second-hand shop in Vauxhall Bridge Road, it had long ago disintegrated. I went to Aquascutum and fitted myself out with a suitably supplicant-looking outfit: heavy flannel, double-breasted, with a faint concession to dash in a scarcely visible red stripe. On the supposed young scourge of the Establishment it seemed likely to invite suspicion of a hoax.

Before my court appearance, I had one more thing to do. Nellie Beatrice knew nothing of my marriage. I had managed, without much difficulty, to keep it from her. She was now working in a rather disagreeable pub, oddly named the Organ Inn, on the Ewell bypass. I decided to give the plaintiff's suit its first public airing and arranged to meet her in the restaurant of Bentall's store, which she regarded as rather posh. I felt I could not allow her to read about Pamela in the newspapers.

As usual with Nellie Beatrice, I either over- or under-estimated her resilience and cunning. She was surprised, resentful even, that she had not been given the rights of confidence due to a loving mother, but otherwise almost insouciant. She asked no questions about my ex-wife-to-be; the incident could be counted a moral victory and swept into discarded memory. She probably hoped that I would not be silly to myself again and would move in with Anthony Creighton on a steadier basis.

She was in a new rig-out: lemon and cream, coral and brown, all to match. What a telling-off brother Jack was going to get from Uncle Sid; Auntie

Queenie kept dropping hints about a pound or two for a drop of brandy; the new barmaid was a common bit of goods; Grandma O. was bedridden above Tesco's. 'Mother, I said, if you don't agree to go into a nice home, I don't know what I'm going to do with you. I said, Mother, if they find you with bedsores, who do you think'll get the blame? I will. And then what will people think. I'm a bag of nerves with it all. My life's been enough rush as it is. You want a bit of peace to buck you up now and again.'

I paid the bill, which irked her slightly, threatening her position of never owing anything to anyone with nothing behind him. 'What's this then? A cheque! I keep telling you. Keep your money for yourself. You're going to need it. Fifty pounds! No, I *can't* take that. Suppose I spend it all at once – you know, go on the razzle!'

When I finally got back to Woodfall Street, Mary was in her nightgown watching an Edgar Lustgarten movie about the grim results of criminal miscalculation. 'Thought you were getting rid of her early,' she muttered. That devout wish was not to be consummated for another quarter of a century.

The following day I presented myself at the Law Courts in my Decree Nisi suit and a blue and red Paisley tie I had bought from Burlington Arcade in my teens for good luck at auditions and interviews. Barwick looked like my Great Uncle Lod, the undertaker, before he got his hands on the coffin handles and the mild and bitter. Oscar was pacing up and down cheerfully. He glanced at my suit. 'Not too bad. Can't have you looking like a Teddy boy, son. Not too sure about that tie. Haven't you got anything less flashy? Well, too late now. Remember, you're a famous man. Press is all here.' I recognized a second-string reviewer who was wearing a huge hat suitable for the Royal Enclosure. Joe Jackson, my counsel, seemed pessimistic about the outcome and aggrieved at the dubious brief. He grilled me as if I were a self-confessed double rapist. He turned to Oscar: 'Well, I hope he does a bit better than this in front of the judge.' He walked off, leaving me with the stain of deadly collusion spilled over the suit. A patently irrelevant purchase.

Huddled groups of rather undernourished-looking plaintiffs, defendants and their relatives sat on benches, hankies held at noses, defensive glares and fidgeting chain-smoking fingers. Now and then a scream would ring out from another court, where more than marital life was being dissected, cut short and condemned in the public sight. The other barristers seemed much jollier than my Mr Jackson. Guffaws sounded. They waved at each other like the Hooray Henrys of Woodfall Street running a sporty abattoir.

The suit became heavier and heavier. I felt I would need to be hoisted up like a bandy knight before the field of Agincourt. Mary, who never seemed to have a nerve to crack, had sent me off with a hip-flask as if I were going out for a day with the Quorn. 'For God's sake,' snapped Barwick, 'don't let them see that.' I longed for a cigarette, but no doubt my black Russian Sobranies would be as damning as the flask. The glands in my neck began to throb like a toad's throat. The lunch-time adjournment came and we slipped over to the pub, where Oscar was eating a huge lunch. I ordered a large whisky, and then another. 'Don't get drunk, son. Wouldn't do at all. Especially in your position.' My position was one in which I needed a drink and no more advice. Like most people who disapprove of alcohol, Oscar believed that one sniff of the stuff made you break into the hokey-cokey.

At three o'clock, an usher whispered in Barwick's ear and we were rushed to another court, the hacks close behind. We had been switched. The atmosphere was torpid, long stretches of silence broken by the scratching of pens, carelessly flung briefs and the whispering of clerks slipping in and out of the room. A red-eyed witness in the box was hunched in misery. A mumble came from her chin, pointing down her cheap print dress. An endless pause before the judge looked up. 'What is she trying to say?' 'I couldn't hear, my lord.' 'Neither could I. Would you repeat the question and kindly ask your client to speak so that the court can hear her evidence.' 'I apologize, my lord,' said the pink-cheeked, portly young Woodfall Street reveller. 'As you will have seen, my client is just an ordinary, uneducated woman, and she finds even simple questions hard to answer at times.' 'Yes. I see that. Tiresome. Well, carry on.'

Jackson rose. He seemed wearily confident. Barwick stared down at his feet. My co-respondent was called. He looked decently dressed enough and answered Jackson's questions loudly in a thick Welsh garble. No one asked him to speak up, although I could hardly hear him myself. It seemed all right, although the accent was one I associated with the equivocations of my own family. When I got into the box, my new Simpsons shirt was stuck wet and tight against me. I blundered almost at once. 'Do you or do you not now live at Number Fifteen Woodfall Street, sw3?' Perhaps that wasn't even the question, but I answered 'No.' Wrongly. My counsel gave me a smart Black Look and the judge smiled. 'I think you mean "Yes" don't you, Mr Osborne?' 'Yes. My Lord.'

Within minutes, a decree nisi was granted without costs, my own adultery being admitted. I was back outside, flanked by Barwick and Oscar. 'No comment, gentlemen, no comment.' No comment was hackneyed enough without having it said for you. Jackson was talking to Oscar as if he had brought off a 10–1 winner. He shook hands with me. 'Hope I don't have to see you again,' he said like an orthodontist showing out a patient who has not been cleaning his teeth properly. 'Yes, one or two nasty moments there,' said Oscar. 'You looked very nervous, son. You'd better go off to your play. You *have* fixed my first-night tickets, haven't you?' It was his first expression of concern all day.

I waved down a taxi. 'This way, John,' the photographers chanted. 'Be a sport.'

When I got back to Woodfall Street, Mary – unlike Oscar – had a large whisky ready for me. It was time to change for the first-night curtain, rid myself of my sodden shirt, toss away my audition tie after my abandoned marriage. I had eaten nothing and felt very sick. As I was throwing up sticky whisky and ginger ale, Mary called: 'Not being *sick*, are you?' Kneeling over the lavatory basin, staring at 'Shanks', I yelled back, 'No.' 'Och, that's all right then.' I felt more lonely than I had for months: the thought of the long evening, so many unfamiliar faces, the stifling scent of such occasions. I never wore the suit again.

In the circumstances, it seemed less deferential to wear a dinner-jacket. I had hardly worn it since the night I had stood on the stage at Bridgwater with my arms clasped shakily round Pamela in her low-dusting-maid's green uniform, waiting for the curtain to go up on *My Wife's Family*. Mary was as cheerful as a bird, as if anticipating the reels at a Highland Ball. I looked around the crowded, tiny foyer. What I had already come to regard as my own theatre was besieged by people who were patently my natural enemies. One voice called out, 'Good luck, John,' and the box-office manager winked at me.

I went through the pass door to find George peering through the curtains in the prompt corner. He was wearing an old velvet jacket and a floppy black tie. I had never seen him dressed up like this before and it was gratifying that he should have taken such unusual trouble. I expected him to be rather grim and soldierly but he was almost gleeful.

'There you are, dear boy, take a look out there.' The serrated rows of sparklers, perfumed earls, belted countesses and the St Michael *mafiosi* in the front of the dress circle was not reassuring. He hugged me and grinned. 'There they are. All waiting for *you*. All of us, come to that. What do you think, eh? Same old pack of cunts, fashionable arseholes. Just more of them than usual, that's all. There's old Harold, thinking about mortal mind. Darlington can't find his ear trumpet. That prick Bessborough. Poor old Neville, that's his mistress, got the same mink on as Elaine. Look at Elaine! Done up like a sofa underneath a Jewish Christmas-tree and twice as prickly. That's what you're up against. That's what we're always up against – *if we're lucky*.'

His fixed-bayonet relish was stunning. I sat at the end of a row seeing little and listening to snatches. I thought idly about other things. Of the people who weren't there. Of Pamela, and Arnold Running ('I wouldn't give him the sweat from my balls'); of my first loves, Joan Turvey, Renee, Stella; and of my father.

The acting is so superlatively good that one could easily be kidded into believing this play to be finer than it possibly is.

Daily Worker

For long stabs it was gin and misery in a show business setting, with no hope in sight for anybody. It's so darned depressing.

Daily Herald

John Osborne is certainly a dramatist of great promise . . . He can write parts for actors . . . He gives Laurence Olivier the chance for a tour de force of impersonation and disguise.

Daily Telegraph

Though maudlin and only partially successful, the new play generates some heat and raw emotion. It is given the immense advantage of being acted by a splendid team of actors led by Sir Laurence Olivier.

Manchester Guardian

The theatrical effect is enormous.

Sunday Times

One of the great acting parts of our age.

Observer

Olivier's presence and the sense of occasion persuaded the notoriously mean management of the Court to allow us the stage and a few bottles of extremely cheap wine for a party. The band played, stage-hands and actors danced and drank. Vivien sang rather sweetly. Mary sang 'Bonny Mary of Argyll.' Richard Pasco and I sang 'Don't be afraid to sleep with your sweetheart', and I forgot the words. Olivier went through his routines from the play. He was happy. He knew he had created a remarkable memory for everyone.

During the early hours, he saw me slumped and buzzed in the stalls. He came over and put his arm around me. 'Whatever you do, dear heart, *don't* ever, ever, get into trouble with the Income Tax Man. Buy certificates.' He sounded like, he still *was*, Archie.

I was thinking, as we came home, that we all talk about the director, the acting, the theatre but no one ever mentions the *play*. I suppose, lucky us, we take it for granted, like some great tree which just exists and we are all pissing round its base. Anyway, thank you for it, once more –
Best love,
G

Letter from George Devine to J.O.

On the strength of Olivier's defiant act of public slumming, *The Entertainer* had sold out at the Royal Court before its opening. To my delight, he agreed to play another limited season at the Palace in the autumn. In the meantime he and Vivien took the suitably vengeful tale of *Titus Andronicus* on tour to Australia, land of benighted strife, and Mary and I went on holiday to Sicily.

We returned for her costume fittings for the second film under her Rank contract. We were summoned to dinner at the Savoy with John Davis, ex-accountant and new Chairman of Rank Films. I had just filled in for a fortnight as film critic of the *Evening Standard*. I had enjoyed putting a cheerful blowtorch, a kind of hogmanay lark, to a lumpen Davis product called *Campbell's Kingdom*.

At the Savoy Grill, Davis, accompanied by his new wife, Dinah Sheridan, had already ordered the meal for all of us. I spotted that evening's copy of the *Standard* on the chair beside him. 'Mr Bogarde is a very good actor with immense personal charm. For years he has been Britain's most popular screen actor, during which time he has never appeared in a decent film . . . *Campbell's Kingdom* is yet another large-budget British film doggedly maintaining a B-picture standard.'

It hadn't occurred to me that my few cents-worth in a London evening paper could affect anyone's pocket or reputation. I was unprepared for Miss Sheridan's loyal wrath. In my perverse relish for shockable middle-class girls, I found her rather attractive. I declined the saddle of lamb and asked for an omelette. Mr Davis, brandishing the *Standard*, demanded what I knew about films. I replied that I knew nothing about accounting but had seen four films a week from the age of four. The lamb and the omelette were quickly dispatched. There was little to drink. I began to feel the silent support of the waiters. Mrs Davis threw back her pretty young head: 'More than anyone I've ever met, I'd like to slap your face.' She looked as if she meant it, and in the right circumstances it would have been an intriguing prospect.

The next production at the Court was Ionesco's *The Chairs*, with George Devine and Joan Plowright playing the Old Man and Woman preparing for the arrival of unseen guests and filling the stage with significantly empty chairs. It appealed to George's dogged Francophilia. The curtain-raiser was a piece of Gallic whimsy by Giraudoux called *The Apollo of Bergerac*, in which the young film actress, Heather Sears, told chandeliers and other objects that they were beautiful, in case they didn't already know. When Tony offered me the tiny part of a grumbling gardener, I accepted at once. I had no wish to begin writing another play, although my head was scrambled with what I might do now. The welcome of the past year had been suspicious and had a cannibal relish to it. The cooking-pot was bubbling away. The prospect of putting on another bald-pate wig and streaking my face with lake liner, a drink afterwards with friends and a weekly brown envelope with money inside it was hard to resist.

One lunch-time in the pub next door to the Royal Court, Mary and I were having a drink. The pub was mostly used by Irish labourers, drunks and guardsmen. A hack came over and sat down beside us. 'Hello, John. Mulchrone, *Daily Mail*!' The dirty-mac reporter from Fleet Street still doggedly dressed the part then. 'I understand that you've just come back from a holiday in Sicily. I don't want to spell it out, do I? But the Queen's Proctor might be very interested.'

Mary was genuinely puzzled, having heard of the Procurator Fiscal but not the Queen's Proctor. 'What's he talking about?'

'After all, your decree doesn't become absolute for a few weeks yet, I believe. I've had a word with Mr Beuselinck. You know, public figures, all that, people are bound to be interested. Of course I'd rather be working on the *Manchester Guardian*. Do you think my colleague could take a quick photograph of you together?' said Mulchrone.

'Tell him to fuck off,' said Mary, so caught by her wee-lassie distress that she was trapped into a four-letter comeback.

'You heard what the lady said,' I replied, stoutly.

Nothing did appear in the *Daily Mail*, but I suspected the incident had set Mary on to determining a wedding date as soon as possible, rather than let news of the Queen's Proctor penetrate the north.

The Chairs went into the repertory and was treated with general caution. Giraudoux was more or less ignored, rightly and to my relief. Nigel Dennis had been so excited by *Cards of Identity* that he had written another play especially for George, with parts for Joan Plowright and myself. The gratitude of playwrights for actors is almost as rare as the reverse. Golden eggs have little time for the mucky feathers that cling to them.

Nigel's offering was a sincere response to the shaky iconoclasm of the Court, under constant attrition as it was from its own generals at the rear looking for easy victories and urging swift withdrawal to the dug-out positions of box-office safety. *The Making of Moo* was the first direct product of George's opening campaign. It must have been sweet encouragement for him, coming so unexpectedly from a middle-aged, rather monkish novelist and critic. All the others he pursued had been almost contemptuous of his overtures, making it clear that the Novel and Poetry would continue their ascendance indefinitely.

Moo's theme was unyielding. God was a Bad Thing. It was torch-carrying atheism with small Shavian clowning. It had been tooled up entirely with the object of giving offence. George was happy. Nigel was delighted. My part as

George's secretary, an amateur musician set to compose hymns as gruesome substitutes for those Ancient and Modern, was patchy but enjoyable. My Ben Travers training came in useful. The machine itself was endearingly wobbly. The only way to approach it was to jump aboard and hang on before falling off – the kind of pleasure that purists find inexplicable.

There was also the attraction of yet another short tour. Back to Brighton, the Royal Crescent and the stage carpenter's welcome: 'Blimey, not *you* again.' The cast, apart from George, Joan and myself, consisted of Robert Stephens and Anthony Creighton (first and second natives), John Wood, John Moffatt, James Villiers and Esmé Percy. Tony directed. His assistant was John Dexter. I had tried to persuade George and Tony to employ both Anthony and Dexter. In Anthony's case it was in the hope of keeping him out of the Sloane Square pubs at my expense. John, I believed, was possessed with a special talent which, if he would overcome a wounded class pride unsuited to his intelligence and his natural bullying ambition, could become a valuable asset.

Most of us had already worked together for over a year and a half. Robert Stephens and his wife, Tarn, lived a couple of minutes away from Woodfall Street and we spent many evenings together eating heartily at the cheap Indian restaurants at the World's End and drinking late into the night. Robert was a rumbustious jokesmith and had a good line in making his farts explode when exposed to a naked match. Actors from the Court, employed or out of work, dropped in at almost any hour at the Stephens' house in Glebe Place. It must have been hell for Tarn. We probably made as much noise as the Henrys of Woodfall Street. But the Henrys were the ruling garrison, we were bandits from the hills.

The Making of Moo was a short play: 'A History of Religion in Three Acts'. It was a pretty snappy tour of the subject, over in not much more than two hours with a couple of disgruntled intervals to bring relief to the weary observers. Everyone, including Nigel, was aware of its deficiencies. George and Tony promoted a feeling of light-hearted scepticism. We would give ourselves a good time for attempting it at all. There was no question of dragging Nigel down from his Essex cottage and beloved earth-closet, of locking him into a suite at the Grand to rewrite the third act. He came down once during the week and, in the way of authors, laughed shamelessly at his own jokes.

Several of the company decided to go to Brighton on Saturday, move in unhurriedly and spend the evening together. We went out to dinner with Esmé Percy as the unofficial guest of honour. With his glass eye flashing and his old dog farting loyally beneath the table, he became movingly expansive in the way of old men who are astonished by the curiosity of the young. We urged him to remember and coaxed out every detail of Lady Cunard or Colefax's days and nights.

His memory seemed meticulous, waspishly accurate about people and events mostly unknown to us, flowing without pause in his almost castrato, fluting voice. My schoolboy memory of him in wide, sloping hats, astrakhan collars, with jewelled fluttering fingers, was enacted before us. Eventually, he reluctantly pleaded tiredness. It was almost 4.00 a.m. when Robert and I saw him up to his room. He embraced us both. 'What an enchanting evening. I have enjoyed it so much. You are all so sweet. And young. I don't know why you are so kind to me. Thank you, *dear* boys.'

When I went down in the morning to look at my lines on the beach, Robert came along with Esmé's dog on a leash. He had been found snuffling unhappily against Esmé's glass eye, the replacement of the one bitten out by his predecessor. The real eye was closed in death.

Immediately, remembrance felt cruelly treated, and so swiftly. I had hardly known him, but it seemed like a warning shot against careless acquaintance. However, to die in work, with your own farting friend beside you in the Royal Crescent Hotel after a jubilant evening in the affectionate company of younger friends, seems as much justice as most of us would probably wish. Robert, no slouch at breaking wind himself, adopted the dog.

7. 'All Russia is my Garden'

Oh, heavens, how I long for a little ordinary human enthusiasm. Just
enthusiasm – that's all. I want to hear a warm, thrilling voice cry out
Hallelujah! Hallelujah! I'm alive! I've an idea. Why don't we have a little
game? Let's pretend that we're human beings, and that we're actually
alive. Just for a while. What do you say? Let's pretend we're human.

Look Back in Anger

Shortly after *The Making of Moo* opened in London for a couple of weeks, the
English Stage Company was invited to something called the World Festival of
Youth in Moscow. Trips to Russia were hard to come by and, even under the
dubious sponsorship underwritten by the British Communist Party and every
shade of left-wing dupe, the invitation was irresistible.

Going for the ride, or being taken for one, were Tony, Oscar Lewenstein,
Lindsay Anderson and myself. We flew to Helsinki and then boarded the train
for the twenty-four-hour journey to Moscow. The excitement was high. Tony
muttered at the great landscape, 'All Russia is my garden.' Oscar, the only
card-carrying Communist, looked more smug with every mile. The train was
huge, almost empty, with samovars on the boil at the end of the corridors and
martial music bursting forth as we drew near the capital. This was the best
part.

The official jaunt was a dispiriting affair, zealous but chaotic, possibly well-
intentioned but glum. There were not enough beds, not much food and we
were assigned a guide and interpreter, Marion, with a passion for official
architecture. She responded to our requests for a beer with a blistering, 'I am
not a drunkard!' We spent a few pleasant unofficial hours in Gorky Park,
where some friendly students expressed their affection for Jack London, A.J.
Cronin and J.B. Priestley. We saw a creaky but scenically weighty performance
of *The Sleeping Beauty* at the Bolshoi and I was impressed by a couple of tough
lady claqueurs who I thought I might usefully take home as a present for
George. I swam the width and back again of the River Moskva to aloof

disapproval from the natives and was nearly arrested on the train journey home alone.

I had to return to London before the others as *Moo* was due back in the repertory. Despite the Queen's Proctor's mackintosh moles from the *Daily Mail*, my decree absolute was waiting for me, and Mary had begun to make arrangements for our wedding with such determination that I wondered whether she might be pregnant and already in dread of brisk finger-counting-months north of the border. Perhaps to wipe out the stain of Sassenach adultery, like the memory of Glencoe, her father, stepmother, brothers and sisters-in-law, cousins and auld nanny had already been notified, travel and hotel arrangements were organized. She had bought a hat with a veil and a dowdy suit from some madam shop in Baker Street. The Scottish guests would approve, but it would photograph pretty disastrously in the departure lounge.

I was powerless to unscramble this great skein of Scottish knitting. A ready complaisance took me over as it sometimes does when I decide to concede a helpless position and retreat until the ingenuity of time or delayed inspiration will rescue me. Like being trapped in an airport queue or at a nightmare of boredom in the theatre, one can only pretend that it is all happening to someone else and that a ladder from the skies will descend for the execution of a perfect and daring escape.

I persuaded the registrar at Chelsea to open his office on a Sunday morning. Our intention of marriage would not be posted outside until the Saturday evening, when Mulchrone and his clones were unlikely to spot it. The ruse worked until a passer-by tipped off the newspapers for the usual fee. Vivienne Drummond, Mary's friend who had taken over as Helena in *Look Back*, was a witness. The other was Tony, who performed the same office for me five years later in Sussex.

The reception was held at Au Père de Nico, a restaurant in Lincoln Street patronized by the Court. George was there, Robert and Tarn Stephens, Anthony Creighton and others. At least half of the guests came from Over the Border. A genial uncle of Mary's proposed the toast and unmarried Nanny gave the bride advice: 'Remember, lassie, if he ever expects, or wants, well you know what I'm talking about, don't ever *deny* it to him. That's the secret of marriage.'

It had been impossible to exclude Nellie Beatrice from the occasion but I saw to it that she would be hemmed in by the noisiest, less respectable guests and preferably not too near the Lowlanders, who would surely find her barmaid's 'get-up-them-stairs' innuendo as spine-chilling as I had twenty years earlier. Someone had arranged for a Chelsea sculptor to present us with a piece of pottery in the shape of a bear with a honey jar and a squirrel with nuts. It was about eighteen inches high and inscribed:

> The bear has found his squirrel
> The squirrel has found her bear
> Honey will flow, the nuts will grow
> And the anger wasn't there.

Mary seemed to like it but, then, Annigoni was her favourite painter.

During the civic mateyness of the registry ceremony I couldn't help thinking of Bridgwater and of Pamela. The vicar had seemed set upon dinning St Paul into us and with me, at least, he had succeeded:

> So ought men to love their wives as their own bodies. He that loveth his wife loveth himself. For no man ever yet hateth his own flesh; but nourisheth and cherisheth it, even as the Lord the Church . . . For this cause shall a man leave his father and mother, and shall be joined unto his wife, and they two shall be one flesh. This is a great mystery . . . auld Nanny.

> Mummy was slumped over her pew in a heap – the noble, female rhino – pole-axed at last! . . . Just the two of them in that empty church – them and me. I'm not sure what happened after that. We must have been married, I suppose.

Look Back in Anger

So, again, I supposed I was.

Mary's elder brother drove us to Heathrow. Mary burst into tears, even now surprised at Mulchrone's men snapping her Baker Street rig-out. 'This way please, Mary.' There was some misunderstanding about whether she should be going abroad while filming *Windom's Way*. '*I'm* not publicizing that fucking film.' By the time we had boarded she had recovered herself like a toddler rising with bloodied knees. We had made no hotel reservations. 'Just leave it to me,' she said, mopping her face. I did. We got to Nice and moved into the Martinez for the night. Mary thought the prices outrageous. As we were returning in two days it seemed pointless to move, but we did, to a small hotel off the Croisette. The Martinez was too grand.

George's petard had blown a hole that was even harder to fill now that everyone was scrutinizing the success of the first assault. 'What do they expect?' he growled. 'If you can get even two good plays a year, you're bloody lucky. How many passing good novels are there a year? Or paintings?'

But the pressure was on. Revolution had to be pragmatic in those days before the Arts – like Sport – had ministers to support them. The St Michael mafiosi were pleased to have Laurence Olivier in their theatre but not to lose thousands of pounds on plays which carried neither cash nor cachet. Mention John Arden, Ann Jellicoe, Donald Haworth or Christopher Logue and they reached for the blowtorch.

In his first true revival, coming as it did so soon, George had disarmed the slings of amateur know-alls with a brilliant stroke. With the production of *The Country Wife* in December 1956 for his unknown protégée Joan Plowright, he had the proper sense of vulgarity to cast a film star whom he hardly admired, Laurence Harvey. The result was happy for everyone. A fine cast (Alan Bates, Nigel Davenport, George himself and Robert Stephens) and a Jack Hylton transfer to the Adelphi which ran for a year staunched the murmurings of the mafiosi and their moneylenders.

This success also blurred for a time the evidence of a consistently uncommitted public which suited itself capriciously whether or not to attend the next production at the Royal Court. This idea of a 'Court audience' was already attracting deluded enthusiasts. The fact emerged as production followed production that it never existed. Star names might coax the West End punter over to Sloane Square for the right play, as with Harvey in Wycherley, but not for the wrong one, like Ashcroft in Brecht.

In truth, there was no systematic policy except that which engaged the various personalities that grew around the original nucleus assembled by George and Tony. Most of these were, in the mild climate of the time, left of centre, though they would now be regarded as soft-meringue-liberals by the drowsy commissars who have long since taken over. There was criticism that this English approach was damaging and incoherent. It seemed to me human, thoughtful, sympathetic and flexible. It was conviction contained by natural sweetness and not mere aggrandizement. Joan Littlewood had this gift in plenty. George and Tony were perhaps more acerbic: unknowing prophets, but not bullies.

In the midst of such energy, to be accused of being eclectic seemed to be civilized. As I found with the Anglican Church, it would be a rich landscape in which to exercise and refine one's unbelief. 'Choose your theatre as you would a religion,' said George, famously. What he produced was often a comically unbalanced broad Church accommodating anti-democratic works like *August for the People* and the reverential French connection. Now, the bony memory of the arse-aching boredom of many of those evenings helps to send me gasping for the interval air and a succouring drink to ease the pains of past and present.

I think it was Balfour who used to pass out from boredom at political soirées. In the fifties I had more stamina and expectation. I didn't know the form book, either. And, anyway, we were off to America.

There were many understandable reasons why American producers had been reluctant to take *Look Back* to Broadway. There were no stars. Because of the embarrassed sensibilities of Mr Albery over the bears and squirrels, it hadn't been given a West End showing. True, it had aroused almost unprecedented attention, but if it was such a smash why wasn't it still doing boffo or even boffola business? Naturally, it was too long.

In reality, it ran for two hours and forty minutes with two intervals, and even less when Kenneth Haigh used to cut certain speeches on the evenings when he declared that he 'wasn't feeling it'. ('What do you want me to do? Tell the audience a lie?' Yes, by all means, Ken. They won't know the difference.) As many of the London critics had commented with grim satisfaction, 'It calls out for the knife.' Length is something both reviewers and producers confuse with time. *Hamlet* is too long. So is *Don Giovanni*. So, sometimes, is life.

Another obstacle was language. Although the immigrant populations have all but lost their native tongues, English is still a foreign field to most Americans. Peter Nichols swears that when he was working in Minneapolis, an apparently literate middle-class couple deduced from his speech that he was a foreigner. When he told them that he came from England, they asked, 'Oh, where's that?' 'Well, sort of up on your left from Europe.' 'Is that so, and what sort of language do they speak there?'

So. Could not this piece be transposed successfully from somewhere in the Midlands to Greenwich Village, or even Minneapolis? And a *sweet*-stall? What about a downtown soda fountain? What if they were all Puerto Ricans? None of this reassured Roger Stevens and Alexander Cohen, then reckoned to be the arbiters of New York theatre. The chances of *Look Back* reaching Forty-second Street seemed remote.

I had met David Merrick a couple of times in London. He was one of the many hundreds who later claimed to have been present at the Royal Court on 8 May. A soft-spoken Jewish lawyer, born Margoles, with a mournful moustache and eyes to match, Merrick had an almost sinister obsession with the theatre which made his conversation quickly pall. He had scarcely any small talk except occasional satisfaction at someone else's out-of-town disaster, when the sad-dog eyes would brighten slightly. It was hard to explain his tenacious fervour as he never expressed enthusiasm, rather the opposite: 'I saw it and I hated it'; unimaginable that he should feel affection for a medium so sustained by its own madcap follies, high spirits and occasional generosity.

'It's a bum and so's he.' With his carefully measured evasive manner, dark suits and overcoat, abstemious, non-smoking Merrick would make an ailing bloodhound seem like a cavorting court-jester. He was a most depressing companion and again reminded me of Uncle Lod.

Like all obsessive characters, Merrick was inordinately boring. He was uninterested in books, music, politics, people or, seemingly, even sex. His studied politeness was a mask that must conceal a slow-boiling malevolence. I can't see what he could have responded to in an irrepressible jokesmith like Jimmy Porter. He could squeeze out a frosty smile only when someone like a lovingly hated star collapsed with a coronary. His undisguised antipathy to actors was planned with glum precision. 'You see, I hate *actors*.' He accented the word as a National Front skinhead might spit out 'Jew'. 'Binkie *loves* them,' he added, baffled that so successful an impressario should possess such an aberration. 'But then he hates writers.'

This was undeniable. Binkie Beaumont took great satisfaction in tearing the wings from writers, especially the rich and famous. Rattigan and Coward had both suffered humiliation from his lizard tongue. Merrick, unlike Beaumont, was indifferent to sexual politics. 'Now *I* like *writers*,' he'd say in refutation of Binkie's preference.

He liked writers in the way that a snake likes live rabbits. Unfortunately they were more difficult to dispatch than actors. They could take their plays with them. It could be said that firing actors was his profession, producing plays his hobby. When he sat beside me at a rehearsal, if I made a note or said something to the director, he would turn hopefully. 'What's the matter? You want me to fire him?' Fortunately, rehearsals seemed to bore, even mystify, him. He preferred the out-of-town previews with the backers to appease. 'It's not going to be like *that*, is it?' 'Don't worry, they're working on it.' This evocation of all-night black coffee and weeping actresses in hotel suites would usually comfort the most alarmed angel for a few hours.

Merrick had gained some attention by producing an ill-received musical, *Fanny*, which he managed to keep going by advertising it in the Paris Métro, with the calculation that American tourists would be impressed by seeing a Broadway show touted in such a chic venue. Later, he was to contact subscribers in the New York telephone directory with the same names as theatre critics (Brooks Atkinson, Walter Kerr etc.) and persuade them for a small bribe to put their names to a rapturous quote. 'A stupendous event. An undoubted masterpiece,' Walter Kerr. Walter Kerr was probably an unemployed window-cleaner from 114th Street.

Later, when the *Look Back* business was falling, he hired an out-of-work actor to get up on the stage and strike Kenneth Haigh in a fit of fury. The audience was delighted, a photographer recorded the event for *Time* magazine, and bookings rose. The bewildered leading man got the sock in the jaw that Merrick cherished in his heart for every actor. For $50 it was a stylish investment.

To me, one of his charms was that he cared not at all how much he was disliked. He once inserted a clause into my contract that (a) I should not travel to America by sea and (b) that I should not expect to see my name on any advertising or programme matter. This did seem rather desperate sadism. However, I ignored the first condition and agreed to the second, assuming that an anonymous playwright might prove to be rather more intriguing. In London he would eavesdrop on the interval conversation of critics like a detective shadowing an adulterous wife. He once gave me a detailed account of a collusive dialogue between the critics of the *Daily Telegraph*, the *Spectator* and the *Evening Standard*. It sounded plausible, delivered with the conviction of a finance revenue inspector intent on promotion.

Merrick had no concrete or practical opinions himself, or, at least, he never expressed them. He merely presided like a silent oracle, a broody boatman into a journey of endless ordeal. His advantage was that he was so awesomely unlikeable. One had no misgivings about hurting his feelings. It was as impossible to humiliate him as it was to move him to the merest show of admiration let alone friendship. He produced five of my plays in New York, and I would have chosen no one else.

8. The October Bonfire

An October bonfire opened last night and lit a blaze on Broadway. *Look Back in Anger* by a 27-year-old British playwright . . .

New York Times, 2 October 1957

The waiter rasped it in my ear with urgency, like a conspirator giving the tip-off to George Raft in a speakeasy. He left the first few inches of Brooks Atkinson's galley proof beside my plate and went off muttering, 'More later.'

It was indeed October. October 1957. I was sitting in Sardi's restaurant on Forty-fifth Street, barely aware that Brooks Atkinson was the theatre critic of the *New York Times* or that the *Times'* building backed on to the kitchens of Sardi's and that in a few minutes the trucks blocking the street would be spreading the news of Broadway's bonfire to the rest of the city. Drink appeared. Suddenly, as Arthur Miller said, attention was being paid, and to a small band of British actors unknown outside their own country.

The waiter kept returning to our table with the wet galley pulls from next door. Later these were followed by copies of the *Herald Tribune*. The *News*, the *Post* and *Journal American* would not be on the streets until mid-morning but, with the *Times* and *Tribune* declared, we were a palpable smash. The bonfire, lit by an unknown candidate, had sent up a puff of smoke from the Broadway College of Cardinals. It was a remarkable contrast to the London reception the previous year.

Merrick appeared, his eyes rather less mournful than usual. He had not been able to fire anyone but he had a hit on his hands. The restaurant, which had been half-empty of opening-night rubber-neckers, began to fill up. A few people who had attended the performance pointed out Alan, Mary and Vivienne Drummond. Mary went to the powder room and on her return was greeted by a round of applause. Some of the men rose to their feet when they saw that the star of the evening was a pretty young blonde with an unforced, happy smile. Kenneth Haigh, on witnessing this amazing tribute, went out of the restaurant and made a fresh, more measured reappearance. He received his reward. He may not have been as cute as Mary but he was the man of the hour.

Fellow diners came up to our table in the out-of-towners' ghetto beside the kitchen swing-doors, shaking us by the hand, saying they heard it was just great, couldn't wait to get a ticket. Someone sent over a bottle of wine. More surprising still, Merrick bought some for us. Leonard Lyons, the famous columnist of the *Post*, tracked us down. Sardi's was his first port of call on his all-night round of New York's celebrity spots and here was this unexpected bunch of young British guys making big news almost literally behind his back. Lennie, whose ferrety eyes never missed a face in any gathering however large or noisy, was sharp, shrewd and knew everyone in New York from politicians to actors, writers and gangsters. He managed never to break an implicit confidence and yet still succeeded in writing an entertaining column every day.

Mary, Tony and I had already moved out of our dull hotel and into the Algonquin, where a rather startled management treated us very politely. Accustomed to sober dress and linked for ever to the alleged wits of the Round Table and famous foreigners like Noël Coward, they were particularly baffled by Tony's appearance. Dressed like a bony eccentric from Sunset Strip in his beloved uniform of sneakers, sweatshirt, bowling-jacket and baseball cap, he was very unlike the Englishmen they were used to welcoming. Nearly thirty years later the manager, Andrew Anspach, told me of the dismay we aroused at the time.

The next weeks were headily confusing. Sleep was confined to a snatched hour or two in the late afternoon. The telephone rang constantly, there were piles of urgent messages, there was an invitation to a party at an East Side address which even I could identify as being very grand indeed. From dark horse we had become front runner on the Great White Way. Excitement didn't merely sustain itself, it seemed to increase, unlike the English response to such a tide of interest: 'Jolly good. Any idea what you might be doing next?' It was a shock to realize the containing sea of phlegm that one had to raise one's head above at home.

It was like being called to play oneself in a vast film with settings you had already inhabited in another dream-life from a past that had now become real and present. Here, on the streets themselves, black and white memories from the Essoldos and Odeons of my childhood were transformed into a darting haze in the autumn air, the warm subterranean steam breathing from the sidewalks as though from the nostrils of a vast animal. New York seemed to be alive underneath, raging to burst forth with more energy. Food itself was a street-life spectacular. Smells on every corner; fresh oranges pressed by men in white forage caps, a mystery called root beer, hot dogs, fried onions, bagels, pizzas, chestnuts, Italian sausages, kebabs all the way up and down Fifth and Sixth Avenues.

Here it all was, teeming with affluent squalor, patrolled by oblong-shaped cops, coats buttoned up to the neck, straight from a Cagney film, as Irish as Central Casting could produce. A rush of men looking like unhealthy lumber-jacks pushed against ladies inexplicably dressed in hats and wraps as if for a lunchtime cocktail party. Newsboys flashed better teeth than mine. Ragged creatures trussed up in newspapers against doorways; black blind beggars with white canes, rattling tin cups, their guide-dogs slumped beside them on sacks. I began to understand why a flop-house was a flop-house rather than a hostel. A bum was just that, and Skid Row was the gutter he slipped into. Failure, which at home often carried its own distinction of inspired fallibility, was unequivocal here. Irredeemably foreign as I was, I felt myself strangely at home, like a cat sharing a huge household of dogs.

Mary soon seemed to be known to all the salesgirls from Saks to Blooming-dales and in all the coffee-shops from Forty-fourth Street up to Carnegie Hall. 'Why, Miss Uray, we hear you're just wonderful in your show!' She reminded me of the beaming girl of my boyhood who appeared at the wheel of an open car, exclaiming brightly to the naked god beside her, 'Oh, Mr Mercury, you *did* give me a START.' Kelvinist and Calvinist, schoolgirlishly light-hearted, she stood out in Manhattan like a Welsh miner at a bar mitzvah.

We had huge breakfasts in the hotel room with buckwheat cakes, butter and maple syrup to soak up the ninety-proof spirit of the night before as it coursed horribly through gates and alleys of the body never before even noticed. We watched the lines of whores perched in the Astor Bar, where the lady got pinched in the song. We raided all-night record shops like Goody's, where you could choose from an Aladdin's cave of LPs unknown in England. At five in the morning we'd go to Stein's and eat Welsh rabbit, served orange and bubbling in stout, or a selection of sandwiches the size of football boots – the Doris Day (honey, lox and sour cream), the Frank Sinatra (bologna sausage, cheese and dill pickle), the Judy Garland (smoked salmon, honey, cream and nuts) – and a jumbo pack of chocolate to take home.

There were downstairs joints selling thick black-bean soup with huge tank-ards of beer, or Dinty Moore's for lunch of Irish stew and strange-tasting bottled Guinness. I began going to a barber who was patronized by cigar-smoking men shrouded in towels who emerged purple, manicured and shoe-shined. An hour after my last visit, the windows and mirrors were smashed, the floor covered in a lake of blood and bobbing hair. Albert Anestasia had been rubbed out by a few passing business rivals before he had time to wipe the lather from his chin.

We all made regular visits to the Apollo Theatre in Harlem, where people like Lena Horne were supposed to have begun their careers. Wednesday nights were Amateur Nights and if a contender didn't make it in the first ten seconds he or she was 'given the hook', in the venerable manner of burlesque, by the entirely black audience. It made the first house at the Glasgow Empire seem like a Young Conservatives dance. White New Yorkers thought we were pretty dumb to venture there, and cab-drivers would leave us at the uptown end of Central Park. I had the fatuous notion that not being a White American I possessed a kind of *laissez-passer*, a foreign passport providing immunity from a switch-blade in the heart.

Mary was not unnaturally beguiled by her new daily round inside the Big Apple, by the lunches with producers, directors and columnists. Now her New York agent began the serious business of launching her into the big time with an apartment in the city and promotion in Hollywood. Yesterday's allegiances – to myself, the Court, London even – were fading. I was pleased to be more or less excluded, like an elderly relative from olden times, but the potential dangers to her and myself were beginning to emerge. Talk of green cards and tax readjustments determined that I should head for home.

I had stopped concealing from myself, if I ever had, that Mary was not much of an actress. She had a rather harsh voice and a tiny range. Her appearance was pleasing but without any personal sweep to it. Binkie had been right to sign her up for his stable of light-comedy fillies. One couldn't imagine her tackling Lady Macbeth, Cleopatra or even Rosalind. Her movie career could lead nowhere very much except to the conventional exile and bondage of a Hollywood 'home', servants, managers and accountants. I would always need a northern bite in my blood if I were to survive the writer's recurrent ailment: exhaustion. A jumbo Judy Garland at five in the morning would not ultimately nourish me as much as a plate of jellied eels in Margate. I felt a stabbing wave of homesickness.

A more disturbing alarm bell was Mary's preoccupation with a new gynae-cologist friend. There was, he had told her, no reason at all why Mary and I should not have a baby without any trouble. I had not anticipated any trouble, beyond keeping my fingers crossed. Like most men and women of my gener-ation, I was so accustomed to 'taking risks' that I came to feel I had not only been amazingly lucky for the past ten years but that my potency might be a little haphazard.

Mary took up a regime of counting days and temperatures, applying cold compresses and assuming uncomfortable positions. Her new manual, the gynaecologist's *Good News Bible*, contained numerous illustrations which bore little resemblance to any sexual activity I had known for many a long, uncompli-

63

cated and pleasurable hour. It seemed to require all the penitential care of administering a successful enema, only without the aid of soapy water. What had seemed a fairly simple process became a tricky piece of athleticism. The illustrations were daunting. That God, in His infinite wisdom, had come to invent such an all-demanding and capricious object as the clitoris made one wonder if He had nodded off around the same time as He gave us the useless but dangerous appendix.

I began to feel a growing unease which might decline into panic. After six weeks of New York saturation, it *was* time to go home. George rang saying that Anthony Creighton had been injured on his Lambretta. It gave me a small excuse to return, although it confirmed Mary's understandable dislike of Anthony. I said I would be back for Christmas, and landed at London Airport. She had slipped some cheap shirts into my suitcase as presents for her brothers and I failed to declare them, together with some already-worn LPs. I was taken away, stripped and meticulously searched.

Back in Chelsea, the welcome was summary. 'Oh? Did well, did it?' The October blaze had not been sniffed in London. It was rather as if a disgraced school rotter had returned from the Olympics with the old country's one and only gold medal. The fairground fever of the Great White Way quickly receded. Things at home seemed stuffy, unfriendly even, but more serious, light-hearted and normal.

5, Norma Villas,
Town Hall Approach Road,
Tottenham

Dear Dolly [family name for Nellie Beatrice],

I have written to John thanking him for his kindness. It was kind of you dear to mention me to him it brought tears to my eyes, I have never had anything like that given to me and nobody has ever asked me how I manage to keep this house going.

Well, dear I had a letter from Mum but not one of her nice kind ones, full of Queenie looking her dear old self but said she was still in bed and could not walk. Sidney said different in his letter didn't he. She was full of Jack and Bessie's kindness. I am not answering that letter. All this *kindness* will soon blow over as before. Well, dear my hand is a bit wrong today with Rheumatism so excuse writing and mistakes it is the weather.

Ever your affectionate,

Auntie Min xxxxx

[PS from N.B. to J.O.] It looks as though his Lordship is now turning

Mother against Auntie, which proves he hates anyone liking me a little but it will blow over, I hope so or else I shall have that on my mind.

Tottenham

Dear Dolly,

Yours to hand. I cannot express my disgust for your so call Brother. He will kill my Sister, it is breaking her heart. He is *bad enough* to stop her coming to me. It worries me, I have had a cry. She is not happy there alone. Cheer up dear God will help us. Don't worry. God pays debts without money.

Affectionately,

Auntie Min.

Tottenham

My dear Dolly,

Your letter just to hand. I certainly cannot understand Mother. I did not think she could be so unkind as to write you those letters. *Do not worry* you will have a Breakdown. I wish I could get about as well as Mum and I am only 88. I have not had a Bed of Roses but I am satisfied, so buck up, do not be downhearted. I will let you know of any trouble at Salisbury.

Love,

Auntie Min xxx

Tottenham

My dear Dolly,

I always thought my Sister such a straight and good living dear. Now she has cast me off. She was always all I had now I am just alone and *not* wanted. This has put the last Nail in my Coffin. Think of me sometimes one thing I have done nobody any wrong.

God bless.

Auntie Min.

PS I have to wait for someone to post this. I would like some new legs.

[PPS from N.B. to J.O.] What a family, I have to laugh really.

Tottenham

My dear Dolly,

Mind do not let it worry you, worrying about other people has got me down. I am alone and nobody troubles about me. When I am gone I

65

expect they might send me a few flowers. Hope you are well there is such a lot of illness about.

　With love.

　Yours affectionately,

　Auntie Min xxx

In those pre-breathalyser days, Anthony had driven into the back of a lorry on his way home from the Salisbury in St Martin's Lane, then the chic theatrical gay pub in the West End. There was also a dive called the White Bear where servicemen and young men from the provinces drank black and tans and sipped green chartreuse. It was a few yards from the gents lavatory at Piccadilly Circus, the most famous 'cottage' of the age. Even the heavy tread of the boots of *agents provocateurs* did not deter its visitors. As one was told constantly, the danger and prospect of humiliation were, like the chase, almost as heady as the conquest.

Anthony also spoke with nostalgia of a club in Soho, the Rockingham, which seemed to be a homosexual Athenaeum, a world away from the sweet liqueur squalor of the White Bear or the discreetly camp surroundings of Victorian mirrors at the Salisbury. Pre-Wolfenden, the Rockingham was very exclusive. Although merchant seamen or still-room boys were discreetly welcomed, members were otherwise expected to be most circumspect. Anthony had been there in his bomber–navigator days on leave from missions over the Ruhr and, he said, Terence Rattigan had promised him a job when the war was over.

As the song goes in *Flare Path*:

> I don't want to join the air force,
> I don't want to go to war,
> I'd rather hang around,
> Piccadilly Underground,
> Living on the earnings of a high-born lady . . .

Piccadilly still held its spell for Anthony and with the £20 a week I had arranged to give him I imagine he had been doing as much hanging about as £20 could buy in those days. 'Give her a shilling and she'll probably be willing' had long been overtaken by inflation, but a chartreuse can last an evening.

Lowndes Cottage was also a world away from the White Bear. When *The Entertainer* transferred to the Palace, Mary was in America and Vivien Leigh and I were both spending evenings alone. She would sometimes ring me up as I settled down in my cupboard-study in Woodfall Street. It was always a shock to hear her voice. 'What are you doing this evening?' There was only one answer. 'Why don't we go to the pictures? Come round now and we'll see what's on.' I dusted down my best suit, best shirt and tie and VLOI would pick me up.

All sorts of phantom possibilities crossed my mind. Did she expect me to seduce her? Surely not. The presumption was absurd. I was neither Rhett Butler, Laurence Olivier, good red meat nor even Peter Finch. Was it a kittenish plot to involve me as a pawn in a game about which I was ignorant? I knew that life imitates melodrama more often than not, but my own profligate and to-hell-with-it nature had not equipped me for this. I had been foolish to myself for too long to be cast as the spare prick at the demise of a very public marriage. I felt crass enough *already* for even agonizing over such self-important guesswork. But the presumption of youth and the sudden appearance of bourgeois caution within me made it all the more baffling and exciting.

We would look down the list of likely attractions in the *Evening Standard* and drive off rather late into the West End. On the first occasion we ended up in the Charing Cross Road watching Sophia Loren. Lady Olivier gave a running commentary in her pleasing, ginny voice on Miss Loren's physical and technical deficiencies. It seemed a long ten years since I was sitting in the circle of the Rembrandt, Ewell, stuck palm-to-palm with Renee.

Afterwards, an autograph signed for the cinema manager, we would glide round to the White Tower or somewhere similar. She had witnessed my untutored tussle with an alien artichoke and always helped me tactfully with good humour over the menu and wine list. Apart from the dressing-room incident at the Court, I never witnessed those moods of manic caprice for which she was well known and dreaded by some. 'The only virtue I possess', John Betjeman once told me, 'is hope.' Vivien's virtue, always a prized one in my book, was enthusiasm, the physical expression of hope, the antidote to despair and that most deadly of sins, sloth.

On our return to Lowndes Cottage I was unsure whether to go in for a drink or not. I had no wish to be churlish nor – wild projection – to be caught *in flagrante* by Larry after his performance as Archie ('I'm a twice a day man myself'). It was a ridiculously comic notion but events had moved in such a headlong and unlikely sequence for the last few months that almost anything seemed possible. Taking Scarlett O'Hara out to supper might be only a starter.

I could only guess at the state of play between the Oliviers, but theatrical royalty, scandal and heaven knows what scorn were certainly beyond my sophistication. I wasn't, as someone with an acute sense of class and achievement later put it, 'ready for it yet'. I felt a certain loyalty to Olivier. I was also racked by curiosity. In St Augustine's words, 'A Stiff Prick hath no conscience.' Maybe it was a Jacobean plot to damage *The Entertainer*? That seemed too vulgar a device. On the other hand . . . On the other hand what? On the other hand, I wanted nothing to threaten the success of my play.

Not for the first time, I fiercely regretted my indecision in such circumstances. Caution is evil medicine to me, even when it seems to guarantee reward. It was a foretaste of my later conviction that the follies which a man regrets most are those which he didn't commit when he had the opportunity.

In the past eighteen months I had not made the fortune everyone assumed, but it seemed pretty good to me. I need not worry about electricity or telephone bills. I bought new clothes and books and became less nervous of restaurants and hotels. Even Merrick could not whittle down the standard Dramatists' Guild contract in New York. *The Entertainer*'s packed eight-week run at the Palace was earning me almost £900 a week. I still made my £.s.d. entries in my pocket diary and Dr Strach, the accountant who a year earlier had advised me to go back to him when I had a little more to show for myself, was urging me to spend money on a chauffeur, even a valet. He was patently baffled that so much could be earned for doing so little.

Shortly after my return from New York, I took a crash course of driving lessons, passed my test one lunchtime in a deserted Acton High Street and bought the 'grocer's car' so despised by George. Anthony seemed more confused and incoherent than usual. I decided that a short convalescent trip for him would provide me with an excuse not to return to America for two or three weeks before I decided what to do about Christmas. I christened the car by taking him to Wales. It was a fine chance to get back to the provinces.

The choice of Wales displeased Mary. It was, I pointed out, the land of my grandfather's father. (Years later I discovered that my Welsh connection only reached as far back as the early nineteenth century. The Osbornes had been migrant artisans who crossed the Bristol Channel from North Devon.) Why wasn't I going to Scotland? When was I coming back? She was talking about New York as if it were home. I told her Anthony was still a bit goofy, though, I might have added, not much more so than before.

I needed a holiday myself. I could feel her mouth tighten beneath the Atlantic waves. From *what*? There was she slugging it out on Broadway and here was I wandering aimlessly around Wales with a cadging homosexual drunk. Like most actors, she was hysterical when unemployed and resentful when appearing every night to full houses. She also entertained the common belief that a writer is only working when he can be seen head down at his desk. Why are you drinking/dreaming/farting/fornicating instead of making typewriter noises?

After Wales and back in London, time and space in which to manoeuvre seemed to be contracting. I was looking for more air to breath and found it in an unlikely quarter. Harry Saltzman reappeared. He was forty-two, plump, with grey short-cropped hair and large, brown, defensive eyes. He had been in the RCAF and the USAAF during the war, had worked in the circus in Paris before that and spoke perfect argot, dirty-talk French. His suits and shoes were expensive, clinging to him with a sort of Italian fondness. His range of knowledge and reading was impressive for a man whose book on a desert island, apart from the Bible and Shakespeare, would be a bound volume of *Variety*.

Unlike most of the American enthusiasts I had met during the past months, he was friendly but not fulsome. He talked fluently, as if we had grown up together, with a familiarity that was neither intrusive nor objectionable. In spite of massive presumptions, he also had an instinct for reticence. His past experience with the English had alerted him that we were easily scared off by admiration and that praise could make us prance and sweat like horses.

Harry had seen *Look Back* again in New York. He talked engagingly of his wild intentions. He also put them to work. He had an amazing profligacy in his enthusiasms and an energy in withdrawing them, whether it was restaurants, girls or hot properties. 'What do you want to eat tonight?' he'd ask. 'French, German, Italian, Jewish? I know the best Finnish restaurant in town.' One always, rightly, chose the best in town. A week later he might ask the same question. 'Well, that Finnish place was terrific. Why don't we . . . ' He would cut you off like some blundering toddler. 'Forget it. I know a much better place.' I don't think we ever went back to a best-restaurant-in-town.

He dropped ideas for films like restaurants. He wanted to make films of *Look Back* and *The Entertainer*. He wanted to buy, or me to buy, the rights of *A Taste of Honey*. He was going to get *Saturday Night and Sunday Morning* from Joe Janni. We – Harry, Tony and myself – should form a production company. We would call it Woodfall Films. In the meantime, why didn't we go to Paris for Christmas and he'd show me the town. I said I was expected in New York. He brushed this aside like last week's best restaurant. 'I'm going over a week later. We'll go together. Hell, let's go to Paris first and have some fun.'

I found myself in the Hotel Napoléon off the Champs Elysées, eating in the small hours at Les Halles and wondering what I should say to Mary. 'Hell,' said Harry, 'we'll send her a cable.' As if that settled everything. Bemused, I watched him dash it off. 'We love Paris, Paris, Paris. Happy Christmas. See you for New Year. Love John and Harry.' It did not go down well.

9. *Broadly Speaking*

By thy great mercy, defend us from all perils and dangers of this night.

Third Collect, Book of Common Prayer

My first sighting of Francine was when she made a brief appearance at a party in Harry Saltzman's New York apartment. This was in an anonymous block overlooking the horse-drawn-carriage park round the corner from the Waldorf Astoria. Tony insisted the building was a warren for middle-priced whores. As most New York ladies seemed dressed for the evening long before noon it seemed difficult to tell.

Early in 1958, George came over to America to give a lecture, and it was a relief to have him with me. I had seen little of Tony who, as usual, was pursuing a full day-and-night timetable. Occasionally we would go to the theatre, but we rarely stayed beyond the interval. Like most directors Tony was an appalling spectator, shifting in his seat at the outset like an uneasy colt, head falling forward, jerking back snoring, then snapping into twitching wakefulness.

His boredom was fierce and accusing. He made one feel like a prisoner under escort. 'Are you *enjoying* it?' he would hiss after five minutes. As the play progressed the interrogation mounted, ending with a bristling show of exasperation. 'I mean, do you want to *stay?*' Usually I didn't. Outside, as often as not, he would mutter something about 'having to see someone'. 'I mean, you will be *all right*, won't you?' he'd say doubtfully. Before I had time to answer, he would be striding off down the street. It took me a long time to realize that his schedule for the evening had been fixed implacably long before we had settled into the stalls.

Tony's duplicity was so sinewy and downright that he was able to deceive friends and adversaries effortlessly. His instinct for the strategy of perfidy was immaculately simple. No deception could be too bold. Simple undertakings became mystifying conspiracies. The prospect of arousing his mockery prevented people from comparing notes. Insinuating cabals and strengthening them with discreet misinformation, he was able to gull the most hardened and

70

cynical of spirits. It was a formidable gift and, even as it grew with comic legend, there was always a band of willing eunuchs prepared to sacrifice their interests, sometimes even their destiny, for the promise of his approval.

George and I, spending lazy hours alone together for the first time, began to compare notes on our dealings with Tony. It was clear that we had been manipulated mercilessly, both of us being coaxed into positions of mutual suspicion. By the expedient of scattering distrust and unease between us on a constant feed of innuendo and specific warnings, he had kept us separately stabled like animals in a stud. We had obeyed the handler's instructions submissively with a trust that seemed bovinely unintelligent.

George's tentative attitude to a younger man and my own shyness had been used like blunt instruments to coerce us into avoiding anything like intimacy or confidence. Now, like escaped prisoners, we exchanged anecdotes of our incarceration in the Richardson conspiracy. Inimitable and uninventable phrases tumbled out like mocking Christmas-cracker jokes, suddenly making everything less humiliating and more comic. 'You mustn't speak to Johnny. You know what he's like. You'll only *upset* him!' 'Don't mention anything to George. He's very *sensitive* at the moment. You'll only put him off.' Lie low and leave it to Richardson. Why? His unique perception of two difficult and irreconcilable personalities would preserve a working balance between us. Remonstrance was out of the question. The only remedy was the laughter of self-scorn.

Harry's party was an untheatrical affair, an almost all-male gathering of agents, lawyers and salesmen. Francine's entrance could hardly have been more startling. Every head most certainly turned. She seemed the embodiment of the silliest of American dreams, the Dumb Broad, all in white and glittering, accompanied by a Texas oilman from Central Casting. She was unquestionably a caricature of every snobbish idea of such a girl, almost bursting apart with the effort she had put into her captivating appearance.

A sublimely trashy, brave innocence pervaded the room. If she were a parody of someone striving to give the appearance of a film star, she managed to achieve an odd pouting dignity. Perhaps it was her intrinsic lack of realistic ambition. It worked most effectively, inspiring an atmosphere of instant affection from everyone. So much care to her image, so transparent and so amateur, was a triumph of narcissism. She certainly had the Monroe effect on her audience that night.

Americans invented the dumb broad as the English perfected the gun dog. George drew me aside, 'Now that's the kind of woman you and I could never even hope to get near.' Our agreement could not have been more complete. Inside George's almost anorexic craving for a hang-dog Giacometti posture was a MacGill man in a ballooning red-and-white-striped bathing-suit. If ever there was a bum-and-tit man condemned to a diet of lean pickings it was George Devine. He would pull on his pipe lingeringly at the sight of a pretty girl. His contemporaries might aggressively admire the androgynous beauty of Virginia Woolf or the Plantagenet exoticism of Edith Sitwell, but there were no fine-boned ladies with broad foreheads and drawn-back wispy hair among the rippling nubiles between the covers of *Seventeen* and *Honey*.

'Not a chance, dear boy.' As he said it he put his arm around me with great deliberation. It was a rare gesture and a sure sign of how relaxed his mood must have been. Doubtless a middle-aged English theatre director would scarcely have roused a glimmer of interest in Francine's appraising eyes. Covetousness was a cool gift that seemed to be admired most by its victims. The Great American Broad was never dumb. She had the heart of a snake and the fervour of a prophet. She was a protected species.

A week later I found myself sharing a huge bungalow with Tony and Harry in the Beverly Hills Hotel. I had easily persuaded Mary that my visit could be useful to her. Hollywood was a dream in all our experiences. Harry was handing out fistfuls of dollars. 'Leave it me. We'll settle later.' Settle what, I thought, and then forgot about it. I knew Tony would soon rebel at being hustled along by this genial, impatient courier. We reconnoitred the Polo Lounge, where Harry exuded a feeling of tetchy over-familiarity towards the Praetorian waiters. He bounced us along Wilshire Boulevard to the emptiest, most expensive shops in what appeared to be the most unfrequented street in the world. He waded his way through counters of 'sports' clothes that would have been scarcely saleable on market-day in Derby. Back in the pink and green bungalow, he retired to his bedroom with *Variety*, shouting down the phone to New York, London, Miami, half a dozen other provincial US cities and a few European capitals as well. His fluent French sounded like a union leader addressing a rioting mob.

Then, suddenly, the air-conditioning seemed clattering and cold. It was shivery rather than sunny California and as a subtropical chill settled over the mid-afternoon I felt my first intimations of West Coast dread. When I later described this very particular unease that Los Angeles aroused in me, Christopher Isherwood rasped, 'Oh, you've got the Pacific Blues.' From the twinkle of his eyebrows, he clearly relished those evening shadows which darken both sunshine and spirit.

Tony, sensing my depression, left abruptly, banging the door of his bedroom behind him. Soon he too was screaming into the telephone. I wandered off to the Polo Lounge and on into the 'Pool Area', which was being closed down for the night by those young men in shorts and sneakers who seem to hang from everywhere in California like bats in Indian palaces. I felt as if it was the end of September in Bognor rather than mid-January in Los Angeles.

A slim, dark figure, hair parted familiarly in the middle, came and lay down a yard from me. I remembered a naked girl crashing through a black and white jungle. No longer naked but cool as a cat drying itself in the watery sunshine was Hedy Lamarr. For a few minutes my bungalow gloom vanished. *White Cargo*'s Tondelayo, I learned later, was working as a waitress in a café and was allowed to use the pool when the Real Customers had retired to the Beauty Parlour. She still outshone them all for my one-and-ninepence.

'So, what do you want to do?' Harry was detailing a possible itinerary for the evening, meaning that he had made every arrangement already. Tony eyed us like a parent confronting a pair of dithering children. 'The thing is, Harry. I've arranged to meet someone.' His knee jerked in impatience. He wanted us out. The foot stabbed the air. His voice rose to a tremolo of exasperation. 'I mean, are you going *out*?' 'Sure, sure,' said Harry.' 'What time's your party coming?' 'Quite soon.' The banging down of his Cutty Sark marked the end of the discussion.

'I've got to pick up Francine from the airport,' Harry said. 'Coming along, John? I thought we'd take in this guy Shelley Berman . . . Bring your friends if you want.' Tony's glare intensified as if there were squalid implications in this suggestion. 'Who's Francine?' 'The girl in my apartment. John's met her.' Well, hardly. The glare turned on me suspiciously. 'Well, I *might*.' Harry was a hard man to insult, but no one could clear a room so peremptorily as Tony.

Then, to my surprise, he offered a weary explanation, dropping his voice so low that it became all but inaudible. 'Someone's coming to see me I used to know. We've got lots of things to *discuss*.' Things beyond the grasp of the likes of old Johnny and Harry. 'I haven't met up with him for a long time.' He was already adopting German–American prepositions like baseball caps. Strange how eccentrics pick up the trinkets of conformity. 'It's somebody called Gavin Lambert.' He spilled the name out like Shakespeare's being introduced to the unlettered natives. 'The thing is Johnny, you won't *like each other*.' How did he know? This was divide-and-rule by a king-emperor who never allowed his eunuchs to meet.

Francine was even more impressive in her travelling clothes. The tweeds she wore were Paris, France, rather than Harris, Saks. She spoke animatedly in husky French during most of the drive back to Beverly Hills. That would have delighted George. I couldn't remember when I had heard such a joyous range of sound. Playfulness was a quality I cherished more than most. The divine gift of dogs and monkeys, it sometimes seemed as if it were being bred out of my own species, particularly here in Pacific Bluesland, where a mere suspicion of irrationality was subjected to the scrutiny of analysis. She also had a command of hooker's patois, much of it unknown to me, which tripped from her a little incongruously. It was endearing rather than offensive. Her call-girl coarseness sounded, to use one of Nellie Beatrice's favourite words of approval, quite dainty.

At the restaurant, Francine was transformed into the image George and I had reeled at. The pleasure of being seated across the table from the unattainable is that there are no attendant anxieties about the outcome of the evening. The greatest-restaurant-in-town lived up to its reputation so far as I was concerned. Francine seemed studiously unimpressed but her reassumed aloofness was soon cast off. I thought I recognized a depressive of the same kind as myself, eager for persuasion. She and Harry swopped gossip. If they had once been lovers, and I assumed that they had, they appeared to have an affectionate memory of something briefly enjoyable and now a pleasurable, if limited, friendship. A talent for disinterested friendship, especially with a beautiful woman, was not something I would have suspected in Harry.

They reverted from her native Swiss-French to English. I didn't feel she was interested at all in Harry's enthusiastic breakdown of my career or the promise of my future if, indeed, she was listening. However she smiled a kind of dreamy encouragement across at me. It was more than enough and preferable to being asked unctuous questions.

By the time we arrived on the Strip at the club where Shelley Berman was appearing, I was convinced that Harry, Francine and I were destined to be lifelong, valued friends. There could surely be few things more pleasurable than the exhilaration of an attractive woman's company without any constraint of possible seduction. Soaked in a cloud of rarest pragmatism, the Pacific pangs of the afternoon had vanished.

Mr Berman was clearly off-form that particular evening. He wasn't helped by a few witless hecklers. Sitting in a crouch over the microphone, his technique of ingratiating intimacy became more and more wounded and alarmed. Harry chewed on his cigar impatiently. It was a relief when Tony groped his way to our table and sat down like the late arrival at a wedding. Managing a stiff smile at Francine, he glared round him and then at the stage.

Comics often welcome latecomers as a distraction and an opportunity to turn their torment on someone else. Rather to my disappointment, Berman didn't choose to victimize this obvious target and quickly finished his act. The evening had wound down with such suddenness that it might have seemed to Tony that his appearance had dispelled either a dull or an uproarious outing. It had been neither. He had evidently made some effort to find us, and now the party was clearly over. Francine refused a refill, saying she was tired. She made an exit which drew some respectful whistles and applause from Shelley Berman's tormentors.

Its abrupt ending was slightly disappointing but I was not going to let the evening be blighted by either Berman or Richardson. When we got inside our bungalow, its strangeness seemed to affect us all, except for Harry who behaved as if he had lived there all his life. 'Help yourself to a drink.' I was hoping he wouldn't leave the three of us together, hoping childishly that somehow I could be allowed to show my gratitude by rekindling the lights for one more game before we went to bed. But Harry was bushed. We were off to Las Vegas in the morning. 'Get a good night's sleep. It's gonna be a long day.' He slammed the door of his bedroom.

Francine smiled and followed him. There was the sound of good-humoured chatter and laughter. Tony fell on to the sofa, which skidded as if an exasperated ostrich had collapsed on it. 'But what did you *do* all evening?' For once, in the mystery game Tony conducted, I was the banker. Anticipating sullen interrogation, I filled his whisky glass with too much ice, mocking his American affectations rather clumsily. Perhaps I was drunker than I thought.

Francine reappeared, still smiling, and wandered into her own room. The door was unclosed. 'But, I mean, who *is* she?' I told him truthfully what little I had learned. I was about to affect boredom with the subject when she made another entrance. This time she was snuggled into an hotel bathrobe. The back of her hair was glistening and wet from the shower. The whiteness of her robe against her skin, from knees to bare feet, gave an impression of a somewhat larky Tondelayo beneath. She walked over to the sofa and sat beside Tony, curling herself into a comfortable parcel.

Clearly the evening was not yet over. It was a perfect final bonus to the day. She gazed at us, dark smiling eyes and shamingly white teeth, waiting. Waiting for what? There were three of us in the game now. Francine, curious and relaxed, the two of us reluctant to show our hands, let alone start bidding. Tony brought it to a swift close. With the snap of a spastic guardsman, he stamped his feet to the floor. 'Well . . . ' he muttered. 'I'll see you all in the morning.' The low conspiratorial tone was there but it could have meant anything, a slipstream of discouraging mystery.

I started questioning her about her Persian ex-husband and her show-biz ambitions, about America and what she hoped to get from it. She made passably funny imitations of her wealthy escorts. 'See here, honey, you and me could make the sweetest music together.' Her contempt was still in control of illusion. Snatches of American Dream dirty-talk somehow emphasized her fastidious foreignness of spirit.

She looked lynx-like and unconcerned beside me until she ran out of

75

cigarettes. Refusing my Gauloises, she went to her bedroom. Her door was partially closed. My provincial musings induced a very shabby-headed feeling: go to bed, wash your face, head on pillow and sweet dreams before the nocturnal gates and alleys bloat up another spasm of the blues. Curbing my suburban instinct to turn off the lights, I crept past her door. 'John?'

We slept very little and, when I did wake, the expected cut and thrust in my head and throat was mild, nothing that a Bloody Mary in the Polo Lounge wouldn't pacify. Francine was sitting up, sheets tucked under her armpits, a packet of king-size Kents balanced on her chest. She began giggling, rather as I used to as a small boy trying to unravel some third-form smut to my patient father. She had evidently interrogated Harry closely about Tony and myself. 'I said, "Jesus Christ, Harry! What are you doing with a couple of English fags?"'

At the airport, Harry greeted us with especial warmth, the immediate past banished by the greater enjoyments to come which, in Vegas, would be lighting up the desert sky. Even Francine abandoned her public languor, smiling broadly at the hostesses who normally would have got no more than a princess's incline of the head. Tony seemed a little detached, squirming less than usual in his seat. 'She seems very charming.' 'Yes.' There was the merest trace of bitterness in his voice as he added, 'She only looked at *you* all evening.' He absorbed himself in a screenplay of Faulkner's *Sanctuary* while I sat speculating on what sleeping arrangements Harry had prepared for us.

At the hotel desk Harry distributed the room keys like spending money on a school outing. 'That's for you and Francine.' She was already in full progress behind a procession of bell-hops and flunkeys. 'See you here, 7.30,' said Harry. 'First show's eight o'clock.'

Francine's application to her evening appearance was a priestly ritual. After a couple of hours watching her at work, silent before the looking-glass, I went below. Like an actor on a vast set, I picked my way through hundreds of intent gamblers, dressed in anything from dude Western outfits to tuxedos. I felt that if I didn't keep on the move I might be arrested or whisked away to an outside alley by a couple of hoods and pinned against the wall. The quiet of European casinos is oppressive enough but this supermarket roar was worse. I found Francine in one of the bars, having a drink with Harry. They appeared to be having an argument.

'Harry's getting Tony a girl,' said Francine. 'I tell him he's stupid. He wants a girl, let him get a girl. The joint is crawling with them.' Her Swiss accent had hardened into Hollywood-French, not a playful note to it. 'Aren't I right, darling? Your friend know what he want. Harry must think he's stupid or something.' Tony appeared, looking confident enough. His 'girl' was a long time coming. Francine grew impatient. 'What the hell, Harry. Let's go in. I'm hungry. So leave her a message.'

Before he could corral us up for the interminable evening ahead with Sammy Davis Jr, Tony's partner for the night loomed impassively over us, indistinguishable from the scores of hefty cactus plants at every turn. Harry gabbled introductions like a referee instructing a couple of prizefighters. The two girls assessed each other. Francine barely acknowledged her. Lorraine-or-Laverne was clearly accustomed to this kind of snub from the hierarchy of her own sex. Tony scuppered Harry's frantic *placement* so that I was trapped beside the unconcerned Laverne (or Lorraine).

I expected Tony to leave almost immediately, exposing Harry or myself to make amends for the other's behaviour. My repertoire of uninspired questioning palled horribly. 'Do you come here often?' (Yeah.) 'Do you live here?' (Where else? There was only the desert.) 'Have you see Sammy Davis before?' A polite, 'Surely.' Francine was flushing angrily and began what looked like a domestic row, in French once more, complaining unmistakably about the presence of our guest.

Sammy Davis intervened, seemingly for ever. Harry and Francine continued to argue. Tony remained expressionless. When the performance at last ended, Harry, hemmed in by the goading glares of Tony and Francine, was addressed by Laverne/Lorraine. Distinctly, but without reproach, she uttered her first constructed sentence: 'You know, I understood every word you and this lady were saying. My mother was French.'

Harry's button-brown eyes swivelled, but he recovered. 'C'mon, let's go.' I stood beside Laverne while he reached into his pocket and brought out a deck of Yankee bills. He flipped one out and crumpled it into her palm. 'Thanks, kid. Goodnight.' She slipped the bill into her purse as mechanically as a hat-check girl and walked away without a glance at any of us.

Before I could absorb the facile shame of being privy to such a brutal exchange or her offhand dignity, Francine pounced on Harry. 'How much you give her?' 'Ten bucks. C'mon.' 'You lie, Harry. How much you give her?' 'Twenty.' 'You dumb, Harry. Twenty bucks for nothing.' She made it sound as if it had come from her own purse. 'So what? I felt sorry for the kid. Maybe we gave her a hard time.' 'A hard time? You call that a hard time – for *that* broad!'

10. *American Panic*

Already Osborne is a professional success here on a big-time scale – almost at the same heights as the grand old days of pre-war Hollywood. And he is also a personal success. I think one reason for this is that he fits into the exaggerated pattern the Americans admire more than anything, the Horatio Alger legend, the boy who rises from rags to riches.

'From the USA', *Daily Express*, 31 January 1958

The Entertainer opened in Boston on 27 January, the anniversary of my father's death, and a week later at the Royale on Broadway, next to the theatre where *Look Back* was still smouldering on.

By this time, I must have agreed to a substantial royalty cut, in the growing custom of mendicant playwrights faced with the option of closure. It would have been impossible, even for Merrick, to extract any concessions from the cast. Mary was earning less than $300 a week, although my New York agent, Harold Freedman, was picking up our Algonquin bill. How the rest of the cast survived, Alan Bates and Vivienne Drummond in particular, was a mystery. Both of them were living in what were little more than red-light apartment blocks in the sleezier streets off Sixth Avenue. Merrick's mask of pain when I suggested he might nudge them just above the New York poverty line was the most frozen expression of pleasure those hard brown eyes and mourning moustache could betray. He looked like an excise man being asked to ignore a false-bottomed suitcase.

The opening of *The Entertainer* was on a different scale. My remembrance of it is little more than a series of sharp images, inconsequential detail, faces, a chaos of narrative. A dream in fact, like most of the coming year, to which I succumbed with a kind of shaky exhilaration and bouts of bleakest disquiet. I was aware of the presence of dangers, of events taking hold of my life, but, as usual, I felt I might ride with them, that I would confront them frantically rather than be driven back or diverted against my will. As in a dream, I was feeling less and less a participant than a bemused spectator.

I left the Algonquin with a good hour to spare before curtain rise. Mary kissed me chirpily at Times Square and disappeared into her own theatre. The sidewalk outside the Royale was already blocked to standstill with familiar-faced Schubert Alley 'fans' and touts reportedly disposing of tickets at $250 apiece, a record price previously held by *My Fair Lady*. Olivier's name had sold out the three-month run weeks earlier. It was a daunting spectacle, the throng voracious and unpredictable like a gathering of anti-hunt supporters. I retreated into the nearby Piccadilly bar, and a few Scotches began to burn comfort into the gape of apprehension within.

A bleep of comic insouciance settled on me, something rather like the moment in so many British films when the senior officer turns his back on a startled wardroom, growling 'Carry On, Number One.' Like Noël Coward, I must Rise Above It. Number One barked a command for another Scotch. I decided that this New York episode would be conducted like a part in a play. It would only be a short run. *Try to enjoy it*. 'Try' was the flaw in that daily injunction to myself.

Sufficiently anaesthetized, I emerged into the bitter February wind-tunnel and picked my way with a sudden rush of agility through a heaving pack of honking cabs and limos, those strangely skinny-looking New York police horses, mink, black ties and Homburgs. By the time I got to the cheerless foyer, smelling harsh and sweet like the cheaper department stores on Sixth Avenue and the flea-pits of my youth, I felt Number One was back on the bridge. There was a wary but elated radar-blip in my head.

The first act seemed pretty cold, similar to one of Mrs Blond's Jewish Charities. Looking around me in the interval, I realized that this was more than exactly what it was. The moody reception lightened a little in the second act. I had already noticed that a number of unwilling husbands felt they had been conned into shelling out $500 for what was little more than a cheap vaudeville show, and a foreign and incomprehensible one at that. But my inner blip scarcely bothered to register this as a scuffle erupted a few rows in front of me. A bulky man was in the throes of a fatal seizure or heart attack, accompanied by anguished moans, suppressed howls and stage whispers that swept through the auditorium and hissed up to the gallery.

What followed was my first experience of American Panic. This exercise in hysteria is so instinctive that it can be set off as immediately by a broken thumb-nail as by an earthquake, preferably in as public a place as possible. A restaurant or an airport concourse is ideal. A packed theatre could not have been more suitable. Everyone was struck with frantic immobility and primal helplessness. No chance here of 'Carry on, Number One': the British may freeze ('Keep calm, old chap'); the Americans explode. They invented a whole genre, the Disaster Movie, based on this national characteristic.

American panic prevented the stage management from bringing down the curtain. There was no officer class backstage to tell them what to do, and even Merrick could not be expected to improvise with sudden death in the stalls. Lowing moans and groaning disbelief grew as the unfortunate corpse was eventually passed from hand to fumbling hand and dragged out of view. The whole business probably lasted only fifteen minutes, but the effect was as onerous as a concertinaed version of the *Ring* cycle.

All this inflamed attention was reluctantly redirected at the intrusive performance on stage. But the play was undeniably over so far as the spectators were concerned, the scented air choked with aggrieved impatience. Olivier's crumpling descent against the proscenium arch met with little response from an audience still transfixed by the extra-funereal drama they had just undergone. The applause was thin, irritatingly grateful rather than polite.

I returned to the now-empty Piccadilly bar, reflecting on the possible consequences of the evening. Would Merrick pull one of his tricks? Could he devise a way of depriving me of my share of the advance? A Broadway première where most of the audience were emotionally absent for half of the evening must be some sort of precedent. I went to pick up Mary. She had discarded the Mary Quant dress I had brought back for her and was wearing a middle-aged, flouncy black number from Saks, topped by one of those skull-cap ornaments favoured by American ladies-who-lunch.

There was a first-night party at some ritzy hotel. I was curious to see if American Panic had subsided; if, indeed, any of the guests would turn up. To my surprise, the huge reception room was full. There were some very famous faces, most of whom had visibly risen way above it. Merrick and his henchmen were gathered in a corner, fidgeting like a bunch of bookmakers after the favourite has romped home. David was staring black reproach, his moustache askew like a disarranged toupee.

I turned for escape to a noisy group led by Frederick March who was hugging Olivier and exclaiming, 'You old cocksucker. You *old* cocksucker!' 'Isn't he?' he demanded. His wife, Frances, nodded cheerfully and so did I. The frowning faces of the night were obliterated by a misty collage of Anthony Adverse, Prince Oblonsky, Robert Browning and Willie Loman, a whooping figure hooting hallelujahs. 'You old cocksucker!'

I found myself shaking hands with Greer Garson. She sparkled with an animal energy of gentleness and delight, pre-Raphaelite golden and pale but gloriously animated and unholy. I was drunk enough to have tried to kiss her arm-length glove in adoring gratitude, but she was gone and I was left with at least one smile from heaven, which looked to be the last. As one whose

1 John Osborne, 1956

FAREWELL TO ANGER
"ANGRY MAN"
"MAN IN A RAGE"
LOOK BACK IN ANGER
"BARGAIN FROM STRENGTH"
A PLAY
by
JOHN OSBORNE

or
"CLOSE THE CAGE BEHIND YOU"
"MY BLOOD IS A MILE HIGH"

APRIL 1955

2 & 3 Pages from John Osborne's notebooks: the original title page and draft of
Look Back in Anger
4 George Devine

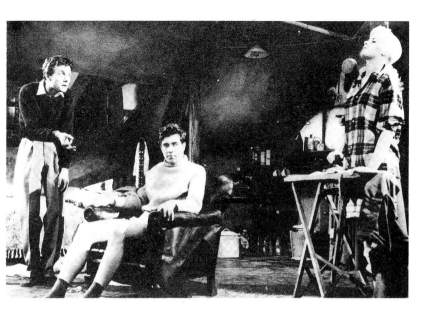

5 Kenneth Haigh as Jimmy Porter, Alan Bates (sitting) as Cliff, and Mary Ure as
Alison Porter in the original production of *Look Back in Anger*
6 *Look Back in Anger*, Royal Court Theatre, 1956

7 Peggy Ashcroft as Mr Shui Ta in *The Good Woman of Setzuan*,
Royal Court Theatre, October 1956

8 The English Theatre Company's production of *The Good Woman of Setzuan*, Royal
Court Theatre: John Osborne is in the centre of the group with, to his right, Joan
Plowright, Rachel Kempson and George Devine; Peggy Ashcroft is on her knees

9 John Osborne, Woodfall Street, 1957

10 Kenneth Tynan

11 Tony Richardson, Oscar Lewenstein, Margaret 'Percy' Harris and John Osborne in discussion about the set for the Russian production of *Look Back in Anger*

12 The golden couple: John Osborne and Mary Ure, 1957
13 Mary Ure in New York's Vegetarian Restaurant, 1957
14 Elaine Tynan and Mary Ure, Sandy Wilson's flat

15 Brenda de Banzie and Laurence Olivier in *The Entertainer*,
Royal Court Theatre, 1957
16 *The Entertainer* at the Royal Court Theatre, 1957: left to right, Dorothy Tutin,
Richard Pasco, Brenda de Banzie, Laurence Olivier

17 Laurence Olivier and Dorothy Tutin in *The Entertainer*, Royal Court Theatre, 1957

18 Laurence Olivier as Archie Rice in *The Entertainer*
19 Cover of the original programme

Royal Court
Theatre

Sloane Square S.W.1

English Stage Company

The Entertainer

by

John Osborne

First performance on Wednesday, April 10th, 1957.

6"

20 Oscar Lewenstein
21 Neville Blond

22 Joan Plowright, George Devine and John Osborne in *The Making of Moo*,
Royal Court Theatre, 25 June 1957
23 John Osborne and Mary Ure at home

It's a Broadway hit!
Playwright John
Osborne and wife
Mary Ure arrive at
London Airport
after " Look Back
in Anger's " New
York success

24 John Osborne and Mary Ure arriving at London Airport after the New York
success of *Look Back in Anger*, as featured in *Lilliput*

25 John Osborne, Jamaica, 1958

Tes joies et tes peines seront les miennes.

Pour John avec tout mon amour.

Francine

26 Francine, 1958

27 Yvonne Mitchell as Ruth and Robert Stephens as George Dillon in *Epitaph for George Dillon*, Royal Court Theatre, February 1958

fame or shame lay publicly in the balance, the problem now was how to catch the eye of the drinks waiter.

The blip was quite blurred. As I was seeking an escape from Merrick's Men, Larry grasped me, kissed me and said with a swift tenderness that was like a slap in the face of my near-stupor, 'Darling heart, they're not good. Not good at all.' He meant the reviews, of course. The critics, like the audience, had clocked off half-way through. 'Well, not good for *you* anyway.' He said it without a trace of irony, only concern and healing recompense. 'I shouldn't read them.'

The old cocksucker held me to him, muttering with clear Crispian diction, 'We'll get out of here as soon as we can and go home for a drink together.' So we did. In the small suite at the Algonquin, his actor's energy, damned by hours of concerted indifference, burst forth into gleeful, all-celebrating anecdote. It was like being expelled from school in the company of its brightest star, repudiating the remaining assembly of dross and prudery and isolating them for ever.

Larry sang loudly, to the tune of 'John Peel':

> When you wake in the morning . . .
> Full of fucks and joy . . .
> And your wife's in prison,
> And your daughter's coy . . .
> What's the matter with the bottom
> Of your eldest boy,
> When you wake with the horn in the morning?

Next morning the usually garrulous clerk at the cigar stall in the foyer looked down as I bundled up an armful of newspapers. The knowing desk-clerk, Mr Puley, handed me a few messages absent-mindedly, the Chinese elevator man was uncharacteristically inscrutable and the bell-captain too absorbed with departing baggage to boom his normal daily greeting. They must all have read the reviews. Olivier had been given the respect due to visiting royalty but Archie had struck no responsive chord. There was a dismissive tone throughout: New York had seen it all before in the thirties. Clifford Odets was invoked, a comparison which made me squirm at the taint of being both second-rate and unoriginal, and tardy to boot.

I stumbled on Tony in the chilly gloom of the Blue Bar, where I was downing a couple of cauterizing Bloody Marys. It was like pouring disinfectant and lighted matches into a blocked sink, a form of drastic medicinal chic which I'd convinced myself might be effective in this foreign battlefield of hard liquor.

I knew well enough by this time to look for no reassurance from Richardson's stony quarter. 'What did you *expect?*' All his undertakings had the precipitate energy that made closed incidents of them even before completion; failure or fulfilment both produced a fidgety, post-coital unease.

As ever, he was completely informed about everything, having been on the telephone for hours, spoken to Merrick and his Men, and probably arranged his life for the coming year. He was certainly in no mood for reminiscence and leaped to his feet with alarming, uncoordinated speed. 'I've got to go now. I'll talk to you *later.*' He paused in the semi-darkness. 'Why don't we go to Jamaica?' He was gone.

I had a dispiriting lunch that day with my American agent, Harold Freedman, in the harsh light and clatter of Dinty Moore's. He was always most kindly in a polite Judge Hardy manner, but I knew that he was of the same mind as the critics. As a founder-member of the Playwrights' Company, a friend of Odets and those other Broadway luminaries of the thirties, Anderson, Sherwood and Hellman, he must have regarded me as a Limey-cum-lately.

Freedman made it plain that I was expected to clutch at the flimsiest offer Hollywood might see fit to extend. His first offering, which he regarded as a prestigious coup, was a remake of *Blood and Sand*. When I refused, rather unthinkingly, his embarrassed disbelief at my ingrate hubris was almost shaming. He was genuinely hurt. But if I was becoming increasingly confused by my forebodings about New York, my reluctance about being sold into Californian bondage was genuine. Woodfall Films had yet to make its debut. What vague ambitions I may have had about films were resolutely chauvinist. It was a snobbish response which was dominant in England at that time. There was a maidenly horror at the suspicion of corruption, of compromise for either financial or critical advantage. At the Royal Court this obsession was an almost hysterical neurosis. What passed itself off as high-minded scepticism and integrity was often mere prig's timidity, the plain virgin with locked knees.

As I passed the adjoining marquees of my two plays, I half expected that Merrick might already be gouging out the flashing letters of my name, but they were still there, like a fairground display dimmed by daylight. Back at the Algonquin, Mary had already left for the theatre. I trundled the breakfast trolley into the corridor, flipped up the Do Not Disturb sign. The bathroom was steaming, with trickling taps, a trail of towels, sodden Kleenex, a wet stain of make-up and false eyelashes that looked like a laboratory experiment.

I was free until eleven that evening. The disorder and sheer bloody mess Mary had left behind filled me with a feeling of nauseous regret and failure. My spinsterish response to the state of the room was ludicrous in the face of my own capacity for squalor and error on every scale. The play itself seemed like a blunder. I had possibly, and foolishly, allowed myself to believe in the Alger Hiss theory. At home, I was conditioned to being jostled by suspicion, dislike and hostility, to being regarded as an upstart, a word which had almost no meaning over here. The American Dream had the upstart as hero; Ellis Island was his Golden Gate. My background drilled into me the discipline of low expectations. It was this loveless mockery of flailing endeavour that incited resistance, however blind and ineffectual.

Salisbury

My dear John,

As I feel a little better I thought I must write and ask how you are keeping. It is so boring sitting all day doing nothing and cold too. I expect you wish you were in warmer climbs. There is nothing to report, only I have lost the sight of my right eye. Yet there's plenty worse off in the world . . .

Uncle Jack

Salisbury

Dear John,

We were so grateful to receive your kind letter and think that we put the contents to good effect by buying Dulux paint and redecorated some rooms out, so you can imagine we have been very busy and not without a few aches.

God bless.

Uncle Jack

Salisbury

My dear Sister,

Have enclosed a few snaps of home and hope you will be interested. Queenie would have loved it and I tried several Charities to get her here. We did not hear of her death until *two months after*. Our letter to her was returned from the hospital where we had arranged to see her. I was sad because Watford did not inform us and think that Sidney should have done. I *have two* letters from her asking that she be cremated with Dad at Putney Vale also saying that Sidney knew all about it and his sister told us that the transport was too dear. In 1945 I got Queen a *free paid up* Cremation Policy No: 13463 from the Cremation Society and *I have her letter* asking the Soc to arrange for Putney Vale. In this letter she said

'I have told Sidney of my wishes.' She paid for that. I thought that you ought to know this dear.

Your ever-loving Brother,
Jack

Dear John,

Shall we ever see you again? I sit about in my chair and think of you and the old times. It always appears my letters are bad news but Bessie's brother died this morning, heart trouble, he was not 70 so you can imagine how it is. I felt I had to tell someone. There is no one to tell and I feel so hopeless and he was such a help and big. He lived at Ringwood. Please forgive me boring you John but I cannot get there in a pushchair.

God bless,
Uncle Jack

Even at the Court, I had been instructed by George and Tony in the guerrilla arts of living off the land, an unyielding landscape patrolled by an enemy that was identifiable and merciless. To have shown feelings of disappointment or expectations of enthusiasm from such battalions as the press, the public or ruling theatrical moguls would be folly and a betrayal of whatever cause we felt we were fighting. It had the excitement of war but also the attrition of wasted energy.

In foreign terrain, I felt untrained and ill-equipped, like a desert soldier suddenly confronted with jungle warfare. The Blue Bar's Bloody Marys were proving ineffective. Lying on the bed, I felt like someone who had foolishly let an undisciplined dog off the lead and watched it hurtle off into an oncoming car.

Harry rang. 'Hi, John, how are you?' He didn't wait for a reply and, to my relief, didn't mention the opening. 'I've spoken to Tony and we think we should all get some sunshine. There's a flight to Montego Bay Saturday night.' I looked up at the ceiling through a tide of tadpoles. Where was Montego Bay? 'Jamaica.' The tadpoles turned into ducks in a shooting-gallery. Jamaica.

I could think of half a dozen reasons why I shouldn't suddenly swoop off to the Caribbean. Mary would most certainly and understandably be displeased at abandonment to the play and the freezing wind-tunnels of New York. I could invent a plausible excuse. I'd done so before. She'd not believed me then and wouldn't do so now. Our relations had never been more than an almost childish game, once pleasurable and now uncontrolled. It was a cruel business.

Could I afford it? Olivier had given me a further lecture about never getting into trouble, like Archie Rice, with the Income Tax Man. As Harry, a natural courier to my anarchy, was rattling off his travel agent's itinerary, my misgivings faded. They were all so bourgeois and cautious. What shall I say to the wife? Can I afford it? Such craven questions should be struck from my record.

For the present I appeared to be caught in a trap of gaudy bungle and sham. I might as well benefit from its enjoyments while I had the opportunity. Gaudy, Bungle and Sham sounded like a firm of solicitors. Recklessness, however dangerous, was preferable to prudence. 'I've booked four tickets,' said Harry. Who was the fourth? 'Oh, Francine's coming. Call you later.' If ever there was a handmaiden to folly, it was surely Francine. Gaudy, yes, perhaps. Certainly a gift-wrapped bungle. A sham, not really. Some certain sadness.

New York seemed a dangerous place in which to pursue an affair which I already regarded as a luxurious, uncomplicated interlude. Francine's currency-wise Swiss soul knew better than to risk the real hard slog of romanticism, but when I arrived at Harry's apartment, she was alone and as excited and apprehensive as I was. Sixth Avenue on that Saturday afternoon was empty and hardly visible under a driving blizzard of snow. I was confident that Harry's arrangements contained some military contingency plan that would see us off to the sun on time, but he rang to say that there was no chance of getting out of the city that day. For thirty-six hours we waited like fugitives for word of escape. Had I blundered into a humiliating, farcical trap? On Monday, Harry rang again. Our flight would be taking off. He and Tony were tied up and would join us in a couple of days. 'Have fun,' he instructed.

So, in the winter of 1958, I found myself the author of two plays running on Broadway, one of them starring Laurence Olivier and the other my wife, staying with a beautiful girl at the Half Moon, Montego Bay. In Glasgow they were all wrapped up in woollies and having colds.

We were the centre of attention among the American tourists, the star honeymoon couple. To my relief, there wasn't an English accent to be heard. Francine spent long mornings on the beach and then would dance under the stars, displaying the most public candle-lit devotion, eyes brimming mournfully across the table. Acting out this cloying pantomime made me think longingly of rain-swept Brighton and anonymous adultery there at Moss Mansions.

Tony would have said, 'I mean, what did you *expect?*' The truth was rather more and a little less. I had not anticipated the leery brutes in Bermuda shorts on the hunt for 'a juicy piece of black ass', their wives cooing over my bride with her 'cute accent', nor Francine's addiction to glutinous Latin love-songs. She would gaze rapturously at the waiters as they warbled '*Amore*' and '*Volare*' into her cleavage. If '*Volare*' could make you blubber, 'Pop Goes the Weasel' must make you weep.

Rescue from 'the boys' in New York was unforthcoming; more pressing things had 'come up'. At least they wouldn't be witness to the spectacle of Montego Bay's most popular young lovers honeymooning the night away to a crass hokey-cokey. I told Harry we'd be cutting it short. I should have known better than to have gone trawling so blindly, but what absurd expectations could Francine possibly have looked for? The heart-melting pramful had become an armful of misery.

Harry met us at the airport. It was the homecoming of a pair of runaways dragged back from a juvenile prank, adulterous but scarcely adult. He didn't throw blankets over our heads but hustled us into a car. He was full of news of the film negotiations for *Look Back*. Everything was fine, fine. Olivier had extended his engagement for another four weeks. That was unexpected. So was the follow-up. 'Mary's telling everyone she's pregnant.' The furry burden stiffened on my shoulder. We drove back to the Algonquin in silence.

'OK then, John, we'll call you tomorrow.' Mr Puley at the desk greeted me with his customary camp eyebrow-lift. 'My, we *do* have an expensive tan.' There was a message from Mary asking me to pick her up from the theatre for supper with Richard and Sybil Burton, Julie Andrews and her husband, Lena (Horne) and Lennie, Rex and Hugh Griffiths, some of them or maybe all of them. I don't remember. When I arrived at her dressing-room, she welcomed me in her absent-minded bubbly way, pouring forth Broadway gossip, details of her non-buying shopping expeditions, the awfulness of Kenneth Haigh and so on. If Harry's news was correct she made no reference to it. She seemed an untroubled spirit as she tumbled cheerfully into bed.

Mary had accumulated a tight circle of friends. Her immersion in them must have eased the gaping deception of the little time we spent alone together. There was Josephine Premice, a Haitian actress in the cast of Lena Horne's musical *Jamaica*. Witty and articulate, she was as arresting as a Masai chieftain and almost as fearsome. Mary claimed that, whenever I was away, she and Josephine would share the same bed. I wasn't quite sure whether this was the dormitory bravado of the Mount School, York, colonizing Manhattan chic, but pale Quaker Oats curled up beside this blue-black warrior seemed a rather forced sort of lark.

Mary's most attentive escort was Robert Webber, a Broadway actor familiar to most of us through his sharp performance in *Twelve Angry Men* and later in *The Dirty Dozen*. He was an unsubtle but effective performer, a New Yorkerish red-neck sophisticate who had made his reputation in several of Tennessee Williams' plays. He was a close friend of Tennessee and of another, less flamboyant, homosexual playwright, William Inge. Most of his circle were famous queens, and these liberal sympathies must have grated against his insistent balls-flexing stance which was then a stock caricature of widespread sexual unease.

He was a regular visitor to Ziggy's Gymnasium on Broadway and Third and tried to persuade me to join him, to pump some manly iron into my feeble frame, among the ranks of sweating body-boys. His absorption in these gentle giants was expressed in gruff-voiced jokes punched up from profuse testicular powers ('just a bunch of hairy faggots'), but was as full of awed tenderness as derision. I believe that, years later, he did at last emerge, like a snorting bull, from the closet.

Webber, with his butch references to his bed as a work-bench marked with the notches of a hundred grateful maidens, must have earmarked me as an irresistible target for cuckoldry. I was unsure whether he had already succeeded. Mary, feeling herself an object of public neglect, might have found some comfort in private revenge.

I found his company quite endearing in its boisterous way for short periods. At his Eighth Avenue apartment one day, he suddenly began to berate me at the top of his deep-balled voice about my treatment of Mary, the Half Moon expedition and my dumb entanglement with a scheming hooker. His condemnation was accurate enough to be damning and left me helplessly mugged by my own criminal indiscretion. He gave chapter and verse of my behaviour, which was, he said, being openly bruited in Broadway theatres, bar-rooms and the columns of Walter Winchell and lesser gossip-writers. The principal object of his harangue became Francine. I was assigned the role of an innocent alien who had been set up for a messy intrigue with a cheap and tasteless broad.

My own behaviour had been patently wanton and inexcusable, but the assessment of Francine seemed vindictive and extreme, more McCarthyite hysteria than puritan outrage. To compound the evidence of my villainy, he told me of Mary's fierce loyalty at some recent party when, after rejecting a clumsy pass from Elia Kazan, the director had taunted her with the observation, 'I hear your husband's a fag.' It was quite believable. There was a teasing softness of style in the English male that baffled and even outraged these guardians of acceptable mannerism. The ambiguity of English maleness was not merely Un-American but downright provocative. Mary had given Kazan a good Yankee smack in his Armenian face, which turned her into an instant heroine, an exemplar of the fire-power of the frontierswoman.

Webber became more solicitous. 'I should keep your head down for a while if I were you.'

Epitaph for George Dillon, the play I had written in tandem with Anthony

Creighton some four years earlier, had just opened to some muted enthusiasm at the Royal Court. Sloane Square suddenly seemed a very friendly, wise and civilized place and even Woodfall Street a pleasant haven from the luxuries of room service and the excitements of all-night New York. I needed to return where I was less regarded and more tolerated.

It was a dismal, cowardly decision but I could think of no other. In writing of one's past, it is an unavoidable pity that there is no one to speak up on one's own behalf. There might be some faint plea of mitigation. Perhaps not. I was born with a contrite heart. This is not a boastful apology, rather it might provide the motive if I have occasionally perjured myself. I hope so.

To the accusation of slovenliness I merely change the plea of guilty to a charge of unremitting and commonplace simpleness. What does it matter? Not very much.

11. 'His own Worst Enemy'

He achieved nothing he set out to do. He made no one happy. No one looked up with excitement when he entered the room. He was always troubled with the void round his heart, but he loved no one successfully. He was a bit of a bore and, frankly, rather useless. But the germs loved him.

Epitaph for George Dillon

I should judge that Osborne has been his own worst enemy. Self-loathing appears to be a driving force of his art. He should control it: he is not as bad as he thinks.

Harold Hobson, *Sunday Times*, 14 April 1958

When I got back to Sloane Square, George had just returned from Buckingham Palace with his CBE from the Queen. He had accepted it 'on behalf of the theatre' and, to ease his misgivings, he would hand around the despised bauble of the Establishment with rather forced mockery, saying, 'Here, feel that, boy. Her Majesty actually touched that.'

It was not a very convincing performance, but his discomfiture was real enough. Her Majesty was, after all, Defender of the Faith and her servant, the Lord Chamberlain (one Sir St Vincent Troubridge), had demanded that twenty-one blasphemous lines be excised from *Endgame*, including Beckett's notorious dismissal of the Almighty: 'The bastard, he doesn't exist.' Moreover, George had dropped the custom of playing the National Anthem before every performance, confining it to first nights to appease the Daimler-and-diamonds brigade.

Apart from the bauble, he seemed in good spirits and a little puzzled by the mild approbation for the opening of *George Dillon*. I had sent him a copy of the play after he first came aboard the *Egret*. He made little reference to it except to imply he found it inferior, and I scarcely thought of it again, although Anthony was disappointed. I was well aware of its deficiencies, in particular the shadows of gauche shabbiness at the heart of it and the impression of irresolute defiance that seemed, even for me, an act of wanton self-denigration, self-manacled Houdini crowd-pulling.

The play's first showing had been a year earlier by the Oxford Experimental Theatre Club, who had written asking if I had an old, unproduced script I might care to let them loose on. On this flimsy proof, George decided to give it an airing at his own theatre. In spite of misgivings, echoing his own verdict, about 'an apprentice work unwisely resurrected', he offered it to the director Bill Gaskill. I was surprised by the choice and, even more, that Bill accepted. I scarcely knew Bill, although I liked him, but felt there must be a natural chasm of taste and temperament between us that would be difficult to negotiate. The low, baiting cruelties scattered all over the piece would surely affront his rather prickly Yorkshire severity. I had been glad to be away in New York leaving him to sort out Anthony's amiable vagaries for himself.

As a result, perhaps for the first and last time, I sat down to watch something of my own with scarcely any apprehension. For once there would be no inner recriminations. The West End triumphs of the day were *The Reluctant Debutante*, *Teahouse of the August Moon*, *South Sea Bubble*, *Sailor Beware* and *The Mousetrap*. I was reassured that *George Dillon* would at least be more stimulating than anything else in London. It was. Bill had cast it extremely well. The curtain line of the first act, 'You stupid-looking bastard,' delivered by Robert Stephens as George Dillon to the photograph of his benefactor's dead son, drew exactly the shocked frisson from the audience I had intended.

Robert was a complex character, exuding actorish high spirits which concealed a deeply divided, embittered soul. Although few could have been aware of this simmering dissatisfaction, it made him an inspired choice. Watching him, I had the needling impression that he might have based his interpretation, consciously or not, on an unflattering observation of myself, even to the extent of physical mannerisms. I didn't brood on it. Robert's innate qualities were more valuable than charm. This letter from him, seven years on, is wholly characteristic:

National Theatre, SE1

My darling, I must say it again I do think *Patriot for Me* truly, truly magnificent! Larry said *he* would give up the National to play it if he were twenty years younger!!! – He said he was *born* to play it!! – And that I was the only other actor who could do it apart from himself! – So that's two of us who would give an arm and a leg!!! – But apart from all that I think it is immense and deeply affecting and as always makes my hair stand on end.

Hope to see you very soon – and show you my Doug Hayward corduroy suit which is smashing! (not a pinch, I promise).

All my best love.

Always.

Bobby

The year before I had written a piece for a provocatively titled book, *Declaration*. This provided an unexploded package to an eager corps of cultural-disposal experts. The only ones certain to suffer injury were its rash contributors, the eight conspirators in this literary gunpowder prank, who were to find themselves and their pretensions blown up in amateurish ignominy.

Declaration was an early example of instant opportunism, put together by the fluently pushy young publisher Tom Maschler. He trumpeted in the introduction that:

> A number of young and widely opposed writers have burst upon the scene and are striving to change many of the values which have held good in recent years. No critic has succeeded in assessing them or correlating them objectively one to another. This volume aims at helping the public to understand what is happening while it is actually happening – at uncovering a certain pattern taking shape in Britain today.

Maschler had been as shrewd as he was opportunistic in his selection of writers. But his literary clout was marred by his endorsement of Colin Wilson, the trusty Outsider from Leicester and sleeping-bag philosopher of Hampstead Heath, and his two altar boys, Stuart Holroyd and Bill Hopkins. This cranky triumvirate had already been unkindly caricatured as a high-brow Lord Snooty and his scruffy intellectual Pals.

Oddly, they were the only AYM who looked especially young. Wilson, briefly buoyed up by accolades from Cyril Connolly and Philip Toynbee, had the appearance of a sinister, bespectacled swot with a catapult dangling from his threadbare trousers. Their academic simple-mindedness and immature arrogance dashed any possibility of the other benighted essayists receiving a token of sympathetic attention. We were all implicated in their doomed manifesto. Prophetic heroism, proclaimed by self-educated lower-middle-class upstarts, pronounced in English and with dodgy Nietzschean flourishes, never stood a chance. Putting Doris Lessing and Kenneth Tynan, Lindsay Anderson and John Wain alongside Lord Snooty and his Pals was fun but unfair even by the fairground-booth standards of Fleet Street.

At least three of the *Declaration* pieces deserved attention. Lessing's essay, written from the standpoint of an ex-Communist, colonial novelist living in England, was more than realistic about the poetic limitations of working-class heroics. Tynan's was full of fanciful certainties, combative, cool and funny. It would have aroused ill-natured envy wherever it had appeared, especially from those whose mincing, mandarin style Lindsay Anderson nailed in his own essay. My own piece, written hastily over a weekend punctuated by Maschler's deadline calls, deserved some if not most of the scorn heaped upon it.

Party Swoop

A cocktail party for the publication of *Declaration* was banned from London's Royal Court theatre over criticism of royalty by the Angry Young Man author, John Osborne. Mr Reginald Poynter got a telegram from Mr Neville Blond, chairman of the English Stage Company, saying: 'We will not permit the party to be held in any part of the theatre.' He also got a call from Mr George Devine who said, 'Members of the Council are shocked at the John Osborne piece and in particular to the references to royalty. They wish to be disassociated from the book in every way.' Lord Harewood, the Queen's cousin, Lord Bessborough and actress Peggy Ashcroft are members of the Council of ten.

And so the party was held at the Pheasantry, Chelsea. The company included Mr Aneurin Bevan, Mr Michael Foot, Hollywood actor Rod Steiger and the authors.

This is what Osborne wrote in the book. 'My objection to the Royalty symbol is that it is dead: it is a gold filling in a mouthful of decay.'

Daily Herald, 15 October 1957

George had joined the party, so hastily switched to a crumbling, recherché bohemian retreat, and gamely offered to send the bill to the Council. The whole episode must have increased his daily burden with hours of ultimatum telephone calls. He never rebuked me for my part in encouraging the hooligan elements ranged against his own serious efforts. He was already hemmed in by detractors and foresworn enemies. I had merely added to them.

Stuart Holroyd, Lord Snooty's Pal, popped up again the following spring at one of the Court's Sunday-night productions without decor. These were presentations of plays by unknown authors, most of whom were to remain so. But there had been some notable debuts by Michael Hastings, N.F. Simpson and John Arden and, later, Donald Haworth, Wole Soyinka, Edward Bond, Christopher Hampton, Joe Orton and Howard Brenton. They were a little like those turn-of-the-century showings of plays by Ibsen and directors like

Granville Barker. The list of actors prepared to rehearse for two weeks for one performance and virtually no money is unthinkable today. Even more fruitful was the recruitment of untried directors including Lindsay Anderson (dubbed by Tony 'the Singing Virgin'), Bill Gaskill, John Dexter, Peter Gill, Robert Kidd and Bill Bryden.

Holroyd's play, *The Tenth Chance*, was directed by Anthony Creighton. How anyone could have countenanced this farrago of talents even as a bad joke on a Sunday night was mystifying. The house was untypically full and there was a discernible impression of assembled factions, including Wilson and his band of apocalyptics dotted among the main body of chafing hostility. The cast included James Villiers (who had replaced me at Frinton Rep and was the object of Anthony's romantic dreams), Bernard Kay, Ronald Fraser and the daily who cleaned Woodfall Street.

The awfulness of the play mounted to a climax, then evened out like the mid-plateau of a hangover before descending into a final tableau of incomprehensibility. Groans and scuffles in the auditorium were drowned out by the superior bombast of Bruckner, which Anthony employed as an extra blanket to throw over the confusion on stage. It was custard-pie anarchy.

I slipped out quickly. Anthony was in the pub next door in high spirits and wearing the Hunting Stewart kilt he favoured when contemplating an evening of seduction. He was surrounded by a group of sympathetic supporters. I decided to leave before any confrontation between the fuming factions broke out. I was too late. There were cries of jubilant aggression from a table in the corner. Colin Wilson, lying in wait for Tynan (who had walked out noisily before the end with his wife, Elaine), pulled the dandy-critic's chair from under him and left him sprawling on the floor.

As I made for the door, a reporter asked me if I had seen anything. I replied that I hadn't. The following morning I read that I had been at the centre of 'an angry young brawl' in a Chelsea pub. It wouldn't have happened at Sardi's.

By 1958 George's adversaries, within and without, could not deny that he had established some kind of bridgehead, however vulnerable. Even the Essenes noted the changes in the desert map of English theatre. The choice of repertory might seem too eclectic for those looking for a clear, doctrinal affirmation of taste, but it conformed to the practical considerations of what was available and possible. It was the application of his insistence that 'all problems are *technical*', a dismal-sounding dictum that might come from a woodwork instructor at an Evening Institute rather than an inspirer of poets. Pondering on it years later, I felt that it was more useful counsel in dealing with women than art. 'There are plays that you do out of passion,' he said.

'There are plays that you do to express your beliefs. And there are plays that you do because the author needs that support at that moment.'

Even if I should wish it, I am not equipped to write a history of the Royal Court. I may have been a participant, but much of the action was going on in other places, other rooms. Rather like a character in Arnold Wesker's *The Kitchen*, I had a fragmented vision of a series of dramas acted concurrently. There was ignorance and indifference to what was going on at the next 'station'. We were too absorbed in our allotted contributions to pay much heed to the troubles of others. The complaints of the vegetable cooks were a hindrance to the pâtissiers. Both were a nuisance to the butcher. Only George had any overall picture. As for the customers, they had no knowledge of the chaos below, and less interest.

So many plays were presented through a system of default, happy and less-happy accidents of fortune: sometimes the stealth of a minority faction, or the apathy of a few, or simply the overnight need to plug up an unforeseeable hole created by a singularly battering disaster. Devine, the Little Dutch Boy of Sloane Square, was obliged to have his finger at the ever ready to thrust into the most shaky of theatrical dykes. John Arden became an in-house joke for box-office disaster. George's triumphant cry at the latest clutch of bad notices was cherished by those below stairs: 'They're worse than *Live Like Pigs*!' Neville Blond, panting for a knighthood, would go white. 'Not *another* Arden, George.'

Arnold Wesker was then living in an LCC block of flats in the Upper Clapton Road with his young wife, Dusty. He had approached Lindsay Anderson outside the National Film Theatre after a showing of Lindsay's film, *Every Day But Christmas* and entered an early version of *The Kitchen* for the *Observer* play competition, where it received neither prize nor mention. The competition was the inspiration of Kenneth Tynan, whose enthusiasm for working-class theatre was not always helped by his unfamiliarity with the idiom of the man in the bus queue or, in this case, the salt-beef bar. Lindsay reported back to Upper Clapton Road that he thought the play 'Important as well as very *good* . . . Can I send it to George Devine to read for the Court? Of course I haven't any idea what their reaction will be! They are rather incalculable people.'

All creative enterprises, at risk from electricity bills, salaries and box-office caprice, are faced with the inescapable contortion of compromise. In George's case the Wesker plays were a classic example. It was a matter of keeping the right balls in the air. When *Chicken Soup with Barley* fell at his feet, he kicked it straight into touch by offering it to the Belgrade Theatre, Coventry. In exchange for mounting it, there would be a week's showing in Sloane Square.

It was the kind of transparent dexterity, limiting financial loss – and loss of face – that cautious impresarios used in similar arrangements with the Court.

The task of directing the play was consigned to John Dexter, then a house guest at the Wesker flat. The two had met on an Aldermaston march, the duffle-coated radical answer to Ascot or Leander-pink Henley. Who knows what ambitions, what plans for plays, novels, between-sheets liaisons and poetry readings were fired on those blustery Easter-weekend route marches? Unlike hot, drowsy pre-1914 summers, Aldermaston weekends were always wet and cold.

JIMMY: Is your friend Webster coming tonight?
ALISON: He might drop in. You know what he is.
JIMMY: Well, I hope he doesn't. I don't think I could take Webster tonight.
ALISON: I thought you said he was the only person who spoke your language?
JIMMY: So he is. Different dialect, but same language. I like him. He's got bite, edge, drive –
ALISON: Enthusiasm.
JIMMY: You've got it. When he comes here, I begin to feel exhilarated. He doesn't like me but he gives me something, which is more than I get from most people.

Look Back in Anger

Webster was one of the twenty-seven off-stage characters referred to in the play who never make an appearance, a breach of the laws of dramaturgy at the time, though for no explicable reason save custom, and often cited as typical of my overall technical ineptitude. Dexter, however, must have been pleased with his non-appearing role because he told everyone *he* was the original Webster. I like to think so, although we never referred to it.

We first met in Derby in 1953. John was no bushy-tailed gay of a later generation and the burghers of Derby had every reason to be resistant to his passing through the stage door of their playhouse. He was a local boy, but he had the mark of metropolitan criminality. He also had a ferocious energy, driven curiosity and a kind of fearful courage which cut little ice in the rink of provincial certainties. His visits were a welcome distraction in Pamela's flat exposed to the year-long chill which swept in from the Dales. Sunday evenings were a dangerous border-crossing of the week, a few short hours infested by my own uncertainties and the usual Sabbath intimations of utter isolation. No one could compound that terror with such finality as Pamela. Oh well, that was another Sunday over. Not much to show for it, and not much promise for the next.

Dexter, like Anthony Creighton, abhorred the mere mechanics of female functioning. No other director could have boomed from the auditorium at a stumbling actress: 'Oh, dear, we know she's got the rags up again, *but* . . . ' It was a vengeful, goading shock to bourgeois gentility under a mask of working-class consensus. He once told me that as a fourteen-year-old apprentice he had been gang-masturbated on the factory bench by a bunch of middle-aged housewives in some initiation ritual.

Later, he was infamously charged with various indecencies against a minor during an audition above a pub in Brewer Street. George, summoned to Bow Street to give evidence of good character on John's behalf, had been sick with disbelief at the detail he had been obliged to hear. The magistrate was a renowned queer-hater ('A Hogarthian monster', according to George), but having to listen to the pornographic plod was the worst of it. Dexter received the maximum sentence of six months. George's liberal kindness took a savage mauling. 'I can't tell you the stuff that came out . . . '

In replying to this letter, please write on the envelope: – Number 2952.
Name: Dexter

H.M. Prison,
Wormwood Scrubs, w12

My dear John,

I think of you back in England now. Hope so, anyway I'll risk a letter finding you. I can't give you many details of life in here, but it's odd: very cold, not as bad as you expect. So many reforms coming into effect, so many yet to come and the place overcrowded and understaffed. The screws are in the main, a decent crowd, most of them seem to be aware that things are changing and are happy to change with them: the only people who *hate* any reform are the old lags, but they are all terrible old Tories anyway. The worst thing here is time; it has no feel, no taste, no shape, length, no, nor no bloody brevity neither. Nick is rather like hell: a climate but no situation.

A ghastly rumour has reached me; it is said that I have taken my bird as a punishment for evil and have gone religious!!! This is not true. I have tried to do my time with as much strength and gaiety as I possess. As for religion, what do people think I am for God's sake? I admit I hope to be in Pamplona next year, but that has more connection with bulls than saints. Worry not, I shall never darken your door, whisky-soaked and priest-ridden. I shall bring nothing out with me but experience which I can use, and which is unique. I shan't write a book and as for the strange langue d'oc of the lags, I fear I shall never speak it with ease. No change, in fact, but that which only those who know me best will see.

Now then, on Dec 5th or 6th, I am due for another visit, would you like to come? Tony V knows the routine and will bring you if you wish. Don't for God's sake come if it is going to upset you. But if you think it would interest you I would love to see you. Let me know, and I'll set the wheels in motion.

I am well and half way now and it's going more quickly. Tony and Doris write regularly. I work hard, and time passes. I love you all very much. You must know this, but I didn't know I was loved back!! It makes the world a different shape. Give my love to Tony R and G.D, Mary, Tony C, Oscar B, Jenny, EVERYONE.

For yourself, thanks, gratitude, oh balls! I am going to be a big success, that will be my thank you.

John.

I was there to take him home on the morning when he was released. I later learned he called me 'Sister Mary Discipline'. Fairly amusing. Not very.

Devine, Richardson and Anderson had all been to Oxford and even to the same college, Wadham. Lindsay was known to chant its Latin prayers along with 'The Streets of Loredo' or 'She Wore a Yellow Ribbon'. Among the actors in the original company, there had been a sprinkling of graduates – Nigel Davenport, Christopher Fettes, Jose Richards – but I was never aware of a conscious clique. Later came Gaskill and Anthony Page. Most of this supposed Oxford bias was little more than pipe-smoking in-filling, like the proscription against homosexuals: it did you no harm and less good. Few of George's playwrights were graduates, with the exception of Arden (Cantab.), Beckett (Trinity, Dublin) and Wally Simpson, who was a teacher. Playwrights who had been to university, let alone Oxford or Cambridge, were then, as now and before, a minority.

As a factor in day-to-day practical considerations, I don't think the 'Oxford' count figured at all. People like Dexter had some reason for feeling intellectually discriminated against, but it was not a substantial one. My own class and credentials were every bit as unpromising as his, or Wesker's, but I didn't detect any evidence of paternalism or impenetrable class chasms between George and myself.

Dexter and George played out their mutual unease in a cross-talk banter, the NCO to the other's Officer. Their shared experience was a bitter dislike of the army. 'Tell me, Dexter, how did you rise from the ranks?' 'I didn't, sir. I stayed on as a staff sergeant because I wanted to be with the boys.' Dexter had looked up the boss's initial assessment in the company files: 'Nice little chappie, not greatly talented, looks like Noguchi.'

Arnold, particularly, found George's presence in the council flat in Upper Clapton Road intrusive and patronizing. I think of George making his way through the gefilte fish dutifully prepared by Dusty. It is a scene rich in comic speculation, but it also makes my heart ache a little. Nothing invites such scorn as good intentions. When George came upon the Wesker's first-born being breast-fed in his office, he delighted all expectations by shouting, 'Get that woman out of my room.' Even the mutual bond of class affinity could be strained, immortalized by Dexter's equally impatient outburst, 'Shut up, Arnold, or I'll direct this play as you wrote it.'

Whether or not directed as written, *Chicken Soup with Barley* opened in Coventry and was received enthusiastically. George honoured his obligation and brought it to the Court, where the phantom audience failed to turn up. A year later *Roots* came in after another success at the Belgrade. Dexter was then able to persuade George and Tony to agree to his Sunday-night staging of *The Kitchen*. Repudiating Tony's verdict that it was 'technically impossible', the result was astonishingly invigorating.

Binkie Beaumont once said as I left the room, 'Well, there goes a million pounds and, probably, good riddance.' George felt much the same about Arnold. Despite Tony's derision and my insularity, there is no doubt that George's favourites in the 1958 season were the French connection: the Romanian Ionesco's *The Lesson* and *The Chairs* and Irish-Sam's *Endgame* and *Krapp's Last Tape*, known to us all as *'Tape's Last Crap'*.

Appearing with Joan Plowright in *The Chairs*, George was nightly stimulated by the cries of 'surrealist rubbish' and the rows of empty seats in the stalls. Those who knew him from his Young Vic days had never seen him happier. He would puff on his pipe from the window of his dressing-room on to a Sloane Square empty of parked Daimlers and sigh, 'This is what I'm here for.'

12. 'Not at his Best'

The body of Jonathan Swift, Doctor of Divinity, Dean of this Cathedral Church, is buried here, where fierce indignation can no longer lacerate his heart.

Epitaph, St Patrick's, Dublin

Donald Albery, who had refused to transfer *Look Back* to the West End unless the bears and squirrels were given the heave-ho, ran the only management of any substance to compete against the oligarchy of H.M. Tennant. Through the patrimony of Sir Bronson he controlled several key theatres. A tall, chilly figure, he walked with a cane and, in the repertory of the time, would have been well cast as an embittered ex-officer who terrorized the small boys in an oppressive prep school.

I was becoming accustomed to condescension, and his was more entertaining than most. It was difficult to believe that he could possibly have liked *Epitaph for George Dillon* and he presented me with a list of his 'demands' in the matter of cuts and changes. Among these was a stipulation that the title be changed to '*George Dillon*'. 'Epitaph', with its intimations of mortality, was a message of death at the box-office. It seemed dull to me but preferable to his other suggestion, which was to use the mocking title of the play within the play itself, '*Telephone Tart*'.

My compliance didn't seem to give him much pleasure. I was fairly sure that a few perfunctory clips here and there would be enough to persuade him, like the critics, that the play had been almost completely rewritten and become something else. So it was, and continues to be.

I returned to New York, braced to improvise some kind of restraint on the disorder I was sure to face. Air travel then still had an element of daring privilege: a twenty-four-hour journey from a large shed at Northolt, couchettes reminiscent of exotic foreign trains (always chivalrously allocated to ladies), drinks in the cosy bar, the arctic blast of air that ripped through the aircraft when it landed at Gander, where health inspectors flashed lights at sleeping passengers as if they were curiosities from a distant world. I drank myself

99

insensible and broke my vegetarian vows by eating something called Cornish Rock Hen.

Wearily sedated against recrimination, I arrived at the Algonquin in mid-afternoon and I was effusively greeted by everyone, including the quizzical Mr Puley, always an accurate wind-sock. Mary, still in her nightdress, was in full-flow of her daily gossip on the telephone. She blew me a cheery kiss and waved at an ice-brimmed champagne bucket on the table beside a gift-wrapped package from Saks. Both resistant to the expensive novelty of transatlantic calls, we had only exchanged a few uninformative letters. If she had received poisonous dispatches from unkindly friends, she showed no sign of suspicion. Her chirrupy ease was almost infectious, even to my wary spirit, and her obsession with the punishing *Kama Sutra* of fertility athletics seemed to have abated.

Algonquin life resumed more or less as I had left it, with the additional hazard of Francine waiting like a mislaid parcel to be reclaimed at Harry's apartment. For the next few months I did no work at all. Margery Vosper, unlike Harold Freedman, had a comfortingly unambitious attitude to advance-ment. 'I think you've done *quite* enough for the moment, dear,' she would say. With Mary's commitments to Merrick, Fifth Avenue, her girlfriends and the English and Welsh Broadway exiles, I saw very little of her, less than I did of Francine.

If it wasn't a double life, it was an exhaustingly packed double half-life. I could detect a strong undercurrent of displeasure. It genuinely surprised me. I couldn't trace the impulse for it, least of all from a profession which should surely have retained its scorn for anti-bohemian outrage. I was as circumspect as was possible within a square mile of New York. I was observing the most obtuse mechanics of propriety. I was realistic enough to know that to calculate the cost of adultery is like enquiring about the cost of running a private yacht: posing the question defines your inability to afford it. But it wasn't the cost – it never has been – that concerned me. It was the matter of what was justifiable as a caprice of short life and affectionate memory. It didn't seem a great deal to ask.

I continued to have breakfast in the room, then a late lunch at somewhere like the Russian Tea Room with Mary, and an early 'Volare' evening with Francine at the Little Club, her favourite, most expensive and boring idea of fun. Tinkling pianos, twinkling Manhattan, why should I begrudge such simple upstart pranks? It was minimal consolation for a twenty-eight-year-old drama-tist with a play running in London and two on Broadway, and assuredly all over by Christmas.

Merrick summoned me to his office. I knew that I was to be presented with some St Valentine's Day ultimatum. The glum look on the face of his chief hit-man, Jack Schissel, as he ushered me in, confirmed it. He rasped out that *Look Back*'s box-office was slipping, as I already knew from *Variety*. I felt as if I had been found guilty of cheating him in a bootlegging racket on the South Side. What was that object bulging below Jack's left armpit? Merrick agreed, with much show of reluctance, to present *George Dillon* in New York. I would be back in October. *Look Back* would never have survived the steaming New York summer and, with the departure of *The Entertainer*, the exposure of the last nine months looked like becoming a tidily closed incident.

On 8 May, again (my father's birthday, the end of the Second World War, the opening of *Look Back* and, later, the death of Max Miller), Olivier gave a last-night party. He had chartered a private yacht, *Knickerbocker VII*, and welcomed the guests in a Butlin's blazer and yachting-cap to the accompaniment of bagpipes.

Vivien was presumably pining in London. Joan Plowright was tucked among the guests, successfully evading the hovering English journalists. Up the gangplank came Douglas Fairbanks, Henry Fonda, Helen Hayes, Cedric Hardwicke, Ustinov, of course, Denholm Elliott, Eric Portman, Anthony Quayle. And Greer Garson, again. There was a buffet of fish and chips, jellied eels, stout and bottled Bass. As we sailed up the Hudson, I spent most of the night with John Steinbeck, also in a yachting-cap. To Mary's dismay, I gave an extended impression of a typical English faggot to Elia Kazan.

> There are bad times just around the corner,
> There are dark clouds hurtling through the sky,
> And it's no good whining
> About a silver lining
> For we know from experience that they won't roll by.
> With a scowl and a frown
> We'll keep our peckers down,
> And prepare for depression and doom and dread,
> We're going to unpack our troubles from our old kitbag
> And wait until we drop down dead.
> Noël Coward, 'There are Bad Times Just Around the Corner'

The following month, Mary and I embarked on an adventure holiday which seemed to be riddled with portent on every hand. I felt she deserved comfort and physical freedom, some recompense for nine months in the poky Algonquin suite and the twenty blocks of exercise yard she had trailed between

Forty-fourth Street and the Park. I also felt what Nellie Beatrice would call an 'entitlement' to luxury in the face of the strange and unexpected.

We emerged from the Beverly Hills Hotel and a Cadillac was delivered to the forecourt. George couldn't have described this as a 'grocer's car'. Red and gleaming, it was already warm from the morning sunshine. It was a car for the likes of girls we had decided we would never find ourselves escorting, girls like Francine. Francine would have descended into this eight-cylinder sphinx convertible-absurdity as effortlessly as into a proferred mink stole. Mary looked at it with dismay. This surprised me, as she had taken enthusiastically to American food, clothing and customs without any of my own resistance. Indeed, I suspected, half hopefully, that she might contemplate citizenship. She slumped into the front, clutching an armful of maps and we glided off.

It took me ages to get us out of Los Angeles and on to Highway 1, an operation a Californian eight-year-old could have accomplished in minutes. I soon wished we were in the two-litre grocer's roadster, gazing at the white sands of the West Highland road to the Hebrides, or even back in New York. Out here, Mary was suspicious and fretful in a way I had never seen her before. Where she had been eager and uncomplaining, she was either tentative or disapproving. She discarded the maps. I knew she was capable of navigating a boat on the Clyde without thinking.

For the next six weeks she said less and less, looked at little, the space between us in the rushing wind widening as the mileage clock plunged into four and then five digits of time and distance. If I had any expectations of exhilaration from following the line of the Pacific coast, they were soon dispelled. There was none of the ferocious vastness of the prospect from Falmouth or the enclosed ghostliness from the dereliction of Gateshead. It was monumentally bland.

We stopped at tourist spots like Monterey, where we spent an evening in a perfect Egyptian art-deco cinema, and Carmel, a Disneyish Cornish village, popular with middling phoneys and film actors. Nothing seemed to engage Mary's attention, nor even her disapproval. I felt we should get away from the placid seaboard and strike inland. First stop Reno. From Reno, to the Blackpool of Las Vegas. Then the lunar cities and tiny settlements of Nevada, Utah, Colorado, New Mexico and Arizona. I had never known such parched exposure and banishment in the constant presence of another.

I was increasingly certain that I had been ham-fistedly cuckolded by Robert Webber. The fact that my coltish liaison with Francine had been pre-empted by Mary's conduct with Webber explained her oddly restrained behaviour in New York. Sexual guilt, like jealousy, had never been more than a passing cloud over any of the tumult of the past. Betrayal might end in the bedroom but I found it naïve to assume it necessarily began there.

The one thing which did rouse Mary from her day-long prickly inertia was her motel inspection in the blue-pink light of the late afternoon. The motels varied from lower-middle-class luxury to American-style squalor. We learned that behind the world of Betty Crocker hygiene, of paper-sealed lavatory seats and post-coital showers, there was a continental closet of trash, unlaundered sheets and cockroaches that would make many a Lancashire landlady retch over her scrubbed doorstep. There were times when we found ourselves groping about, after the sun had snapped out in the limitless distance, in ghostly rooms lit by broken lampshades, aired by stale air-conditioning and the presence of the last occupants. The basic rule was never to stay anywhere that was uncarpeted. That could reveal all manner of disagreeable surprises to the most exhausted traveller.

Town after town seemed an exact replica of the one we had just left. The empty diners confirmed Brendan Behan's observation that 'You can tell the richness of a country by its bread and its whores.' In Main Street there would be a general store, a barber's shop, a saddler's, a bar and a sheriff's office. We would retreat to our motel room and hope to make the television work without summoning the Anthony-Perkins-look-alike in reception. No doubt if we had not each been constrained by the listlessness of the other it would have been very different.

One afternoon, late into our venture, after driving in silence through an insanely twisted, cruel landscape, Mary suddenly asked me to stop the car. We were heading for Yuma, the town with the hottest recorded temperature in the United States. The Gila Desert lay to one side and the ridge of the San Bernadino mountains ahead. We had not spoken for hours. 'Can't you wait a bit longer?' 'No. I can't.' Her reply was so terse there was no mistaking its urgency. She got out, scanned the swimming haze of emptiness surrounding us and, without looking at me, snapped, 'I want to be fucked.'

I decided that if it were to be done, it were best done quickly. The back seat looked as if it might start blistering and burst into bubbles. I didn't care for the prospect of an icy lunar night among rattlesnakes and coyotes. I put up the hood. I could have sworn that the sun was actually making sounds as I joined her. It is hard to think of a more unforgiving spot on earth for a loveless coupling, two desert insects locked in the lifeless dust.

Without a word, she got into the front seat and I drove us back on the road to Yuma, thankful that we hadn't trapped the hub-caps. I stumbled into the barber's shop, Mary cooled herself at the soda fountain. The barber looked at my soaking frame. 'You're foreigners, ain't ye? You're from New York.' I nodded and closed my eyes, pounding from the sun and my gasping exertions beneath it. The temperature at noon, he said, had been a record 138 degrees. That was a record. Yup. Even for Yuma.

In the motel it dropped to almost freezing as we climbed into bed in silence and mercifully fell asleep at once.

> To thirst and find no fill – to wail and wander
> With short unsteady steps – to pause and ponder –
> To feel the blood run through the veins and tingle
> Where busy thought and blind sensation mingle;
> To nurse the image of unfelt caresses
> Till dim imagination just possesses
> The half-created shadow, then all night
> Sick . . .
>
> Percy Bysshe Shelley, fragment: 'Igniculus Desiderii'

We returned home from New York with Tony and Harry. For most of the flight Mary remained as silent as she had been for the six weeks of our self-capsuled moon-holiday. Going through Customs I was obliged to pay £10 for some trifle. None of us could find the necessary cash, except a hovering reporter who produced a note and said, 'Here, John, have this one on me.' Mary immediately, and to the delight of the spectators, broke into a loud and tearful denunciation of Harry, informing him – and the press – that she might well not agree to appear in the film of *Look Back*.

Harry, fumbling in his pockets, turned to the eager note-flasher, 'Ridiculous. Sure she'll be in it.' 'If I don't appear,' she announced, 'my reasons will be personal. I may have other commitments. Personal ones.' The note-flasher's inevitable next question startled her. She flushed and mumbled, 'No. There's no baby.' I waited for my duty receipt and Harry pushed Tony and Mary away. 'Miss Ure is under contract to Rank,' he puffed. 'I'm trying to borrow her, that's all. We'll have it all sorted out by Monday.'

The four of us drove off in a blanket of sandy silence. No one had been fooled by this toddler's tantrum but it didn't augur well for life in the house from which Woodfall Films took its name. Any hopes I may have had of cauterizing rankling bitterness had vanished in the calcining desert.

During Mary's absence I had acquired Helen Henderson. Anthony had met her when he was working at a debt-collecting agency off Oxford Street and he brought her round for supper. She was small, frail, with a fine, slightly pinched face and a gentle intensity that matched her voice. She made the most ordinary utterance sound like a line snatched from some ancient Scottish ballad. I guessed her to be about fifty and she lived in a small north-London flat with her elder sister. She was also an active and lifelong member of the Communist Party, although she was losing heart. As with every imagined aspect of her life, one longed to offer the simplest comfort but there was none, except silence.

She had an unsickly, still fragility that I had recognized in my father, and I persuaded her away from the sweat-shop job at the agency to become my secretary. In those early days I had not yet learned to throw away and ignore letters or to refuse to answer the telephone. I was still constrained by a doggy amiability and politeness. The prospect daunted her but I hoped it might awaken some new confidence in her. It was a makeshift proposition. I installed her at a toy-like desk in the tiny upper room in Woodfall Street and she insisted that she would improve her typing, learn shorthand in her spare time and cultivate a stern telephone manner.

I was uneasy about Mary's reaction to Helen's presence in the house, but she took to it quite happily. Their common tongue and background made Helen a more suitable lady's companion to Mary than secretary to me and she was a helpful distraction during the few hours we spent in the house together. Mary immediately reverted to her daily routine, Knightsbridge standing in satisfactorily for Fifth Avenue.

Harry had somehow requisitioned Lowndes Cottage, where I had first dined with the Oliviers, which he used as a production office for the film and accommodation for himself and visiting friends. One of these, he implied, was Francine. It was one of his gestures of offhand friendly service, but unhelpful at the time. Mary's hostility to Harry was implacable. Tony and George were busy rehearsing the Ionesco double bill. I saw less of George during the rest of that year. I never even had the opportunity of discussing Francine with him. Perhaps I wouldn't have done so anyway. After the nightly satisfaction of outfacing *The Chairs* audience, there was the beginning of his adventure with Samuel Beckett.

If Ionesco's discordant wilfulness intrigued him, Beckett's temperament inspired him with almost apostolic awe. Even the peremptory sourness of Brecht couldn't match the incomparably bleached bone of Beckett and his liturgical 'toneless voice'. Uncle Sam had the monstrous good fortune of actually looking like one of his own plays, a graven icon of his own texts. The bristled cadaver and mountain-peak stare were the ultimate purifier that defied all endeavour, pity or hope. If the head of a Balzac or Ionesco or a dozen other sybaritically fleshed-out masters had been put on to the Irishman's torso, the response to the purity of that 'toneless voice' might not have been so immediate. Furthermore, for George, he had the impeccable credentials of French cultural hauteur.

George tried unsuccessfully to persuade Alec Guinness among others to play Hamm in *Endgame*. He was reduced to having to attempt it himself. It was not a happy choice and he knew it. Wrapped up nightly in his rug, cap and blackened spectacles, he would tremble at the enormity of the theatrical task of stepping unfalteringly into emptiness. It was brave but unmoving. It seemed a pretty long chew on a very dry prune. I would never have dreamed of saying so.

Mary was then technically under contract to H.M. Tennant. Binkie Beaumont was still very much the *éminence lavande* and she was awed and enthralled by his undoubted leathery, matinée charm. So when we received an invitation to dine at his house in Lord North Street, she was as flustered as if she had been summoned by a reproving ex-headmistress. The clear purpose was to subject her to a smooth dressing-down for her ingrate behaviour in joining the barbarians and marrying the ugliest voice of them all.

It was an inimitable, taffeta-edged performance: the measured reproach, the hint of avuncular sarcasm and then wise forgiveness. Unlike Merrick, whose greatest pleasure lay in baiting or humiliating actors, Binkie had a consuming itch to make himself indispensable to his actors and, especially, his actresses. They were smothered by his courtesy and discreet air of slightly alarmed concern and admiration. He held out the promise of benign power and sanctuary against the perils of a vulgar, predatory world.

During dinner he was in sprightly command at the head of his table and lobbed several deftly primed grenades in my direction. He had not yet reached that stage when he was to become more or less incoherent after six o'clock. I was made to feel a little like a mud-wrestler being complimented by a duchess.

His housekeeper was a woman called Elvira, who reminded me irrepressibly of the old crone who appears at the top of the stairs in the film of *The Old Dark House* shrieking, 'No beds, no beds!' At one point, as she put a plate in front of me, he turned to her and in an arresting tone said, '*Now*, Elvira, tell us . . . ' There was a long pre-Pinter pause while he leaned forward. 'Tell me. Mr Brendan Bracken, as you know, has just died, and his house across the road is up for sale. Don't you think . . . it would be *splendid* if Mr Osborne should buy it?' She gave me a gimlet glare and replied emphatically, 'No!' Binkie's lizard lids fluttered beneath the folds of a perennial sunlamp tan. 'But why on earth not, Elvira?' 'Because, 'e's not *ready* for it *yet*!' Game, set and match to Mr Beaumont.

13. 'Letting down England'

Now I have to turn my memory back over thirty years to recapture my first vision of John and Mary as they returned from New York. It is no exaggeration to say they took my breath away, because they did . . . Mary's hair was like corn silk, her skin matt and flawless and, although she was thin, her limbs were exquisitely rounded in an Eighteenth Century fashion . . . A briar rose – natural, honest and wild . . .

The same evening John was a physical Oberon to Mary's Titania, very lean and sunburned, his light hair streaked by the sun and his eyes a truly blazing blue . . . They were both so high with pleasure to be home, competing with each other in their Truman Capote impersonations and, for that evening, they were both full of laughter. I was the only person there unknown to them, but nothing could have blighted their gaiety and pleasure and it left me free to observe and wonder at their outrageous vitality and glamour.

Letter from Don Bachardy to Jocelyn Richards, 1986

Filming of *Look Back* was due to begin at Elstree in September. Tony and Harry had persuaded Richard Burton to play Jimmy Porter. It was a calculated move on his part to reverse the tide of his career and possibly the last time his shrewd intelligence overrode his duplicity. His most recent films, which had concentrated in Cinemascope on his splendid knees beneath Roman kilts, had failed to establish his surety as an international star. That wouldn't happen until Elizabeth Taylor flipped her Cleopatra's ball from the film scrum into his waiting hands.

He was a huge asset to our modest undertaking, which was regarded with general suspicion from Wardour Street. Burton's presence guaranteed dignity if not commercial success. Harry's principal obstacle in setting up the production, apart from distaste for the play's reputation, was my insistence on employing Tony as director. This was based not on blind loyalty but on my untutored faith in his flair and his being the only possible commander to lead Woodfall's opening assault on the suburban vapidity of British film-making.

Rank had offered me £30,000, which Margery urged me to accept immediately, but insisted on using one of their high-street directors. Eventually, Harry was able to persuade Associated British Picture Corporation to chance its reluctant arm, provided Burton dropped his Hollywood fee to a Celt-chastening minimum, which, in the face of all augury, he did. I was to throw in the rights for nothing except a 'returnable' £2,000.

In spite of the concerted press campaign to transform me into some upstart wordsmith who had inexplicably won the pools ('Osborne mellows now he's on £1,000 a week'), I was not earning great sums from any of the three plays now that two of them had finished their Broadway runs. What had come my way I had largely spent, much of it on travel and the Algonquin, and now I had committed myself to buying the rights of *A Taste of Honey* for Woodfall's next film venture, a considerable gamble and one which was to cost me £30,000.

Although my ambitions for Woodfall and Tony were almost headlong, those for myself were more contained. Film-going had been a secondary education throughout my life, as it was for so many of my unschooled generation, but the technicalities and the organization of it intimidated me, particularly the necessity of becoming an inferior among equals, which is the unacknowledged status of a film-writer. So, in spite of some unenthusiastic prompting to write the screenplay (for nothing), I was relieved when Kenneth Tynan suggested hiring Nigel Kneale and Tony willingly agreed.

Kneale had made a reputation as a skilled writer of science fiction with his creation of the enormously popular *Quatermass* series. It was soon evident that, though he had readily accepted the task, the material was not much to his liking. He and Tony decided to 'open it up'. It seemed to me they were ripping out its obsessive, personal heart. I protested without much authority and Tony agreed to let me rewrite some of the dialogue scenes, particularly those of Ma Tanner, one of the many characters who were discussed but never appeared in the play. We went to the South of France for ten days to – most dread to me of all wasteful activities – 'work on the script' and watch Harry's day-long dealings between plage and pedalo.

Ma Tanner was a treacherously difficult role with almost no immunity against mawkishness, which was the reason I had banished her off-stage early on when writing the play. But working on it with Edith Evans turned out to be one of the few pleasurable privileges film-making ever offered, and between us I think we more or less got away with it. She insisted on going through the text word by word, which she also did later with Miss Western in *Tom Jones*. Her ear was miraculously tuned. 'I have perfect pitch,' she said. '*And*, I am *really* a Cockney.' She took the unresisting costume designer, Jocelyn Rickards, with her round the second-hand shops of the North End Road to choose her costumes, including accessories. Even Tony was unable to argue with that.

From the first moment I met Jocelyn Rickards at Lowndes Cottage, I was intrigued by her. Neither sphinx nor tantrum child, she suggested a passionate intelligence and emotional candour. Small and dark with wide, appraising eyes, she had an almost comic air of uncombative lethargy which I found immediately attractive. It reminded me of Stella's impatience with my own similar affectations of indifference. The ironic temperament always seemed to me the most admirable and bravest of attributes, however little I had managed to achieve it, and an especially English one. Jocelyn was also vulnerably opinionated on almost any subject, as if driven by mischievous dissent. This irritated many people, including Tony, but I found a warmth of irreverence in her drawled commentaries that was reckless and endearing. She knew only too well that she had at least one layer of skin missing when she exposed herself to the cutting edge of adversarial intellects more vain and brutal than her own.

She nurtured, and still does, an immutable affection for men. Her feeling for her ex-lovers was abidingly loyal. As one of them, Graham Greene, observed thirty years on, she has 'an outstanding capacity for friendship – rare in the jealous world of art and letters'. At this time, in the summer of 1958, although I didn't know it, she was attending daily to the needs of Raymond Chandler, dying alone in a basement flat in Eaton Square, where she herself lived with another ex-lover, the photographer Alec Murray.

Along with their friends Loudon Sainthill, the theatrical designer, and his partner Harry Tatlock Miller, Jocelyn and Alec had formed an early advance guard from Australia to a cold, unwelcoming London where they were duly registered with ration books. They soon established themselves with the recidivist ease that is the inheritance of all expatriate Australians. Jocelyn's emergence had been the most leisurely, decorating galleries on commission, painting murals in private houses of the more or less famous, and designing the costumes for a musical which had boasted nine directors before its quite showy collapse.

The professional aspect of her life may have been patchy and tentative, but she had discovered and entered a rather loose fifties-cum-Garsington world of writers, philosophers, painters and eccentrics. The list of her friends in this exclusive – and, to me, suspect – circle was formidable. It made the stern endeavours of Sloane Square seem rather provincial and unworldly. I never really explored it. Although at the age of twenty-eight I had become preposterously famous, I was still partially gagged by the indoctrination of aggrieved lower-middle-class humility. In my work I had not dissembled, I was sure of that, but the nagging inheritance of 'Who do you think you are?' is hard to drown out in the presence of those who seem to have an ironclad awareness of who *they* are.

During the weeks to come, I found myself drawn to the large top-floor flat in Eaton Square at increasingly earlier times of the morning. Jocelyn would put down her paintbrushes and we drank black coffee laced with brandy. I soon gave up the pretence of talking about the film and encouraged her easy flow of energizing gossip. Sometimes she would be interrupted as a visitor passed through to see the occupant of the third bedroom, the ballet critic Peter Williams. Frequently it was a young journalist on the *Daily Express*, later to become drama critic of the *New York Times*, Clive Barnes.

Jocelyn seemed a cliquish, literary-circle kind of name, suitably attached to her namesake Herbert, with her Auntie Virginia Woolf profile, but not to the oddball Rickards. In Australia they had called her 'Joybells'. 'Joy' seemed an acceptable diminutive, so that's what she became.

Look Back began shooting and I went to some of the locations: Stratford East, Deptford Market and Dalston Junction, where I found Oscar Beuselinck and my accountant getting in everyone's way. They seemed to regard it as some expensive game which they had generously allowed us to play. Everyone appeared to be in good spirits. Richard was behaving well, apart from being discovered in his dressing-room *in flagrante* by a startled actress, and the ensuing drama kept Mary happily absorbed. I left earlier than necessary for the opening of *George Dillon* in New York in the first week of November.

Watford

My dear Dolly,

Lots of thanks for your letter I had this morning. Was pleased to hear your Back has eased up a little. I have to see the Chest specialist a week today. I think the trouble was when Queen came home once or twice and would not have a Bed downstairs. I had to take the weight of getting her upstairs on my Stomach and Chest. I used to gasp for breath by the time she was up. All she thought of was herself. For a long time after I met her, I *never* knew she had a mother, father or any relations. I don't mind writing you like this, as I know she was *never* a good Sister to you. No one knows what a life I've had since I married.

I've just done some washing, put in Garden. Thought I would go out in Garden this afternoon, and do a few odd jobs, but the wind is too cold. Do hope dear ole John does *not* overdo things with all the work he has to do. Was pleased to hear you feel better. I felt so very depressed last Sunday night, here alone.

God bless.

Sidney

[PS from N.B. to J.O.] Poor Sid, still washing. I feel sorry for him as they are mad at him for writing me. Good God tell me *what does one have to do not to be hated* like me. I don't feel that *rotten*. Who cares. I *don't* any more. Still, it's not a crime not to come up to others expectations.

Watford

My dear Sister,

I have your letter before me, which I had yesterday mid-day. Sid is upstairs in Bed. He had had all his *bottom* teeth out on Wednesday 5 o/c, they were devils to get out and he had a bad time as they were so large. The Dentist looked as if he'd had a rough time himself.

Ever your loving sister,

Queen

Watford

Dear John,

Lots of thanks for your letter and the suggestion that you will see what you can do from your end, as regards a woman to come in and help. I could get a Home Help here but Queen will *not* agree. You know what the Groves are, just b–obstinate. I also thought of the WVS for meals, but still Queen will not have it. Ah well, why worry. She will not agree to a Bed downstairs, and I have to heave her up and down each night. Have had terrible pains in my stomach. When you write please do not say anything about this as I have to read letters to her.

Love,

Uncle Sidney xxxxx

Uncle Jack and Grandma Grove saw me off at Southampton. As I sat fuddled in a corner of the tender in the midst of a force-eight gale, I was so drunk that I believed I was already aboard the *Isle de France*. The last time I had been in the town was to watch my father's coffin disappear behind the clattering curtains of the crematorium.

The voyage was my first and last glimpse of travel on the grand scale and I loved every moment of it. The setting was operatic and vast and gave me a feeling of liberty and anonymous fame I never experienced again. I dined at the captain's table, surrounded by French aristocrats whose snobbery made that of my own countrymen seem quite matey. There was an elegant Maugham-like character who claimed to be a professional caviare-taster. Like a priestly diviner, he would dangle a small gold instrument over the black slime in its diamond ice-bed and pronounce it acceptable. I was pursued to my cabin nightly by a couple of very rich American widows. They looked like ladies with powerful connections and vindictive appetites. Life was in enough snarl. I might not be exactly a gent, lounging like a deluded film extra in this departing show, but I didn't fancy being leaped on like an Italian waiter.

Anthony Creighton met me in New York with his new American lover, Bernie. They were in a state of ecstatic excitement about the play. The word was around, said Bernie, that it was going to be the biggest hit since *Abie's Irish Rose*. This information steadied my sea legs a little. I liked Bernie and I was glad that he was clearly helping Anthony to enjoy some of the romantic delights denied him since his wartime, high-kicking days in *Boys in Blue*, but I had no trust whatever in his taste. The other source of their excitement was the discovery of Fire Island.

George Dillon opened in Baltimore, going on to Atlantic City, where we played in a 3,000-seat picture-palace of the thirties. It was an Italian palazzo with cypresses and copies of Michelangelo's *David* in every niche. The Royal Court set filled only a third of the surrounding blackness. From the back it looked like a small television set.

The drabness of the Boardwalk made me yearn for Brighton's promenade, Stella, Edlin's bar and cockle stalls. In spite of this, the production was fine. Hurling their performance at a vast amphitheatre, the whole cast preserved a lightness and sublety. Eileen Herlie was a considerable improvement on Yvonne Mitchell. Alison Leggatt was near-perfection and Robert Stephen's performance was quite remarkable. 'What have we heah?' He smirked like an arch-conjuror as he unwrapped the typewriter, destined to tap out a lifetime of 'Telephone Tart' plays. He trapped the audience in a trembling moment of heart's agony.

Atlantic City had been invaded by half a dozen conventions and the hotels were full, so I found myself sharing Robert's motel room. We drank late into the night. His grief and anguish, mingled with a powerful comic intelligence, were terrible to witness. It was truly *endoganoid*, as I believe the Greeks have it, the very style of Philoctetes, an inheritance of creeping malignity. In bed at last, I listened to the sound of his teeth meshing and grinding in the pole-axed death-throes of oblivion. I had never heard such an alarming sound but, then, few ladies possess either the teeth or the temperament for it.

The first night in New York at the John Gorden Theatre was a classic example of Broadway disaster and its comic ritual, which remains unchanged and unchallenged. The astonishment of writers like Arnold Wesker and David Hare when they find themselves its sacrificial victims is hard to understand. It was ever thus. The cab-choked street, the PR men clutching their ulcers, the jewellery displayed like medals on the chest of a Soviet general, the snoozing men from Wall Street, the Sardi's supper entrance. As always, in any enterprise, Americans travel hopefully, fuelled by a thirst for adrenalin not experienced by most Europeans. I felt that the odds were much the same as punting at the Sands' in Las Vegas.

The reception was barely short of rapturous, or so the house manager told me. He hadn't seen anything like it since *My Fair Lady*. Some little whisky-wise worm of instinct told me that we might just be less than a palpable hit. Merrick was glaring. Bernie was weeping copiously, his gaze fixed bravely upwards. 'Well, John,' said my friend Sam Zolotov of the *Times*, 'I'll just read over to you the opening paragraph of Brooks's notice. I'm afraid it's not very good, John.' It was clear that Anthony's dreams of permanent residence in the poofs' paradise of Fire Island were not to be fulfilled.

I decided to go straight to the party at Josh Logan's in Sutton Place, where there must certainly be drink. I felt rather cheerfully exhilarated. A dozen swerving waiters holding champagne-laden trays swooped aside with the nimbleness of a fly-half and whisked their trays further aloft into uncontaminated hands. Mine were leprous with the contagion of failure. I managed to wrench a glass from an unguarded table.

Bill Gaskill had already been there for some time and explained the state of play:

> Josh greeted us at the party like heroes. 'The show is a hit,' he announced. 'I thought you should never say that in New York till the notices came out,' I ventured. 'Look, young man,' he roared, 'when I say a show is a hit, it's a hit.' ... Not long after it was noticeable that the room was emptying or rather that there was a mad rush to the door like water running out of a bath. The notices had arrived. I went over to Josh and said, in effect, 'I told you so,' perhaps not the most tactful thing in the circumstances. 'I knew there was something wrong in the third act. You should have done something about it.' 'Why the fuck didn't you say that before?' I wasn't exactly thrown out but I did hit Walter Winchell's column the next morning.

> William Gaskill, *A Sense of Direction*, 1988

To Bill's everlasting credit, he refused to back down in the face of a recriminating gathering, swelled by a bizarre group of British patriots led by

Oliver Messel, accompanied by a noisy Danish sailor who shouted at me, 'You've let down England!'

Shortly after this doleful night for the Fire Island heroes, I went for lunch in Sardi's with the Roberts Stephens and Webber, Marty Balsam, Robert Preston, Sam Levene and Christopher Plummer. Apart from Stephens and myself, all were famous faces at the peak of their fame. Marlene Dietrich was at the number-one table, the first banquette on the left. Beside her sat a bald, bearded man who was, I was told, Leo Lehmann, editor of American *Vogue*. The outline of Dietrich's unique profile beneath a small, pointed black hat and short veil outshone even the impact of Greer Garson. As we all tried to direct our attention from one of the century's icons to the menu, a waiter laid down a small salver with a piece of folded paper in front of me. I picked it up. On it, written in a bold hand, were the three words 'Who are you?"' Signed, Marlene Dietrich.

I passed it across to Robert, who exclaimed in his George Dillon voice, '*What* have we HEAH?' I craned sideways to see if the sender was still in her place. He passed it round the table to the accompaniment of low whistles and 'Good gods!' He thrust a pen at me and dictated, 'Just write this: "My name is – and may I have the pleasure – no, honour – of meeting you?"'

We dispatched the waiter. I shifted my chair further behind the pillar. If I were about to receive a rejection slip, I had no wish to see the signatory. It returned within minutes. Robert snatched it: 'Any time. Any place . . . My number is . . . ' It was a Yukon exchange and I memorized the digits almost at once. I scarcely ate and pondered the next move. The restaurant was almost empty by now. I stepped unsteadily beside Miss Dietrich and announced myself. Her smile was unaffectedly kindly and curious. She said something like, 'Of course, I've heard about you. Forgive me, I didn't know what you looked like.' Lehmann invited me to sit down but I excused myself, never having felt so shamingly inadequate in my life, publicly or privately.

For days, until the last moment before I left New York, I hovered over the Algonquin telephone with the Yukon number beside me. I didn't rise to it, an act of craven timidity that I have regretted ever since. In the words of Binkie's Elvira, 'I wasn't ready for it yet.' Thirty years later I met Lehmann, who confirmed every detail of the occasion. 'She really had no idea who you were. She just admired the look of you.'

When I returned to Woodfall Street Mary greeted me, as I had come to expect, affectionately like an absent-minded parent confronting an offspring returned from school, suspicious at what it might have been up to but soon losing interest. Shortly after, one night about 2.00 a.m., we were awakened by the sound of laughter and heavy thumpings on the front door. 'We thought we'd drop in,' said Tony, more drunk than I had ever seen him. His counter-tenor bounced off the cobbles. With him was Robert Shaw, who was reeling. 'Where's poor little Mary?' Poor little Mary was standing at the top of the staircase, startled but not displeased.

'How *are* you? I mean, *are* you all right?' She shivered in her nightdress and smiled bravely. 'Robert and I were talking about you and we thought you might like to see us for a drink.' She switched on the bars of the electric fire while I poured whisky for the three of them. They all settled down, Mary happily curled up, knees to chin, pleased as a welcoming dog. I left them and returned to bed. I wasn't angry, mostly surprised that Tony should employ such a clumsy ruse and with such an unlikely carousing companion.

Helen Henderson was left alone for most of the day in Woodfall Street. Mary's attention was fixed between the Knightsbridge daily run and her new *Sons and Lovers* co-star, Dean Stockwell. Jocelyn suggested that she, Alec, Mary and myself should spend Christmas in Rome together. I was astonished when Mary agreed readily. Perhaps she too was keen to avoid the chilly house by the Clyde, her nephews and grim stepmother. Woodfall Street seemed progressively colder and comfortless, a small box that defied decoration or warmth.

We stayed at the Inghilterra in the Via Bocca del Leone. It was delightful. Some of the rooms had terraced gardens overlooking the city. It was warm and sunny, and on Christmas Day we had lunch in the Borghese Gardens in rolled-up sleeves and sunglasses.

Jocelyn was signing off a painful affair with an Italian lover. She returned one evening distraught and tearful from a protracted, nostalgic farewell. She fell on to Mary, who put her to bed, promptly and efficiently sedating her. It was an odd sight, like watching a bossy toddler playing doctors and nurses with a truthfully sick adult for a patient.

For days I sat beside Alec and Jocelyn dreaming that something would summon Mary home alone. Suddenly, she decided that Italy was no place to spend Hogmanay and returned to Scotland to 'first-foot' with her brothers and Auld Nanny.

14. *A Night to Remember*

When you go out into the world, among the birds and flowers – count
your change.

Max Miller

Most of my attention during the following weeks was directed towards securing
a licence from the Lord Chamberlain for my next venture, *The World of
Paul Slickey*, permanently labelled with the preface 'ill-fated'. Thirty years on,
arguments about its worthlessness are of little interest, but the uniform weight
of the vituperation it aroused and the hysteria accompanying my own tumbrel
ride to the public scaffold in an idiotic and vindictive pantomime still make
one pause.

When George padded on to the *Egret* four years earlier, I was tapping away
at what I intended to be a modest but amusing 'comedy of manners'. It was
titled *Love in a Myth*. I was to find that modesty of intention is never an
acceptable mitigation of failure. When vilified for not having achieved something on the scale of the Sistine ceiling, it's useless to plead that you were
only attempting a palm-sized miniature.

I decided to question George Goetschius, an American sociologist, eunuch
and guru-in-residence at Lower Mall. I liked George very much and knew
that he was privy to all that went on politically and emotionally in the Richardson–Devine camp by the river. He told me frankly and helpfully that neither
George nor Tony thought much of the play. They were both anxious, he said,
not to cause me pain or rouse me to anger, which might be destructive to us
all and enduring. I was hurt by their lack of trust in my stability. Perhaps they
were right? But I also believed they were wrong, narrow and snobbish. They
had confused lightness of heart with frivolity. I was not downcast or aggrieved.
Rather to my surprise I was excited.

I can't quite remember why I decided to turn *Love in a Myth* into a musical.
Perhaps I had seen so many in New York by this time, good and dull, that
the incitement to reach a 'popular' audience was attractive. With the departure
of Ivor Novello's highwayman's jinks and lovers-in-lederhosen the English

musical had more or less died, although Lionel Bart, booted by the genius of Joan Littlewood into soupy crash-bang-wallop success with *Fings Ain't What They Used to Be* had achieved a knees-up for the nobs, and Sandy Wilson's pastiche *The Boyfriend* flattered its audience into a trance of indulgent sophistication.

The subject matter of *Paul Slickey* was the disagreeable exploits of a newspaper gossip columnist. This nasty species, originating from the snob reportage of obscure landowners, debutantes and duchesses, was almost unchanged since Edward VII had enlivened things with the introduction of royal mistresses, Jewish bankers and upstarts from the Turf. Recently an underclass of mountebanks, including photographers and ballet dancers, American comedians, interior designers and the 'Princess Margaret Set' had proved a new, decidedly 'camp' addition to the Edwardian City and racing fraternity.

Money spoke all right, and no one heard it more clearly than the gossip columnist snooping on the edge of a semi-private world of celebrated nonentities. I was not uninterested in this rising phenomenon and I possibly exaggerated its importance but, like royalty-worship, it seemed to reveal an alarming change in the British character that was cruel and ugly. The most successful agents were William Hickey in the *Daily Express* and the *Mail*'s Paul Tanfield. Each had a coven of malign moles. The title, *Paul Slickey*, had them sniffing for months.

What's Osborne up to behind those locked doors?

Only one thing succeeds more than success in fascinating the entertainers – failure. Which explains the speculation now buzzing in the world of show business over *The World of Paul Slickey*.

This is the John Osborne musical which goes into rehearsal behind closed doors today. Last night he pulled on his Sherlock Holmes pipe and puffed out this definition of his first musical comedy: 'A show about modern archetypes in a schizophrenic setting.'

It is even more. Its fate affects a theatrical phenomenon of the fifties – the Osborne legend. Already Shaftesbury Avenue is asking: 'Is fresh triumph in store for the author of *Look Back in Anger*? Or, switching to a new and more difficult medium, will he stumble in the pitfalls of British musical comedy and come a spectacular cropper?'

Daily Mail, 9 March 1959

George's gnomic throw-away that all problems were technical was especially appealing to me at the time. It implied defiance and cool indifference to almost certain pain. Some simple adjustment, like the use of an old screwdriver or a kick at the faulty mechanism, might turn reversals into triumph. With *Slickey* the first problem was to find a management prepared to be identified with it. The fact that the Royal Court and George, from whose rib I had sprung so unwelcome, were not prepared to endorse it was damning. Even those implacably opposed to the disruptive ambitions of the tiny upstart theatre had been forced to accept that it had made an astonishing impact in little more than a couple of years. Even Beaumont's Bourbons had been shaken by the ugly outbursts of the mob and were now unashamed to nip off the tumbrel and clamber on to a careering bandwagon.

I approached Jack Hylton, the only producer who had ever shown me a hint of geniality. A cheery, popular bandleader of the thirties and a famous Lancashire lecher, he had been a successful producer of gamey twice-nightly plays, variety shows and the abominably popular *Kismet*. More significantly, he had transferred George's production of *The Country Wife* to the Adelphi. He was a happy gambler, read the script and talked about it intelligently. 'I think it's a bit too highbrow for the British public, John,' he concluded. 'I may be wrong and I dare say it's jolly good, but it's too highbrow for *me*.'

So, it was back to Albery, who had taken a short ride on the tailgate with *George Dillon*. He agreed to give his backing, if not his blessing, for an undefined term of trial. His assistant, Ann Jenkins, was as encouraging as her dedication to her boss allowed. He accepted that I should direct the piece myself. This was not surprising, as he must have known that it would be difficult to find anyone of useful reputation to take it on, especially as the score was barely complete.

This was being written in some haste by a young man who had been recommended by Margery. Only my impatience could have persuaded me to consider her judgement seriously. His name was Christopher Whelen. No one, apart from Margery, seemed to have heard of him. He was rather solemn and smoked a pipe in a maidenly, Anthony Creighton manner. But, again, I was grateful prey to a little old enthusiasm, especially as there wasn't much of it about.

It was soon clear that, if the book might be patchy, the music would be more so. However, with the myopic faith that seems to grip people when they get involved in musicals, I chose to assume that the whole process in itself would create an organic mystery. The bit was in my mouth. At last, for the first time since sleeping in crab-infested blankets in the dressing-room at Hayling Island, living on evaporated milk and biscuits, swanking about as a peroxided Hamlet to an audience of geriatric holiday-makers, I had contrived some sort of personal control over the whole brash enterprise. I would only have myself to blame. The release from benign paternalism was firingly enjoyable.

Auditions were a daily encouragement. Ann Jenkins had no difficulty in assembling an impressive number of actors backstage at the New Theatre, eager to take part in a production for which every augury pronounced disaster. Only two characters really required a fine singing voice, in particular Slickey himself. Slickey also needed someone with a strong sexual presence, or so I thought, as well as the ability to be 'unsympathetic' – not something most actors are prepared to take on. I made a monumental misjudgement by dismissing Sean Connery, who turned up one morning looking like my prejudiced idea of a Rank contract actor. It was a lamentable touch of Royal Court snobbery.

The final choice was a young South African singer called Dennis Lotis, who worked with the better big-name bands and had a loyal following. He had a sweet, lyrical voice, more Mel Tormé than Frank Sinatra. As an actor he was only adequate, but he had grace and a casual sexuality. Perhaps, even in 1959, he was *too* nice and polite to excite admiration, let alone frenzy.

With Dennis, the bet was indisputedly on. To my amazement, I then secured a jewel of Edwardian theatre in Marie Löhr. She embodied everything we could steal from a tradition the piece itself partially mocked. In the dodgy circumstances it looked like a small triumph. Her mere presence would be an asset to the younger actors and, from beginning to end, she behaved with such grace and circumspection that it was difficult to believe my good fortune. It was comparable to having Edith Evans on the team. For the rest, I depended on whim and experience. Philip Locke was one of the Court actors I knew was special and reliable. Harry Welchman was a veteran musical-comedy idol and the original 'Red Shadow' of *The Desert Song*, and Adrienne Corri deserved a chance for sheer profligacy of nerve. In her chaotic way, she managed to inspire a schoolgirl bravura which was helpful at the lower moments to come.

Jocelyn R.'s costume drawings were practical but startling. Through her intervention, Hugh Casson agreed to design the sets. But the happiest and most valuable recruit was the choreographer, Kenneth MacMillan. It was a haphazard choice. I knew nothing about ballet or 'the dance' as it would now be called. I had seen *Swan Lake* at the Bolshoi and used the odd free ticket from the likes of Dexter to touring companies in the provinces or accompanied Anthony on occasional hunting-trips to his favourite Ram Ghopal Indian ensemble and the more dreaded Ballets Nègres, which brought so much relief to deprived outposts of homosexuality in Streatham and Hammersmith. Faith, as we are supposed to know, is not the same as certainty, and my faith in

MacMillan's theatrical genius and originality, notwithstanding my unrepentant ignorance, was as devout as a housewife's in the pin stabbing a racecard.

Asking for trouble

If ever a drumming was invited in advance it is the one John Osborne has taken with *The World of Paul Slickey*. Mr Osborne and his supporters are not in a strong position to resent the discovery that his big guns have the calibre of pea-shooters.

Daily Telegraph, 7 May 1959

There is something I call 'Window-cleaner's Nose'. On a day when every minute is physically unendurable, when in the silent, darkened room even the touch of the sheets feels like a cattle-prod, when you disconnect the telephone and curl up like an exhausted louse to oblivion, that will be the day when the window-cleaner's nose twitches and summons you to the front door. His untroubled spirit whistles and hums as he clatters his buckets and ladders, asking for an extra cloth, some more warm water. He hounds despair with his optimism and health, making retreat even more furtive and ashamed.

Will it be a signal for others to come sniffing at the entrance to the burrow? The lady from the Conservatives ringing doorbells which refuse to be disobeyed? The old man with his tray of Remembrance Day poppies? A briefcased gauleiter from the Social Services tracking down your unkept records for thirty years past? Or, worst of all, Archie's Income Tax Man?

There must be a saint assigned to this happy army of window-cleaners, blessing their gift of intrusion into the blackest dates of the calendar. Albery had been endowed with the nose, if not the innocence, and had a magical knack of appearing at rehearsals on the darkest of days. It must have been one of them that finally decided him to withdraw from the management. A fresh look up at the surrounding hills of antagonism gave no further sign from whence any help might come. But come it did, and indirectly through my connection with Merrick.

David Pelham was an improbably effusive, red-haired young man, who had worked as one of Merrick's 'assistants'. He came to London to exploit the experience he had gained as one of Schubert Alley's hired hit-men, wrapping leading ladies in concrete-lined mink coats and slipping them into the East River. I was sceptical at first. He had little familiarity with the West End. But English managements, with their gentile caution and suspicion of shameless enterprise, might gain from an injection of mobster strategy. In my present circumstances there seemed little to lose.

Pelham's enthusiasm was unquestionable. His reactions to everything were shrewd and thoughtful. His grasp of the immediate 'technical problems' was impressive. He delivered his first coup by persuading Emile Littler, licensee of the Palace theatre, to promise a booking in May. In *Who's Who*, Littler listed himself as 'Theatrical producer, racehorse owner and play-doctor'. Sawbones and butcher would have been nearer the mark. Even Margery, most generous fudge of playwright's enemies, felt constrained to down an extra Guinness and gin-chaser before telephoning him.

Then, most vitally and almost overnight, Pelham persuaded three backers to invest in the production. One of these was a rather mysterious but affable Russian with an undistinguished entrepreneurial past in films and theatre; another was a Jewish furniture manufacturer who had no show-biz connections at all.

Mr Osborne is a figure of anxious speculation at the moment. Like someone silhouetted on a cliff-edge one gets a sudden feeling he is going to jump over. He is as fascinating as a firework on November 4. Tense as a photo-finish. His new musical will either be the biggest fallen hope since airships, or such a success they'll start selling Anger on the Stock Exchange. Mr Osborne has been playing with fire too long not to get his fingers not simply burned but amputated – if he's lost his touch.

In the chill dark of the auditorium as he comes on-stage, sits his most vulnerable audience. The backers of the play. He stands, back to the footlights. His is a narrow, leaning figure that he props up like a ladder against light and shadow.

The chief of the angels comes forward to be presented to the young man who has become one of the portents of our time. The angel is wearing that becoming and unmistakable indication of wealth – a tan. He is rich. But he is shy. And it is difficult to know *what* to say to the brilliant and wicked Mr Osborne.

He proffers the kindest, meekest, best-meaning phrase he can remember from his schooldays. 'Very promising,' he tells Mr Osborne, encouragingly.

Anne Sharpley, *Evening Standard*, 11 April 1959

A budget was agreed almost on the nod. Even by the deflated standards of the time it was bone-spare. With a cast of twenty-four actors, ten dancers, a musical director, a choreographer, set and costume designers and an orchestra of a dozen or so, Pelham proposed an astonishing budget of £20,000 with a £5,000 overcall. Today the cost would be terrifying.

The Russian and the Jew kept an anxious, respectful distance. The third backer, Gilda Dahlberg, responsible for the possible overcall, was not so easily corralled. A rich New York widow and former chorus girl, she was reputed to have been engaged to the English director Anthony Page and saw herself as the successor to Irene Selznick, who had produced *A Streetcar Named Desire* in America. Short, plump and teetering, she would clop down the aisle at rehearsals in open-toed lamé shoes with shimmering matching pants topped off by a mink coat. She caused some comic diversion but her flabby fidgeting and incessant notebook-scribbling soon became irksome. Merrick would have had her efficiently dispatched in the direction of the East River.

I was summoned to her Dorchester suite. Pelham was an untried mountebank bumming a few thousand pounds from a prominent widow. I was a jumped up bus-boy, or whatever the British called it, with a couple of questionable Broadway hits behind me. I agreed to most of her objections, but she wasn't to be taken in by my Limey smooth talk and when she discovered I had ignored every one of her instructions her neckless head slumped in fury as she clattered to the exit doors.

She struck back by turning spy and informer to our most eager enemy, the press. Excited reporters waited outside the Dorchester and delightedly set down her complaints of our ineptitude. She was the only passenger on board shouting 'Iceberg!', and the captain was pouring garbage on her. Pelham tried to persuade her that if anything guaranteed us sinking it was her own renegade campaign. But she was content. She had achieved her ambition and become an overnight celebrity. The more the Slickeys scribbled, the more detailed her invention. She had brought with her a considerable wardrobe for her role as star impresario and was photographed at first nights and night-clubs. She was a miraculous gift, a rival to Lady Docker, Zsa Zsa Gabor and the Princess Margaret set.

Will success pacify John Osborne?

No post-war musical has been awaited in London with such excited speculation as Osborne's *The World of Paul Slickey*. Will *Slickey* succeed and consolidate Osborne's soaring reputation? Or will it – together with its adventurous author – come a cropper in the West End, following other off-beat song-and-dance offerings into Flopsville?

Well, we shall have the answer in a month or so. Meanwhile Britain is not lacking in prophets waiting to display a gloating glee if Osborne this time encounters a disaster. He has, after all, sired three major successes in a row. And this is, in some ways, an ungenerous land which resents uninterrupted triumphs and finds satisfaction in witnessing a downfall... Many of my Fleet Street colleagues when they interview

Osborne inevitably tabulate his cars, suits, shoes and other evidence of wealth. As though, somehow, they were corrupting influences. As though, somehow, nobody that angry has any right to luxury.

'It's impossible in this business to do anything interesting without making enemies,' he said. 'Too many people want to be loved, you see.' He lit another cheroot and looked very sad.

Herbert Kretzmer, Daily Sketch, 8 April 1959

Apart from Gilda, rehearsals became increasingly encouraging. Dennis was still irredeemably sweet-natured, but there was a month or so to fit him with a set of fangs. MacMillan, Jocelyn and I spent many evenings together, partly to work and also for pleasure. Mary was in Nottingham filming *Sons and Lovers*, scripted by Tony's mysterious visitor in Beverly Hills, Gavin Lambert. Late at night in Woodfall Street we discovered that one of those yellow fogs had descended on London, thick beyond Hollywood legend. Kenneth, hardened by the workhouse discipline of his profession, decided that he could find his way home. Jocelyn sensibly refused to set out in these Captain Oates conditions and stayed.

It was mid-morning before she returned to Eaton Square. Alec Murray was waiting for her with a laconic open eye. 'Oh, Jocelyn, you bloody fool.' She limped off to bed. She told me, 'All I could say was: "Don't nag, Alec. I don't exactly feel full of wisdom, but no one's going to get hurt." '

> I'm just a guy called Paul Slickey,
> And the job that I do's pretty tricky,
> I'm twenty-eight years old
> And practically everybody, anybody, anything
> You can think of leaves me
> Quite completely
> Newspaper neatly,
> Quite, quite cold.
>
> *The World of Paul Slickey*

I was braced for a rough opening in Bournemouth. Famed for its wheelchair garrison and huge Conservative catchment, it seemed a disastrous choice. The air itself was notoriously enervating. Half of Fleet Street had made the journey. I recognized many faces feigning friendship. 'Hello, John,' they trilled, like men bellowing at a badger cornered in its set.

Dennis began the show with a brisk number called 'Don't think you can fool a guy like me.' His voice was confident and subtle and the audience responded quite gratefully. There were two and a half hours for them to lose patience. Marie's magisterial entrance was greeted as if she were about to wind up the Proms; Harry, the 'Red Shadow' of many a Bournemouth bosom, was applauded for his nervous stumblings. At the interval there was a general reaction of enthusiastic relief. Kenneth, Jocelyn and I could scarcely look at each other for our disbelief.

The second act was a minefield of what had been prophesied as monumental bad taste. The high – or low – point was a scene in which Philip Locke as Father Evilgreene led a satanic dance which would, we were assured by Hickey and Tanfield, enrage the most agnostic sensibilities. It didn't. Even 'Bring back the axe,' drop-kicked at the groin of feminine Toryism, got an odd cheer from the shrine of primitivism. Half-way through the curtain calls, I heard the sound of 'Author, author!' It was so unfamiliar, I thought it was 'Off with it! Off with it!'

That Musical

And what did respectable Bournemouth think of John Osborne's first musical which opened there last night?

Lady Cobham, wife of Sir Alan Cobham, who lives at West Overcliff Drive said: 'I thought the whole thing was dreadful. Not at all artistic. It is shocking to put on anything like that and call it entertainment . . . The ballet where the parson sings hymns and there is all that rock'n'rolling reminded me of the reptile house at the Zoo. Give me the potted palms of Bournemouth to these Angry Young Men.'

Mr Philip Tridmore, manager of the Norfolk Lodge Hotel told me: 'I didn't think it was so bad. After cutting it could be slick.' Finnish Baron Godot Wrede, who was staying at Norfolk Lodge, said: 'It is very nice to see in England something naughty, like we see in France.'

I am sure Mr Osborne is delighted to have disturbed the still Bournemouth air.

The Star

Shocker

While columnists sat in the lounge of the Royal Bath Hotel, Bournemouth, discussing John Osborne's musical, he was sleeping soundly upstairs. He didn't care what they said about him, or his effort. 'I am surprised that more people didn't walk out.' Only three years ago Osborne filled in his income tax return: 'No income. No tax.'

Evening News

Mr Osborne Sprays Weed Killer

Mr Dominic Elwes, in the only dinner jacket I saw, and his wife Tessa, represented the biceps of society. Mrs Gilda Dahlberg was there in jewels, and Mr David Pelham in a sports coat. But they are financially involved. And any masochistic gossip writers who made the trip had to buy their seats.

Evening Standard

Slickey Makes Them Seethe

Christopher Whelen, composer of the music for *The World of Paul Slickey*, John Osborne's controversial play now running at the Pavilion, has had a nervous breakdown. He is at present being looked after in the Parkstone home of his mother, Mrs W.E. Whelen. She told *Bournemouth Times*, 'Christopher always gets like this after a first night. This time he has not slept for four days and has hardly eaten anything.'

Bournemouth Times & Directory

The effect on the company's morale was tangible – even the Equity representative looked happy. Leeds, the next week, was even more encouraging. They laughed knowingly at the jokes Bournemouth missed. But I was apprehensive about Brighton. We were playing the old variety house, the Hippodrome, home of Max Miller. There was an elegant, glass-enclosed bar at the back of the stalls. It must surely attract a better class of audience. They turned out to be a little rowdy and unpredictable. Towards the end of the week a strong claque of local queens dominated this bar promenade with scattered bouts of sniggering barracking. They were being urged on and orchestrated by Patrick Desmond, Stella's ex-husband.

All-time Low

Sir: – In my opinion the British Theatre sinks to an all-time low with this week's offering at the Brighton Hippodrome. I consider John Osborne's so-called musical comedy to be blasphemous and disgusting – an insult to decent-minded and intelligent theatre-goers.

Evening Argus

Why Does Slickey Make Them Froth?

So this was *Paul Slickey*. Before I saw John Osborne's calumnied, castigated and near-crucified piece, about 25 people had described it to me in terms ranging from atrocious to zymotic. Certainly Osborne leaves nothing out; nothing is sacred. But I must admit I cannot understand the vitriolic, bitchy, almost unbalanced opposition the thing has aroused . . . Mr Osborne's startler is far from being the horror it is painted. *Expresso Bongo* was much worse.

Worthing Gazette

We were to open at the Palace in London on a Tuesday. On Monday we had an all-day run-through. Emile, play-doctor and horse-fancier, sent one of his minions to tell me that, unless certain adjustments and cuts were made, Mr Littler would not allow the performance to take place the following night. Robin Fox's invaluable advice came to mind. We went on rehearsing, waiting for the house lights to be snapped out and the doors barred. They weren't.

Such night in England ne'er had been, nor e'er again shall be.

Thomas Babington Macaulay, 'The Armada'

I must be the only playwright this century to have been pursued up a London street by an angry mob. Like most battle experiences, my own view was limited by my vantage point at the back of the stalls. There was an inescapable tension in the house. The theatre itself took on a feeling of rococo mockery and devilment, too hot, a snake-pit of stabbing jewellery, hair-pieces, hobbling high heels, stifling wraps and unmanageable long frocks.

First nights brought out duchesses in those days. I had never seen so many black ties. The public-relations girl insisted on letting me know who was trooping in: the Duke of Bedford, Lord Montague, the Marquess of Milford Haven, 'Bubbles' Harmsworth, Cecil Beaton, Noël Coward, Jack Hawkins, John Mills, Michael Foot and the Profumos. Worst of all, George, on his own. Whatever the outcome, it could only bring him grief.

These occasions were made more hazardous by the now-defunct 'Gallery First-nighters'. This group of self-appointed deputies queued for hours for the fifty or sixty gallery seats of most London theatres. They were organized and hierarchical. Their leader was Nellie (another one). Surrounded by carrier-bags, sandwiches and flasks, she would loll over the edge like a poised gorilla. Nellie was the final arbiter. Thousands of pounds, investors' sleep, actors' careers were in ransom to her sticky thumbs. Her supporters were as intimidated by her as the managements.

Nellie set off a few exploratory skirmishes. Dennis had the misfortune to utter the line: 'God in heaven, it's like a pantomime.' 'Hear, hear,' roared the first-nighters. 'What we want is a return to commonsense.' Nellie and her henchmen rose in applause. The dowagers' humps settled back in comfort to enjoy the sound and smoke of battle. In the redoubt of the pit, the MD whipped the orchestra into a thunderous barrage. It was magnificent, and war. The cast faced front and hurled their lines like grenades.

At the curtain-call, John Gielgud was booing, not waving. So was Coward. Adrienne shouted a scarcely audible, 'Go fuck yourselves.' The cast was sheepishly elated. Marie embraced me regally. '*What* a silly audience.' She boomed at Pelham, 'Where *did* you find them?' 'Take no notice, my dear,' she said to me. 'They can't stand originality in one so young.'

I wandered on to the stage, looked up at Nellie's firing-position and then at Casson's set, shivering in the stare of the working light. A photographer, concealed in the curtains by an exit door, snatched a flash picture. It appeared in the *Evening Standard* the following day, captioned 'Lonely Moment'. The front of house seemed the only likely exit for dignified escape. But the foyer doors were still open, flooded with light. There was no question of retreat. I hoped I wouldn't lose my balance from a hefty punch or whisky vision. I could hear cries of 'Tripe' and 'Bloody rubbish'. I tried not to hurry up Charing Cross Road but the footsteps were coming nearer and I broke into a halting run. I imagined a few public-school scrum-forwards who would bring me down in a flying tackle before Foyle's.

Astonishingly, a taxi-driver threw open his door. I hopped in and he revved off like a bank robber. Fists banged on the window. Woodfall Street was dark, silent and empty. It was very cold. I switched on the electric fire and opened a gift-bottle of champagne. I fell asleep and dreamed of lying half-clothed with Stella at Moss Mansions, the sea roaring beneath the girders of the Palace Pier. I fancied she might have had some sympathy with the audience at the Palace Theatre. I awoke, shivering. Mary and Jocelyn were helping me upstairs.

Mary must have had a difficult evening but she said very little. Helen Henderson arrived early to deal with the continuous telephone calls, Mary's polemics about Albert Finney's cruel behaviour towards his wife and child and Charles Laughton's misery and trepidation at the reception of his forthcoming Lear. She was returning to Stratford that afternoon. I clutched the edges of the lavatory basin, feeling as if the inside of my head had been scrubbed with a rusty cheese-grater.

The high and low spot of my London visit was the opening night of John Osborne's musical *Paul Slickey* at the Palace. Never in all my theatrical experience have I seen anything so appalling, appalling from every point of view. Sad lyrics, dull music, idiotic, would-be-daring dialogue – interminable long-winded scenes about nothing and above all the amateurishness and ineptitude, such bad taste that one wanted to hide one's head.

The Noël Coward Diaries

15. *Surprised by Joy*

He Should Have Known Better!
The first night audience at the Palace seemed to be about equally divided
between those who loathed it politely and those who hated it
audibly ... The final curtain came down to the most raucous note of
displeasure heard in the West End since the war.

Milton Shulman, *Evening Standard*

Extraordinary dullness ... manifest failure ... vulgar mockery ... lack of
skill ...

The Times

An evening of general embarrassment ... three boring hours ...

Manchester Guardian

Osborne has been his own worst enemy ... *Slickey* isn't slick enough ...
everything is out of proportion ...

Observer

It has almost every fault.
    New Statesman

> I want to hear about beautiful things
> Beautiful things like love
> I don't want to hear of emotional wrecks
> Of people who practice peculiar sex
> I want my love to be pure
> My income secure
> I don't wish to wallow in a spiritual sewer.
> *The World of Paul Slickey*

Gilda was having a field day with her press boys. 'Sipping orange juice in her
seventh-floor suite at the Dorchester, 52-year-old, 4′ 10″ Mrs Dahlberg said,
"I've never known a show take such a terrible beating from the critics but,

believe me, the beating was well deserved. I put thousands into the show." '
Not yet, she hadn't, nor did she. ' "I was meant to be the associate producer.
I made notes and notes on every page of the script. *Now* perhaps they will listen
to my suggestions." ' One of her pals from Fleet Street left the Dorchester with
a couple of mink stoles, valued at £2,000 each. Ten days later, Gilda moved
into the London Clinic, suffering from 'nervous exhaustion'.

There seemed little point in hanging on in London for any possible reprieve.
The cast were cheerful enough. They had received praise and unaccustomed
offers, and Pelham had promised to keep things going for a minimum of six
weeks. Mary was immersed in the daily domestic routine of Stratford. Jocelyn
R. and Alec had been invited to stay in Graham Greene's villa and so, a couple
of days later, I picked Jocelyn up at Eaton Square. In my new racing-green
Jaguar XK150, unobserved by Fleet Street's 'has-been' spotters, we swept into
the tiny concourse of Lydd Airport and drove the car on to the ferry-plane,
en route for a leisurely journey to Naples and then Capri.

Moving south slowly down the secondary roads of France through the
horizon points of the poplar trees, Jocelyn was the perfect companion. She
possessed that most powerful antidote to opinion, joyful curiosity. With the
hood down, the squalor and play-acting of the past year blew away as we drove
from long lunches at tiny inns along empty, unbending avenues. We dined
early, falling sated and inflated with food, wine, folly and fresh air into a goose-
feathered well of forgetfulness. We were halted for a week by a fierce, enclosing
storm in a fishing-village on the Camargue coast. The shutters clattered ill-
temperedly for hours but the respite from driving was welcome and the sunny
stillness that followed, with bowls of bougainvillaea and platters of lobster,
almost convinced me that the French could be likeable, when they were off-
guard.

By the time we snaked our way along the Côte d'Azur and into Italy I began
to feel that the wind, sun, garlic, even the angry *mistral*, had flushed out all
the poisons of ill-nature I had absorbed. For the past ten days, life had been
marked out in Michelin spoons and it doubtless showed, but as we crossed
the Italian border, I felt as young as only the old can remember feeling: lean,
lithe and swift. In Rapallo we drove up to an Edwardian wedding-cake of an
hotel and were welcomed like milords on the Grand Tour. Beaming over my
passport, the concierge declaimed, 'Oh, Signor Osborne – the World of Paul
Sickly!'

In Rome we joined Alec at the Inghilterra. The English press had been
seeking us out and Mary seemed to have dealt with their descent on Stratford
with blindfold skill. Paul Sickly it was indeed.

While John Osborne was moving towards Paris with his friend Jocelyn Rickards, his actress wife Mary Ure talked to me about this latest in the line of unusual theatrical holidays. Mr Osborne is driving Miss Rickards, *Slickey*'s costume designer, while Miss Ure is stuck with the rigours of a season at Stratford. 'John is utterly exhausted. He's got the feeling, you know, when one simply has to get out of England'. With Miss Rickards? 'Jocelyn is my oldest, dearest friend,' said Miss Ure. 'She and John and I have known each other for years. She was going to Paris – so John said he could give her a lift.'

Daily Express, 18 May 1959

It was all very game. I couldn't make out whether she was being blithe or brave and it seemed mean not to give her the benefit of the doubt.

The *Express* continued:

'This is one of those theatrical holidays where one partner goes on holiday – I'm afraid I can't join him – I'm up to my neck in it in Stratford.' Mr Osborne's holiday will keep him away from the première of his film *Look Back in Anger* at which he was due to meet Princess Margaret.

This set the features editors to work: 'Does Show Business Have its own Marriage Code?'

In show business married couples taking their holidays apart is not an eyebrow-raising experience. Not since those well-known style-setters, the Oliviers, did it a couple of years ago. But the Osborne-holiday-alone raises rather an interesting issue. Supposing Osborne wasn't a successful playwright but a milkman? And supposing his wife Mary wasn't a successful actress but a secretary? Would we be so ready to accept the situation where the milkman suddenly takes a Continental holiday while his wife stays at home sharpening her pencils and taking dictation? How many people go along with the Oliviers, the Trevor Howards and the Osbornes?'

Daily Mail, 1 June 1959

It was still 1959.

Long before I was confronted with the task of giving witness to it, I regarded my childhood as not so much unhappy as devoid of happiness. 'What you've never had you'll never miss,' was a calumny on my life. Myth is just as admissible as history, and my sense of lost inheritance was as powerful as any downright deprivation. Happiness when it did come, snatched from the air in provincial corners, was so rare and irreversible it could survive every avenging assault upon it. I decided not to ring Mary and hear the latest progress of Finney's marriage. That could wait most contentedly. Its postponement was an additional spice to the happiness that had sped past in the fugitive progress south.

As the three of us drove on the autostrada to Naples, I nudged the needle past the 100 m.p.h. mark for the first and last time in my life. The misty rain, mingled with the scent of the countryside, slammed into our faces in the open Jaguar. Jocelyn's question to Alec, shrieked above the wind, was as characteristic as his reply. 'Isn't the wild thyme marvellous?' 'I don't know,' he said, knees clenched and teeth clamped on his cigar. 'We're travelling faster than the speed of smell.'

We spent the next two weeks at the Villa Rosario, Greene's house high up in Anacapri. They had both stayed there before and knew the locals. The house was low, bare and full of light, the perfect fortress against the infelicities we had left behind. We lay in the sun, reading and staring out over the bay of Naples, lunching simply at a restaurant in the square, occasionally bathing from the rocks below Gracie Fields' swimming-pool. Nino, an Italian friend of Alec's, joined us and in the evenings we would sit in the opera-house setting of the piazza and watch the new arrivals, their luggage trundled up by flamboyant porters, or the black-tie set bawling from the yachts moored at the Marina Grande, a gaggle of sound from well-goosed Wentworth-Brewsters.

On our last evening, Alec suddenly rose and drawled, 'Time we were leaving.' His professional ear had picked up the click of a Sickly camera. Grabbing Jocelyn's hand, he sauntered away. The following day dozens of pictures of them appeared in the London newspapers, strolling like a pair of dozey lovers. You could see Nino's head in the rear and most of my legs.

When we returned to London, Eaton Square was staked out with waiting reporters. Jocelyn managed to dash through the front door. I was less lucky. Woodfall Street was jammed from its entrance in Smith Street to the brick wall at the end. I parked the Jaguar, battered by alpine rocks, at the corner and made my way to the front door. 'Come on, John. Be a sport, John.' I fumbled with my keys and was photographed as if I were caught breaking into my own house. Helen was upstairs looking panicked and frightened. Jocelyn was on the telephone. She sounded pretty shaken herself.

Angry Young Man's Mother Pulls Pints

The charming lady I found pulling pints at the Spring Hotel, Ewell, laughed and said, 'I don't work as a barmaid because I'm hard-up. I like doing it. My son makes me a very generous allowance indeed.' Mrs Nellie

On my way to Stratford, I noticed in my mirror a large Rolls Royce of the same royal vintage as the Oliviers' VLOI. As we emerged from the usual crawl through High Wycombe, it began to make bold attempts to pass me. It was TR100 and behind its impassive chauffeur were lounging Terence Rattigan and Mr Beaumont. I was determined not readily to be overtaken by such lordly opposition and I managed to keep in their eyeline all the way to the Memorial Theatre, where my satisfaction was slightly spoiled by Peter Hall's Jaguar, identical to my own, parked importantly outside.

Mary had already opened in Hall's production of *A Midsummer Night's Dream*, in which she played Titania to Robert Hardy's Oberon, with Charles Laughton as Bottom and Vanessa Redgrave and Albert Finney romping away listlessly as the juveniles. It had been an earthbound, schoolmasterly business, unhelped by Laughton's unease. He was a useful addition to Mary's corps of self-kneecapped wounded; a most suitable case for her busybody brand of concern. Thirty years on, she would have made an admirable 'counsellor'.

Laughton was one of the most pugnaciously morose men I had ever met. His huge talent seemed to endorse his implacable resentment. His Caliban self-portraiture must have been further agonized by being incarcerated, like so many of his unhappy generation, in that closet which dared not speak its name. Even his large collection of Klees and Kokoschkas was displayed as trophies of martyrdom rather than joyful plunder.

After the absorbent tranquillity of Capri, the return to Woodfall Street had a head-on impact of instantly returning fatigue. However, I could scarcely avoid the brick wall of Mary's first night as Desdemona. Tony had directed it. He and Oscar Lewenstein had winkled Paul Robeson from his McCarthyite bondage to play Othello. His legendary appearance with Peggy Ashcroft twenty-five years before ensured that expectations were running high. Loudon Sainthill had designed the sets, and Tony provided one of his proscenium menageries of hooded birds and Great Danes. The expectant energy that a rising curtain bestows even on the likes of myself quickly wilted. Robeson, the beloved volcano, rumbled thrillingly, but the eruption was choked back, the fire gone cold, banked down by age and the extinguishing weight of neglect and cruelty.

Mary was unimpressed by my mother's Cockney gush. She and Nellie Beatrice disliked each other and they were both too artless to be capable of pretence, let alone artifice. In a mood of idle vengeance, I invited my mother to stay. Mary's rented house in Stratford was bright, Edwardian and airy, but the days were stifling now that she was no longer rehearsing. The town had the unfriendly, philistine air that most centres of tourist culture seem to radiate. We had less than ever to say to each other, and I was straining to try to work. Mary had made few friends, apart from Jane Wenham, Finney's wife, and her newly born son, both objects for counselling and homely comfort. We went to the twenty-first-birthday party of an attractive young bit-part player, Diana Rigg.

I took Nellie Beatrice to see *Othello*. Afterwards Robeson joined the three of us upstairs for supper. Perhaps it was as well that my mother was not wearing her favourite outfit, what she might have described to him as her coral and nigger-brown rig-out. We waited apprehensively for his appearance, a handsome but exhausted giant. Nellie Beatrice was genuinely admiring, in awe of this massive, Blakean figure, possibly wondering why he wasn't clad in one of Lord Sandy's left-over leopard skins.

She hardly spoke until we came to the main course, when she piped up in her most ingratiating-the-head-waiter voice, 'Oh, Mr Robinson,' she said, 'it's such an honour for us to meet you.' Mr Robinson acknowledged this sweetly. 'Especially for my son. He's such an admirer of yours. You see . . . ' She looked around the restaurant, graciously drawing her audience, then said with deferential confidence: 'You see, Mr Robinson, he's always been very sorry for you *darkies*.' A large, gentle smile spread over his face. In those days, innocent of racial policing, cheerfulness did have a way of breaking in on simple prejudice.

After *Othello* Tony was to direct Vivien Leigh in Noël Coward's translation of the Feydeau farce, *Occupe-toi d'Amélie*, retitled *Look After Lulu*. The combined force of Vivien, Noël, Binkie Beaumont and Citizens Devine and Richardson was prickly and suspicious from the outset, as doomed an attempt to contradict the emnity of history as an allegiance between France and Albion.

Tony rang me from Nottingham, where *Lulu* had opened in an atmosphere of divisive conspiracy and recrimination. 'You've *got* to come up.' I was accustomed to this kind of urgent pleading when he was merely bored with his present company or wanted another hand at bridge. But I was curious to be an observer of the whole explosive enterprise. It also provided me with an acceptable excuse to get away from Stratford and the aimless defeated days Mary and I were spending together. As usual she was unconvinced and possibly relieved, and cheerfully waved me off without any pressure on when I should return.

I picked up Jocelyn and we set out north to watch the progress of the faltering Grand Alliance. We booked into the Turk's Head where Tony was waiting, enjoying every moment of intrigue and sub-plot. 'Thank God you've come. I think I'm going mad. Vivien's gone to pieces because of Joan, George is in a *state*, and Noël insists on being fucking *witty* all the time.'

A supper had been arranged after the performance and Tony insisted that we must be present. Binkie presided over the table that included Vivien, George, Meriel Forbes (Lady Richardson), who was also in the cast, Noël and a posse of Vivien's reinforcements, among them the preposterous agony-journalist, Godfrey Winn, who had been hearing her lines and comforting her as she sat by the telephone waiting for Olivier to call from Stratford, where he was about to open in *Coriolanus*. There was common anxiety about her health and state of mind. She had been in an almost unbroken condition of shock ever since Larry had peeled off his Archie Rice eyebrows in the Palace dressing-room and, addressing her image in the mirror said, in a reversion to Coward-like delivery, 'Of course, you know I'm in love with Joan Plowright, don't you?'

Coward himself, though increasingly impatient with what he considered to be a vulgar circus of tedious procrastination, was possibly more helpful than anyone. His cold eye saw quite correctly that Vivien must somehow reconcile herself to the divorce Olivier was set upon. His anxiety was prompted by fears for his leading lady's endurance, but also by his loyalty and affection for them both. Unlike most of the spectators to the whole miserable indignity of their situation, including Larry's forced hole-in-corner dalliance with Plowright, he appeared not to stoop to the silliness of 'taking sides'.

I found myself at the far end of the table, next but one to Coward. Perhaps this *placement* was Binkie's way of demonstrating Elvira's assessment of my social standing. Listening to this undaunted ornament of the century, born in the same year as my father, I remembered Binkie throwing a few chips of encouragement to me as he said with a gleam of disaffection, 'Of course, Noël's *quite* uneducated.' Whether it implied that the Master was as unashamedly ignorant as myself, expelled and barely literate at fifteen, con-demned to a fixed condition of 'not being ready for it yet', I hadn't resolved. It merely seemed a piece of clumsy treachery, a fair example of the reverence for academic skill and a classic misapprehension of its link with creative imagination. Even Binkie, from his own more distinguished productions, could have deduced that from Shakespeare to Shaw a little Latin and less Greek, or none of either, did no damage to untutored dramatists.

I could see what Tony meant about Coward's compulsion to be 'fucking witty' all the time. Fortunately, Jocelyn, with her salon experience of abstruse table talk and literary gossip, was adroit at stirring the vanities of opinionated celebrities into the illusion of making conversation rather than dominating it. She asked him intelligent questions about himself which he answered amusingly, pinning down each one with an exact date, place and relevance to the Coward calendar of first-night triumphs and occasional disasters. I was tempted to ask him about his own confrontation with Nellie of the first-nighters, but decided against it. The evening ended amiably.

As we went to bed, I suggested to Jocelyn that it might have been trying the Master's patience to run her fingers over his head as we left. She said she was so overcome with affection that she couldn't resist his careful crewcut. 'I loved him so much.' 'Oh well,' I said. 'I suppose you *are* Australian.'

Lulu continued acrimoniously in Nottingham and then opened at the Court, where it enhanced no one's reputation and drew rather gratuitous scorn for the incompatibility of the two theatrical factions. It must have seemed to Vivien that we, George, Tony, even myself, were the instruments of her present misery and Larry's disavowal of the whole courtly progress of the legend surrounding their love and lives. However much one sympathized with Olivier's desperation to escape the destruction of her magic alchemy, it was impossible not to be affected, like Coward, by the pain cascading over both of them.

The most generous assessment of the whole miserable enterprise came from Harold Hobson in the *Sunday Times*: 'The trouble is that Mr Coward is too witty and Miss Vivien Leigh is too beautiful. For the kind of play that *Look After Lulu* is, beauty and wit are as unnecessary as a peach Melba at the North Pole.'

Vivien's presence ensured *Lulu*'s transfer to the West End, justifying George's derided intention of using the proceeds to pursue his own theatre's proper course. Whether or not the rewards of his pragmatism were worth so much hysteria, he was running a corner shop which demanded speedy turnover, improvisation rather than adherence to fixed principles. Some people never forgave him for it. Perhaps they were already dreaming of airport-like buildings whose very existence would create a sacrosanct brotherhood of public 'funding'.

Even Tony's resilience had been tested by Tennant's battalions and he insisted that we should go off to Ischia to work on the screenplay of *The Entertainer*. It was a kind of second-time-around bonus. The chance to return so quickly to the Naples skyline and a further reprieve from Stratford was welcome. It was out of the question to take Jocelyn with me. The flat landscape of Ischia provided less chance of concealment than the lush hillsides of Capri.

Apart from a fairly attractive secretary, who might be an amusing decoy, there would be no female accompaniment. Another respite.

We stayed at a barely opened new hotel overlooking the sea. We seemed to have it almost to ourselves. Ten years later it was overrun by huge Germans grunting and wallowing in the volcanic mud baths. In the mornings we sat by the pool chatting, working swiftly. I scribbled while Tony's knees jerked in reflex to his own inspirations. One jab for yes, three jabs for no. Before noon, we would have a drink, perhaps an unwise Negroni, and wander off to the veranda of a simple beach restaurant nestled in a cove round the corner. We would lunch on fruit, smoked meats and pasta with a couple of carafes of the local wine. Apart from a few noisy Teutons blubbering away in blue-black wells of mud by the rocks, we were undisturbed. I would write up what we had discussed in an agreeable haze before a cool snooze.

Most evenings we took a rattling scooter-taxi across to Porto d'Ischia, twinkling with lights but fairly deserted. Our fellow diners were usually groups of Englishmen in blazers and striped socks, all oppressively self-conscious, shouting at each other to keep up morale. Their unresponding audience were middle-aged couples, retired soldiers, housemasters or husband-and-wife authors of children's tales. To Tony and me, both in relaxed humour, their performances were open to infinite speculation and salacious fantasy.

One night we had to pick our way through crowds to the courtyard entrance, revealed by the lights of a fiesta, the Victorian bandstand sparkling in the square and white-uniformed musicians tootling out Verdi. Euphoria and grappa flowed upward into the shimmer of the Neapolitan night.

There was a newcomer at one of the café tables. He was flabby, debauched and was being fêted by a group of New York faggots and the local passing trade. Tony stared at him with a kind of repelled excitement. It was Chester Kallman, long-time companion to W.H. Auden. Not for the first time, I found myself leaving Tony at a street corner and going back to the hotel alone. All the same, the days that followed were probably the most careless and stimulating that I was ever to spend with him.

Grand Hotel, Ankara

My dear John,

I am sorry you feel so bitter. I feel bitter in some ways too but they're not the most important ones.

The trouble is that you have a one way morality as far as films are concerned. You don't really like writing them, you don't give of your whole self and heart but you expect other people to treat what you do as if it was one of your own plays. You don't really value the writing in the same way but you can't bear others not to.

I'm sure this probably won't help our relationship only exacerbate it because I feel increasingly that what you want from a friendship is not real loyalty which is based on truth or on knowing each other but sycophancy and adulation which I can't give, and despise anyway.

I hope your present feelings will change soon. Whether they do or not they won't change mine. I love you.

Tony

Letter from Tony Richardson to J.O., 1966

16. Viva Mexico!

I am a worm and no man, a byword and a laughing stock.
Crush out the worminess in me, stamp on me . . . I am alone,
I am alone, and against myself.

Luther

When I was in New York for the opening of *George Dillon* in November 1958, I had seen very little of Francine. Robert Webber made a somewhat sinister reappearance to tell me she was 'a mess, bloated with booze' and spending all day in Harry's apartment on Eighty-second Street with the blinds drawn. He was not exaggerating. When she opened the door to me, she was in her underwear, barefoot, with a glass in hand. Her face was puffy, her body had a stiff, swollen look and the apartment was thick with an accumulation of tobacco and marijuana. She seemed bewildered.

After a while she had settled against me, comforted and tearful, then chattering as if she had spoken to no one for weeks. I rang Harry, who was sympathetic but unsurprised. 'Give the kid a good time, if you can.' I couldn't think what I could do to ease her fragile mood. The only thing which seemed to give her pleasure was dancing the night away in deafening night-clubs. After which she would spend the next few days in the apartment, clutching a glass and rolling joints, her eyes brimming as she listened to numbing Spanish love-songs in the darkened room.

I tried to coax her into recapturing her high-spirited playfulness, but, whatever had taken place, she was reluctant to talk about herself any longer. She was still disarmingly affectionate, but the tiny pearl of innocent lustre she had preserved beneath the mink-and-diamond drag had gone. She was intelligent and realistic enough to know that there was no chance of or even desirability in continuing our affair for long.

I was anxious to get back to England, to the filming of *Look Back* and my headlong fling with *Slickey*, but I felt wretched leaving her curled up in the smoky pool of light by her bed listening to some mawkish variant on *Volare*. I knew little about her or how little there might be to know. If her heart-strings had cracked slightly, they might also have hardened. I felt as if I was already something half-forgotten.

When I got back to London I instructed my accountant to send her some money, not in expiation but because she would expect it. The size of the cheque might reassure her of my small-time English stinginess. With true accountants' insight, he observed, 'I think you've got off very lightly, John.' I would not see her again for almost a year, and then in circumstances so surprising they confirmed all my instincts about her Swiss resilience.

The film of *Look Back* opened in June 1959 and was fairly politely received. Someone wrote, 'In essence, it doesn't amount to a row of beans eaten with a knife straight out of the tin.' There was some carping about Burton's age and 'very unlovely people living jaded and appallingly crude lives in the filth of a Midland garret'. And, more damning, it was described as 'beautifully made', a certain euphemism for dull and arty.

Harry had tried unsuccessfully to bribe the organizers of the Cannes Film Festival to accept Woodfall's first-born in competition. He had hosted an elaborate dinner for the French dignitaries, headed by the Chef du Festival, Fauvre LeBret, and afterwards dealt out pound notes like a croupier to the gaiety of a circle of outstretched hands. He was pipped at the post by *Room at the Top*. As some sort of recompense, in November we were invited as the official British entry to a film festival in Acapulco, of all places.

This was a banana-republic fiesta with no cultural pretensions. It was organized to provide the President with the company of desirable foreign actresses. Dozens of countries sent representatives, directors, producers, starlets and that army of vagrants who can sniff out free food and carousing from across continents. Most of the films 'entered' in the non-competitive 'festival' were already commercial or artistic failures. Or both. Each was awarded a prize.

Tony and I had been attracted by the comic possibilities of the event and the agreeably tangible prize of freeloading Mexican sea and sunshine. Apart from the Rank and ABPC front-office boys, Sandy McKendrick was there and Peter Brook, preparing his film of *Lord of the Flies*. The President entertained at his hacienda in furious El Gatsby style, the gardens, beach and palm-trees popping with female flesh of all nations and ringed by a detachment of the army, all armed to their gold teeth.

The films were shown at midnight under the stars in the courtyard of a disused fort as little more than an afterthought to the principal proceedings. The British participation was sulkily mismanaged by the Rank contingent. Perhaps because of this, Tony decided he must make a speech from the platform on the night of *Look Back*'s presentation. A Mexican interpreter was coaxed into translating it into phonetic Spanish which Tony would learn by heart. As she rehearsed him in delivery and pronounciation, she kept repeating, 'Maria! He can't say that. He can't!' It seemed he was in danger of being badly mauled or even lynched. She would accept no responsibility for his safety. As I was to appear with him, I would be in danger of the national wrath myself.

Under the spotlight of a bright moon, I stepped forward, bowed and acknowledged the audience's mild applause. Then Tony thrust himself forward and launched into his strangled Spanish harangue. They were silent throughout the whole arm-waving, uncoordinated mime, until he came to a shrill crescendo, proclaiming with clenched fist: '*Gracios muchos. Viva Mayheeho! Viva Mayheeho. And – Viva Buñuel!*' At this, everyone in the courtyard stood, whistling and booing, and the interpreter dragged us off into some dark passage in the fortified walls. 'I told you not to mention Buñuel.'

Whether it was the Mexican sun, day-long parties or his headlong determination to master water-skiing, Tony was in an odd mood. Our next brush with physical danger was by the pool of the El Presidente Hotel. In an idle moment, I mentioned to Tony and Oscar Lewenstein (another Woodfall free-rider) that I was thinking of writing a play about Martin Luther. Oscar immediately bristled with Marxist certainties. Tony said he felt I was ill-equipped to pay enough attention to the historical and social background of the bloody events which took place and changed the face of Europe. My heart went cold within me as we sat under the bruising sunshine. Apart from my own hesitancies about belief and doctrine, I began to feel that I was embarking on something which would have been better left for a few years, when my own confusion might have resolved itself into some coherence.

The conversation turned to the matter of Luther's undoubted anti-Semitism, a favourite weapon used against him by his detractors. I had planned to avoid this aspect of his character, from artistic rather than moral timidity. My own crude perception is that the Jews, rather like the Irish, are essentially a cold-hearted race. Sentimentality, which they both have in abundance, is the sugar-armour of the hard of heart.

I relapsed into silence by the pool. Oscar, as usual, was waiting for someone else to make something happen. Tony raised his shiny beak and fixed us with a peregrine stare. He has spent a lifetime thrusting his face provocatively at the sun. Suddenly, in a castrato shriek which bounced back across the Olympic-size pool, he bellowed at Oscar. 'Sometimes, Oscar, when I look at you . . . ' Oscar stiffened as the inflection rose skyward. 'When I look at you, I think Hitler was right . . . ' The flight straightened out into counter-tenor, then ascended. 'You fucking little Jew.'

The pool-side silence seemed interminable, cigar butts drooped limply. Oscar frowned, more in irritation at gratuitous frivolity than at intention to wound. 'Oh dear, oh dear. You really shouldn't say things like that, Tony. You really shouldn't.' Tony was uneasily exhilarated. The silence around us had not yet broken. I decided it was time to leave and strolled off as unhurriedly as I could. Tony's outburst seemed like some prankish madness, a device to cause instant pain and disarray. It had certainly worked.

Tony had hired a water-skiing boat on a daily basis from one of the many plying beachboys. He selected José, beautiful, about nineteen, with the kind of rippling iron-spare body that few of us ever glimpse outside an athletic stadium. He was unquestionably the noble savage among the others. He spoke little English but he seemed free and independent, breathing out the air of sanguine, grave delight. Watching him made one feel like an unwholesome face-flannel.

José would pick us up about eleven and we'd go round the bay. Learning to water-ski with a careless driver at the wheel can be a painful business. Half an hour of this bone-pounding keel-haul was enough for Oscar and myself, but Tony snapped and catapulted into the foaming wake for hours until he reluctantly agreed to pause for lunch. We went to the same restaurant each day, a dark hut with an ill-stocked bar which served delicious langoustines, octopus and shellfish. They had a reviving effect after the morning's buffeting. We suggested to José that he might take us somewhere else, cleaner and with a less restricted menu; he smiled charmingly and continued to take us back each day. The sullen owners were his relations. Apart from a few ferocious-looking locals, we were the only customers.

After a week of listening to Tony's scornful analysis of my athletic disabilities ('You look like some old porpoise'), I was beginning to get bored with all this obsessive effort for such intermittent excitement. José revved up at furious speed towards Acapulco's inner harbour; as we bumped and crashed over the water, Tony asked him where we were going. He throttled up, shouting into the wind, 'You see. I take you someplace else.' We weaved in among the moored fishing-boats, missing them by inches.

José brought the engine down to a croak and the boat's nose back to the water. We were heading for a beach crowded with Mexican faces. Screaming children splashed and waded. It was palpably not a tourist beach and our arrival aroused some lethargic curiosity. It was the shanty-*sur-mer* end of town. As we approached the jetty, I saw a figure waving a ritual greeting. She was wearing a bikini. Even a hundred yards away, it was apparent that she would have been more than acceptable in Cannes. An abandoned tourist? As we staggered ashore, aided by the beaming José, she walked towards us, unhurriedly and gracefully. It was Francine.

Her skin, naturally dark, glistened like a coco-bean sheath, not quite what Nellie Beatrice called 'nigger brown' but a shade darker than José's, her eyes marbling an almost independent life of their own. Her teeth seemed to foam with the bright, hardening polish of the sun. There could be no doubting her pleasure at seeing us. I was so astonished to see her on that dirty, native beach that it was a while before I realized that her delight was as much centred on Tony as on myself. I had never seen her so unguarded and free or, indeed, so beautiful. I felt a wave of happy relief, almost of justifiable pride. When we had last been together, she had been so broodingly despairing. It was difficult to reconcile that with this bounding, uncautioned creature.

She took us by the hand and led us to a primitive beach café which also turned out to be run by José's relatives. Francine's tone changed when she addressed orders to them, as if she were the proprietor and they disorderly children. They were in grudging awe of her, their Latin torpor broken by her Swiss proficiency. She had retreated from the hooker's gutter to this tiny, peasant dominion.

A plump, barefoot, middle-aged woman banged down some bottles of wine. She was probably not much older than Francine. Her flesh was wizened and hung in folds beneath her knees and armpits like a lizard's throat. She pushed her belly forward as if she might bite the bottle-tops off with her yellow teeth. Francine watched her with open distaste. 'This is José's mother. Hey, Maria. Say hello to my friends from England.' Maria ignored her. Francine snapped at her in Spanish. She responded by pulling her stained dress up to her face and wiping it. José flashed a proud smile. Francine's disgust mounted. 'She's my mother-in-law too. Yes. My little old mother-in-law. Aren't you?' She turned away. 'Don't you think me and José are lucky to have such a creature to look after us?'

Tony pressed her with questions. Yes, she had married José six months ago. The boat was hers. 'He's pretty, my little monkey boy. He's beautiful, don't you think?' She looked over at him as if she might leap astride that powerful body. 'So strong, so beautiful, not like American men.'

Tony persuaded her to take us to their house. 'Is nothing to see, I tell you.' It was true. Their married quarters were a few streets from the harbour, a pedestrian run of sleeping drunks, black pigs and chickens. Their home was like all the others, little more than a mud-and-stone-built hut bleached in the sun. An antique oil-lamp burned all day, the floor was covered in rush matting and the furniture consisted of a large divan and a couple of peeling armchairs. But Francine's dressing-table, covered by a large Mexican shawl, was prominent, laid out with huge bottles of expensive scent and all the working tools of an expensive courtesan. Where could she keep her wardrobe? Her furs, her scores of shoes? What about her jewellery? Perhaps she had sold them all to buy the boat, the cafés. And José.

The others left. 'What have you done with all your smashing things?' I asked. 'No worry. I keep. They're around.' She winked. 'I'm quite a smart, Swiss girl. All those dumb Americans were wrong, weren't they, darling?' She slipped her arms round me and kissed me unhurriedly. It could swiftly have become a case of grievous bodily pleasure. I disengaged myself with some difficulty. I had no wish to confront the iron-willow power of her young brown god, nor his vengeful relatives.

She smiled a mock-reproachful smile. 'You no want me no more?' 'Of course I do. Still, you *are* married.' 'So what? I take care of José. He's like a child.' I felt a tremendous relief. It was the assurance that in spite of her surroundings, she was in control of her life, perhaps as she had never been before. She was redrawing her lipstick in the gloom. 'José, he's sweet. Can't read or write. None of them can. I teach him English. Just enough.' She kissed me again, less avidly but assuringly, like a flimsy but tender seal.

Francine and José came to dine at El Presidente. He was in a swamping borrowed suit, she was quite startling in white with long gloves and a pricey-looking evening-purse. Dozens of heads, fresh baked from the beauty parlour, turned to study this incongruous couple. We ordered several bottles of horribly sweet American champagne. José left. 'He's OK,' said Francine. 'He's gone out to play with the boys.' She was slightly drunk but fired with craving energy. 'You all look so miserable. This place . . . ' she addressed the other diners, ' . . . all these mother-fuckers from Hicksville. C'mon. I take you someplace else interesting.' She rounded us up into a taxi.

After twenty minutes we found ourselves in the outer suburbs. There was no street lighting and the few prosperous houses disappeared as we swept up a dusty track and stopped outside a small, bare fortress. There were figures of rifle-toting soldiers – or policemen – silhouetted at various vantages. Francine went over to the entrance to talk to a couple of lounging guards. Presently, she waved us to one of the dozen or so tables scattered around the forecourt. A plump mustachioed girl waddled towards us and laid down a tray with a bottle of Spanish whisky and a muddy-looking carafe of what might have been orange juice. Apart from a slumped body in a sombrero, we were the only customers.

Francine filled our glasses. 'Well, guys? OK? What you think?' A cluster of girls emerged to lean over the low balcony. The doors behind them opened and more appeared, singly and in groups. Tony sniggered rather loftily. 'Well, it's obviously a *brothel*!' His mocking falsetto cackle echoed out into the chilly stillness. Oscar looked more like the Gandhi of Threadneedle Street than ever before. We were being observed closely both by the soldiers and by the girls above. Some of them wandered down in pairs, stared at us and sprawled at the other tables.

Francine grinned. 'They want you should buy them a drink.' She immediately anticipated suspicions that she had lured us into an enterprise in which she had a percentage stake. 'Don't worry. I see you not cheated. You have a good time. You afford it.' She had adopted a pidgining of her English as phoney as the strangled Americanization of Tony's Shipley vowels. She waved at the girls, stabbing her cigarette-holder like a farmer at a sheep-pen. 'What you think, eh?' She was beginning to sound like an auctioneer. 'Yeah, well these are pretty much all dogs.' She shouted across to the soldiers in the porch. 'He says all the good things inside. I show you.'

A very bored madam or head girl led us into a whitewashed cave strewn with large cushions, low tables, chairs and rush matting, with bare coloured bulbs slung across the walls. It smelt of cigars, stale spirits, a glutinous sweet scent and things I thought it better not to identify. She went over to a rickety bamboo bar and opened several bottles of something masquerading as champagne. Francine was concentrating on the girls who paraded in and out, naked except for what were then called 'baby dolls'. Open at the top and transparent below in pubic-catching, greasy nylon, they concealed nothing.

I half expected Francine to be incensed by our undissembled, absurd dismay. Instead, she turned her thwarted fury on the head girl, 'Don't you worry. I take care of her.' They screamed at each other, fingernails flashing, noses almost locking. I feared we should all be rifle-butted. She broke off breathlessly. 'We make a mistake. However, she say she show you something.'

The girl led us upstairs into a bare pink cell containing a large bed covered by a rumple of grey sheets. A broken lamp glowed on a wooden orange-box, a hole in the wall led into what was presumably some kind of washroom. There was a large crucifix above the bed and a low bench beside it. A baby doll, reading a film magazine, watched us sourly as we were pushed down on the bench, scarcely long enough to accommodate the three of us. Another baby doll, red-haired, plump and even less wholesome than the first, was hustled into the room. She crawled reluctantly on to the bed, lugging her leg over the other girl outstretched beside her.

The raw squalor and enslaved inertia of the pantomime that followed were quite literally paralysing. Admittedly the local whisky and champagne were flailing my inside like a blunt propeller and I concentrated on the thought of the gleaming haven of the washbasin at the El Presidente Hotel. I looked straight ahead. I thought of the English Stage Company Council watching the three of us cramped together in silence confronting the heaving bed.

Francine, exasperated by the girls' sloth, became an hysterical ringmaster. 'For Christ's sake, go down on her! No, not that, *do* something. Whistle the Marseillaise in her. *Viva Mexico*, you bitch! What's the matter with you? You think we pay money for *this?*' She was almost collapsing with rage, prodding and punching them. Fortunately, it ended as quickly as it had begun. 'Let's go. We finish the shitty champagne and go someplace else.' We stumbled downstairs, Oscar shaky and muttering in appeal, 'Oh, dear. Oh, dear. It's so degrading. So degrading.' An Artistic Director of the Royal Court, its most profitable playwright and a highly regarded West End producer sat in silence on the journey back to the El Presidente.

For a few more days we met José at an appointed place, water-skied and had lunch at Francine's beach café. But Tony had begun to show impatience with her, and Oscar was increasingly wary. She made some effort to be amusing but we had intruded on her life and it had unsettled her. I began to feel that she would not be sorry when we went.

The day before we left for New York, as we were dropping her off at the harbour, she embraced me, the sea dragging her away by the knees. She whispered, 'I'm not saying goodbye tomorrow. Bye, l'il monkey! I see you sometime. Don't forget José. See Tony don't cheat him.' She ran up the beach, turned, waved and disappeared among the crowd.

There were rumours later that she had left José, clutching the proceeds from the sale of his boat, and moved back to New York or, possibly, Paris. For some years I looked out for her in likely migration places, Cannes, Geneva, Venice. But I never saw or heard of her again.

17. Pushing Thirty

The glass is falling hour by hour, the glass will fall for ever,
But if you break the bloody glass you won't hold up the weather.

Louis MacNeice, 'Bagpipe Music', 1937

Woodfall had raised the money for *The Entertainer*. In spite of Olivier, it was
to be a tightly budgeted film. His recent attempts to make a movie of *Macbeth*
had been humiliatingly rejected. We were offered the alternative contenders
of the English-speaking French star Eddie Constantine and James Cagney,
who turned it down on moral grounds.

Tony and I had gone to Rottingdean to persuade Brenda de Banzie to
repeat her stage performance. Her put-upon husband, employed as one of
Binkie's stage-managers, and her aspiring-pop-singer son listened obediently
as minuscule drinks were poured and she made her demands. Her Gilda-like
'suggestions' centred on the importance of 'developing' the part of Phoebe.
We readily agreed. Tony shot most of her embellishments with a camera empty
of film. He later played the same costly trick with Laurence Harvey in *The
Charge of the Light Brigade*.

The rest of the casting was cautiously agreed by the principal investors,
British Lion, headed by Sir Michael Balcon. Tony cast Roger Livesey as
Archie's father. I would have preferred a less cold actor with fruitier, pre-
1914 resonance. Not wishing to add to the splashing waters of unease, I didn't
pursue this. Shirley Ann Field, a young actress who had attracted attention
for her alleged association with Frank Sinatra, was to play Olivier's girlfriend,
a part which didn't exist in the play. Thora Hird, Morecambe's most famous
daughter, would be her pushy mother.

The only choice that was certain to incite fatuous controversy was that of
Archie's daughter, Jean. There was a consensus that the part was underwritten. In fact, Jean is herself a somewhat insubstantial girl, expending her
vapid emotions on cloudy universal concerns rather than the comfortless
tragedy of isolated hearts. She had an obstinate, docile earnestness which,
twenty years on, would have led her to the barbed-wire theatricals of Greenham

146

Common. Beneath those woolly hats beat conforming, mousy hearts. The image of Jean prefigured them all.

It was tricky ground. Joan Plowright, already agreed upon by Tony and Olivier, would fire the gossip columnists' tedious speculations still further. All those concerned gathered in a viewing-room in South Audley Street to look at Tony's rushes of the tests made for Geraldine McEwan and Joan. Geraldine had taken over the part at the Palace after Joan, who herself had succeeded Dorothy Tutin, and in my opinion she had been the best of the three.

The lights went up to the usual apprehensive silence that hangs over these occasions when Talent is kept waiting at the tradesman's entrance of Power. Balcon growled bad-temperedly. Harry looked sweaty and anxious. Tony was poised in one of his defensive knots. Geraldine was pregnant and an insurance liability but she had no scandalous or even kitchen-sink associations. I was certain that Balcon would plump for her. He did, quite vigorously, adding, 'That other girl simply won't do.' In the hush that followed came Jocelyn Rickards' puzzled drawl, 'Why are you against her, Sir Michael? She's a marvellous actress, will play well with Olivier and won't be intimidated by him. Why don't you settle for her?'

I managed to scoop Jocelyn off to the American Bar at the Dorchester, leaving Balcon to rage at Harry. 'Who is that girl?' he demanded. 'I won't be spoken to like that by anyone.' 'Jesus Christ, Michael,' Harry pleaded. 'She's the costume designer. And it's not just that – she's the author's mistress.'

When we all went up to Morecambe to scout for locations, a more significant rift appeared, the first of many that marred, and finally ended, my Woodfall partnership with Tony. We booked into the unwelcoming art-deco Midland Hotel. I was looking forward to wandering round the empty Winter Garden theatre and the rep where I had appeared in *Seagulls over Sorrento* while scribbling the end of *Look Back* in a deck-chair on the pier.

At dinner, talk again returned to the matter of the Plowright casting, which I had by then accepted as a *fait-accompli* in the complicated Olivier circumstances. Argument seemed to have become a daily exercise and it was not a stimulus I sought in friendship. I had little taste for public bickering and I looked to my friends for the balm of complaisance. I heard Jocelyn's voice, blown like a distracting smoke-ring. Tony's reply seemed too swift to disguise his eagerness to wound. 'You're employed to design the costumes, not to intrude your opinions on the rest of the film.'

It was an arguably deserved rebuke, but delivered with such satisfaction that I instantly took the blade as directed at myself. We all hastily agreed to meet at the Palais de Dance. In our room, Jocelyn said she would stay behind. 'You must go, but I'm not. Nor am I going to work on the film.' I was angry and didn't argue. Downstairs, Tony was waiting. 'I had to stop Jocelyn.' He sounded like a schoolteacher who has broken up a fight in the playground. 'She does go too far, you know. I mean, you must agree.' I didn't, not with the manner in which it was done, and said so.

Harry took me over to the Palais. Tony persuaded Jocelyn to join us. A lone couple were dancing under the green flashing light of the ballroom. I thought of the Gaycroft School of Dancing in North Cheam, Mrs Garret who had set me on the road to Morecambe Pier and Renee whose only expressed preferences were in the matter of Bravington rings.

I was puzzled by the fearfulness of Harry's anxiety. My own contribution to the film was virtually finished and replacing Jocelyn wouldn't be more than slightly irksome. But he looked as if the whole venture had collapsed. We travelled back to London in icily separate compartments. When we got to Lowndes Cottage, Tony made the best show of contrition he could manage. He said he had allowed his love for us both to degenerate into jealousy. He asked me to persuade Jocelyn to stay on the film. Harry poured out a rare vintage. Jocelyn agreed to carry on. But the inducements to drift in and out of Morecambe in expectation of fun and irresponsibility during the filming were effectively withdrawn.

If diffidence is the weakness of right-thinking men, I had it in abundance. However it may have appeared at the time, especially to myself, my inability to act decisively and put an end to the charade of marriage to Mary was not sustained by timidity or inertia. The debilitation of petty dissembling was humiliating and the indulgence of guilt was repugnant. My behaviour had been idiotic rather than wicked, a drift into a state of gracelessness rather than palpable sin.

Vainly, I assumed that the pains of inadequacy chafed more heavily on myself than on Mary, whose most serious wound was pride. My instinct was that if I presented the proposition to Mary that our life together was fraudulent it would only stiffen her obstinacy. Procrastination, wasteful though it was, might precipitate her into grabbing at a dignified and happier alternative. If there were other Roberts, Shaws or Webbers, cluttering up the wings, she was at least free to cue them in without loss of face.

For the time being, she still derived pleasure from presenting our faces together, particularly if they could be caught in the light of social worthiness rather than show-biz frivolity. The marriage of true minds, brains and beauty, exemplified in the Miller–Monroe honeymoon visit two years earlier, still lingered in some simple imaginations. A unique medium for its expression appeared in the recruiting exploits of the Campaign for Nuclear Disarmament, which declared itself in mid-September.

Mary determined that we should be seen together in the vanguard. The fact that our propagandist value must be negligible eluded her. She was committed to joining the public picket of Downing Street. Refusal to be alongside would be interpreted as marital disloyalty, a politicized act of adultery. Convenience was more persuasive than conviction and I agreed. Tramping up and down Whitehall, strapped to a sandwich-board, on a Saturday was preferable to an empty weekend in Stratford. We were photographed parading past the Cenotaph, sportily dressed, looking penitential and foolish, caparisoned in our message to humanity. I had once applied unsuccessfully for a job as a sandwich-board man for London Transport's Lost Property Office, and I wished I was touting cheap umbrellas and briefcases rather than self-consciously hawking peace.

I suppose each generation has its quota of prominent prigs and dupes. The learned, the gullible, the senile and vainglorious stride out to be counted. It is unsurprising that a previous generation should have responded so numbly to the contributors to *Declaration*, or that my own should feel a rheumatic chill at the giddy praise heaped upon today's *nouveaux naïfs*. But some of us, like those who preceded us, had fugitive gifts discernible to those whose principal commitment was to literature, poetry and drama rather than to pamphleteering politics.

From 1956 I had abused my intelligence and, more seriously, instinct with frolicking priggism. After 1961, came an abstemious hangover. By 1968 I was quite reformed and vilified by the priglets as 'Tory Squire'. 'Mellowed blimp', they exclaimed wittily. But, for the meantime, I played the fool fairly prettily and consistently.

The Committee of 100 held its first meeting in Friends' House on Saturday. Those present had responded to Lord Russell's invitation to come forward to form a committee that would sponsor acts of civil disobedience . . . From all accounts, its deliberations were inconclusive. The first disappointment was that there were not more well-known names among those present. Lindsay Anderson, Reg Butler, Alex Comfort, Doris Lessing, Christopher Logue, John Osborne and Arnold Wesker were there. [Not yet a first eleven. Reinforcements were promised.] Alex Comfort objected that there were not enough scientists; Rev Michael Scott was sorry there were no other clergymen and Reg Butler thought the list lacked very important people in general. [Lindsay, Arnold and the likes of myself, who had put ourselves forward as openers, were insignificant.] It was decided that the list should be longer and more impressive before any names were released for publication. [I decided to accept a half-hearted invitation to Scotland from Mary's parents, after all.] But many ideas were put forward. It was suggested that there should be direct action against military installations and centres of authority – even the Houses of Parliament. Others thought of disrupting official functions such as the Opening of Parliament or the Trooping of the Colour, or capturing the Chancellor of the Exchequer on Budget Day, or jamming the BBC and setting up pirate radio stations. The collection of funds is said to have gone well.

Manchester Guardian, 25 October 1959

This is when I should have left, hands firmly in my pockets. Once again, diffidence and ingenuous belief in some organic flexibility of human spirit led me to the same wasteful inaction with which I was conducting my personal life. But I'd no intention of associating with lunatics intent on disrupting theatricals like the Trooping the Colour, still less of throwing myself beneath the well-trained boots of British squaddies.

Mary's father, Colin, was a retired engineer and had recently moved into a mullioned, stained-glass Edwardian house on a hill above the Clyde in a suburban outpost of Glasgow called Kilcreggan. It was the coldest house in which I had ever stayed and made more comfortless by the stewardship of Mary's stepmother, a Scots Mrs Danvers, who decreed that no fire should be lit before 6.30. If you were cold you 'put a woolly on'.

Colin Ure had made a great deal of money from the manufacture of concrete pipes, had no interest in the theatre and, happily, seemed quite unaware of newspaper gossip or anything published outside the *Glasgow Herald*. His wife was scarcely friendly to me but then, like Grandma Osborne, withholding approval was one of her principles, bestowing it only on the dead or barely living. She more or less ignored me, recognizing at once a shivering southern upstart. She reserved her asperity for her stepdaughter. This reached its apex when she discovered us rising from bed in the morning wrapped in overcoats, something I hadn't done since Stella and I shared a room in Scunthorpe. Mary fumed over this domination of her father and the breach it had caused between them. However, he seemed content and waved us off cheerfully on our journey following Dr Johnson's Hebridean route.

In the same way that we had set off up Highway 1, I had no idea of any objective. I entertained some vague notions of her being comforted and invigorated by the return to familiar landscapes, that it might reassure and recharge the resilience, as I saw it, of her Scottishness. But, as we drove towards Loch Ness and Fort William, she seemed just as indifferent to the soft white beaches, inviting and protective, as she had been to the hostile glare of Nevada and Colorado. We relapsed into a misty, narcotic progress up to Oban, where Mary decided that that was enough of Scotland and we returned to Woodfall Street.

1960 began unpromisingly enough with my submitting a commissioned television play, called *A Subject of Scandal and Concern*, which was turned down with peremptory haste by Granada and resold almost immediately to Associated Television. Mary accepted the offer of replacing Claire Bloom in Christopher Fry's adaptation of Giraudoux's *Duel of Angels*, opposite Vivien Leigh and opening in Boston in late February. It was an opportunity to shine in New York and regain American interest which had not yet resulted in anything concrete in Hollywood. It was an almost perfect temporary arrangement, offering us respite from the attrition of our present pretence and Mary access to the trappings she had come to covet.

> Were it not for imagination, Sir, a man would be as happy in the arms of a chambermaid as of a Duchess.
>
> Samuel Johnson, 9 May 1778

It seemed inappropriate to go on living in what lawyers call, in their charmless way, 'the marital home', especially if I should feel constrained to invite anyone to stay. It was a prospect that offended every canon of taste. Even more important was the realization that Helen was becoming increasingly unhappy working for me. Her affection and loyalty were inviolable, but it was evident that the pressure and squalor of so much that had taken place in the preceding year had troubled her to the extent that it was affecting her health. She had become so frail-looking that I found myself feeling guilty for thrusting her into a world of such bewildering chaos and vulgarity. I could feel her pining for release like a dog.

Jocelyn had found a flat in Lower Belgrave Street and we agreed it seemed sensible for both of us to move into it. When I put this to Helen she responded as I knew she would, saying that she didn't feel able to join us. I knew that she was motivated not by dislike of Jocelyn or moral disapproval, but by relief at being offered an outlet from a burden that had become a nightmare.

She had made some practical provisions for herself. Her sister had retired from the Civil Service with a pension comfortable enough to keep them both. So she told me, and it would have been hard to disbelieve anything she ever said. My accountant devised a legal hand-out (less than sympathetically, as there was no sex involved) and I could supply her with whisky, untipped cigarettes and theatre tickets. It was a tearful parting for us both, one of those death-in-life leavings. I felt wretched watching her patter up Woodfall Street for the last time. How differently my throat had cleared as Mary disappeared through the flight-gate to New York. How bitter is lovelessness both to suffer and to inflict. More than anything I have dreaded the despair of its remembrance and the threat of its repeat.

The flat in Lower Belgrave Street consisted of a tall, windowed drawing-room adjoining the dining-room, which looked on to a terrace garden which Jocelyn soon filled with climbing roses, honeysuckle and clematis. It was only a few yards from Ebury Street but it was quiet enough to lunch in during the early spring days to come. Above the kitchen were a large study and a smaller one for an incoming secretary. I had few possessions and Jocelyn left most of hers in Eaton Square, so the move was like little more than changing digs. It was extremely cheerful and we settled in gratefully.

It was the first time I had shared this kind of domestic comfort with anyone, and the next six months were the most uninterruptedly private I had known since the year at Arundel Terrace in Brighton with Stella. Jocelyn cooked huge, elaborate lunches, which were followed by long, lazy afternoons. Occasionally we went to the theatre, the cinema or a restaurant, but we ventured out rarely and there were few visitors. Most evenings Jocelyn would curl up with Henry James while I worked or turned on the television, which she resolutely refused to watch.

The rare visitors were usually figures from her recent past. I liked most of her male friends and ex-lovers. Her taste in female companions seemed to me pretty execrable. None of them appeared to exhibit any of her generous gifts of affection and loyalty. Most of them seemed snobbish, avid, calculating star-fuckers. Women who are encouraged to complain of 'harassment' have never felt the nasty draught that whistles round a man subjected to female scrutiny. The masculine leer at least is warmed by the breath of inquisitive lust. It may be tedious, even offensive, but it must be preferable to the rubber-glove approach of the female National Health Medical: one's brains as well as balls are up for grabs. However, I could always escape and walk down the street to Lowndes Cottage for a drink and a chat with Harry or Tony.

One visitor who didn't drive me from the house was Barbara Skelton, ex-wife of Cyril Connolly and George Weidenfeld and ex-mistress to King Farouk, a hat-trick whose taste alone aroused mild curiosity. She would arrive at midday looking as if she had been aroused by the all-clear siren after a night crouched in an air-raid shelter. Jocelyn has described a typical ensemble: a pair of man's striped flannel pyjamas, a cashmere pullover covered by a djellaba and several shawls, thick woolly socks and fur-lined slippers, the lot topped off by a sheepskin-lined suede coat and a pair of mittens. It was the perfect outfit for weekending with the Ures at Kilcreggan.

Barbara would fall, bleary-eyed, through the front door and make directly for the kitchen, muttering, 'My God, I'm ravenous.' Once in there, she would open the refrigerator and methodically finish off all the leftovers. She was an upper-class version of the woman in N.F. Simpson's *One Way Pendulum*, who 'came in' daily to 'clear up' the debris of food left behind from the previous night. Like Simpson's lady who 'did' for food, she was undaunted by bulk. Refusing to acknowledge defeat by a surviving jar of pickles, she'd say, 'I'll come and finish them up for you tomorrow.' In spite of this vacuum-cleaning talent she was always Jack-Sprat lean. I found her amusing in her remote fashion, although too thin for my fancy. I was unquestionably not fat or worldly enough for her own.

The male exception to my acceptance of Jocelyn's drop-ins was Professor Freddie Ayer, who would invite himself to lunch from time to time. It was simple enough for me to find an alternative engagement; my presence would have been intrusive and indelicate. I had nothing to contribute to their trips down the groves of memory and could only inhibit something that both of them wished to preserve. It was a principle of continuity that I thoroughly endorsed, even though I felt it was misplaced in this case. I was in no position to pass judgement on such inexplicable lapses.

After one of these extended lunches I found Jocelyn, her face streaked with tears, more upset than I had ever seen her. It confirmed my view that Ayer was possibly the most selfish, superficial and obtuse man I had ever met, spitting out his commonplace opinions to an audience mystified by the tricks of manipulated sleight-of-mind. He had announced that he was contemplating marriage to an American, but was undecided whether the match fulfilled his standards of wisdom and self-esteem. He offered his ex-mistress a two-card choice: he was prepared to marry the American unless Jocelyn should feel impelled to offer herself as an alternative. Anyone less kindly would have kicked this pear-shaped Don Giovanni down the stairs and his cruel presumption with him. She could find nothing to say except, 'But, Freddie, it's too late.'

Meanwhile, back on the Rialto, Woodfall's activities began to attract attention, although it was not until the release of *Saturday Night and Sunday Morning* that the attention became friendly.

Woodfall is *British*. The brains behind it belong to John Osborne and Tony Richardson, men who are willing to sink their last sixpence – and their hearts – into the films they make. [Willing to sink my last sixpence, alas, and stupidly.] When rebellion is in the air, Osborne is pretty sure to be in on the act.

Alexander Walker, *Evening Standard* 27 October 1960

It's surprising how patriotism is bestowed on commercial success, particularly when it looks like penetrating the foreign market. Before this our Britishness went for very little. *The Entertainer* was dogged by rumour and auguries of disaster. Negotiations with the censor, John Trevelyan, dragged on for three months. He hobbled us with an X-certificate – 'a borderline case, not as X-ish as some' – which ensured that it would be turned down as the entry for the Royal Film Performance, which might have helped its general release.

Then there was the matter of 'those bloody seagulls'. A legend had grown, encouraged on both sides of Wardour Street, that whole sequences of dialogue were inaudible – a calumny against deserting the studios for location shooting. Finally, there was a newspaper invention that Olivier had confiscated the print because he refused to allow Tony to supervise the soundtrack. Even Oscar Beuselinck managed to bring a successful libel action against that one.

A Taste of Honey ended its West End run and, mercifully, my own disappearing supply of all-British sixpences. We were free at last to start casting the role of the young girl in the film version. Several hundred were auditioned and we were obliged to test all the unpromising starlets who were under contract. There were plenty of talented young actors worthy of a calculated gamble but there was a dearth of actresses. There was no equivalent of the so-called 'northern' school of young men spilling out of drama schools or slogging away unseen in remote reps.

As it was, the part found the right candidate, a young, inexperienced seventeen-year old from Liverpool. Her name was Rita Tushingham. As with Albert Finney, the money-men went into a frenzy: 'Jeez, you can't put that up over the marquee.' Film financiers have an illiterate belief in the power of words. But we had some fun out of their useful publicity: 'Kitchen Sink men discover their Ugly Duckling.'

18. Off the Peg

A Gentleman is one to whom discourtesy is a sin and falsehood a crime.

Richard Brathwaite, *The English Gentleman*, 1641

The spring and summer of 1960 passed even more pleasurably and unevent-fully than the days splashing about on the deck of the *Egret* five years earlier. There was an almost sybaritic sense of siege comfort in Lower Belgrave Street and my first taste of the pleasures as well as the constraints of a sustained domestic regime.

I had to overcome my natural indolence and start writing again, to prove to myself that my nerve was only faltering not failed. Martin Luther was with me still. I wanted to write a play about the interior religious life. I was not yet reconciled to an inheritance of the perpetual certainty of doubt. This effort alone linked easily with the uncertainty of faith, and Luther's explosive revel-ation of its precedence over good works was irresistible.

Justification by faith and not works, the notion that good intentions are not enough, seemed like a justification for any anarchy I might have imposed on my own actions, some key to plunder. Applied, or reduced, to daily experience, it might be a case for the supremacy of imagination over doing good, of sceptics over the 'carers', of the undissembling over the radical pharisees. It pointed the way to resolving the severest doubt of Christian faith, which, to me, was its taint of insurance, of guarantee. In whatever form faith revealed itself, it was emphatically not the same as certainty. 'Oh, Lord, help thou my unbelief.' A modest request, surely, reasonable and dignified.

I managed to discard some of my natural engaged unease, working quite robustly on the play, my head buzzing with visual images as much as history and argument – the frightening *Garden of Earthly Delights* of Bosch and Bach. It was essential to find a replacement for Helen Henderson, and an efficient one. I wasn't sure of the kind of secretary I was seeking. Certainly not one who could be smooth-talked on the telephone, intimidated by pressmen or saddened by the vagaries of my personal life.

Jocelyn came up enthusiastically with a girl lately off the boat from

Melbourne. I liked her immediately and took her on. Joy Parker was frank, funny and strangely friendly for a native of that suspicious, benighted land. I think I was the only pom she spoke to apart from bus conductors and the man who read the gas meter in the flat she shared with three compatriots in Earls Court. At work there were Jocelyn and Alec, whose remembrance of and attachment to their homeland were very separate.

It was an arrangement that worked well for all of us. After Helen's granite gentility, there was heady pleasure in employing such a cool bouncer; Joy could blow the Slickeys off the telephone within seconds.

She spent most non-hairwashing evenings at the Down Under Club. From here, she introduced me to Fosters lager and the early records of Barry Humphries and I immediately took to them both. It intrigued me that she should have responded so heartily to Humphries' material, which mocked girls like her who had got on the P&O liner and wrote home complaining letters before it had left the shadow of the Suez Canal about the unbelievable price of lamb chops and the Brits' hygiene – or neglect of it.

In 1969 I was asked by some intermediary to write a programme note for the sleeve of Humphries' latest recording. I couldn't think of any reason for the invitation but, partly as a tribute to that early discovery made for me by Joy, I sent it off. It was used, although I never received any acknowledgement from Humphries. The Australian mystic turned megastar was then, as now, a true son of his native land.

> Writing their parts has too often been like serving a puffed-up actor, [or] bedding a plain woman out of kindliness rather than lust . . . It only excites their fury and revenge.
>
> Handel, in *God Rot Tunbridge Wells*

The whips and scorns to be expected by an unknown playwright are nothing to those endured by those who discover that neither reputation, success nor standing will prevent them being sandbagged frontally, publicly, privately or from behind. The unexpected blow from a stranger is more easily dismissed than some young Hal you once caroused with giving you the frozen lip from beneath his critic's crown, clutching his orb of Nomination as he plants a passing whack from Bankability's sceptre. Actors bear the ceremony without forfeiting the heart's ease those that serve them must forgo. Inside every playwright there is a Falstaff, gathering like a boil to be lanced by his liege employers – fashion and caprice. That discovery was still to come.

John Osborne is being unusually quiet just now. What is he up to? I'm told he has a new play on the stocks – a play about Martin Luther.

Evening Standard, 11 March 1960

John Osborne has been tuning himself both spiritually and physically . . . a visit to the Community of the Resurrection at Mirfield at the invitation of Father Trevor Huddleston. He has also become a regular visitor to a London gymnasium where he spends about an hour weight-lifting and skipping. He is expected to surface in a couple of weeks I am told.

Daily Express, 6 April 1960

How anyone had come by these two unremarkable items was a little puzzling and depressing. Edward Bolton, the proprietor of the gymnasium, had befriended George after a recent illness and helped him in his recovery. Oxford-educated and reticent, he seemed rather austere to me and not the kind of man who would discuss his clients with gossip columnists. I could see that his soft manner and monkish gravity would be persuasive and comforting to George. In the face of the ever-open beaks of the young Royal Court company and the dying battle-fatigue of life with Sophie coming to an end in Lower Mall, he looked for more gentle affinity among the male, middle-aged and stoic.

The gym attracted other acolytes, like Olivier and Robert Stephens. Keen to undergo some reasonable spiritual and physical rigour, perhaps to penetrate the clouds of unknowing thickening above my head and scourge the spreading flesh from Jocelyn's afternoon-long lunches, I set out a couple of times a week in the early morning for my solitary work-out against flab of form and spirit. The exercises, mostly pulling weights, emphasized strengthening the spine against all the strain the world imposed on it. They seemed admirably lucid, but extremely punishing. On my return, I would grasp at Jocelyn's remedy of black coffee and brandy. Both flesh and spirit were stubbornly unwilling as well as weak.

Bolton told me that my frame and size demanded more muscle, more strength to sustain their engagement in an alien space. I could believe it. The evidence seemed only too obvious. After several weeks I seemed to feel minimally less ill, with undiscovered muscle appearing on my neck and chest. My collar size changed from 14½ to 16. No longer Aubrey Beardsley on a crash diet, I looked bloated without and felt coarse within. I decided that whether it was a mutual allergy of conflicting psychic temperament and physical metabolism, the combination of gym and Jocelyn was inimical. A flirtatious

American reporter told me that I reminded her of a quarterback for the Chicago Bears. It was back to Jocelyn but never again to the gym.

I also met Trevor Huddleston through George's intervention. I can't remember the exact circumstance that brought them together, but Huddleston was the very sort of radical populist the Court's few followers and many detractors wished to see sweeping up the steps of Sloane Square. South Africa and apartheid, that golden gift to the radical conscience, were among the company's pet obsessions. Oscar Lewenstein raised no smiles when he pronounced that hotels should replace the Gideon Bible in their bedrooms with Genet's *The Blacks*. I had placed an embargo on productions of my own work in South Africa, to the chagrin of Margery Vosper and the dubious cultural deprivation of Capetown and Johannesburg.

Huddleston had roused attention with *Nought for your Comfort*, a best-selling polemic about his adopted homeland. He was a member of the Anglican Community of the Resurrection and a commanding figure even to foot-slogging unbelievers like George. I almost wrote 'even to Christians'. He was very much an emergent figure of that time when the tide of secular absorption was beginning to submerge the Church of England. Glamour was one of his most seductive credentials as an acceptable front man for the humanitarian infantry impatient to break heads in Whitehall. He was handicapped by elitist vows of poverty, obedience and chastity, but his physical appearance and demeanour enabled him to achieve that gift for universal ministry which became identified as 'charisma'.

It also helped to explain George's response to such vulgar appeal. Like Beckett's, Huddleston's persona of saintliness, even more than his undoubted gifts and sincerity, had been blessed by his very facial sculpture. The turbulent priestly head might have been cast from the same block as Sam's, cropped, scarred to the bone of suffering, with the same unblinking gaze of fallen sainthood, gouged by anguish, impervious even to grace. It was the mask of transparent nobility. Few masks of virtue can have been so miraculously fashioned, and George knew all about the uses and authority of the mask. He had been preaching its potential for integrity and power for twelve years.

At this time Huddleston was Prior of the London house of the Community in Holland Park. He was about to return to Africa to take up the bishopric of Masai. He invited George to dinner, and George suggested I might like to come with him. We had an excellent soufflé, salad and, I think, red burgundy. Like many priests, most bishops and all politicians, Huddleston, it seemed to me, was possessed by a driving vanity. Such a frailty underlined rather than diminished his inhuman perfection. Perhaps it even justified the technique of George's comic half-mask, which transformed the inner persona of vanity into an equally valid expression of saintliness, a convincing case of the right actor having found the exact mask. It was not such a preposterous speculation, even if it illuminated George's theatrical apprehension of character rather than the nature of charismatic priests, which was occupying me at the time.

Huddleston had been Novice Master at Mirfield and suggested I might care to stay there. I took the train to Huddersfield and for the next week relished a kind of indolence in a setting of minimal rigour. It was a brief respite from the languor I had been enjoying in Lower Belgrave Street, an invigorating outer world that was also a state of retreat.

The house, built by some Victorian iron-master, was dark with wide rooms and long corridors and overlooked a fiery, smoky landscape of scarred hillsides and forests of satanic mills jostling the Community's Dunsinane. Its prospect was a shivering rub-down of the senses. Only plainsong rose above the muffled wind of croaking birdsong. The silence observed in all communal rooms was broken by the sounds of sandalled feet on stone, utensils on wood and the single bell ringing the offices of prime, terce, sext, none and compline. It was as bracing as the view from my small window.

In the mornings I would read and wander around the grounds, where it was permitted to speak to those working in the gardens. One especially garrulous novice showed me the open-air theatre he was building in a grotto. I would walk over the moors, descend on pubs tucked away in hillsides and listen to the Priestley, non-priestly conversation of the customers, smoking my pipe in a corner and drinking enough of the local brew to ensure a decent snooze on my narrow iron bedstead.

After the opening prayer at supper the restrictions of the day broke. Fifty or so straining tongues slipped their lips into a noise that gave fresh resonance to the very onomatopoeia of 'chatter', a mixed Babel of high table, saloon bar and chorus boy's dressing-room. The palpable sense of relief created an instant conviviality. Some of the visitors were incense-queens and Mary-fetishists who came on holiday to Mirfield from one-room lodgings in towns like Rochdale, where they lived surrounded by ecclesiastical kitsch, vestments and assorted liturgical campery. Affectionately known as the Walsingham Matildas, their annual pilgrimages were a source of kindly amusement. In return for a few simple tasks they enjoyed an ecclesiastical breakaway comparable to an alcoholic weekending in a brewery.

One was merely required to put anonymously what one could afford in the box. I assisted one of the brothers twice with the washing-up, which was all chatter and no hardship. On leaving I stuffed £50 into the Guest Master's receptacle, which seemed about right for the best value I could remember.

The only office I attended was compline. This end to the day seemed to invoke not only rest but a sense of soothed watchfulness, which I might do well to remember, as in the antiphon to the *nunc dimittis*:

> Take ye heed, watch ye all and pray, for ye know not when the time is. Watch thee, therefore, because ye know not when the Master of the house cometh, at even, or at midnight, or at cockcrow, or in the morning; lest coming suddenly, peradventure, he should find you sleeping.

> Tedious, mostly class-conscious stuff . . . Osborne, the acknowledged head of the Angry Young Man school (or racket) of dramatists . . . Ought to have had the kind of education which encourages people to think for themselves: all this blether about the Wicked Establishment is the new, off-the-peg clothing of the mind.
>
> Reader's report on *The Entertainer* to the British Board of Film Censors

The film of *The Entertainer* opened at the end of July at the Odeon, Marble Arch, not exactly a prime site for a film starring Laurence Olivier. The general impression was that we were lucky to be tucked in at all at the wrong end of Oxford Street. The notices were predictable. 'How did Olivier get mixed up in this farrago?' 'Not even Olivier can make this entertaining.' The posh papers, even when polite, couldn't be described as money-notices. 'The film is gloomy. Gloom is not my cup of tea. Osborne is not my plate of biscuits,' said the *Observer*. 'But I think it's a film that should be seen.' Thank you, Miss Lejeune.

The film was either too close to the original or not removed enough. 'Mr Osborne is at once too Brechtian and not Brechtian enough.' As my school-friend Mickey Wall used to favouritely quote: '*Ira furor brevis est*' – 'Anger is a short madness.' I had begun to learn that George's half-mask, the comic one, was more effective than the full tragic one.

> I am not interested in the past but only in the future. But I do believe in the inspiration of tradition.
>
> George Devine, New York lecture, 1960

It is invariably those who have detested or distrusted your work from the outset who complain most vehemently of their sense of betrayed disappointment at your subsequent efforts. Having begun to assimilate this rule, I was in no hurry to finish *Luther* and press it on George. As ever, he was meticulous in concealing any hint of anxiety or impatience. Margery, for different reasons, was almost discouraging me to present myself again after the garish indignities of *Slickey*.

My prevarication in completing the play was only partly encouraged by a determination not to be goaded into a precipitate denial of the popular rumour of my creative death. I was excited by the way in which I had, I believed, resolved the 'technical problem'. I was at least certain that I had infused some vitality into that moribund genre, the English 'historical' play. I was confident that it had enough brawn of language. I forgot that no one *listens*. Fry and Eliot almost got away with it until their 'language' was exposed as the cumbersome armoury of the feeble warrior-poet. It was not my writing arm that was holding me back from the lists but my exposed inner and religious uncertainties.

In May, Vivien had issued a press statement revealing that Olivier had asked for a divorce in order to marry Joan Plowright. Later she had appeared on television looking pale and ill, wearing the fullest mask of Betrayed Wife *and* idolized Star. There was no reason to believe that the grief behind it was dissembled. Her rabid devotion to Larry, however ruinous, was incontrovertible.

When Olivier and Plowright opened in Ionesco's *Rhinoceros* at the Court they were hemmed in by newsmen within minutes. Joan went immediately to a 'safe house' and left the play. It was understandable but undignified to be driven into hiding. George and Tony were deeply immersed in the ensuing public melodrama, almost comparable to the abdication of Edward VIII. 'What's that coming down the street?/ Mrs Simpson's ugly feet.'

Of course, I was intrigued, and also concerned for Larry, whose glimpse of freedom from Vivien's mounting madness was blighted by the vulgar furore which enveloped his hubristic sense of National Dignity as much as his hopes of deliverance from years of guilt and unhappiness. This was clear when I visited him in his temporary foxhole in Glebe Place. He confided little that was not public knowledge, but even the unease of his more trivial preoccupations, like royal esteem, were consumed with wild, terrible pain. It was as if Nelson had been caught with his hand in the Admiralty till.

By the end of the summer it was inescapable that I should break my retreat in Lower Belgrave Street, that I would have to summon some sort of resolution to pump out the blocked drain of matrimony. I braced myself for what must surely be an acrimonious and wounding encounter with Mary in America. There had been little communication between us since she joined the cast of *Duel of Angels*, where she was in harness with the famously wronged Vivien. I was concerned that she would try to adopt the same tragic mask. She could not hope to match Vivien's authentic effect but it would be disagreeable and, although remarriage was not in my mind, would cause Jocelyn mischievous distress. I could already hear Beuselinck: 'No, son, I'm afraid she's got you by the short and curlies there!'

The run of *Duel of Angels* in New York had been interrupted by a strike of technical workers. The management decided to send it on a national tour, starting in Los Angeles. Mary had accepted Tony's invitation to stay with him at the house he had rented from Zsa Zsa Gabor in Westwood Village. George and Jocelyn Herbert were also there. George was badly in need of respite from the tit-swingers at the Court and was shortly to lecture in New York and give master-classes in Restoration acting.

Tony had contrived a deal with Merrick which only he could have achieved. In the evenings he would rehearse *A Taste of Honey* in Los Angeles and open there before a brief tour and its Broadway première. During the day George would deputize while Tony was filming *Sanctuary* for Fox. It was impossible to think of any New York producer contemplating such a split commitment, let alone Merrick. Persuasion was Richardson's most deadly gift.

As always with his urgent invitations, one's flattered delusion that they were an exclusive mark of favour, seductively revived in the soil of past-remembered chaos, was immediately dispelled on arrival. It was further confounded by *his* half-mask of injured astonishment, protesting that all other guests, like Joan Plowright, who was playing the lead in *A Taste of Honey*, were self-invited. 'I mean I don't know *why* he's/she's here! They just *arrived*. They won't say when they're *going*!'

He had assigned Mary the master-bedroom overlooking the swimming-pool. Joan was obliged to swelter in a tool-cupboard beside the boiler-house. In the August humidity, it can't have been much fun. George and the terminally tired Jocelyn Herbert had been packed off elsewhere. Jocelyn's 'tiredness' was a refinement of her mask of 'saintliness'. It assumed, and still does, a Goya expression of inner suffering.

Zsa Zsa's house – 110 Montana Street, West Los Angeles – was the kind of Hollywood 'home' that always surprises outsiders like myself by its suburban scale. There was the obligatory bar in the drawing-room and just enough room to accommodate a baby grand. Visitors wandered in and out at all hours. They were mostly tanned young men from Malibu or Muscle Beach in uniform T-shirts, white shorts and sneakers. 'Hi, John,' they would say politely. 'Pleasure to meet you. I'm Don.' Or Bob. Or Rick. Or Dick.

Regulars round the pool included Zachary Scott, a saturnine young actor called Tom Tryon who later turned up as Tony's companion at the Broadway opening of *A Taste of Honey*, Yves Montand and Simone Signoret. Montand was appearing in *Sanctuary* and was about to co-star with Marilyn Monroe in

Let's Make Love. Signoret was present to keep a very cold, Gallic eye on him. This simmering drama fired Mary with excitement and loyal indignation. It also deflected any immediate attempts to rationalize our own less starry dilemma.

Tony's more intellectual friends tended to 'drop by' around midnight. This was unusual in Los Angeles even then. Hollywood's Cinderellas had to be up for make-up at six o'clock or back at the rewrite desk by eight-thirty. Only the Ugly Sisters could stay up drinking. These were headed by Christopher Isherwood and his long-time companion the portraitist Don Bachardy, unkindly dubbed 'the Frozen Madonna' because he rarely spoke above a breathy whisper. I enjoyed Christopher's company, and his predator's gaze and impish, schoolboyish enthusiasms, although his reminiscences of England and Berlin were more intriguing than his anticipations of the 'gay rights' crusade.

A stranger arrived during one of Christopher's visits. He was tall, wearing high-heeled expensive cowboy boots and matching hat. His name – Lyall Flewitt – was as striking as his appearance. As he listened to Christopher's fancies, his disapproval became clear. When he left, he drawled feelingly: 'Well, it sure has been something, listening to this goddam bunch of English liberals. Guess you none of you know what the fuckin' hell you're talking about. Goodnight to you all, *gentlemen*.' Tony recrossed his tireless legs and gave out that shrill neigh of disbelief. 'Well, what about *that*!'

It transpired that Lyall Flewitt, far from having dropped in straight from Dodge City, was a highly rated Wall Street financier, which might have accounted for Tony's current fascination with stocks and bonds. He turned up later in the role of Master of the Horse in the film of *The Charge of the Light Brigade*, another recurring figure in the Magical Mystery Life of Tony Richardson.

I decided to delay any confrontation with Mary until *Duel of Angels* moved to San Francisco. On the Sunday evening before her departure we attended the technical dress rehearsal of *A Taste of Honey*. It was the usual stop–go process of seemingly insoluble hold-ups and delays, abetted by American panic. After about ten hours, Tony went backstage to give 'poor little Joanie' her notes. He suggested that the four of us should meet in a nearby bar. I explained to Mary that it would be better to leave them alone, but her sense of rivalry was intense. She had her own 'notes' about Joan's hair-style, skirt length and cack-handed use of Leichner, and she was intent on delivering them.

Increasingly drunk, she did so, ignoring Tony's pumping foot and Nellie-Beatrice black stares. Finally, I hustled her out of the bar into the dawn of downtown Los Angeles. She shrieked like a Kelvinside housewife resisting rape as I pulled her across a drab square littered with slumbering wrecks. She wrenched away, screaming with a cry which almost rivalled Olivier's legendary Shylock shriek of a mink with its tongue frozen to an ice-cap. On she plunged, fortunately in the direction of Westwood Village, scattering astonished early-risers on their way to work.

I walked back slowly in the clearing smoke. Tony was already home, drink in hand, revved up by the hysteria of others. Poor little Joanie had gone to sleep in the taxi and was safely tucked in beside the boiler. Mary was in the bedroom. '*Well!* And how are *you?*' We began talking about the play. I assumed that tears, rage and drink had done their trick, until Mary appeared at the doorway, quite naked, and waddled with drunken deliberation across the room and out on to the patio. Tony shot me one of his astonished head-jerks. We went on talking.

There was a resounding splash from the pool and then silence. We listened. 'What do you think she's doing?' he said in his accused-fascination tone. 'No idea. Can't say I care.' 'I mean, do you think she's *drowning* herself?' 'Quite possibly.' There was no sound at all from the pool. 'I mean, don't you think *you* should *do* something?' 'No.' Then. 'I mean she's not swimming.' 'Maybe she's just waving.' 'Don't you think you should go and see?' 'No.' 'Perhaps she's gone *under*!' 'Let her drown. Have another drink.'

It did begin to seem a long time since that one peremptory splash. Tony snapped his legs together and strode out into the garden. The sound of furious splashing came through the French windows. Tony reappeared with Mary's dripping, apparently unconscious body in his arms and stumbled with it into the bedroom. I could just make out her gasping voice, and then it became silent again. 'She's gone to sleep,' he said, as if an exhausting day had ended happily.

When I went to bed she was sleeping heavily, thumb in mouth, curled up beneath a towel. In the morning I was woken by her cheerful chirruping as she splashed in the pool. As I fumbled towards the Gabor bar to mix the first Bloody Mary of the day, I glimpsed her smiling indulgently at little Joanie, who was engrossed in dipping bread into a huge plate of kidneys bubbling beneath the noonday haze spread over sweltering Westwood Village.

19. *Never to be Seen Again*

I lived a very long time in a very flattering, very artificial, very insincere
kind of world – the world of an actress.

Vivien Leigh in Tennessee Williams, *The Roman Spring of Mrs Stone*

It is indeed depressing about the play & it has been a horrid time but I
am sure the decision not to bring it to London is the right one. It is not
John Osborne, darling . . . I think John Osborne would be very surprised
if this particular play were attributed to him!!

Vivien Leigh in a letter to her first husband, Leigh Holman,
on appearing in *La Contessa*, by Paul Osborn

I stayed in Los Angeles a few days longer for the opening of *A Taste of Honey*,
while Mary went on to San Francisco. When I rejoined her there, I found she
had booked into a very scruffy hotel near the port, partly for reasons of
economy but also because it had a Scottish-sounding name. It was the sort of
place where it was always night-time in the lobby and the desk-clerk looked
like Elisha Cooke Jr. For me, luxury had become an easeful necessity against
foreignness and especially the suicidal anxiety which the West Coast induced
in me. I had a dread of collapsing in some bar with no one to supervise the
handling of my corpse on to a British plane home. I could easily imagine
Richardson's satisfaction as he watched me being lowered into the Californian
sod. 'The trouble with you, Johnnie, is that you're so fucking British.'

When Mary saw my genuine dismay at the prospect of spending the next
three weeks in such a dismal dump, she telephoned Vivien, who immediately
sent someone round for our luggage and booked us into a suite in her own
hotel, the Huntingdon. Vivien was installed there with her twenty pieces of
luggage, her Siamese cat, a Renoir, a Picasso and the bewildered man in her
life, the actor Jack Merivale, who was also appearing in the play.

My panic at the idea of death or divorce in the Hotel-of-Scottish-origin
subsided and I set out quite cheerfully for the performance of *Duel of Angels*.
I have a tendency to allow myself to become over-affected by the nature of

audiences. Their pleasure enflames my prejudice, their indifference stirs my rage. I remember George's words: 'Look at them! *That's* what you're playing to.' This piece of French puffery had been sprinkled with fairy dust by the director Robert Helpmann, and at least the San Francisco audience responded to his unmistakable signposts. The Los Angeles promenaders regarded any visit to the playhouse as a gruelling intellectual marathon.

Kenneth Tynan, who had described Leigh's Blanche du Bois as 'a Hedda Gabler of the gin palaces', had mounted a crude campaign to belittle her frail gift and prove that she was personally hobbling Larry's flight into giant destiny. He mocked her Lady Macbeth as 'more niminy-piminy than thundery-blundery . . . quite competent in its small way'. Olivier never forgave him for this kindless strategy. He feared such attempts to drive a wedge into their royal status would exile her permanently to Harley Street and make his own desperate attempts more exhausting and damaging than ever. When Tynan proposed himself to Olivier as the National Theatre's dramaturge, Larry passed the letter from his prospective Duke of Clarence to his new wife rasping, 'How shall we slaughter the little bastard?'

Except as Blanche, it had always seemed to me that Vivien adopted a breathy, lisping intimation of comic gentility which transformed her from the lass-unparalleled into an enunciating doll. Her Cleopatra at the St James's had sounded less like flutes than like a pussy-cat purring through the treble end of a mouth-organ. She sounded like Violet Elizabeth Bott as she mouthed, 'If it be love indeed, tell me how much.' She threatened to scream and scream until she made herself sick.

Now, she appeared to have undergone a transformation. The pitch had given way from kittenish wheedling to the slicing, raw-throated buzz of her off-stage natural voice. She strode the stage, a reborn Scarlett with the fires of Atlanta and despised love within the eighteen-inch waist newly let out. It was defiant, desperate and moving as she swathed her way through the fog of French bombast and twaddle. She almost redeemed it by naked personal courage.

Vivien was revelling in the hospitality and privileges accorded to a monarch-in-exile. It gave her an opportunity to enjoy her gifts as a hostess and 'leader of the company'. She took them out on fishing and sailing trips, picnics in the redwoods. She bought an open white Thunderbird, upholstered in black, and, to the horror of her agent, gave it to Jack Merivale, much to his embarrassment. In daylight she covered her rather thin hair and part of her face from the brutality of the light with a scarf, Blanche-like. After the performance, she would drop the scarf and organize a party at a restaurant.

One night she took us, Saltzman-style, to the grandest Chinese in town. It overlooked the bay in a fishing village called Sausalito, an American attempt at St Ives and a hive of every imaginable full-time phoney. It confirmed all Vivien's enthusiasms. We sat down at a large table, exquisitely decorated, in the middle of which a tower of dishes revolved. She set it on a happy roar. Suddenly bedlam broke out among the diners, hitherto silenced by the spectacle of the banqueting glitter of Scarlett's court. I identified the sounds of American panic: splashes, screams and sounds of drowning. Waiters, hat-check girls and restaurant 'captain' were about to jump ship like the crew of a doomed Italian liner.

There was a long bout of utter confusion. The police and fire department jammed the foyer. Vivien's men stood firm and British, trying to order drinks from the distraught barman. A searchlight finally picked up two figures floundering in the water. I half expected Merivale to nonchalantly strip off his dinner-jacket and plunge in. The police looked gun-happy.

The fire department dumped two wet bodies distastefully on to the floor like a pair of palpitating fish. Downing her drink, Vivien – followed obediently by Mary – parted the awed spectators and, with the dexterity of trained nurses, peeled the clothes off the two gasping survivors. Vivien ordered her wrap and Mary's coat. They covered the bodies with mink and tweed. They rubbed the limbs of these local illicit lovers until the woman came round, screeching, 'That's *my* man! You *leave* him.' Mary and Vivien returned to the bar to some scattered, guilty applause. Merivale muttered, 'Bit like the Battle of Britain, eh? That kind of style's pretty foreign to them.' He took Vivien's sopping mink from her with a casual kiss.

One of her current enthusiasms was a young stand-up comedian called Bob Newhart. She was infectiously elated at the prospect of introducing us to her new discovery and took a large party to a place called the 'Button Down Club'. Since her last visit, a new act had been inserted before Newhart's. I was sitting beside her. Presently, to great applause, a young man appeared dressed as Archie Rice. He proceeded to give an atrocious parody of Olivier in *The Entertainer*, ending up with a grotesque version of 'Why Should I Care?' I could feel her frame tighten. When the act came to a merciful close, Vivien, defying any expectation that she might justifiably walk out, politely joined in the rather puzzled American reception. It was like presenting a mother with her dead child. I grasped her hand. When Newhart appeared, she sat through-out the performance she had brought us to share, attempting to laugh with so many eyes on her, pressing her fingers deeply into my palm.

Back at the Huntingdon, I found myself alone with Helpmann in the drawing-room of Vivien's suite. From the bedroom there were sounds of genuine hysteria and Merivale's soothing tones. Helpmann offered me a drink and spread himself in a pouting pose of balletic elegance. Possibly the demands of his craft had reduced him to a thin bloat of spiderishness. His many-ringed fingers stabbed at me. The huge, swivelling eyes spat out distrust as he made it plain that it was my own presence that was mostly responsible for Vivien and Jack's distress. It had been a cheap attempt at ill-disguised seduction.

As I tried to restrain my anger, he shifted his target to Larry with a series of anecdotes illustrating his pathetic delusions of grandeur and his gratuitous cruelty to Vivien. I knew all of them to be distortions but, before I had time to escape this invidious web, he sent a fluttering little boomerang into my lap, which must have been directed to the next room. 'I hear – from everyone – that you've got . . . ' bristling pause – 'a huge – cock.' He went on accusingly, 'Well, that's what *everyone* tells me. Of course, you know, Larry's got a *very* small one. I've slept with both of them.' The bedroom door was closed by now.

When I saw Vivien the following evening it was as if the incident at the Button Down Club had never taken place. A few days later, she gave a farewell party for Mary, who was leaving the show at the end of the San Francisco run. She kissed me goodbye with unfeigned affection and asked me to come and see her when she returned to London. I was glad that she might want to see me, I couldn't believe that she would dissemble, but I suspected it was an unlikely eventuality. I was right. I never saw her again.

English Stage Company

To: CO Jewish Rifles.
From: CO Jewish Brigade.
Priority: Most immediate.
Classification: Slightly less than most secret but more secret than most.
Subject: Great news. Stop. Refer Corinthians 2 chap 3 verse 7 and keep your muzzles repeat muzzles clean. In other words, I was thrilled to hear you had got it down so quickly. We ought to be able to get it on as scheduled if we can have the script as soon as possible. Longing to read it, 'peculiar' or not.

Love,
George

George, returned from champagne receptions and ovations in New York, found himself quickly deflated by renewed assaults on his stewardship. The newspapers sniffed out the merest signs of setback and disaffection. The *Daily Mail* typified the pitch: 'The Royal Court is in the hands of a clique. Good playwrights are being squeezed out by the policy of badly written left-wing plays which belong to the 1930's.'

Luther, which I had finished weeks earlier, was all set for production, but Albert Finney, who was seemingly indispensable to its commercial success, could not be released from his contract with Lewenstein in the long-running production of *Billy Liar*. George's plans for a European tour of seven countries had also collapsed after the British Council's bland withdrawal of financial support. It was a bleak homecoming for him.

His only two fancied runners for the coming year were staked on Finney and, now, Rex Harrison, whom George had persuaded to star in Nigel Dennis's eagerly awaited special baby, a 'dark', misanthropic comedy called *August for the People*. Mary, cast out of work in mid-November, was left loose in Woodfall Street and Harrods until she began rehearsing with Tony for *The Changeling* in the New Year. I decided to accept an 'insistent' invitation from British Lion to take part in the pre-publicity campaign in New York for the première of *The Entertainer*. I was growing weary of this expedient transatlantic commuting, wanting more than anything to return to the slothful calm of Lower Belgrave Street. Gripped, temporarily at least, by catatonic procrastination, I went back to idle away the rest of 1960 between the Algonquin and Broadway or some-where, although it was made clear that I should have to return dutifully for Christmas at Woodfall Street with Mary.

Before I left, I had a farewell meeting with Harry, who had decided that it was time to end his association with Woodfall. I hoped he hadn't regretted it and I don't believe he did. But Tony and I had become like last week's greatest restaurants. Tony may have been instrumental in persuading him to make newer, more lucrative discoveries. I was a little sad. I had enjoyed Harry's company when he was at his effervescent best, before marriage tamed his bravado. Without him Woodfall would never have got started. He had fair-ground flair and uncanny taste. *Saturday Night and Sunday Morning* and *A Taste of Honey* both saw the light in Harry's bustling brown eyes. He never disowned the rest, although failure to make money was the most damnable sin of his trade.

He told me, shoulders twitching with excitement, about his next big venture. 'I've bought the Bond books,' he declared. I had just about heard of James Bond and scarcely of Ian Fleming. 'All of them. Who do you think I've got as Bond?' I tried to be interested. 'I don't know. James Mason?' 'Hell, no.' 'David Niven?' 'For Christ's sake.' Harry paused. 'Sean Connery.' 'Harry, he's a bloody Scotsman. He can hardly read!' I think my reaction pleased him. So much for my gifts of prophecy.

But you, gods, will give us
Some faults to make us men.
William Shakespeare, *Antony and Cleopatra*, v.i

The year drew to a close. Among those who had died in the past twelve months was my friend from the Savile and Brighton, Gilbert Harding, as well as Clark Gable, Vivien's bad-breathed Rhett Butler, Aneurin Bevan, Oscar Hammerstein, Edwina Mountbatten, Lewis Namier, Melanie Klein, A.E. Matthews and Dornford Yates. Peter O'Toole had 'set the Avon on fire' with his Shylock and Petruchio. By October *Saturday Night* had become the first Woodfall film to be in profit. In December the Oliviers were divorced. On New Year's Eve Mary and I went round to Robert Stephens's house and Mary got as wholeheartedly drunk as she had been *chez* Gabor. I supported her back to Woodfall Street and managed to get her to bed, where she sat up briefly and brightly told me that she was pregnant. She then went to sleep.

I awoke with an Algonquin-sized hangover and crouched in front of the electric fire feeling sour and very feverish. I was half-convinced that Mary's announcement was no more than a piece of drunken bravado, like her plunge into the pool. When she came to in the late afternoon, she clearly had almost no remembrance of her first-footing capers the night before. It was soon obvious that we were both stricken with not only hangovers but severe flu. I took our temperatures, which confirmed the diagnosis.

Apart from a general feeling of physical defeat, I had not yet been lucid enough to marshal the facts denying my possible responsibility for her condition. I made a dazed consultation of my diary, laboriously comparing dates of the previous months with my absences in New York, and the likelihood of my having fathered her child seemed far-fetched if not impossible. I needed a woman's expertise in these matters and could only conjecture uncertainly until I consulted Jocelyn. If my suspicions were well founded, it was at least to my advantage as far as determining my next and overdue course of action. I was in no position to take up any stance of outrage, but it facilitated the task of choice, existential or not, considerably. I also knew that Mary was certain to maintain a course of ambiguity and evasion.

Remembering the small-hours descent on Woodfall Street by Tony and Robert Shaw, it was not difficult to hazard the beginnings of some makeshift plot which had led up to the present dilemma and its consequences. Mary's apparent connivance also clarified her restraint over my affair with Jocelyn, adding the thrill of retribution to whatever other satisfactions she gained from Shaw. I dosed us with hot whisky and a couple of sleeping-pills. It seemed the only practical way of facing the first onslaught of the New Year. We were both asleep long before midnight.

A few hours later I was woken by the sound of barking. Snoopy, our lively but neurotic dachshund, was thumping his paws on my chest. The bedroom was thick with smoke. The well of the staircase was consumed with flames taller than a man. I grabbed Mary, who was still asleep, thrust a pillow into her hands and dragged her to the study, opened the window and perched her on the sloping roof. She clung there dazed but fairly calm while I picked up the telephone, which was miraculously still working.

Within minutes we could hear the bells of the fire-engines entering the street. Then there was a delay and a great deal of shouting below. A fleet of Hooray sports cars blocked the approach. Snoopy's barking had stopped and flames were visible beneath the door. Suddenly a figure appeared through the smoke, flipped Mary over his shoulder and covered her in a blanket. I clutched the window-frame, burning from the heat behind and wondering if I should resign myself to jumping and the certainty of a broken limb or two. A helmeted figure scampered up a ladder at astonishing speed, held out a strong arm and guided me down.

I was bundled into a waiting police-car where Mary was crouched unhurt, crying for Snoopy. It seemed unlikely he could have survived, but he was found later curled up beneath her dressing-table and returned to us at the Goring Hotel, where we were efficiently installed. It was almost light when we sat down in our Edwardian suite, congratulating the dog and drinking coffee laced with whisky.

It turned out that Woodfall Street had not been seriously damaged but it would be uninhabitable for weeks. During the morning I tried to persuade Mary to acknowledge the practical realities of the immediate situation, at least as it appeared to me. I had established a stable base of loyalty and affection in Lower Belgrave Street which I had no intention of abandoning because she found herself pregnant by persons unknown. I was prepared for her to insist on my fatherhood of the child, even vehemently to deny the existence of any other liaison, to declare her commitment to our wedlock and launch into a bout of self-righteous reproval for my own callous conduct. On the other hand, she might come clean, confirm my calendar notes and, more important, acknowledge the utter sterility of our masquerade marriage. It was too much to expect. She did neither and adopted an ice-fairy bland chillness. She would admit nothing, not even her own possible pain.

I rang Joy Parker asking her to gather some clothes together so that I could at least walk the hundred yards or so round to Lower Belgrave Street. Mary said nothing until the telephone rang. It was the costume designer for *The*

Changeling. She became immediately elated, explained her predicament, naked-
ness, poor Snoopy's gallantry and asked him round for a costume fitting for
both stage and street. Joy sent up a parcel of clothes and, while I put them
on, Mary returned to bed, absorbed in the 'notices' of our fire in the evening
papers. I slipped out and walked back to Jocelyn, who was happily preparing
a welcome-home celebration.

The following day, Neville Blond gave his annual lunch for the press and
critics at the Savoy. I was feeling especially spiky because of the obtusely
vicious reception they had given to Shelagh Delaney's second play, *The Lion
in Love*, then playing to poor houses at the Court. It was a classic example of
a second play being demolished on the grounds of feigned admiration for a
first play's privately resented success. None of the women playwrights who
followed Shelagh possessed a fraction of her four-square plain gifts and poetic
realism. Yet, at the age of twenty, she was savaged with such deliberation and
spite that her successors would have run howling to some lunatic Equal
Opportunities Tribunal.

I had been tempted to skip Neville's lunch, but his bemused loyalty to
George persisted against all the aggrieved mutterings and threats from the
Zionist heavies, especially from his wife Elaine, who regarded us as a bunch
of down-and-out opportunists cynically manipulating Neville's naïvety, despis-
ing his happy philistinism and using his secretary and mistress as a Mata Hari
to manipulate his decisions between enseamed sheets. Neville resisted even
Elaine's scorn, although he still blanched at the whispered name of 'Arden'.
I had grown very fond of him as each renewed blow from the front-of-house
returns diminished his dreams of knighthood. Knowing that the straight road
to the Honours List was the simple foot-slog of charity, he pleaded apologet-
ically for the English Stage Company's survival as if it were a respectable
community centre for recidivist Jewish youth.

In his address to the critics, Neville spluttered his testimonial to our unimpressed judges and George, in full curmudgeonly mendicant style, spelled out
the company's disputed achievements and tersely announced the details of the
coming season with the grudging correctness of a captured prisoner of war
giving only name, rank and number. The fume of reproach would have been
chastening to an audience of minimal sensibility; it produced no more than an
air of sour defensiveness. A Savoy lunch with port and cigars, the cost of
which would have matched the loss on Shelagh's play, brought a shaky, sulking
truce.

Luther was palpably George's ace in the hole, its ambitious production might
be the company's urgent 'financial saver'. His rumbustious excitement when
he read the play was not the gruff Devine demeanour of everyday. He lifted

his arms aloft at the open window of Lower Belgrave Street and cast a fine growl down at the passers-by. 'By God, boysie. You've done it! You've done it again!' I never saw him so thoroughly justified and joyful, like a man acquitted by a torn jury. 'I always say to them: it may take time and a lot of sweat but when Johnny finally does bring one out, he really *shits* it out!' He was the only person whom I could forgive for using the diminutive of my name.

I went on my own to see Mary in *The Changeling*. Tony had assembled a fierce cast. Apart from Mary and Robert Shaw, it included Jeremy Brett, Mary's rival Zoë Caldwell, Annette Crosbie, Alan Howard, Charles Kay, Robin Ray and Norman Rossington. All of them were excellent except Mary, who seemed out of her depth in the midst of all this Jacobean tooth and claw, which Tony had directed with chilling power. During the run there were prominent announcements, together with smiling pictures, of Mary expecting a baby in the summer, one of them posed in a night-club with her friend, the kitsch royal-portrait painter, Annigoni.

I suggested that we should meet now that she had moved into her new house in Cliveden Place. It was eccentrically shaped, like a triangle, and one of its 'features' was a rather unwelcoming hall designed with original Eric Gill frescos. It reminded me of the foyer of Broadcasting House and seemed to demand a saluting commissionaire.

Mary looked vibrantly healthy and glowed in the spring sunshine pouring through the uncurtained windows of the bedroom. She chattered without pause about how much she had enjoyed working with Tony, the awfulness of Zoë, her visits to the doctor, her decorating plans, her confinement in Welbeck Street and then, to my astonishment, about Shaw, his latest novel *The Sun God*, how he had introduced her to *Middlemarch* and, finally, his considerable prowess as a lover.

Beginning to undress, she added, smiling, 'Not as good as *you*, dear,' and turned down the lilac-coloured nylon sheets. I followed her obediently, feeling that the whims of an expectant mother should be indulged without quibbling over matters of propriety and taste. I had never made love to a pregnant woman before and she seemed impatient with me in an amused way. Her usual practicality and doggedness made it briefly pleasurable. She leaped up to go to the bathroom. I noticed a letter, several pages long, on the bedside table. A quick glance revealed it to be a very explicit and erotic love-letter from Shaw, full of excitement about the baby and the mechanics of quickly following it up with another one.

It was the first time I had read a letter addressed to someone else. When Mary returned to the room and got back into bed, still quite naked, I slipped it into my trouser pocket while I dressed. If she noticed, she said nothing. I had been in the house for less than an hour. She sat up comfortably, putting on a shawl, as I leaned down and kissed her goodbye. She said not another word and waved as she settled down to read her magazines. It was as if I had dropped in to hang the new bedroom curtains.

I never saw or heard from her again, except through her solicitors and accountants. The acrimony she displayed through them and publicly at the divorce surprised me after the casual circumstances of our parting. She repeatedly refused to return the postcards so sweetly drawn by my father and sent to me as a child and which I treasured alone among my belongings.

She died ten years later, choking on her own vomit in the hotel room she was sharing with Shaw after opening in a mediocre thriller in the West End.

Some time earlier, I had been apprehended by Shaw in the Savoy Grill. As he rolled and roared across the floor in the early hours, a fascinated group of waiters circled round us and he launched into a blundering apology for having calculatedly seduced my wife, who was about to ring him from their home in Spain. I told him to think nothing of it, but he persisted, berating himself for having since impregnated her too often or too quickly. Blessedly, Mary's call came through and I never saw him again either.

When he died in 1978 of a massive heart attack, leaving ten children, four of them Mary's, I broke the news to Nicol Williamson, who was staying in my house, as I took him his breakfast. He paled. He had an envious respect for Shaw's commercial stardom and his athletic drunken ambition. He proceeded to execute a persuasive mime of the manner of his death as he strode from his Rolls Royce into the Spanish sun to be struck down by a pitiless god.

It didn't seem such a waste as that of Mary, whose destiny dragged her so pointlessly from a life better contained by the softly lapping waters of the Clyde.

20. 'Do your Nuns Decline?'

Sometimes I have to console myself with the fact that he who has lived a lie loves the truth.

Ingmar Bergman, *The Magic Lantern*, 1988

How much do we believe of these memories? How much does it matter? All autobiography is fiction to a greater extent.

J.O. reviewing *The Magic Lantern* in *New York Review of Books*, 27 October 1988

I was grateful to be installed in Lower Belgrave Street, but I soon began to find myself disturbed by dangerously incontinent flushes of restlessness. I don't know whether Jocelyn detected this itch. I suspected she did, although she said little, for which I was grateful. She had an almost witch-like pre-science, shrewd rather than suspicious, and I imagine I was a poor dissembler. Apart from a natural resistance to emotional coercion, I was in a mood of prickly assertion of my independence. It was not long before she exercised her 'ethic of frankness' and sent up a few warning flares, in a tone of amused knowingness, about my jay-walking urge.

We had struck up some sort of acquaintance with Roger and Penelope Gilliatt at Tynan-like gatherings in their flat in Lowndes Square. He was a rather stern, saturnine neurologist, who had become an overnight celebrity on account of the reluctant part he played in the melodrama that had been created when it was sniffed out by a creepy hack that Tony Armstrong-Jones's best man at his wedding to Princess Margaret, Jeremy Fry, had once been involved in a youthful homosexual scandal. The subsequent clamour of outraged moral-ity was deafening, threatening to become an issue of constitutional proportions.

Fry was dumped overnight and replaced with desperate haste by Roger, whose respectability was ironclad. Penelope, a staff writer on *Vogue* and, later, *Queen*, achieved some popular fame as Wife-to-the-Best-Man at this most gaudy royal occasion, a living seal of irreproachable official heterosexuality.

The only mark against Roger was that he was a Roman Catholic, albeit a lapsed one. However, there was no time to cast about.

Penelope had acquired a repertoire of Wedding anecdotes, from the early-morning vigil in the Abbey to the scenes behind the balcony at Buckingham Palace. Roger looked a little uneasy at these mocking breaches of confidence, but she told them well enough to set smart, radical tables a-titter. They were genuinely amusing: speculations about the travail suffered by the mighty but incontinent trapped in the nave without hope of escape for hours; of the magnificently uniformed Master-at-Arms barking at a rigid young lifeguard, 'Don't *breathe* on the GLADIOLI! You're turning 'em YALLER!'; and the old Duke of Gloucester, absenting himself hungrily from the waving chorus line on the balcony to munch through a plate of cucumber sandwiches, finally enthusing, 'Bloody good sandwiches you get here. Real *butter*! Only get margarine at 'ome.'

Jocelyn's hostility to Penelope's demeanour and ambitions was soon plain. If she had any doubts about the likelihood of inciting defensiveness on Penelope's behalf instead of my assumed disinterest, her temperament disallowed caution. The decorative style of the Lowndes Square flat, which was very much Penelope's own, came in for instant scorn. '*Nothing* to displease the eye, like Syrie Maugham's, all white on white.' As did her clothes ('Unpressed azalea-coloured chiffons') and her catering, which admittedly was only adequate: 'Curling bits of smoked salmon and watery pools of scrambled egg.'

Jocelyn's strictures were justifiable, but I was dismayed and then irritated by this insistent venom expended on such trifles. What seemed far more important was Penelope's exhilarating display of two qualities I prized most highly: energy and, yes, like J. Porter, enthusiasm. And there was also her fierce curiosity, always titillating to those who find themselves its object. As someone put it less kindly, 'Penelope always greets you as if you had just suffered a grievous loss.' Like Susan Sontag, as described by Gore Vidal, she was 'awesome in her will to understand'. What I admired as divine vitality, Jocelyn and others damned in a single word – gush.

I had met Penelope for the first time five years earlier and saw her quite frequently at gatherings which must have had connections with what she called 'London's Intellectual Life'. Later, when she complained of the working and social pressures which were hindering her development as a novelist and short-story writer, I suggested the solution might be to move away from them physically and live in the country. My uncouth naïvety tried her forbearance terribly; her eyes and tongue snapped together, 'You mean – give up London's *intellectual life*!'

Muddle-headed Johnny, as she cared to call me in the hearing of first-class minds, had no idea of what she could be talking about. Her impatient reply reminded me of the old joke about the dismay of the circus worker who, informed by his shivering, wet, starved and miserable colleague that he could no longer endure the prospect of more years spent scooping up elephants' droppings and was finally quitting, cried out, in disbelief, 'What! You mean quit! And give up Show Business!'

Our first meeting was in a small pub in Lower John Street, just off Hanover Square, where Penelope was making her early mark in the cultural show-ring at the offices of *Vogue*. *Look Back* was about to open and George Fearon, amazed at his own persuasive powers in arousing interest from what he regarded as a classy publication, had arranged an interview with one of *Vogue*'s brightest young stars. Being judged 'terribly bright' as a lady journalist was the equivalent of the thumbs-up from the casting-couch. If anyone was prepared to shovel up brightness by the bucket, whatever the circus privations, it was surely Penelope.

When I arrived around noon in the empty pub, she was crouched over the bar, caught in the light like an insect dropped on to a lampshade. I was unused to being quizzed by journalists, and by ladies not at all, but public houses were the only place where, as the son of a performing licensed victualler's assistant, I felt a certain advantage, particularly over an attractive middle-class young woman. Since parting from Pamela, celibacy had seemed almost a soothing comfort of mourning rather than a further imposition on pain and confusion. It was not so much chastity that troubled me, but the withdrawal of feminine intimacy. And, now, here I was, giving a routine interview to a young, animated woman, seemingly very informed and quick to laugh. The twinge of a limb so recently lost insisted that a significant part of me was not yet dead after all.

By the time we left the pub to go round the corner to *Vogue*, where Richardson was joining us for a photo-session, I suppose I was already engaged by the prospect of mild and easy flirtation. I hadn't marked Penelope down in any appraising way as a future sportive fancy, but I had always been addicted to flirtation as a game worth playing for itself. Unconsciously, perhaps, I calculated that this was someone whose path I would cross more adroitly when I was in a more robust state of health.

Penelope was a redhead, as was Pamela. In my fanciful projections, I took red hair to be the mantle of goddesses and priestesses who craved not obedience, like Ayesha, but a siren enjoining flight up into the firmament of life itself. It was the copper-headed helmet of destiny of those who would hurl their challenge against the very centre of creation and, having struck, plummet and explode upon a disbelieving world. It was lifted by the winds from the north-east, breathing like warspite Hotspur. It was the shade of the imagin-ation's crimson twilight, punitive and cleansing, the colour of communing voluptuaries, of pre-Raphaelites, Renaissance princes, of Medicis and Titians, of Venice and Northumbria, of bloodaxe and vengeance, Percy and Borgia, of Beatrice – Dante's and Shakespeare's – of hot pretenders and virgin monarchs. A red-haired Doris Day was unthinkable.

Robert Webber, who had recently seduced a young, auburn-haired English actress, was emphatic that even the most vapid redhead possessed an entirely different set of biological, sexual, neurological and glandular responses. In specific circumstances of fear or passion they gave off an acrid, foxy smell, sweet to the discerning and repellent to others. A few years on, I brought up this theory with Penelope's obstetrician, himself married to a copper-haired beauty, who solemnly confirmed my dubious theory, adding that they also possessed a lower pain-threshold than their fair or brunette sisters. Whenever I have sought the view of the 'sisters' on this, it has always been greeted with either outrage or laughter.

Six years later, during those early months of 1961, I was infused with that mixture of redemptive joy and apprehension that almost always anticipates a new production, a gale of dayspring from within and on high to contain, and I had until June to snort and stamp all this reined-in starting-gate eagerness. I was straining with the sense of speed and power. I felt the leap of it not simply from on high but even within my eye. Walking down Cork Street one afternoon, I astonished myself by entering the Waddington Gallery, which was given over to an exhibition by Elisabeth Frink. On display in the window was a figure of either a Cock or a Fallen Man, I can't remember which, but either would have been an appropriate subject of interest, and I was intrigued.

Inside, the room was empty and still, I felt like an interloper in one of those madam's shops that used to post a single hat in the window like a challenging sentinel. Retreat was beyond me now and I was handed a catalogue, which, to my instant relief, had the prices pencilled in. If any one had carried an additional nought, I would have been daunted but unsurprised. There was the sound of laughter from downstairs. I had never bought a painting, let alone a piece of sculpture, and I knew almost nothing about either. But these objects seemed to match my own mood with hammering ferocity. I wandered from one to another, and then again, beginning to feel a creature of some bronze myself.

I rejected the Cock after a while. Perhaps there was too much bombast in its poised stride, and that was not how I was feeling at all. It would have to be the Fallen Man or the eighteen-inch-high Harbinger Bird, a bandit creature, swooped for attack or sudden flight. It seemed full of mystery and mockery.

The Fallen Man writhed like a shattered bolt from the sky. I wanted both, which seemed like a costly compromise, and I could scarcely afford one. A hundred and fifty pounds was more than I had spent on anything in my life. For the first time, I would buy myself a gift, a consolation against whatever soot and abuse might be hurled down my chimney at the play's opening, a tangible tribute to myself. If I had nothing else pleasurable to retain from the experience, I would at least have this fearsome trophy as remembrance. Like the play, it would be my own.

I paced between Man and Bird. I settled for the bird. I checked again that I had got my noughts right and announced my decision. Miss Frink, it seemed, was downstairs and would be delighted. Would I like a glass of champagne? No, I had an urgent appointment with my dentist. Just a moment, I'll ask her up. Damn it, I wanted to pay and get out. She would spot me as a footloose philistine and mark me as having chosen her own least favourite piece. She would feel affection for her runt but despise its buyer.

She appeared immediately, like someone summoned to an accident, authoritative and comforting. There could be no question that this big-boned, warrior-faced young woman was the right arm in the creation of these fables. 'Which one have you bought?' I nodded towards Harbinger IV. The response was immediate. 'Oh, good.' She turned to Leslie Waddington. 'He's chosen the right one.'

Caught in my present flight, I had already invited myself round to the Gilliatt flat to talk to Penelope alone, but chastely. I interpreted her avidity as high spirits, like my own. But a small, wormy voice was saying, 'If not you, who else?' One day, ascending the Lowndes Square staircase, I met Penelope arm-in-arm with a most famous academician bearing an immovable post-coital smirk on his face. She furiously denied any reason for his well-being; such secrecy and recklessness increased her attraction.

She admitted to an evening spent with another ill-concealed scalp, 'Freddie' Ayer, Juan Don, in his rooms at New College. She described his appearance as he divested himself of his trousers while she sat at the dining-table finishing her College Pudding, *and* the condition of his underpants – the kind of confidence I had only known from homosexuals in the dressing-room hours of reminiscence. It seemed as if I was making a habit of climbing into the Juan Don's still-warm sheets. As a sought-after cocksman, Ayer had one unenviable advantage: a cold heart. If a stiff prick hath no conscience, the dirty don when detumescent had scarcely more. His organ-grinder's monkey brain was an undoubted aphrodisiac. It was hard to believe that Penelope would have refused the offer of such a coveted college sweetmeat.

Jocelyn insisted later that she had never watched anyone make such a concerted, unadorned play as Penelope did for me. During the admittedly unappetizing dinners at Lowndes Square her intent was plain. Even Roger, creased with fatigue from a galley-slaving day at the Middlesex Hospital, must have noticed it, as inexorable as one of his EEG readings. I was in a mood of importunate bravado. The fact that I was not yet in love and fearful of rejection, nor apprehensive of causing anguish, pumped my confidence. Sadly, the comforts and unfamiliar domesticity Jocelyn had provided incited rather than restrained me. If Penelope was culpable, selfish and ruthless, I was no better.

One bright morning, the page proofs of *Luther* arrived. Excited, as always, by this tangible confirmation of work done, the transformation of my scribbled shorthand notebooks into authenticated, irrefutable *existence*, I rang Penelope. For no reason, I assumed not only her interest but her pleasure. I invited myself over for a celebratory drink. As usual, she was crouched on the floor. I began the badly fluffed masquerade of reading passages aloud from the play. I had never before committed adultery beneath the cuckold's own roof. I had an alarming vision of Roger appearing at the door, haggard from a night-and-day session at the Middlesex. Penelope seemed unconcerned and I committed myself to the magical hands of the eternal redhead of my spellbound dreams. As I walked back to Lower Belgrave Street, I practised contorting my face into the most unsmirklike post-coital half-mask I could devise.

Penelope's behaviour and my own during the weeks that followed were probably grotesquely indefensible. I am no more able to interpret mine now than I was at the time, caught in a narcotic flight of conviction that I could soar above the groundlings who dare not leap at the abyss and be borne up triumphantly. No doubt my hindsight judgement of her Icarus intentions, that they were a trial run for a similar sequence of frantic expeditions fuelled by a kind of spastic ambition, is uncharitable. However, her succeeding journalistic and personal careers, which were not always separable, do seem to bear this prejudice out, notwithstanding pussyfoot feminist apologists.

Her series of 'pieces' or interviews with the likes of Jean Renoir, Buster Keaton, Tati, Hitchcock and Nabokov and, most famously, her plagiaristic interview with Graham Greene seem pretty convincing testimony to this driving avidity wearing the full mask of critical appreciation. Later, these pieces, presented as exercises in creative insight in well-paying magazines like the *New Yorker*, extended themselves into domestic involvement. Penelope, flattering as she was to her hosts, became the Critic Who Came to Dinner, most especially in the cases of Mike Nichols and Edmund Wilson. I was even privy to her selection of Nichols as an essential weapon of her ambition, although I was not aware of it at the time. Oddly, almost all her icons were old men with ravaged reputations, ancient oaks standing in lofty isolation, waiting for the preserving skill of an ingenious tree-surgeon.

Jocelyn told me that she had never seen me so out of control of my life. Even the recent record of my mishandling of events with Mary and Francine might have alerted her to the fact that I often confronted problems like an improvising chimpanzee faced with the dashboard of a jumbo jet. What she did not grasp was that old muddle-minded Johnny was trying, above all else, in a spirit of life-long caprice, to re-establish his own authority and get his simian claws on the levers.

It seemed essential that Penelope and I arrange an uninterrupted weekend away, a bargain-break from Roger's looming presence and the gloomy intuitions around the corner in Lower Belgrave Street. To this purpose, Penelope, by now the film critic of the *Observer*, invented the Folkestone Film Festival. The Slickeys were still alerted for the merest sniff of indiscretion; we settled on a small, unstarred hotel in Sandgate.

It faced the beach and was indifferent rather than unwelcoming. Encouraged by its overbearing anonymity, we went straight up to the cold bedroom. There was an air of practical discomfort that could only promote instant sexual revival between the sheets. The bed was our single necessity and, united in intent, we swooped into it, shivering but well pleased. We were interrupted within minutes by a loud banging on the door. Penelope sat up smartly, impervious to the springtime chill off the Kentish coast. A lugubrious voice announced that there was an urgent call for Mrs Gilliatt from the *Observer*. Grabbing a tactically placed kimono, she scrambled barefoot out of the room.

There had been some queries about her proof. She slipped back into bed. From her frowning expression, it seemed that the problem was not quite resolved. I was slightly puzzled that she had given the number to her high-minded employers. Twenty minutes later the asthmatic porter was thumping on the door again. She sprang away. After an even longer interval, I masked my nibbling exasperation and asked what could be so important for the *Observer* to ring her so close to the time when the paper was put to bed, and frustrating our own similar endeavours. Her patient smile implied that it was something I shouldn't bother my fluffy little head about. Our own presses had begun to roll again when her head drew back, fixed by the sound of the porter's plod up the corridor. Before the *interruptus* knock, she was out of bed and gone.

When she returned, she was exultant as she threw off the kimono. 'How was it for you?' I was tempted to ask. She had achieved a climactic triumph over a disputed spelling and a couple of colons. In trying to affirm autonomy on my rights to chaos, I was scarcely helped by these Feydeau incursions. It was my first close intimation of her manic pedantry. It was only a review of a fairly commonplace film, which was unlikely to be scrutinized for stray commas by somnolent Sunday-morning readers. Semi-copulation seemed a disproportionate price for a couple of colons, but not, patently, to the *Observer*'s fearless film critic.

As the room took on an early summer chill, we ventured out for an evening in festival Folkestone to the local repertory theatre and Benn Levy's comedy *Clutterbuck*. The whole apparatus of clandestine festival seemed, suddenly, comically worthwhile and physically promising. We huddled together in enjoyment, even Penelope seemed confident that all arts editors and libel lawyers would be settled in their unadulterous beds, leaving us with a bottle of whisky between damp sheets.

We returned to London on Sunday evening. I was in a state of some dread at the thought of Jocelyn's catechism. Penelope was terse, detached and determined. She instructed me to appraise the state of play in Lower Belgrave Street. She would wait outside for ten minutes. Jocelyn was pale, drink in hand, smoking one of her cheroots. She concentrated with the authority of a referee just openly fouled by the players. 'I've had Roger on the phone for hours,' she drawled in that Australian uprise that Nellie Beatrice called her 'beautiful speaking voice'. 'Where's Penelope?' 'Outside.' 'I think you'd better ask her in.' Adding, in an it's-going-to-be-a-bumpy-night inflection, 'She's going to need a drink.'

In the scene that followed, I was a silent spectator, a spare prick at the funeral as Jocelyn and Penelope squared up as if they had been rehearsing the match for weeks. I remember Penelope, propped up against the mantel, unusually erect, her brown eyes eclipsed into black as she spat out, 'You've both got to realize the fact that – John and I are in love.'

Like a spectator in a dream, I found myself following her downstairs and arranging to meet her the following day after her morning film-showing. I watched her stride crablike towards the corner of Eaton Square, where she turned to wave and disappear, thinking how fortunate I was to remain with Jocelyn's tear-stained complaisance while she confronted Roger's cadaverous outrage. He'd had the whole weekend to assemble epithets, and 'jade' and 'Jezebel' were the very first. So she said the next day, and I didn't disbelieve her.

Later that year, in November, Tony and I decided to accept another invitation to Acapulco's film festival. Penelope was eager to come along. By this time we were being swarmed on by the British press from all sides. To my dismay, I discovered that she had arranged to file a 'piece' on the festival. She spent the afternoons tapping away at a report for London on a film festival that was only a little less spurious than the one she had created in Folkestone. I began to wonder if Francine was still in residence with José.

Tony erupted in a fury of boredom. He insisted that the three of us go to Yucatan to inspect the ancient Mayan ruins. The athletic agony we could hear from the room next to ours, which he was sharing with Diane Cilento, may have driven him to move on. The prospect of a back-breaking archaeological tramp didn't appeal to my lazy spirit of historical enquiry, but the thought of remission from Penelope's clattering machine persuaded me to go along.

After a bone-bruising drive to Yucatan, we arrived at a filthy hotel where, for the second time in my life, I was stricken by a plague of crabs, which were in full training session on the trampoline blankets of our bed. These Slickeys of the microbe world, first encountered in Hayling Island, do not simply squat and observe vigil in the pubic parts, but dig their vampire gums into the merest hirsute sprout on the body, from a few clusters on the chest to the fuzz of an inner ear. For days, Penelope and I shampooed, scrubbed and impaled these bleeding-mouthed creatures, clenched to every follicle. It was the kind of shared physical squalor, like childbirth, which, some people claim, bestows a definitive lifetime bond; relinquishing all pretence of fastidious secrecy, true love is established for ever. Or not.

Itching from earhole to crotch, we rose at dawn before the full humidity of the peninsula enveloped the day and obediently clambered behind Tony's leaping figure up the steps of the ceremonial towers of the ancient Maya civilization. Cursing myself for my indulgence of the overbearing whims of others, whether writing idiotic reports of a fatuous festival or alleviating sexual panic through archaeological exploration, I barely listened to the querulous lilt of our Mexican interpreter. Penelope, panting behind him, considered his every word. As we all paused for breath above the Courtyard of the Holy Virgins, she closed in on him with a question of syntax of that lost world.

'Tell me, señor . . . ' What could she possibly want to know? Tony glowered from the cruel steps beyond. 'Señorita?' 'Tell me, how do your nouns decline?' An expression of desperate fear clouded the guide's sweating face. 'No, señorita,' he pleaded. '*Our* nuns do not decline.' Tony turned upwards, his cackling echoing below in the ruins. 'Nuns! Decline!' Penelope's eyes clouded with impatience. 'It's a perfectly proper question.'

I should have interpreted the signs then. Or earlier, back in out-of-town Sandgate.

21. *Holy Moses*

For a writer, success is always temporary. Success is only failure – delayed.

Graham Greene, 1963

Protest is easy. Grief must be lived.

Notebook, 1980

Will it be a *success*, George?

Neville Blond – any time

George must have known that the part of Staupitz in *Luther* had not exactly been written for him but was a tentative tribute to a possibly romanticized account of our relationship, or my own view of it. The point was never made, but I felt that he had immediately responded to the intimate resonances drifting from the exchanges between the young Luther and the Vicar-General of the Augustinian Order as they strolled arm-in-arm – as George and I had often done in Sloane Square – around the garden of the Eremite Cloister in Wittenberg. The mentor's combination of sympathy and rigour spoke through Staupitz in a clear voice.

STAUPTIZ: I've never had any patience with all your mortifications. The only
   wonder is that you haven't killed yourself with your prayers, and
   watchings, yes, and even your reading too. All these trials and
   temptations you go through, they're meat and drink to you.

During rehearsals and the run of the play, Staupitz's admonition to Luther – 'Don't think that only you are right' – became a running gag in the company, to be used whenever a disagreement was in need of speedy defusing. It worked unfailingly.

Rehearsals for *Luther* could not begin until June, when Lewenstein released Finney from *Billy Liar*. It was frustrating for me, each passing week seeming to shorten the breath of what had been brought to life with such difficulty. I was not yet accustomed to this extended period of limbo after a work's exhausting struggle to achieve existence, the half-life of anxiety before its lusty proclamation of health and survival in production. These are the playwright's heaviest days, when the play seems poised between life and death, remote and still-born. I had been unusually lucky with *The Entertainer*, when both star and director were on stand-by to slap it into life almost before it emerged.

However, the delay did provide valuable time to protect *Luther*'s hope of eventual life against the unexpected threats of the Lord Chamberlain. Neither George nor I had anticipated such a stern renewal of opposition, particularly as the comic activities of theatre censorship were now widely ridiculed, even in the popular press. It seemed as if a high-ranking decision had been made that the principle of censorship was the strategic redoubt of the Establishment, to be defended at all cost and certainly not to be abandoned in the face of a barrage of laughter.

In March, George sent me the list of cuts demanded by the other side's commander, Sir Norman Gwatkin. There were fourteen of them, none disastrous, but, having gained some ground in public opinion, it appeared faint-hearted to concede without furious resistance. I was reluctant to impose on George the added burden of yet another foray with Lewenstein into St James's Palace, but all our past struggles would have been dishonoured if we abandoned the small advantage we had gained. I dispatched a letter to George, a bluffing ultimatum, in which I said that I found the proposed concessions unacceptable '*under any circumstances*', and refused to agree to any substitutions on the questionable grounds that they were 'severely damaging to the structure, method and interest of the play'. Piling self-righteousness upon rhetoric, I claimed that the principle involved was too important for me to be influenced by the possibility that the English production might be indefinitely postponed. 'I don't write plays to have them rewritten by someone else ... I am quite prepared to withdraw the play from production altogether.' George tucked the letter into his folder for presentation at the Palace, doubtless with a weary sigh, and set off for another clash with the guardians of morality and, now, religion.

To everyone's surprise, the Assistant Comptroller relented almost at once and passed all but four of the passages he had banned two weeks earlier. Remaining obstacles were reduced to: 'convent-piss', 'piss-scared', 'monk's piss' and, most wondrous of all, the 'Balls of the Medicis'. I was able to refer to references to 'piss' in Shakespeare – 'Master, I do smell all horse piss' (*The Tempest*) – and, in response to the helpful suggestion of substituting 'testicles' for the heraldic balls of the original, to the historical fact that balls of bronze were the famous emblem of the Medici family. It was a swift capitulation, although it offered little encouragement for the future.

I didn't attend many of the rehearsals for *Luther*. After the dread ritual of the first read-through, I kept away. These obligatory occasions are detested by everyone involved but no one seems to have come up with a satisfactory alternative. They have to be endured like the Opening of Parliament and tolerated as a piece of theatre in itself, like Black Rod knocking on the door and the Lord Chancellor stamping up the steps to the Queen on her dais. It is an official opening of proceedings, a bit of low pageantry before the real work begins. The ceremony invariably starts late, actors greet familiar faces with relief, something passed off as coffee is handed round by ASMs, trembling or surly. Someone calls out, 'Right, shall we make a start?' and hopes of a quick dash to the pub are abandoned. Then, unless a self-important management or administrator decides to open the batting, the director addresses an uneasy company.

For *Luther*, neither George nor Oscar took advantage of this opportunity. In Oscar's case it was just as well. A St Crispian call from Lazarus, looking as if he was undecided about his own revival let alone the prospects of the production, would have sent the cast rushing to the stage-door telephone to contact their agents, begging for release. George, the indisputable leader of the gathering, properly decided to cede the kick-off to Tony, who mowed down suspicion and lived up to his genius for summoning up enthusiasm. He gave a brilliant account of the play, its intentions so far as anyone could know them, the historical background and so on. The rather wan group laughed nervously in more or less the right places and the reading began with the NCO production staff at a long trestle-table and the actors facing them.

When it all ended, I felt quite happy to leave them to it. I could feel Tony willing me to disappear so that he was free to go through the masquerade of wilful tampering with my work. I knew that he was implacably protective of it, watching for signs of disaffection from any querulous actor. Besides, I had George there to act as warder to my interests.

Many people, other playwrights in particular, are sometimes puzzled by my infrequent attendance at rehearsal, suspecting it to be indolence or even indifference. In America especially, where such trust in the company would indeed by folly, I am asked, 'But don't you *care* about your play?' The answer is that I care more than inordinately, being the only one who has lived, possibly for years, in the travail of bringing it forth, bloody and bawling. I also know when my presence at its nurturing is unnecessary and even intrusive. My experience with Tony on *Look Back* and *The Entertainer* had set an unusual and exhilarating precedent of directorial *in loco parentis* that would have been impossible without fierce mutual confidence.

Putting a director on his honour can be chastening in itself. Most playwrights at rehearsals are of as much use as a father, all masked-up and sterilized, at the delivery of a child. 'All you want to do is sit there fretting over your fucking old golden words,' Tony would say to me. It was an unjust accusation, but many writers do sit in the stalls drooling over their precious syllables, inhibiting and even antagonizing the faltering actors with their proprietorial scrutiny.

Very few playwrights possess personal experience of the practical problems confronting an actor. The same can be said of many young directors, fresh from university where amateur excess is more highly prized than technical precision. Most of them haven't enough improvisatory experience to *demonstrate* to a bemused or maladroit player how to cope with an intractable doorknob or make a clean exit. A minority of writers *are* capable of interpreting their work better than anyone else, including Pinter, Beckett and Coward. But they are the masters of their own meticulous notation. In Harold's case, he has the irreplaceable advantage of having worked in the kitchen as an actor, making do with inferior, tame material and giving it life. Most playwrights should observe the same constitutional rights as the Queen: to be consulted, to advise and to warn.

I knew the play was good. That it could have been better was certain, a routine assumption that would be unhelpfully seized upon by the advocates of the 'Flawed Masterpiece' school of creative thinking: a blemished jewel, suitable for sale, but knocked down as 'slightly soiled'. There's no satisfying some punters, and there's no point in trying. Berating someone for failing to achieve what they never set out to do is one of the most elementary gambits of criticism.

My own view has always been that a play that is susceptible to crucial rewriting in rehearsal should never have reached that stage. Some people, particularly Americans, regard a 'finished' script as a contradiction, little more than a blueprint for the cast, director, backers and any bossy busybody to transform into a demonstrably complete product. The model for this creative approach was Moss Hart and the legend of his all-night pit-stop repairs in out-of-town hotel rooms. These were executed in deference to the producers' timidity, the terror of the angels and, above all, the dubious taste of the audience, whose every cough was slavishly monitored. This was the revered Broadway-bespoke method of playmaking, and it had its less capable practitioners in England. Texts were measured, pins-in-mouth, against the intransigent dummy of the imaginary audience. The most miniscule indication of an ill-fit demanded immediate attention:

They: definitely get restive round about that line.

They: don't understand the joke.

They: aren't prepared.

They: are offended.

Such is the skill of turning out comfortable 'hits'.

As I see it, from the doubtless despotic view of the one and only architect and tailor, democracy goes out of the door the moment the writer has thrown his pen through it. You don't launch a ship with a leaking hull, however much fun it may be for those who've clambered aboard at the last moment. Tony, in spite of his mischievous teasing, understood this very well. He had assembled a fine cast, exemplifying the kind of gritty actor the Court had already made its own: Finney, Peter Bull, fearsome as Tetzel the bovine, bullying indulgence salesman, John Moffat, all silky first-class mind as the Papal Legate, Julian Glover as the Knight and Charles Kay, a rakish Charles V.

For once, Tony's scatterings of plainchant, drums, banners, falcons and Afghan hounds were not cosmetic flourishes disguising unease but a blast of exuberance. He had coaxed Jocelyn Herbert to throw her famous brown paint over the peasants' costumes instead of the scenery. Gauzes, pinched Gothic arches, a lowering figure of Christ, twisted and broken, shadows banished by scalding light, luminous colours, rich red and orange courtly dress were all manipulated with gripping fluency just as I had indicated, usefully for once, in the extended stage directions: 'The medieval world dressed up for the Renaissance, in the brightest sunshine of colour, bold, joyful . . . '

I was slightly sorry that Jocelyn H. had not followed my pointers towards the sickly, frightening nightmares of Bosch, but even so the result burst upon the cramped, versatile stage of the Court, beckoning the spectator with a dazzling garden of earthly delights. My head buzzed with the physical demonstration of my rehabilitated imagination. Not only did it work, it palpably took flight. Instead of dreading Tony's peremptory summonses to rehearsal ('You've *got* to talk to Peter Bull. He's terribly *upset*. He's very *shy* and, because Tetzel's such a beetling shit, he thinks nobody likes *him*!), I longed to be consulted, advise and warn.

Because of this growing absorption, I agreed with Penelope that, after the melodrama of our Folkestone outing, we should give some pause to our regular meetings. Roger's righteous anger was certain to abide for some time, and was most likely to be permanent. In the meantime, they maintained a kind of bitter truce beneath the same roof. Further Scandinavian discussions in the forenoon at Lowndes Square were out of the question. Jocelyn R.'s constraint was chastening enough to deter me from further isolated acts of offensive, ill-bred behaviour, at least for the moment. I could no longer bring myself to concoct contemptible, puny lies about my whereabouts, but I stubbornly rejected any obligation to submit myself to probing catechism. It seemed best to let the air clear itself before entering into any charged debriefings. Penelope and I arranged to make our next rendezvous in Paris, where *Luther* had been invited to play at the International Festival of Arts.

Meanwhile, Jocelyn and I travelled to Nottingham, where it opened at the Theatre Royal. Once again, we stayed at the Turk's Head, scene of the ill-tempered clash–alliance between the Binkie–Coward–Vivien brigade and the disorderly Court guerillas. Tony was as taut as a whippet outgrowing his strength. He greeted me with a huge, bony grin: 'We've cut *whole* passages. I wonder if you'll notice where they are.' I would have been alarmed by this opening shot in earlier days, but this time I was fairly sure it was prompted by irrepressible euphoria rather than sharpshooting sadism.

As I watched the performance, the reason for his outburst became clear. Like the play, it was an endorsement of justification by faith rather than works. Of course I spotted his tinkerings with the text, even anticipating their exact location before they unfurled. Afterwards, when their gnomish intent had made such small impact, he even restored some of the tampered passages.

The following morning I faced Tony's routine note-giving to the company quite free of any qualms about cautionary back-tracking that often emerge from these occasions. The cast responded eagerly to his unique gift of incite-ment. Only Oscar Lewenstein rose predictably, Lazarus-like, to offer a dissent-ing note. He was twitching rabbity glances of anxiety in my direction. As we passed through the darkened front of the theatre into the sunshine, he came out with it: 'Have you seen the *Manchester Guardian*?' 'No.' 'It's not very good.' 'Fuck the *Guardian*.' He looked at me with pained disbelief as we walked in silence to the bar of the Turk's Head, where I presented him with a consoling orange juice and ordered a large whisky for myself. I was sure that Harbinger Bird IV had better news to provide than a provincial stringer from the *Guardian*.

Happily, the actors were as unaffected as myself by those auguries from the north that cast Oscar into such gloom, and by the time we reached Paris the general mood was unchanged. I had never seen George in such joyous form. Sitting at café tables, Jocelyn H. beside him, he was massively relaxed, liberated from the tit-swingers of Sloane Square. 'If this doesn't go, we can't pay the actors,' he growled from ear to ear. 'You'll have to find your own way to Amsterdam [the following date].' Once more, he was a lounging player among players. Some of the actors were astonished by their first glimpse of this concealed expansive core within him. Paris had revived his old French fevers and, as I watched him setting the café on a roar, I felt a stab of gratitude that I was partly responsible for this discarding of the half-mask of responsibility.

After the snooty inertia of the first-night festival audience, Jocelyn R. seemed genuinely tired and elected to go back to the hotel and bed. Whatever intimations she may have had of my plans, she accepted my decision to stay up with the others, drinking into the night and listening to Albert Finney's whore-hunting adventures. I saw her into a taxi and kissed her, my conscience well fortified by the reasonableness of the actors having a prior call on my attendance. The pre-planned liaison with Penelope seemed an after-irrelevance at this stage.

We were all heady with battle-readiness and the bravado that so often infects actors on the road and binds their disparate temperaments, even the gloomiest, into a temporary, headlong bout of high spirits. It is one of the occasional joys of my profession, scattering all my ungregarious inclinations. If it is incompatible with my other longing for perfect containment within the daily domestic stimulus of a woman's entrenched presence, it is equally essential. Unlike those who pursue the thing they declare they most cherish and are left still unfulfilled by its attainment, I thought I at least knew the nature of the two things that could provide me with a working wholeness of spirit and enterprise. That night in Paris, I had a refreshed affirmation in the supremacy of my sanguine powers over the disabling inheritance of bloody melancholy.

There was a pink ridge of first daylight over the skyline when I finally left the café, the others still sitting, cheerily immune to the early chill. It took me a while to find a taxi and the driver refused to believe in the existence of the address I gave him. When I eventually arrived at Penelope's hotel and was admitted by a surly concierge, it was almost daylight. I realized with some pride that it was to be a night without sleep. And so it was. Penelope was in bed when I knocked at her door but she rallied with no show of reproach. To my surprise, she seemed to regard my dutiful carousing as a holy obligation rather than eager participation in a thumping good time with the lads.

It was mid-morning when I set out into the street, dappled with sunshine that must have warmed even the surliest Parisian a little. I strode to the nearest *tabac*, revelling in my energetic step after the renewing exertions of the night, bought the English Sunday newspapers, sought out a sunny bench and began to read them.

Oddly enough, no reviewers from London had been sent to Nottingham to report pre-emptive disaster. They had all come to Paris like an official British delegation. Their reports back home on the prowess of our boys abroad were loyal, almost glowing, at least in the *Times*, *Observer* and *Telegraph*, which were the only ones of sidelong interest or influence. I thought of Harry's ill-received cable to Mary: 'We love Paris, Paris, Paris.' I didn't love it any more now than

I did then, but it had provided me with the most freely happy evening I could remember. A strategic dream of delights.

Sometimes, it might seem that I conducted my life, or steered its lurching progress, rather in the manner of my overboisterous rendering of Hamlet on Hayling Island. Why now, 'e that was mad and gone into France, was set to return to Denmark, sicklied o'er by the pale cast of muddle-headed thought.

> Moses has my great respec's,
> For up his rod he grabs
> And, getting lip from Pharaoh Rex,
> He scourges him with crabs.
>
> For flight and freedom then he bids,
> The Red Sea route he chooses,
> Shakes off ten tribes of fucking Yids,
> Three cheers for Holy Moses.
>
> From the poetic works of Ben Travers

Back at the Court, it was bruited that expectations were high. In other words, malign speculation was growing to the accompaniment of unstifled yawns. Cavalier and Roundhead joined forces to identify and condemn the misguided alliance with Brecht, to protest against the deployment of insufficient historical data and, of course, the dearth of 'explanation'. They may have regarded such an over-extended production as a last chance to repel and crush George's unfortified outpost of rebellion. But they seemed to have lost heart, even if they didn't exactly turn and run.

> Perhaps someone will be bold enough to suggest that Mr Osborne has added pretentiousness to his shortcomings as a dramatist, though there is a risk of being blinded by Tony Richardson's brilliant direction and Albert Finney's most moving performance. [Par for the course.] But let us be fair. [Why?] There are long speeches and brief flashes of theatre in *Luther* showing a sense of beauty and a depth of intelligence of which I admit I did not think Mr Osborne capable.
>
> W.A. Mitchell, *Press & Journal*, 5 August 1961

Slings and arrows with added riders. Others shifted the blame for the evening's failure to Tony, implying that he had travestied a play they didn't like anyway. T.C. (Cuthbert) Worsley, who had surprisingly taken up arms on behalf of *Look Back* in the company of Binkie and Rattigan on the first night, delivered a schoolmasterly reproof for the ineffectiveness of the ending, but acknowledged 'the anguish which Mr Osborne has known and felt'. Perhaps it wasn't the Teddy boy's con-trick after all.

> The seal on *Luther*'s excellence is Osborne's language. No one in the English theatre can write prose like him, dramatic prose designed for the voice and the ear, and he has now proved what an adaptable instrument that prose is.
>
> Bamber Gascoigne, *Spectator*, 7 July 1961

So, it wasn't the concerted output of a million simian fingers tapped out in a flashpast thousand years.

> The seemingly effortless fluency of Mr Osborne's writing has its effect not only in the great set pieces . . . We at any rate can be certain that *Luther* in terms of pure theatre (in the widest sense of the phrase) enriches Mr Osborne's reputation and our stage.
>
> Bernard Levin, *Daily Express*

> Every stage picture seems to have been cut from a frame in the Uffizi, and set into motion. Just so should the Afghan hounds stand beside Pope Leo. It is a mistake for Osborne to tell us too much too often in explanation of his hero. [Now, that's an odd retreat.] Still, it remains a hammer-blow of an evening.
>
> Alan Brien, *Sunday Telegraph*

Tynan, in the *Observer*, sounded his proprietary incantation to Brecht:

> In form, the play is sedulously Brechtian, an epic succession of tableaux conceived in the manner of *Galileo*. [Too Brechtian, or not Brechtian enough? Anyway:] . . . the prose, especially in Luther's sermons, throbs with a rhetorical zeal that has not often been heard in English historical drama since the seventeenth century, mingling gutter candour with cadences that might have come from the pulpit oratory of Donne.

It began to seem that some people had actually listened to the old golden words. Harold Hobson in the *Sunday Times* was almost alone in recognizing that the piece was concerned with religious experience rather than political history, and chided the other reviewers:

28 Jocelyn Rickards, 1959

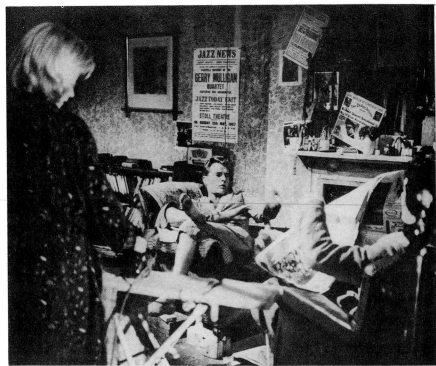

In " Look Back In Anger " Jimmy Porter rages at his wife Alison and their friend, Cliff: " I hate Sundays! Always reading papers; drinking tea; ironing ! "

LOOK BACK
IN ANGER

In scenes from the new film, LILLIPUT captures the sad and eloquent loneliness of one Jimmy Porter. Is he the prototype of a new 'lost generation'?

When Alison finally leaves him, Jimmy consoles himself with Helena, her best friend.

LILLIPUT

29 Richard Burton and Mary Ure in scenes from the film version of
Look Back in Anger

A man's loneliness takes many forms.
With Jimmy it's in the soar of a trumpet.

Jimmy: " This girl's silence twists your
arm off ! I've sat in the dark for hours.
And, knowing I'm feeling as I feel now,
she's turned over and gone to sleep ! "

" Why did I marry him ? " muses Alison.
" . . . . he looked so young and frail."

" There are no good brave causes left to fight " is his epitaph. But Jimmy Porter
knows, here in a clouded jazz cellar, a man can find certainty and a splendour of sorts.

30 *The World of Paul Slickey*, discussions at the Café Royal, 1959: left to right, Christopher Whelen, Kenneth McMillan, Jocelyn Rickards and John Osborne

31 Rehearsals for *The World of Paul Slickey*, 1959: left to right, Kenneth McMillan, John Osborne, Christopher Whelen, Jocelyn Rickards

32 Vivien Leigh in *Look After Lulu*, Royal Court Theatre, July 1959

33 John Osborne, Nuclear Disarmament Week, September 1959
34 The first Aldermaston March passing through Kensington; the banner is carried by Christopher Logue (left) and George Devine (right)

35 John Osborne, Lower Belgrave Street, 1959

36 Giuglietta Masina, John Osborne, Joan Plowright and George Devine in Rome for
'An Evening with the English Stage Company', 1959

37 The poster for the film of *The Entertainer*, starring Laurence Olivier

38 Tony Richardson and John Osborne with Rita Tushingham at the première of the film *A Taste of Honey*

39 The 1961 protest at the Royal Court Theatre against the arrest of Wesker, Bolt and Logue: left to right, Keith Johnstone, Bill Gaskill, Miriam Brickman, Pauline Melville, Anthony Page and Derek Goldby

40 Publicity material for the film *Tom Jones*

41 Nicol Williamson in *Inadmissible Evidence*, 1964

42 Mark Dignam, Vanessa Redgrave (standing), Rachel Kempson, Peter Finch, Tony Richardson (standing), Peggy Ashcroft, Peter McEnery and George Devine in rehearsal for *The Seagull*, 1964

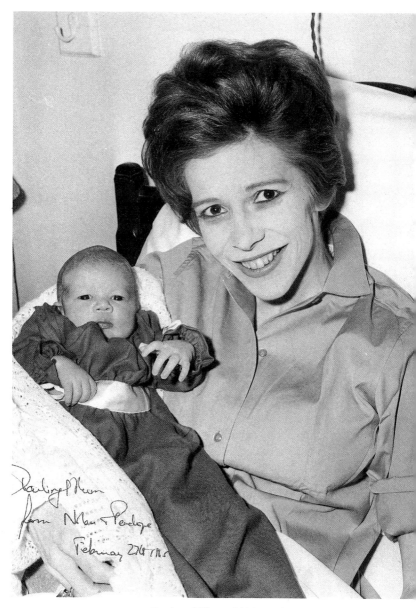

Darling Mum
from Nolan & Penelope
February 26th 1965

43 Penelope Gilliatt and Nolan, 1965

44 Jill Bennett

45 Jill Bennett as Countess Sophia Delyanoff in *A Patriot For Me*,
30 June–14 August 1965

46 Ferdy Mayne as Judge Advocate Jaroslav Kunz and George Devine as
Baron Von Epp in *A Patriot for Me*, 30 June–14 August 1965

47 John Osborne the day after the opening of *A Patriot for Me*, 1965

They will fail to notice the astonishing fact that this play leaves as the last thing in the audience's mind the words of Christ, 'A little while and ye shall not see me, and again a little while and ye shall see me,' finishing, actually finishing, with a tender and timid hope of immortality.

So it did. All that concerned our more immediate hopes was the fact that the production was booked out for the season at the Court and the transfer to the Phoenix in September was guaranteed. We were home, if not altogether dry.

Stoneleigh

Dear John,

Well, *what do you know* at last my Luther has made it – how delighted I was when it came over on the 7 o/c news yesterday morning and the 10 o/c official. *I was so happy* as I had always adored Luther and must try and see it again, once was *not* enough to see such a wonderful play. Full marks again for the reward you certainly deserve. It said '*that it is the first British play to ever have received the Oscar in New York*'. What an honour. Just off to the hair-dresser so forgive my haste. Weather *not* too bad – but it could be *better*.

Always in my thoughts,
Mother xxxx

22. *Grey-haired Youth*

All that is personal soon crumbles away and to this destitution one has to submit. This is not despair, not senility, not coldness and not indifference: it is grey-haired youth. *Only by this means* is it finally possible to survive certain wounds.

Alexander Herzen, *My Past Lives and Thoughts*, 1891

If you can get through the twilight, you will live through the night.

Dorothy Parker

I am rather tired of democracy being made safe for pimps and prostitutes, the spivs and the queers.

Sir Cyril Osborne, MP, in the House of Commons debate
on theatre censorship, 9 June 1967

During the six years that had followed my first meeting with Tony up in George's workroom on Lower Mall, my love for him had grown into something taunting, mysterious and quite inexplicable. In spite of all my regular outraged efforts to repudiate and expunge it in the bitter course of a lifetime, I was slowly forced to concede that this was a phantom which had penetrated my heart inexorably and, however fiercely I tried to banish it, I would never be finally rid of its implant. So it has proved and remains in the present silence between us now, thirty-six years on.

Utterly dissimilar to my passionate friendship for George, it is a chaste, severe love circumscribed by some mutually agreed attachment of alienation. It is cool, circumspect, and no exchange of mockery or disillusion can dislodge its binding brace of respect. No one has inflamed my creative passions more tantalizingly than Tony, nor savaged my moral sensibilities so cruelly. Whatever wayward impulse of torment he inflicted, his gangling, whiplash courage, struggling within that contorted figure, was awesomely moving and, at the last, unimpeachable. The rewards are recorded in scars rather than the stars, but

I shall never regret one moment in his company, nor our scabrous *mariage blanc*.

After *Luther*'s opening it seemed the most logical solution, or easement of our separate constraints, that we should spend the summer in each other's company and in some sort of luxuriously managed isolation. Jocelyn R., with her invaluable access to the upper as well as the intellectual classes, had negotiated the rental of what seemed the perfect retreat, a secluded farmhouse in Valbonne, perched in the dusty hills between Nice and Grasse.

> There was little I could do except watch. Whenever he [J.O.] entered a room or spoke to her, she [Penelope] would light up like a one-armed bandit when someone hits the jackpot. Quite funny, though at the same time totally humourless, she was absolutely determined, come hell or high water, to secure John for herself. It was as pre-ordained as night following day.
>
> I couldn't pretend that I didn't know what was going on. Her behaviour was too blatant. I had told John that I would not, indeed could not, be manoeuvred into leaving him; if my leaving him were to be done it would not be done by me. I was still in love with him and had no feelings of pride, no matter how much the rest of me might hurt.
>
> Jocelyn Rickards, *The Painted Banquet: My Life and Loves*, 1987

Such was Jocelyn's perception, and I doubt that if she had expressed it so plainly at the time it would have diverted me from the course I had stabbed out for myself. I had no clear, ultimate intent, only a wilful determination not to be thwarted. At first she insisted that she would prefer to remain behind on her own in Lower Belgrave Street. I felt that she deserved the least reward of a few weeks' of Riviera sunshine, the company of those she liked and some respite from the flights, uncertainties and harassments of the last year, all of which she had endured on my behalf. I didn't express it as kindly as that. 'I'm fed up with your mute attrition. I've been waiting for you to say that. Don't be so ridiculous, you need a holiday and you shall have it.' So she reported my friendly persuasion, and I don't disbelieve her. With a canny forbearance, she responded with constraint more chastening than any reproach or demands for clarification she might justifiably have thrown at me. Gracefully, she agreed to come.

According to my finger-counting calculations, Mary's baby would arrive by the end of the following month, when Lower Belgrave Street would come under press siege once again. However Valbonne might turn out, it must surely provide Jocelyn with some refuge from that dismal doorstep vigil. With this in mind, we set off in something like hopeful heart in my newly acquired, custom-built Alvis, which even George must surely approve for its Swiss Graber-designed body. Fortified inside fifteen hundredweight of Park-Ward, Armstrong-Siddeley blue coachwork, hood down and open to the wind, we lurched south, white leather gleaming in the sunshine. A grocer's car it was not: an upstart's *bella macchina*, almost a gentleman's motor. It is the only car for which I ever felt affection, and I have it still.

When we arrived at Valbonne, we must have both been in a state of triumphant fatigue, like a pair of bandits locating their mountain retreat. *Luther*, Mary's baby, even Penelope, had been nimbly eluded as the barriers of privilege, astutely planned, closed behind us. The Alvis pitched its weight against the rugged drive that led for the last half-mile up to the house. Hemmed in by a dozen acres of pinewood, La Beaumette was almost buried among grapevines, olive-trees and an overhang of dry greenery, heavily sweet and scented, surrounded by a hedge of lavender. It seemed like the dream of a secret place, but any fugitive fancy I may have held of inaccessible seclusion was smartly dispelled. Tony was already installed, impatient and full of plans for forestalling the threat of isolation or boredom.

Jocelyn and I settled gratefully enough into our bedroom overlooking the swimming-pool, wondering how we might best organize ourselves against whatever regime Tony had set in train. For the rest of the summer, well into September, a succession of his hapless or voracious guests (they came in two categories, we decided) bumped up the lane, usually in the drowsy late after-noon, bewildered, ill-tempered or both. Tony's response to their arrival was ever the same, shrill astonishment. 'I don't know *why* they're here! Do *you*?' How long will *they* be staying? 'How should *I* know. I mean, *you*'ll have to find out. Jocelyn will have to make the arrangements. I don't know *where* we're going to put them . . . ' Jocelyn, of course, did, swinging into an extremely proficient partnership with the resident housekeeper, Mme Voisin.

Oscar Beuselinck turned up, all chippy and confident that he had established some kind of bridgehead into our chaotic lives. He strutted around the pool in the early morning, slapping his belly, bellowing, 'Well, what are we going to do today?' He brought with him his teenage son, later to become a television star, Paul Nicholas. George arrived later with Jocelyn H., saintly-weary as ever, followed by her three teenage children. The middle one, a boy, was quiet, solicitous and very agreeable, but the two girls were, with the restless torpor of youth, openly peevish that they were obliged to share the pool and the sunshine with a bunch of battle-scarred convalescents in their thirties, even forties.

George was clearly in a very bad way over the miserable humiliation of

August for the People, over Rex Harrison's brutal superstar behaviour and, most woundingly, over the bitterness of his rejection by its author, Nigel Dennis. It was hideous to witness his agony at being accused of treachery by one of his most loved writers. The pantomime of events had been cruelly familiar. Caught between the actor's famous vanity and the author's indignation, George as director had more or less given up. In the face of their implacable strategies, he had lost his nerve, turning for solace from the acrimony of rehearsals into the evening's comfort of his part as kindly, integrated Staupitz. 'He fled into that like a wife who can't face the washing-up,' was Dennis's sour observation.

After a fractious opening in Newcastle, *August for the People* stumbled on mutinously to Edinburgh, where Kenneth Tynan denounced it as the 'dead duck' of the Festival. This should have been consistent with the whole tradition of George's fingers-up camaraderie. The production arrived in Sloane Square with the sort of pre-opening reputation associated with most of his past offerings. In spite of the first-night diversion of Lindsay Anderson bearing a banner demanding the release of three newly gaoled CND-affirming Court playwrights and the inevitably grumpy reviews, thanks to Harrison there was no reason for the play not to continue its sell-out run.

Dennis sulked in his earth-closet in Essex; Harrison's irascible panic mounted. His time and costly talent had been squandered by a bunch of dithering amateurs, and he announced his intention of leaving the play in mid-run. He had been offered the part of Caesar in the Burton–Taylor epic *Cleopatra*, and Twentieth Century Fox and its legal battalions happily bought out his contract from the cock-a-mamie Royal Court. George pleaded with Harrison, the finest light comedian of his generation. Sexy Rexy, international star, refused to budge.

The cupidity of rich actors is usually tinged with self-righteousness, but Harrison was too stylish to apologize for claiming his portion of the greed and disloyalty the peaks of his profession may bestow. George knew only too well that no contract is enforceable and that his only course was to take the silver Fox dollars, hand them to Neville Blond and cancel the run. Dennis, in his turn, pleaded with George to take over Harrison's part. Only a contemptuously abandoned playwright would fail to see that this was an impossible demand. George could only refuse, and the rancour between them was sealed for ever.

When George arrived in Valbonne in the midst of the Herbert contingent and adolescent clamour, he collapsed into fits of uncontrollable weeping. The atmosphere at La Beaumette was already strained with Jocelyn's personal uncertainties, my own, the rapacious behaviour of our guests and the parching, dusty heat of the Côte d'Azur in August. Even the shade from the overhanging vines created a mood of chill unease.

So it was perhaps wise of Tony to cordon George off into a kind of quarantine for the next ten days. It was managed with his usual swift skill, successfully and even physically dividing his friends and ensuring his own control. When I protested at George's summary whisking-away into Tony's intensive care, he accused me of insensitivity. 'You've got to be reasonable, Johnny. I mean, you only *upset* him.' It seemed presumptuous to suggest that I might have done the opposite. 'He doesn't want to see anyone. And, besides, the doctor says he's got to rest completely.' I was out-manoeuvred and inflamed that Tony should appropriate responsibility so blandly. I also knew there would be no appeal to Jocelyn H.

Pitched into this swelter of variously aggrieved feelings, there was the daily irritant of registered 'express' letters from Penelope. Each morning, either from timely effort or accident, Jocelyn – mine own, then – would sign for them, tip the *facteur* and mockingly deliver them to me. I took to leaving them around unenveloped. It was a shabby gesture but then the circumstances were wearisomely vulgar, like the whole venture, the South of France, August, even George's breakdown and, above all, myself. I could persuade myself I had been uncommonly goaded.

Worse came later. My secretary rang in what I presumed to be innocence and told Jocelyn the whereabouts of the bank where I could collect the *lire* I should need the following month when I met Penelope at the Venice Film Festival. This time, Jocelyn abandoned all mime and pursued me deadly to the pool. 'If you're going to Venice, you must talk to me.' 'I don't *have* to talk to anyone,' I know I must have snarled back, diving into the pool, and so she says I did.

Afterwards, like Rex Harrison, I made no apologies for my conspiracy, only exacting a promise from her to remain at La Beaumette until I returned. It was an astonishing request and, astonishingly, she agreed. Tony, naturally, sniffed all this out of the air, when he didn't actually witness the melodrama. He asked Jocelyn about the letters. 'You mean the Collected Letters of Mrs Gilliatt,' she replied. He then told her that he had already asked Penelope to marry him.

Two figures appeared mercifully at this stage in the Valbonne farce: Christopher Isherwood and Don Bachardy. Their arrival could scarcely have been more timely. They had a nicely sanitized Californian detachment from the incestuous, provincial preoccupations of their English friends, so trivially inspired in comparison with the earnestness of West Coast campus matters. And they both had the hardest heads for alcohol I have ever encountered. Even Robert Stephens was a mere corporal to these gentlemen.

One early morning, I discovered them both fresh and dazzling beneath the vines, shaven, in white sneakers and as well groomed as their upstanding healthy heads of cropped hair. I could just remember that the three of us – at some time earlier, hours or days before – had disposed of at least three bottles of Ralph Richardson's favourite tipple, Marc-de-Bourgogne. He gave me a bottle of it as a present for the publication of the first volume of this book. It was – once more – the last time I saw him.

Feeling almost euphorically ill, I found myself blurting out eagerly an urgent yet insignificant secret I had told no one, not even Jocelyn. I was feeling driven by indecision about everything in view, my choice of work, where I should direct my energies, both seething and troublesome. The nag of disquiet and all the inescapable forebodings with which I had been born were so rooted that they couldn't be dismissed by the pleasure, the luxuries, the companionships and liberations that I felt I should have been enjoying at this point in my life.

One thing, however, did divert me and obviated some of this fever of tedium and apprehension. It was a small thing, not yet mine own and little more than a figment. It was no more than the impression in my head for a scene in a play which I knew would have to bide its time before it was written. Beneath the trees, in the early coolness of the morning and that oddly pharmaceutical smell of French breakfast coffee, I outlined to Christopher and Don the Drag Ball scene in *A Patriot for Me*.

The hangover pulse hammered away at my neck glands and the frictions of La Beaumette receded as I tried to describe the pattern and the setting of the ball and its slow effect on the audience as the gloriously dressed characters revealed themselves to be exclusively male. Christopher's animated response was rewarding, especially from a homosexual novelist who didn't seem suspicious about an 'outsider' poaching territory he might have regarded as his own.

He remembered the grand drag balls of the thirties, including annual occasions presided over by the famous performing aesthete Bunny Rogers. George told me he had attended one during his Oxford days when his companion was the actress Hermione Baddeley, a jewel of campery hotly pursued by his fellow undergraduates of all persuasions. 'What did you *go* as?' I had asked him. 'Nelson,' he growled. It seemed a tasteful compromise and I consequently wrote a Nelson into the final stage directions of *Patriot*. He was played by Ferdy Mayne. 'It is a measure of my love for you, dear boy,' said George later, 'that I consented to appear on the same stage as one of my least favourite actors.'

Christopher went on to talk about the scene's implications. 'You know,' he said, 'it reminds me of the other night. Know what I mean, Don?' Don smiled beatifically. 'It was in the Negresco. In Terry Rattigan's suite. The company could all have been characters in your play. It was quite a glittering cast: Terry, Cuthbert Worsley, Binkie Beaumont, Michael Redgrave, John Perry, Don and myself. And *then* there were the bit players. Lots of them. Oh, and of course, Tony. Quite a tableau for you, don't you think?' So that was why Tony had made one of his unexplained trips immediately after dinner, roaring down the drive alone in his careering Thunderbird.

It was an oddly encouraging footnote, a small omen, and I felt I could safely put the play away in custody at the back of my head for a couple of years, when I might be 'ready for it'. But not yet.

In August the Cold War escalated with the Berlin Crisis, and the proliferation of nuclear weapons seemed certain.

A Letter to my Fellow Countrymen

This is a letter of hate. It is for you, my countrymen. I mean those men of my country who have defiled it. The men with manic fingers leading the sightless, feeble, betrayed body of my country to its death. You are its murderers, and there's little left in my own brain but the thoughts of murder for you . . . My hatred of you is almost the only constant, satisfaction you have left me. My favourite fantasy is four minutes or so non-commercial viewing as you fry in your democratically elected hot seats in Westminster, preferably with your condoning democratic constituents . . . You have instructed me in my hatred for 30 years. You have perfected it and made it the blunt, obsolete instrument it is now. I only hope it will keep me going. I think it will. It may sustain me in the last few months. Till then, damn you England. You're rotting now, and quite soon you'll disappear. My hate will outrun you yet, if only for a few seconds. I wish it could be eternal . . .

Your fellow countryman,
John Osborne
Valbonne, France

Tribune, 18 August 1961

I had written intemperate declarations of this kind before and, indeed, have done since. Usually, I tuck them aside, soothed by the quick expectorating exercise itself. 'Damn you England' was written without pause, as it plainly shows, when I sat beneath the vines sipping my forenoon Ricard. I knew it to be a slovenly, melodramatic misuse of my so-called gift for 'rhetoric'. Unfortunately, I libelled my own passionate confusion by omitting any grace notes of rigour or irony. I foolishly hoped that a few perceptive souls might recognize the naked outrage at the heart of its posturing self-dramatization. If I had not believed that it partially reflected my overwhelming mood of agitated disaffection, I would never have popped it in the post.

The style was deliberately overheated because I knew that would be the only way to gain attention, to adopt a different tone from the tame blandness of left-wing journals like the *New Statesman*. If this tone was misjudged, it was because my soft-headed liberal analysis of the political realities of international Communism was pitifully naïve. My duped perceptions exactly matched the sentimental orthodoxy that has since shifted its bleeding heart from Atomic Destruction to even dreamier preoccupations like rainforests, United Nations resolutions, the Third World (happy hunting-ground of the eternal liberal) and, lately, the holy relic of the cardboard box.

I had sent the letter to *Tribune* because I knew it was the only journal which would even consider publishing such a seditious piece. What I had not expected was that the editor, Richard Clements, would present it as a message delivered in self-exile from a sybaritic retreat in the south of France, with my address at the bottom. There would be no doubt that I had undergone some kind of brainstorm, to the delight of many and the dismay of my friends. Muddle-headed Johnny had hurled his marbles in the air and, this time, on a bridge far, far too far.

Only a few days after the Glorious Twelfth the Silly Season in England exploded into life and banged on well into September. For weeks holiday-makers opened their airmail editions of the *Telegraph* and more popular papers to find selections of pro- and con-Osborne correspondence (surprisingly weighted one against the other), editorial comment, cartoons and pronounce-ments of respected journalists like Peregrine Worsthorne, who gave discursive judgements on the present state of the nation and myself. His interpretation of the letter and the flood of response to it covered almost the whole centre page of the *Sunday Telegraph* on 20 August:

> I have an uneasy suspicion that Osborne speaks for far more people than we care to recognize . . . For his hatred of Britain is much more than a mere personal idiosyncracy. The murderous language, of course, is per-sonal, but the feeling behind it is shared, I believe, by a frighteningly large number of his fellow countrymen. The truly significant conflict today is not between the rich and poor but between those over thirty-five and those under . . . The friction it causes at periods of acute crisis – such as the present – when the young feel that their fate is in the hands of men whose values they do not share, gives rise to precisely the feeling of passionate despairing resentment which John Osborne so virulently articu-

lated in *Tribune*. Here is the driving force of deep social bitterness – a basic conviction in the young that the established order neither reflects their faith nor protects their lives.

That same Sunday, the *Sunday Times* carried its own 'Critics and Disciples':

JOHN BRAINE: I agree with every word Osborne writes.

HUGH TREVOR-ROPER: I never read things written in that kind of language. I think I might read it if it were translated into English.

JOHN BRATBY: I can't think why he's written it at all. It can only damage his reputation.

J.B. PRIESTLEY: I haven't read the whole thing, but is it all that important?

SHELAGH DELANEY: John has had the courage to say something a lot of people have been thinking.

ARNOLD WESKER: I know what he feels and so do hundreds of thousands of others.

JOHN WHITING: I thought John Osborne's letter was very funny. The whole thing was a bit overwritten and sending it from the South of France wasn't exactly tactful.

RICHARD HOGGART: Oh, dear!

M A I L B A G

HAVING read John Osborne's "attack" I want to say how much I and most mothers I know agree with it.

I have two small children and another baby on the way. I go to bed every night, my heart filled with fear for their future. I'm not brave. I'm frightened to death, but most of all I'm frightened of it for my children.

I, too, wish to God that all the statesmen of the world would get blown up if it meant the end of the Bomb and the fear of our children's destruction.
MARJORIE DENT.
Keighley.

WRONG BASIS

JOHN OSBORNE was right to voice his feelings about warmongers and public apathy.

But he has done a poor service to the cause of peace by expressing himself in terms suggesting the hysterical ravings of a psychopath.

He does not speak for the true pacifist element in this country, which is based on reverence for life and not on corrosive hate.
ISABEL SUTHERLAND.
London.

HE'S HONEST

MAY I suggest that all those who, like John Osborne, want us to lay down our arms and surrender should be equally honest?

It is far easier to respect a man who confesses to being afraid than one who hides his fear behind a smoke-screen of sanctimonious hypocrisy.
DESMOND ALLHUSEN.
Beaminster.

PITY HIM

WHAT a pitiable state John Osborne is in ! Little left in his own brain but thoughts of murder, and fearing death, but clinging wretchedly to life !
(Mrs.) B. JACKSON.
Goole.

SO RIGHT

THANK you for John Osborne's brilliant and much-needed attack on our tinpot, grouse-hunting politicians' handling of the Berlin crisis.

He expresses so correctly the feelings of the younger generation.
Pentraeth. **K. G. KING.**

Daily Mail, 21 August 1961

The *Mail*, obviously taken aback by the weight of response and surprised that its readers were by no means unanimously condemning, delivered a ponderous leader on 23 August:

202

John Osborne's letter of hate reads like that of a betrayed lover . . . This is the cry of the individual who feels powerless to affect the world he lives in. But nobody can change the destiny of the world by going to a village in the South of France and crying 'The Game's Up!' Osborne should be shouting in his own country . . . Men like Osborne should be speaking in Trafalgar Square, as Bertrand Russell does. They could be arguing in the columns of newspapers or on television. They could be standing for Bristol South East . . .

The principal beneficiary from all this nonsense was *Tribune*.

Every true Socialist should roar with applause at Osborne's letter. We five navvies have not read anything like it since Nye Bevin's 'vermin' speech. Hell's bells, you're a *great* newspaper to print it. In the name of God, wake up, wake up, you weak-kneed, sheep-brained sons and daughters of a land that has never cried out so loud in its history for salvation, and has never appeared such a stupid and cowardly shower. All our hate, along with Osborne's.

Jack Jones and the Four Navvies.

Tribune, 21 September 1961

23. 'Don't Cry for Me, Nicaragua'

Everyone in the world has as much as they can do in caring for themselves and few have leisure to really think of their neighbour's distress, however they may delight their tongues in talking of them.

Samuel Johnson, 1783

A mistress should be like a little country retreat near the town, not to dwell in constantly, but only for a night and a day.

William Congreve

Fly if your pigtail catches fire,
Dive down the nearest sink,
Remember if you wash a pancake,
Its underwear is sure to shrink.

How do I live? On the Parish.
Where do I sleep? In a tomb.
I was born in a sardines' graveyard,
Where treacle and sausages bloom.

What does it matter if rock cakes rock,
And pineapples fly in the air?
'Cos at death I shall cheerfully cry,
But he'll say Pontoons only, 'I'm sticking'.

Billy Bennett, 'Devil-May-Care', 1926

Major Colin de Vere Gordon-MacLean (retired), thirty-three years old, who had served in the British Army as a regular soldier in Germany, Hong Kong and Malaya, arrived on the doorstep of La Beaumette with his yellow labrador, Simla, and a rifle under his arm.

He had had to negotiate our next-door neighbours, a rather louche nudist colony, and make his way on foot up the dusty, broken drive for a mile or two. He was lightly dressed in an open-necked white shirt and a pair of old bags, as fresh and eager as when he set out. In the breathless buzz of the airless August afternoon, he must have felt that the farmhouse was deserted. No doubt the plains of Salisbury and Hanover had taught him how to kick up some action from entrenched local inertia during a hot siesta. Sure enough, he discovered Jocelyn R., nodding over Henry James. Major Colin de Vere Gordon-MacLean knew how to sum up a situation smartly and act on it at once. He instructed Jocelyn to seek me out. 'Just tell him I've come to accept his apologies to Britain – at once.'

Jocelyn, in a drowsy state of late-afternoon Calvados, Henry James and the sight of Simla, the Major and his rifle, found me asleep by the pool. 'He's got a gun and a sweet labrador. And he wants you to apologize to England.' 'Tell him to fuck off, or we'll tell the gendarmerie we've got an armed foreign intruder trespassing on the Glenconners' property.' She pottered back happily to deliver this message.

After a while, when she hadn't reappeared at the pool, and there had been no sounds of shots or scuffle, I decided to go and look for myself. The Major had proceeded to reconnoitre the interior of the house while she returned to her bowered hammock and left him to it. He set up a tactical observation post in the drawing-room. What followed could have been nicely worked up by that intrepid farceur Ray Cooney and performed by the splendid Donald Sinden. I acted true to all the conventions of the game. Assuming the golden Simla would spot it at once, I scribbled on a piece of paper and slipped it beneath the door. It read: 'I am tied up at present. Please go away.'

Not a particularly defiant response to a demand for unconditional surrender, but I felt that the Major had made his point for England and would feel no dishonour in accepting such a mild entreaty. Jocelyn pattered back with the major's reply. 'We progress, it seems. I wanted to let you know what many people feel about your disgraceful outburst. I have taken some pains to find you in order to do so.' 'Tell him to fuck off. If he's a British officer, he's not likely to take his rifle butt to an unarmed lady.' 'Well, Simla's frightfully friendly.'

Colin de Vere Gordon-MacLean was a product of the modern post-war British army. He conducted a careful debriefing operation from the Post Office in Valbonne.

OSBORNE: You are a complete stranger. Why should I receive every lunatic who comes beating at my door?
MAJOR: I am not a lunatic.
OSBORNE: I didn't say you were. You are probably an intelligent person. You

no doubt are. But what makes you think you have the right to come to my house and expect me to greet you?

MAJOR: When a gentleman calls on another gentleman, he ought to be received at least.

OSBORNE: You've come bursting into my life.

MAJOR: I didn't burst in. I wanted to discuss these sweeping statements you have made about the British people. What do you think their reaction is?

OSBORNE: I know what the public reaction is. I am not interested in your reactions. I am losing my temper.

MAJOR: A lot of people are losing their tempers – with *you*. Are you sincere or not?

OSBORNE: That's impertinent. I'm a writer.

MAJOR: Writer? Writer? You use a lot of hackneyed phrases like hanging out dirty washing. You are a disgrace. You seem to like hiding behind pencil and paper.

From then on the house was in a state of intermittent siege from stray local stringers of British newspapers and phone calls which Jocelyn R. dutifully answered. Tony said nothing, but his cool, quizzical glances only made me more furious with myself for having visited these squalid indignities on what should have been a healing gathering of friends, all tired, fretful but united in their concern for each other.

A week later, on 31 August, Mary gave birth to her son, Colin, in a Regent's Park nursing-home. Tony came back from his morning foray into Cannes and scattered the English newspapers on the floor, along with his own preferred copies of *Le Monde* and the *Herald Tribune*. There were huge blow-ups of Mary looking more radiantly effervescent than she had done even during our Roman Christmas. The headlines and stories were almost as uniform as the accounts from the Mad Major. 'For Mary Ure – a son. While Osborne stays Abroad.' 'John Osborne is a Shy Dad.' 'A New Son for Osborne – but he stays away.' 'The Strange World of John Osborne – He stays on holiday in France as his son is born in London.' Mary herself was being almost chillingly circumspect, as were her unfortunate parents.

During the evening of the following day, the three of us – Tony, Jocelyn and myself – dined indoors for the first time. The damp, evening chill had begun to set in, driving us inside as well as within ourselves. It was a dispiriting occasion, all nuances confused but oppressive. It was as if each one of us wished to escape the others. Jocelyn's gossiping fluency was almost stilled, and even Tony's spinning core of energy seemed depleted. A heavy pall of leave-taking, a sense of vague misadventure, hung over the table. There was none of the pursued frivolity or wanton speculation of the previous weeks we had spent in each other's company. I could detect a sense of repressed bafflement and disappointment from both of them.

Almost at once, we became aware that we were being observed at very close quarters. In the overhanging foliage of the terrace we began to make out a twilight Tenniel-like vision of faces and the steely reflection of camera lenses trained on the table. As we rose together, the trees erupted into little flashes of white light. We had been ambushed like bandits in a mountain fortress. Paparazzi of all nations hung like bats from the branches. Tony and I shook the trees and they dropped to earth, squealing, clutching their cameras, and disappeared into the darkness. Tony left early the next morning for the airport to oversee the transfer of *Luther* to the Phoenix Theatre and the West End première of *A Taste of Honey*.

I didn't know whether he was aware of my own intended departure and arranged rendezvous with Penelope at our next shared film festival, in Venice. Nor did I really want to. His relief at extricating himself from a steamy mess of emotions must have been profound. Left alone together, Jocelyn and I lapsed into a grateful armistice of humane reticence. During the late siesta, I rose, dressed and packed little more than a change of clothes in a bag. I hoped I was being discreet, not furtive. I also hoped that she would wake with a long, drowsy intake of relief when she found that I had gone.

I don't think I ever asked Penelope why she had chosen Folkestone for a fictitious film festival and the *venue* (in popular tradespeak) for our opening bound into adultery. But, arriving at the tiny Da Vinci airport, I felt as inexplicably in control – at least in the principle of choice – and powerful and lusty as the winged lions of St Mark's. I was as aware of this seizure of euphoria as I was of the blast of concrete heat and the mist from the lagoon.

Penelope was waiting for me behind the barrier at the concourse, a smudge of bright yellow in her frock, northern pale, the large brown eyes bleached from any black. Her hair out-Titianed the arrival gate to Venice. What others would nail as her greeting gush felt to me on that September morning more like the embrace of a voluptuous goddess. It is tempting to deride and disown what may have been howling fits of delusion. But the abandonment of sense and judgement cannot honestly repudiate it, just as my passion for Pamela had been a folly and, most demonstrably, a delusion. That one took more than thirty years before she stamped on it finally with her own authority.

Penelope had booked us into a discreet, that is to say cheap, room at the Europa Hotel on the Grand Canal, almost opposite the magnificently baroque Santa Maria della Salute. It was Germanic, efficient, anonymous – if anonymity is possible in Venice. Unlike Folkestone, Venice's festival showed films, hundreds of them, an astonishing number of which Penelope was determined to attend. As film critic of the *Observer* she felt constrained to present herself at press showings, press conferences and general promotional junketings. The giddy romantic lustings of the Europa paled in comparison.

The piazzas and palaces of Venice were not merely coursing with the international lava of tourists but, as every September, were bobbing with the flotsam of film-reviewers, show-biz columnists, gossips, commentators, stray stringers, baggage-trailers, photographers, directors, producers, actors, starlets and their minders – the hungry international train which followed and scavenged off the whole calendar of festivalizing for a living and as a way of life.

It was an almost blind dementia of hopefulness for the newly respected film critic of the *Observer*, wife of Dr Gilliatt, most publicly approved and vetted best man, and John Osborne, angry young playwright, notorious less for his plays than for his spoiled, intemperate attacks upon his own country, to contemplate the possibility of enjoying lunch unseen together at the Fenice restaurant or Torcello, mingling in the crush at Harry's Bar or sipping midnight coffee at Florian's and traipsing through the pigeons hand-in-hand. And yet we managed it.

I spent long periods on my own at the Europa, either asleep in our bedroom or drinking on the terrace while Penelope toiled across to the Lido to load herself with an armful of bumph from the festival press office. After the grapplings of a long night, I did not want to set out before breakfast to watch ideological dramas about peasant passions among Romanian villagers at the turn of the century or Kurosawa's latest, *Yojimbo* [who he?].

Penelope, however, was hell-bent on appeasing her critical conscience by attending everything on offer. I chose to excuse this as quaint dedication rather than undiscriminating avidity. At this stage, I was still able to stifle my irritation at her rigid priorities which gave misty art-screenings precedence over the tangible passions smouldering in our hotel room. For my own part, I was in no mood to squander precious hours of proven delight by enduring boredom-until-death with a thousand frames of prize contenders for that year's Golden Lion like *L'Année Dernière à Marienbad*.

Of course, I should have spotted the phoney gambler then, weeks before I heard the call 'Do your Nuns Decline?' Yet when I heard affections like 'I shall never, never have to look for anyone again,' the deepest nerve within me was shot through. No one, not even Stella, had seemed to proclaim themselves with such joyous effrontery. Cheap music it may have sounded in other ears, but in my ravenous condition it had the clangour of Mahler, full of frenzy and, here in Venice, a tragic preoccupation with longing and joy in the shadow of the Salute.

I was in the grip of an abiding resolution that I would reject nothing that might be thrown at me, however inadequate my resources. My five years at rest with the Court had provided me with an escape from the wilderness, and I had a premonition of some certainty that the most recent sequence of absurdities and illusions was entering a new stage of haunted apprehension. There was no way I could be rid of it. I could only obey what I must accept as my nature, put my head down and God Rot them all, either to fade or to survive. Redemption of some sort might even break in cheerfully now and then.

Penelope and I left each other at the airport. She went on the 9.00 a.m. plane to London. My flight to Nice had been 'delayed', and I was sweetly told by the nubile Alitalia girls at the desk that it would not take off until four o'clock in the afternoon. I had no money at all. I had given my change to Penelope for her cab fare from London airport. This was in the days before jumped-up clerks and salesmen affected 'executive' calling-cards along with their armoury of briefcases, faxes, lap computers, ties, pens, even homes. 'Lifestyle' had yet to be coined for the man utterly bereft of style. There was therefore no 'executive' lounge. I settled down for the next seven hours on a sweaty leatherette sofa in a hut perched on the marshy edge of the most glorious commercial outpost in the world. Where on earth was I? Perhaps it was God's off-hand reproof for the folly of Folkestone.

Two years later, just after Penelope and I were married, we returned to Venice, accompanied by my mother, Nellie Beatrice, who complained of the city's sparse amenities and its mysterious lack of pubs and Mackeson's cream stout. Penelope, who made an elaborate pretence of liking her and called her 'Mum', was insistent that it would be such a good thing if 'Mum' could be shown that there were other horizons beyond Margate and more enriching alternatives to the Laundry's Day Out on the coach.

My own mock forbearance, as so often, provided me with scope for manoeuvre I might not have been able to exploit had we been alone together. Roving Posh Paper critic, hitched to muddle-headed but acceptable playwright, having drilled lovable old working-class Mum into the cross-over family-shared experience of a publess town, might be put off by the simple bureaucratic difficulties of dragging her unwillingly to the next Resnais or Truffaut press showing. Old Mum's reluctance would give me an excuse to stay away.

One afternoon, after lunch at the Fenice, when old Nellie Beatrice had demanded to know the price of every dish so that she could compare it with her remembrance of the wartime bill at the Strand Palace Corner House, we were on our way back to the hotel. Quite suddenly, Penelope made a crabwise leap through the crowds outside St Mark's and disappeared. For once, I reacted fairly quickly. 'Wait here,' I said to Nellie Beatrice, black-looked and sweating irritably. One of the advantages of being an Englishman in Italy, and certainly in the Basilica, is that you can see above the heads of everyone else.

I shoved my way through the final set of doors leading into the church, looked down the nave and spotted Penelope's copper head bobbing above a sprawling ruck of gawpers and church officials. Everywhere there were signs in five languages requesting ladies not to enter with bare arms or uncovered heads. Penelope had sprinted down the nave bereft of necessary covering. She was tackled by several vergers like a pack of floor-waiters arresting a shoplifter in the food hall. Caught up in the crush were dozens of sightseers, all bawling in the full throat of American panic.

Mercifully, a cool, calm, mid-Western voice could be heard. 'Come on, my dear. Can't you see? There are notices everywhere. You have to cover your head inside this beautiful place.' 'Go and fuck yourself.' 'Come my dear, you must be reasonable. It isn't much to ask of you. Here, cover yourself with this.' A scarf was thrust under her nose. 'Fuck off. Fuck off. All of you.' By this time she was in the grasp of five panting officials of the Basilica, who looked like frog-marching her through the crowd. 'Now, be reasonable, my dear. Surely you can read. It's only ordinary politeness . . .' 'Fuck off, all of you.'

Like the firemen who had raced through Woodfall Street to snatch Davy from my side, I plunged through a cordon of people some twenty deep, grabbed Penelope's bare upper arm and wrenched her from the grasp of the Basilica's men. In the Piazza, Nellie Beatrice looked on almost approvingly as I dragged Penelope towards the safety of the Inghilterra.

Stoneleigh

My dear John,

I promised to drop you a few lines, after I got home made a cup of tea and went to bed as usual thinking of all the nice things there were instilled in my mind. First thank you for my nice lunch and drinkies – also for helping to put right the mess I got myself into through misunderstandings.

How right you were when you said I was wicked. I have known this for a long time, and selfish and self-pitying, you have only confirmed what my brother told me long ago: but I was too much of a coward to admit it this afternoon. There is no crime in being any of these things. It's beyond my control to adjust myself. I have tried – its failed, so please don't ask me to do the impossible. The truth is I'm afraid, *really afraid*;

and must face up to my own selfish stupidity and fight this out alone. Somehow. I ask for no forgiveness or make any excuse for my bad behaviour. You come from fine stock, The Osbornes, gentle – sweet and kind: hold on to these . . .

Dear John,

I know how you feel towards me: and you have reason to dislike me so – and I have never been much of a Mother; and so only deserve and to know how you have felt towards me for a long time now. I make no excuses; only ask you not to be bad friends. I feel terribly sad and unhappy but I deserve to be. Please try to forgive me. I think I have been punished enough. I am not self-pitying myself its the guilt that lays within that makes me realize what a horrible person I have been and am.

My dear,

How are you: I think of you so much. I don't blame you for hating me so much for the hurt I have caused you. I *hate* myself too; believe me – I have suffered so much. I'm nearly going mad knowing that you have cut me out of your life. Please John I beg of you to help me in my great distress, I know it is unforgiveable, and it is a big thing to ask of you . . .

My dear dearest John,

What a relief to get your letter. Oh God so understanding, how rotten can a mother feel. My dear boy I feel so dreadful, you will never know how cheap: selfish to know I treated you so cruelly I cannot offer any excuses. It's unbelievable one's utter selfish and cruel temper. I have indeed suffered and quite rightly too, John, nearly gone mad thinking what for God sake have I done to hurt you so much. I can't ask you to forgive me, it is too much to expect for the cruel treatment I have given you. Moods are so hard and difficult to explain. I hardly know what to say to your kind and sad letter. I am now crying. Oh dear God do understand and believe I do not mean to hurt you: it just boils down to the truth lets face it: I am and feel the most horrible creature alive cheap and low: here I am living on luxury by your brains and in return you receive such cruel and unkind treatment. It sounds so dam stupid and does not make sense. Hughie Green was on television last night. He was out in India and showed us the picture of a beautiful temple. He said it was the loveliest thing he had ever seen. I thought of you . . .

Your loving,
Mother

24. *Crimson Twilight*

Voltaire, who was in a torment of envy for the universal esteem in which Congreve was held by men of all parties, felt irritated by the Playwright's disclaimers for his gifts as a poet of the theatre. When he had called on Congreve, the Englishman declared that his plays were trifles, produced in an idle hour, and begged Voltaire to consider him merely as a gentleman.

'If you had been merely a gentleman,' said Voltaire, 'I should not have come to see you.'

Notebook, 1957

DORN: (*alone*) I don't know, maybe I don't understand anything, maybe I've gone off my head, but I did like that play. There is something in it. When that child was holding forth about loneliness, and later when the devil's red eyes appeared, I was so moved that my hands were shaking. It was fresh, unaffected . . . Ah! I think he's coming along now. I feel like telling him a lot of nice things about it.

Dr Dorn in Anton Chekhov's *The Seagull**

Joceyln R. met me at Nice Airport. We decided to let the evening Croisette cut-up chariot race abate a little and had a drink in the shade of the roof-terrace bar. We were pleased to see each other. She said not a word of reproach, implying that she had enjoyed having La Beaumette to herself without the daily flood of letters from Penelope.

I was able to relate news from the Rialto, quite literally, and provide her with a few choice ends of gossip which gladdened the eager spite we shared towards certain figureheads in films and journalism. I had enough malicious scraps of disasters, clowning, tales of aborted narcissism and duplicity gone

---

* Produced by the English Stage Company at the Queen's Theatre, March 1964, directed by Tony Richardson, with a cast including Peggy Ashcroft, Ann Beach, Mark Dignam, Peter Finch, Rachel Kempson, Philip Locke, Peter McEnery, Vanessa Redgrave and George Devine as Dr Dorn.

awry to keep her stocked with the pleasure of several weeks of dinner-party recounting. Open, ill-natured gossip was one of our devout bonds. Although much of my stay in Venice had been spent in idle hours in the bedroom at the Europa on my own, I had been too preoccupied to read the newspapers or take account of what had been going on at home. Jocelyn filled me in on the confrontation in Berlin, the Oder–Neisse line, and the prospect of imminent nuclear destruction.

It was well into the second week of September 1961 and the Committee of 100's campaign for a mass sit-down in Trafalgar Square on Sunday the 17th had been shrewdly stage-managed. The preliminary meetings I had attended were overlorded by experts in dissidence, those who would have been most at home in the days of Babylon, locked in canonical disputation and Deuteronomical intrigue among the tribes of Israel.

The beginning of the fanaticism that was to expand and impose itself on every aspect of life – from the anti-smoking lobby to animal rights – was stirring, a rabid, venomous and neurotic collection of factions, united by their frightening brand of righteous ruthlessness. I had never believed it could take such hold among my temperate, lazy-hearted countrymen.

Like many others at the time, and for many years to come, I had a sentimental, indulgent attitude towards the adherents of CND and even its militant wing. It was the popular view of a substantial minority of high-minded folk driven to unremitting extremity by their sense of helplessness in the face of the wickedness of those who had seized dominion of their lives. The familiar image was of well-humoured, peaceable folk, pushing the prams of a doomed generation and singing their gentle defiance to the accompaniment of a jolly marching jazz-band.

The reality was somewhat different. The inner heart of the movement was cynical, sophisticated and rigidly political. The simple, idealistic, apocalyptic visions it aroused among the mass of good-hearted adherents were ruthlessly engineered and exploited by professionals who were dedicated, born enemies of their own country. They used all their fanaticism and skill at arousing panic and dissatisfaction among the ranks of decent, respectable, dim liberals who were genuinely dismayed and alarmed by the way the world seemed to be heading for hideous destruction.

In the week before I returned to Valbonne, the government's alarm at the rising tide of feeling, which could no longer be ignored, began to make itself plain. Embarrassment at the revelations of incompetence on a grand scale at the George Blake trial in April and, particularly, its effect on American confidence, was still biting hard. The economic situation, grim enough at the Budget, had worsened still further during the summer. Unemployment, running at the then 'unacceptable' figure of over a million and a half, had remained static and, by mid-July, the Chancellor of the Exchequer, Mr Selwyn Lloyd, had been forced to increase taxation by £70 million before a shot had been fired on the Glorious Twelfth.

All of this was as meaningless as usual to most of us, immersed in peccadilloes at film festivals from Folkestone to Venice, but the climate of panic seemed clear to all, and it might have been this that prompted Mr Harold Macmillan to make one of his grandiose pronouncements at the end of July, that his government had decided officially to apply for full membership of the EEC. It didn't seem to have much effect on the public mood, even to those who were happily contemplating a new era of frantic common enterprise, accompanied by the civilizing influence of French cuisine and German poetry.

Nearer to the homely realities of our own lives, Tony had rung Jocelyn R. to report on the opening night of *Luther* when it transferred to the Phoenix. British Prime Ministers are not remembered for their enthusiasms for literature or drama, although Macmillan was already highly regarded as an Edwardian eccentric with his addiction to bedtime with Trollope. He seemed to have gone out of his way to be present at the opening, taking his young grandson with him. The newspapers were mystified. Was this not an unlikely gesture from a Premier burdened with the gravity of the developments in Berlin, economic pressures at home, sustained unemployment, the unease of the trade unions at his government's disputed intrusion into the negotiation of wage agreements?

Not at all, he had said to amazed reporters during the interval. Just the thing to take his grandson to see. But what about the play, Mrs Lincoln/Mr Macmillan? Written by the author of an infamous letter, damning his own countrymen? 'I thought the play was wonderful,' he said. Whether he did or not, Tony confirmed his public reaction, having been cornered by him in the bar. 'I mean, it was very weird, Jocelyn. He just went on and on very emotionally. All Johnny's old Edwardian wilderness stuff, and then the young men dying in the trenches, the dole queues, the soup-kitchens. I mean, Johnny would have loved it.'

The subsequent declaration of the government's intentions over the proposed Trafalgar Square demonstration was not so benign. A couple of forgotten mid-Victorian Acts relating specifically to public order and vagrancy had been winkled out of the statute-books and, by the invocation of these, summonses were served on several of the most prominent Committee members, including the stridently frail Chairman, Bertrand Russell, and playwrights Arnold Wesker, Robert Bolt and Christopher Logue. They had all duly appeared at Bow Street and been required to enter into recognizance not to breach the peace on the big day in question. All of them refused and were sentenced to a month in gaol in Brixton.

Jocelyn had a copy of the report of the proceedings in one of the more ponderous dailies. When I finished reading it, she said very simply and with no satisfaction, 'You'll have to go back, won't you?' Her restraint was as helpful as everything else she had said while we sat in the noise and glare of the Aeroport Côte d'Azur. 'I was hoping you'd say that,' I replied.

For once, there was no room for equivocation, which made my next act, even its physical execution, strangely easy. The following day, in the taxi from Heathrow to Lower Belgrave Street, we stopped at traffic lights beside Chesham Place, where Penelope had moved. I opened the door unhurriedly, in those days of unlocked cabs which didn't thank you for not smoking, got out and said, 'I'm sorry, my darling. I'm afraid I'm going to behave rather badly yet again.' It was odiously expressed and odiously executed. Perhaps I felt too numb even for self-disgust. I could only think of Sir Henry Irving's legendary desertion of his wife in a brougham after the first night of *The Bells*. 'Are you going on making a fool of yourself like this all your life?' Lady Irving asked him. Jocelyn might have justly repeated the question.

Meeting Penelope again in the thirtyish nastiness of her new mansion-flat was as dispiriting as joining a long bus queue in the airless mid-September heat. She seemed suddenly remote after the stifling closeness of our room at the Europa. She was not taking part in Sunday's pantomime and made dutiful noises about joining me. But I would have done my best to dissuade anyone from going near the whole ludicrous event. Her relief at being absolved was so clear that I couldn't possibly hold it against her, any more than her prepared defence of Kenneth Tynan's alibi, that he was supervising a filmed television account of this momentous event in popular British politics.

'Of course, he feels so awful,' said Penelope, 'not being in there with you and everybody else.' Sensible, crafty old Ken, I thought. They would probably cuddle up together while I spent the night in the nick. It was just enough, the way things go among the birds and flowers.

The morning of 17 September seemed very long indeed. Penelope and I slept late, until noon, but the day still seemed like early morning. There was a breathy, aluminium haze over the London sky that I couldn't remember before. Like every other reluctant bit-player that day, I assumed that within twenty-four hours I should be starting a gaol term of at least twelve months. There was no reason to think otherwise. Both government and press had made it very clear that none of us could expect any quarter and that the public was impatient to see us all dispatched and forgotten for a decent period of time and the whole incident properly contained by firm action. Ordinary, right-thinking people had been imposed upon enough by presumptious, self-advertising 'intellectuals' and other odd folk. That was indeed becoming my own view.

By one o'clock, the rain had begun to drizzle down. Of the few clothes I had brought from my Valbonne wardrobe, I laid out my raincoat and filled the pockets with packets of Cojene, for my palpitating head-glands, to smuggle somehow into the Scrubs (John Dexter would have been too spry to get caught up in this amateur nonsense), some pious small book and a half-bottle of whisky.

Penelope and I walked through Belgravia, on to Hyde Park Corner and down Piccadilly. London was not then blighted by tourists but, even so, Piccadilly Circus itself was almost empty and the resonant hum that every great city must contain at any moment of the day or night seemed to be stilled. Somewhere opposite the Garrick Theatre, we went into an empty Italian restaurant and poked at some pasta, which seemed to have been reheated repeatedly for weeks, with a bottle of Post-Office-inky wine. She went on about how 'Ken' was going to keep tabs on where I was and how I ended up. Soon we were both longing for me to go.

By 2.30, ignoring Penelope's solicitous irrelevancies, I had many times gone through in my mind the ritual mime of handing over my watch, keys, money, lowering myself into a humiliating, uncleansing bath and so on. Imprisonment seemed as inescapable as death or despair. Penelope continued to twiddle her spaghetti. I began to anticipate the pleasure of being locked up against the petty legal harassment we would both face from the newly maternal Mary and the righteously vengeful Dr Gilliatt – the naming of names, the closing in for costs. *She* would have to sort that out on her own while I was pressing shirts in the prison laundry.

With hung-over fatigue from Valbonne and Venice, I kissed her farewell in the north corner of Trafalgar Square, Sir Henry Irving keeping a watchful eye on the right, and the hopping lust of barely a fortnight earlier almost forgotten. Trafalgar Square seemed vast in expectation and emptiness. I skipped up the steps to the National Gallery. Inside, the faces upturned to the famous paintings were almost all equally famous. We were like figures in an old spy thriller. All-night companions were pretending not to recognize each other. It was a dumb-show of bizarre, conspiratorial behaviour.

I spotted the vague, unfocused stares of Bill Gaskill, Anthony Page, Lindsay Anderson, Keith Johnstone and Ann Jellicoe, and then of John Arden, John Berger, Shelagh Delaney, John Neville, Alan Sillitoe, George Melly and Vanessa Redgrave. And these were only the people I knew personally. I was beginning to wonder what my next instructions were and where they would come from. Should I be wearing a buttonhole and carrying the *Daily Telegraph*?

Then I spotted Doris Lessing poring over an Impressionist painting. I knew her a little and was extremely fond of her. She possessed an extraordinary delicacy and eroticism which touchingly discounted all her White Rhodesian liberal tedium. I knew she wouldn't disown me with a vague smile but that she would embrace me, which she did. As we joined arms and descended the steps into the Square, I felt as if I had selected a bride. I cannot think of a public entrance more cheekily stage-managed or carried off with such enjoyment. Doris looked so innocent and sweet underneath that charmless sky that I would happily have married her there on the spot. I half expected one of the chief inspectors to ask, 'Bride or groom?'

Within minutes, Doris and I were sealed off and settled in among the damp patches below Landseer's lions. A pall seemed to descend, distorting sound and sight, a very little like battle without danger, blinded and deafened without knowledge of what is happening. In the throng around us I could identify Arden, Sir Herbert Read, in his seventies and clearly suffering pain from a kidney disorder, a very worried Lady Read, Sillitoe and, somewhere beyond Doris, Vanessa. They were talking about deadlines on various commissioned works until the surrounding roar and thrust put paid to the pretence. Doris and I consigned ourselves to a mime of passionate public intimacy.

Young men in leather jackets fell on us, shouting instructions to make a thrust down Whitehall. A cry went up: 'They've got Vanessa!' I think I saw her being passed, hand over hand, like a plank, above the edges of the inner circle around the lions, and on towards a surge trying to charge its way to Downing Street. By around 6.30, the mob had made some kind of breakthrough as sounds of shouting receded. Around the lions it was comparatively quiet. Strutting pigeons had returned and, rather to my relief, most of my disconsolate companions had dispersed, including Doris. I sat it out, as instructed, and no one took the slightest notice, neither patrolling policeman nor preening pigeon.

The air seemed heavier than ever, mixed with a sickly sense of torpor and anticlimax. It only needed more rain to make the remnants of the demonstration even more despondent. The clamorous folly of it all, the gritty pounding of my eyeballs and an enormous thirst tempted me to walk away. But I decided against it. Arrest seemed certain, but I'd no wish to precipitate it. The police were busy rounding up the hard-liners at the front. They would leave the defeated core for the time being. I settled down with the half-bottle of whisky I had rather meanly kept in reserve for myself.

The glum consensus in the Royal Court barracks, before we showed our colours, had been that we could all expect to be treated much more severely than the unfortunate Wesker, Bolt and Logue. If they had been sent down for a mere month, it was certain that the Heavy Brigade could expect no mercy from Macmillan's merry magistrates and were assured of a minimum of six months. Did one get remission on such a short sentence? I tried to remember if Dexter had served his full term. I might even find myself up before the theatrical-hating Sir Laurence Dunne, VC, who had dismissed George's testimony to John's good character with such Hogarthian loathing.

My speculations became gloomier as I swigged the whisky. I thought of poor Oscar being jeered on the platform of Clapham Junction on his way to the treadmill at Reading Gaol. Sodomy began to seem genuinely brave, even romantic, compared to sitting down wanly on a wet London pavement. I lay beside the lions, growing chilled in my thin south-of-France finery, my thigh-bones bruised from the damp stone, wondering how I – with the pride of my cold view of simple faiths – could ever have let myself be gulled as any other fat-headed seeker after true happiness. I made an almost formal vow to myself never to do so again.

By the time I heard the midnight chimes from St Martin-in-the-Fields, the effects of the whisky and ten hours without food had brought me to that condition of near narcosis which I used to induce to persuade myself that I was not actually taking part in something disagreeable, like a double period of maths, a bad play or an aircraft flight. It was all happening to someone else. I was fading into a buzz when I heard a voice over my head.

'Mr Osborne?' I saw an extremely dapper police superintendent wearing gleaming leather gloves and sporting a silver-headed cane under his arm like an RSM pausing on parade. 'Mr Osborne?' The voice was quiet and polite. 'Yes.' I began to raise myself up, until I was lifted with careful firmness by about half a dozen silent constables. I had the pleasant sensation of being gently suspended and carried away. Looking up at the stars, I felt mild irritation at having been disturbed, however discreetly, and then a flood of relief. When should I look up at the stars again?

I heard a voice, surely Alan Sillitoe's. 'They've got John.' It was Alan. Other voices, friendly and excited, took up the cry. 'They've got John! Good luck, John. Good old John.' As an exit, it was a very exhilarating curtain-call. After fifty yards of being borne up like Hamlet on the stage at Hayling Island, only more expertly, we reached a waiting police van and I was lowered to the ground as carefully as I had been lifted. 'Now, Mr Osborne, do you want us to put you in the van or will you walk into it?' I struggled with cramp. 'Oh, I'll walk. Certainly.' I clambered into the empty van and they left me, the doors still wide open. Perhaps Mr Macmillan had enjoyed the play after all.

I waited for twenty minutes, when some policemen arrived with more arrests, young men, kicking and yelling. They refused to 'walk' aboard and each landed with a hefty thump on the floor beside me. I huddled in the shadows. They were full of pretty-fair hatred for the rest of the world, peace-lovers or not. I tried to will myself into a further trance. The police returned with more struggling passive-resisters and threw them in a heap among us. When the van was full, the door slammed and we moved off at speed.

Past a few streets, and we were bundled aboard a waiting coach with other detainees. For the next hour or so, we stopped off at police stations all over the West End as a few weary protestors were led off to be charged and booked for the night. It must have been around dawn before we drew up in a tiny street at the back of John Lewis. The station looked like a rather cosy Victorian cottage with a dinky blue gas-lamp outside.

I found myself standing beside John Calder, the distinguished English publisher of Samuel Beckett. He looked as grim and dour as I felt myself. Inside it was not so pretty, and the police at the desk were tired and bad-tempered after a leave-cancelled weekend. When I had been booked, I was shoved into a windowless cell. Again, I was happily alone. There was nothing on the extremely cold floor, so I bunched up my raincoat once more and tried to sleep.

Presently, there was a great deal of scuffle outside, the door opened and three or four wild-looking men were shoved with extreme force into the cell. They shouted abuse at our captors through the door. They spat out eyewitness accounts of monstrous acts of police brutality past and present. Their credentials as veteran peace-protestors were immaculate. As their professional euphoria wore off and a tiny sliver of light appeared, peace-loving grunts and snores rumbled in the shadows. They were all in their early twenties, wearing expensive leather items. They looked like a group of Millwall supporters, tired out from a happy afternoon smashing up the away team.

The door was opened at about nine o'clock. By this time, my tongue was clamped to my palate and I asked the desk sergeant if I might have a cup of traditional police-station tea. His expression implied that I had possibly committed a further chargeable offence. I didn't press it. I glanced at his copy of the *Daily Express*. It was headlined in huge type: '1,140 ARRESTED INCLUDING JOHN OSBORNE [top billing], FENNER BROCKWAY, VANESSA REDGRAVE, SHELAGH DELANEY AND CANON COLLINS TOO . . . THE WEARY POLICE VICTORIOUS AND NELSON DEEP IN DEBRIS.' No wonder I didn't merit a cup of orange-coloured tea.

I was finally disgorged into a huge room below the court in Bow Street. To my dismay, Oscar Beuselinck came waddling over, with his clerk, Charlie Barwick, beside him. Trying to look grave, his familiar vindictive manner made me instantly suspicious. 'Just plead guilty, son. Just plead guilty.' Twenty-four hours spent on stone surfaces had eroded my patience. 'What else would I do, you cunt.' 'Come now, come now, language,' he rebuked in his avuncular voice. 'You're in a police court now.' 'No, I'm not. I'm in a fucking police cell.' He looked around as if he expected me to be arrested and charged all over again.

I found myself speedily in the dock before I had to suffer much more of Oscar's puffed-up gravity. The magistrate, Mr Bertram Reece, looked more like Rob Wilton's music-hall magistrate, Mr Muddlecombe, than a Hogarthian bully. 'This is a court of justice, not a court of politics,' he muttered amiably. Within minutes my turn came and I pleaded guilty.

Mr Reece smiled at me over his half-lenses, like any competent character actor. 'Fined. Twenty shillings.'

25. *Bad, Sad and Mad*

We loved, sir – used to meet;
How sad and bad and mad it was –
But then, how it was sweet.

Robert Browning, 'A Death in the Desert'

I tell you, hopeless grief is passionless.

Elizabeth Barrett Browning, *Sonnets* – 'Grief'

Sir: – The *Daily Telegraph* was always a footman's paper. Since its amalgamation with the *Morning Post* it seems to have progressed as far as 'What the Butler Saw'.

Nancy Harrison, Dulwich (letter to the *Spectator*, 13 October 1961)

Earlier in that summer, on a stifling day just after *Luther* opened at the Court, Jocelyn R. and I drove down to Sussex in the open-topped Alvis, buzzing with morning hope, clear sky and sunshine. I was intent on finding a place in the country where I could spend most of my time and work without hindrance. I felt that even an hour's drive away from London would discourage people assuming access to my life. Up to a point, I was right. I knew that the ultimate decision of where to park my bones permanently in England would probably take years of searching to achieve. When I asked John Betjeman to suggest the most perfect resting place, he snapped back with utmost seriousness and good faith, 'Middlesex.'

Fired by the symbolic attributes of having acquired Frink's Harbinger Bird, I was convinced that somewhere, in the no-man's present, I would find a place that would be more than a temporary refuge against all the froth, sham and enmity that had pursued me for the past few years. I had no clear idea of whether Jocelyn or anyone else should want to share it with me. I craved solitude but I didn't want to be alone.

I remembered that Vivien Leigh's last retreat had been Tickerage Mill, at Blackboys in Sussex, only about five miles from another mill-house which I had seen advertised. The Old Water Mill at Hellingly, near Hailsham, just off the main Eastbourne road, was about an hour and a half's drive from London. It was attractive enough for my purposes, within my West End playwright's grasp at a price of £10,000, and Jocelyn, whether or not she was considering the likelihood of moving in with me, was enthusiastic about its possibilities.

The property was contained within a few acres of fairly wild but tameable garden and enclosed by two running streams of the River Cuckmere. The main house was small and mid-Victorian, with a happy, reassuring feel about it even though it was functioning as a simple boarding-house for stray geriatrics. There was a cluster of outbuildings – always a special attraction to unpropertied townies like myself – that included an eleventh-century mill recorded in Domesday Book which had been active up until the early thirties, a large, unused granary and a rather twee little cottage by the mill-race. They could all be easily and modestly converted.

I immediately rang Beuselinck and tried to impress on him that the security of my immediate future depended on his instantly acquiring the Old Water Mill for me without any petty lawyer's haggling. By the end of the month, and to my great surprise at having my simple wishes executed so swiftly, contracts were exchanged, the owners moved out, the place was empty, waiting and my own.

Penelope's choice of a flat in Chesham Place as what journalists like to call a 'love-nest' was not a happy one. Its Belgravia location alone confirmed the squalor of the course in which we had trapped ourselves. I was anxious to clear my presence from Jocelyn in Lower Belgrave Street, and Penelope was yearning for her portion of the Gilliatt library in Lowndes Square, her small wardrobe and the tools of her voracious trade.

Within a week of the Trafalgar Square sit-down we had made arrangements with Jocelyn and Roger to extricate both our lives and simple props from their own. Jocelyn took herself off for the afternoon while my secretary and her husband stripped Lower Belgrave Street of my books and few belongings. Reluctantly, I then accompanied Penelope to an empty Lowndes Square where she went through her own larger and more disputed inventory.

Anthony Creighton had borrowed a small van from one of his fellow late-night workers at the Chiswick telephone exchange. Penelope and I spent hours puffing up and down the adulterous stairway of Lowndes Square, clutching her collection of review copies, and thankfully filled the van before Dr Gilliatt returned, when he would most surely have contested her claims of total ownership. By the time she had finished, the flat looked whiter, more Swedish and too bare to be habitable without a great deal of refurnishing and book-buying. It was almost midnight. Anthony went on ahead in the van with his driver–telephonist companion and, after a reviving hour of drinks at Chesham Place, Penelope and I set off for Sussex in her new, snappy Triumph Herald.

As is usually the case with the mere mechanics of this kind of strategic withdrawal and domestic disintegration, the dreaded process had proved more swift, simple, almost satisfying, than anyone could have hoped. Penelope drove through the night, showing off her pointless double-declutching skills, and we arrived at Hellingly in a mood of triumphant relief at our nimble resourcefulness.

This was immediately dispelled as we nosed into the narrow lane that was the only approach to the house. Our path was blocked by dozens of cars; we were dazzled by battalions of light from all directions. Had we suddenly come upon a huge film-crew engaged in an ambitious night set-up? Figures and faces advanced on the little roadster. Hemmed in by cameras, microphones, flashlights, notebooks, we stumbled our way across the creaky, narrow bridge that straddled the stream beside the Mill. We were pelted with questions by a couple of dozen reporters and cameramen. Having only visited the place once before on a blazing afternoon, I was just able to guide Penelope to what I remembered as the back door.

The house seemed drab, deserted and much smaller than my dim recollection of it. When we stumbled into the kitchen, all the doors and curtainless windows were open. Every room seemed to have been invaded by shouting, joking journalists. Anthony reeled towards us like a drunken host welcoming a pair of deprived late-comers. He had invited the press unit inside and they had gratefully presented him with cases of drink which they were all joyfully knocking back downstairs, upstairs in the geriatrics' bedrooms and in shadowy corners of the garden. It took the better part of an hour to persuade, cajole and bully his guests from the house and then the garden and, finally, the lane. We managed to avoid saying anything, and least of all 'no comment', to the hundreds of light-hearted enquiries after our health, domestic intentions, personal and professional plans for the future.

I would have lost my temper with Anthony, but he was soon blissfully collapsed in the protective arms of some equally sodden hack. When the last car sprinted away up the pitted lane and the morning light began to show up the dirt and debris on the floorboards, the stained markings of pictures past on the walls, Penelope and I were left feeling equally soiled and derelict, as if we had been burgled, defiled and humiliated.

I half expected her to make a crablike Lucia di Lammermoor descent down the bare, creaking stairwell, presaging her mad dash to the altar of St Mark's. Her eyes were flecked black beneath the bare light-bulbs. Perhaps the sheer volume of pressing hysteria had restrained her own. We retrieved an old blanket to shield the upstairs window of a room containing an abandoned mattress. We dropped down on it and fell asleep.

Shortly, we woke, fully clothed and shivering in the smoky light of a late September day. Piled up with tea-chests and scattered piles from the Lowndes Square library, the otherwise empty, unheated rooms were stung with the first winter chill. Sidling up to the windows, like holed-up gangsters in a remake of a classic French movie, we peered out. Dozens of cars and vans had returned, scattered all over the lawn. Reporters and cameramen were wandering through the garden or lolling beside the stream.

Anthony's press party had re-established itself during our short bout of unconsciousness. Having discovered Penelope's hoard of coffee, he was already busy in the kitchen greeting his guests through the window. Blessed with a toxin-proof head as impenetrable as Christopher Isherwood's or Robert Stephens's, he had shaved with great care and sprinkled himself with Old Spice. He was as skittish and lively as he must have been playing one of Terry Rattigan's famous fairies in *Boys in Blue* during the war.

There seemed little to be done except keep out of eye-line and make sure that we had enough food and drink to get through the day. Most urgently, Penelope needed the assurance of seeing her byline in the *Observer*. Only Anthony could run the gauntlet thrown round us. He was more than eager to do so, having scored a huge personal success, as he saw it, which overshadowed all the triviality of my own marital mess. Having sworn him to speak to no one, not even the most godlike young reporter, I sent him off down the lane with a fistful of money and instructions to buy all the newspapers, cigarettes, two bottles of whisky for us and a bottle of gin for himself.

A couple of hours later he returned, explaining that he had dropped in at a nice little place down the road called The Wheatsheaf, where he had been obliged to have a couple of drinks with a few chaps who were actually quite decent and hated hanging around and being a nuisance but had a job to do, however much they disliked it. One of them, like himself, had been in Bomber Command and had also flown Halifaxes.

For the next few days, indeed weeks, life was once again measured out in column-inches rather than coffee-spoons. There was an odd compulsion to read them, not from squeamish vanity but to find out what we had apparently been up to. That first Sunday, it was spelled out that every movement we had made during the past twenty-four hours had been observed and noted down for what the Press Council had just announced a 'Warrant of Public Right'. Anthony Creighton's van had been followed, the Triumph Herald had been followed and an inventory had been compiled of goods removed from assorted residences around Belgravia. It could hardly have interested those that read it, and probably not even those who recorded it.

The following Friday, 29 September, Cyril Ray in the *Spectator* and Francis Williams in the *New Statesman*, gurus to the cleverer classes, made things clear about the press handling of a case of commonplace adultery. What emerged, to those who might care, was the louche behaviour of the footman's newspaper. Mr Ray, although himself of the Left, summed up for the Right:

> When I refer to the sensational gossip-mongering papers, let it be clear as to which they are. The *Daily Express* gave the story seventy-nine lines and one single-column photograph of the lady concerned, and the *Daily Mail* gave it sixty-nine lines, a similar single-column picture and a small photograph of Mr Osborne. The *Daily Telegraph* gave it 162 lines on its middle page, opposite the leading articles, a bigger picture of Mr Osborne (across two columns) and one of the lady.
>
> I have always thought that one measure of a newspaper's dignity is whether *any* of its stories could have been undertaken by *any* member of its staff without his feeling ashamed of himself and his calling. I wonder how the *Telegraph*'s editor or political correspondent, say, would have liked to hang around Mr Osborne's house, asking him impertinent questions about his marriage that elicited the answer, 'I do not wish to discuss these matters,' and about his friendship with another lady which forced him to say that, 'All I want is some peace and quiet.' I cannot believe that the high-minded Peter Simple would have enjoyed chasing the unhappy lady in question from cab rank to railway station or that the urbane Peterborough would have relished snooping around Mrs Osborne's front door, making an inventory of the furniture that was being removed. I should have thought that a paper with the *Telegraph*'s pretensions to gentility would have hesitated before exposing even the lowliest of its staff to having to report that he was told, 'She doesn't want to talk to you. Nor do I. Now go away.'

The Spectator's readers the following week joined in:

> Sir: – Cyril Ray's sneer at the *Daily Telegraph* is not justifiable. John Osborne has recently sought, and obtained, wide publicity for a virulent attack on the morals of his fellow-countrymen. For a proper evaluation of his opinions, it is a matter of public interest that his own morals should be under equally close scrutiny.
>
> W.I.D. Scott, Chester

Sir: – The gossip-mongering papers, which Cyril Ray had the courage to list, have now stooped to a new level of prying that almost defies satire. It brings to mind Oscar Wilde's comment: 'In centuries before ours the public nailed the ears of journalists to the pump. That was quite hideous. In this century journalists have nailed their own ears to the keyhole; that is much worse.'

B.R. Jones, Chelsea

More surprising was the spirited response of that week's *New Statesman*, which, apart from Cuthbert Worsley's schoolmasterly critical attentions, had always ignored my existence:

The *Sunday Pictorial* [tame equivalent of today's *Sun*] was the first to answer the call of 'the public right'. Determined that no one should be able to accuse it of being 'faithless to its trust', it announced on its front page in large white type on a black background, 'John Osborne and Friend in Mystery Midnight Move'. This was flanked by a four-column picture of 'Playwright John Osborne and his wife Mary' and a two-column picture of 'Dr Roger Gilliatt and his wife Penelope'. 'John Osborne, Britain's bomb-squatting playwright, has made a sudden moonlight move from London to his new country home down by an old mill by the stream in Sussex.'

The story by *Pictorial* reporters opened dramatically. 'Just after midnight yesterday, he drove down to Hellingly in Sussex accompanied by a beautiful woman in a light coat'. He was, 'a dark-haired woman who said she was Mr Osborne's secretary' explained, in a phrase that deserves to go down in history, moving from London 'to get away from all the publicity'. He evidently misjudged the high ideals of public service that animate Fleet Street; he should read *The World of Paul Slickey* some time. The *Pictorial* was on his tail.

Indeed, it seems to have had reporters lurking behind every third lamppost for hours while fast cars stood by. At all events, every movement of Mr Osborne, his secretary, Mr Anthony Creighton (his friend) and a small removal van were watched by *Pictorial* men, who followed the van in a fast car. Eventually they reached the Old Water Mill, where their vigil was rewarded: 'An hour later, Mr Osborne drove up. With him in his hard-topped sports car was the beautiful woman wearing a light coat.' End of First Episode . . .

So that was what had happened.

... On Monday the story was taken up in the *Daily Mirror*, the *Daily Express* and the *Daily Mail* and, somewhat surprisingly, the *Daily Telegraph*. One had tended, apparently wrongly, to assume that the *Telegraph* governed its affairs by somewhat different standards. Not so. Only *The Times* and the *Guardian* took the strange view that the private life of a well-known playwright is his own affair and not a matter for hour-by-hour journalists playing the part of disreputable private detectives.

The *Mirror* took up where the *Pictorial* left off. By Thursday Mr Osborne and Mr Creighton were finally persuaded to appear ...

Thank God, in his enthusiasm for the venture, Anthony had forgotten to pack his kilt.

... 'I have nothing at all to say,' said Osborne, 'and neither has Mrs Gilliatt. Now go away.' Go away indeed. Hadn't he heard about the freedom of the press? Who does the man think he is? Neither the *Telegraph* nor the others were prepared to stand for this sort of nonsense. The *Telegraph* man spoke out straight and proper for the right of the press to poke its nose where it wishes. 'I asked him', he proudly informed *Telegraph* readers, 'about the future of his marriage'. Also, 'had Mrs Gilliatt left her husband?' Osborne – an uncooperative man if ever there was one – while remaining polite but firm (why he should have been polite I do not know) – actually refused to answer. If he is not careful he will be making an enemy of the press.

No doubt the Press Council will in due course explain to us the 'warrant of public right as distinguished from public curiosity' that governed this operation. I can only say that this seems to me to be one of the most disreputable and degrading examples of what passes in some parts of Fleet Street for newspaper enterprise I have come across in years. I consider the editors, news editors and reporters involved showed themselves in this matter a disgrace to journalism. I should like to think that in due course they will feel a little ashamed themselves. But that, I am afraid, is too much to hope.

28 SEPTEMBER: The entrenched guardians of press freedom and purveyors of news to footmen of the gentry were startled by the appearance of a demonstration by local residents outside the Old Water Mill.

During the morning a car drew up, driven by Captain Vivian Hancock-Nunn. Major Colin de Vere Gordon-MacLean may have felt unable to put Simla into quarantine in order to join him, but the captain was accompanied by his wife, Mrs Eileen Hancock-Nunn, who was described as a 'prominent Sussex personality' residing at Lealands, Hellingly. Also with them in the car was Mr Fred Livingstone, a scientific and technical writer, together with his wife, Mrs Florence Livingstone, of South Lodge, Lealands.

Led by the 'snuff-taking' Mr Livingstone, each produced large placards in a dignified demonstration before the front gate. The placards, displayed for the benefit of the photographers present, read: 'DAMN YOU OSBORNE', 'HELLINGLY'S ANGRY OLD MEN OBJECT' and 'HELLINGLY WANTS MARY URE.'

Mrs Hancock-Nunn, whose placard supported Mary Ure, told reporters, 'I think a man who says "Damn You England" deserves anything.' Mrs C.C. Brunning, of Little Gates, Hellingly, wholeheartedly agreed with her. They had planned to sit down in the road but decided against it, although Mrs Brunning had brought a raincoat just in case. Mr Livingstone added that they were in a public place, were entitled to protest and were prepared to call the police. Then they climbed back into their cars and drove off.

4 OCTOBER: One or two newspapers report that Robert Shaw – Dan Tempest of the television series *The Buccaneers* – 'is being cited in the divorce petition being brought against Mary Ure by her husband, John Osborne. Mr Shaw is in New York, where he is about to open in Harold Pinter's *The Caretaker*.'

Two days later, the *New Daily* comments, 'How little the newspapers know about Osborne's life is shown by the fact that it is he who has filed a petition for divorce against his wife, citing Robert Shaw.'

13 OCTOBER: Only the *Scottish Daily Mail* carries the story that Robert Shaw – old Dan Dare – has become a father for the fourth time. His wife, Jennifer, has given birth to a daughter in Charing Cross Hospital.

14 OCTOBER: Mary Ure flies to Philadelphia with her seven-week-old baby, Colin, and a nurse. She is travelling under an assumed name, 'Mrs Fisher', and is met at the airport by a cordon of photographers. Asked why she has come to America, she replies, 'For a rest.' Refusing to say if she would be meeting Robert Shaw, she came out of the airport alone, leaving the baby with its nurse, and leaped into a taxi which took her to an hotel. After two hours, she left in a black, chauffeur-drive car, headed towards New York.

26 OCTOBER: Tony Richardson announces Woodfall Film's £500,000 production of Henry Fielding's *Tom Jones*, which he'd read at Oxford. It seems a wonderful opportunity to get away from the kitchen sink and a chance to work with friends, practically a Royal Court camp.

1 NOVEMBER: Mary Ure reveals her intention to reply to allegations of her adultery and will defend the suit.

11 NOVEMBER: Dr Roger Gilliatt files a petition against his wife, Penelope, citing John Osborne as co-respondent.

18 NOVEMBER: John Osborne best man at Oscar Beuselinck's wedding.

30 NOVEMBER: John Osborne and Penelope Gilliatt, attending the Acapulco Film Festival with actresses Mary Peach, Billie Whitelaw and Diane Cilento, are photographed on the beach. A cameraman from the *Daily Express* attempts to punch Mrs Gilliatt.

2 DECEMBER: Mary Ure cross-petitions, alleging Osborne's adultery with three women and denying that he is not the father of her child.

8 DECEMBER: After an investigation into John Osborne's friendship with Mrs Gilliatt, *Tribune* declares: 'It would be difficult to think of any more impertinent and disgraceful intrusion into the private life of two individuals than the pursuit of these two people by certain gallant gentlemen of Fleet Street.'

And then the *New Statesman*, again: 'These stories were unique even in the annals of popular slime for their piling up of detail and in their reports of every movement of the two individuals to whom it had been decided to give the full treatment.'

10 DECEMBER: Osborne, returning from New York and unaware of the existing strike by technicians, appears on the arts programme *Tempo* and is immediately expelled from Equity.

25 DECEMBER: My mother comes to stay at Hellingly with Penelope, her sister Angela and myself for Christmas.

Laurence Olivier rings up from Brighton to ask us over for a drink in Royal Crescent, where he and Joan have just moved. I use Nellie Beatrice, whom he has met once, as an excuse not to go. He won't hear of it, and insists we bring 'Mum' along.

During the celebrations, he opens a huge jar of the most luscious, oily caviare. I watch Nellie Beatrice as she takes a portion from him. Instead of refusing it politely, she executes a dextrous mime, watched by all, and Joan in particular, during which she slowly and slyly deposits a creamy black stream of finest Beluga on to the newly laid, purple-pristine carpet.

She slowly grinds it in with sole and heel. The Oliviers watch this performance with well-mannered horror. Nellie Beatrice enlivens the whole pantomime by looking down at the lake-sized stain and blaming Penelope's sister. The Oliviers will remind me of the incident for another decade.

31 DECEMBER: A more than usually large number of public figures seem to

have died. They include Gary Cooper, Peter Dawson, George Formby, Bransby Williams, Thomas Beecham, Ernest Thesiger, Percy Grainger. All of them had some special meaning for me. And then, of course, there were others who left a resonance of one kind or another: Hemingway, Moss Hart, Jung, Augustus John and James Thurber, whom I used to talk to in the lift at the Algonquin.

Worse, 1961 had seen the introduction of the New English Bible. It had condemned even 1 Corinthians 13 as irrelevant 'to modern minds and a changing world':

> Though I speak with the tongues of men and of angels, and have not charity, I am become as sounding brass, or a tinkling cymbal. And though I have the gift of prophecy, and understand all mysteries, and all knowledge; and though I have all faith, so that I could remove mountains, and have not charity, I am nothing.

No longer. So much for the marvel of language.

In the New Year, Penelope and I took a flat in Hertford Street, around the corner from Woodfall's offices in Curzon Street, while the builders made Hellingly habitable.

26. Then Whom Have I Offended?

And I will put enmity between thee and the woman, and between thy seed and her seed; it shall bruise thy head, and thou shalt bruise his heel.

Genesis 3:15

I am troubled; I am bowed down greatly; I go mourning all the day long . . . I am feeble and sore broken: I have roared by reason of the disquietness of my heart . . . My lovers and my friends stand aloof from my sore; and my kinsmen stand afar off. They also that seek after my life lay snares for me: and they that seek my hurt speak mischievous things, and imagine deceits all the day long.

Psalm 38:6–12

I believe the notion of a 'love-nest', so beloved of Fleet Street's hackettes, was first coined during a sexual scandal involving America's President Harding. I had always coveted one, ever since I heard the phrase as a young boy. My image of it had been quite precise. It was subterranean and windowless, with child-size furniture, a huge open fire and a patchwork bed. The floors billowed with brightly coloured eiderdowns for bare feet to tread. It was eternally tea-time, and vague doctors-and-nurses games went on all day in this enchanting Mrs Tiggywinkle whore-house.

The service flat Penelope and I rented in Hertford Street was, alas, not like that. It was built and furnished in tawdriest fifties style, the kind of place where lesser executives from the North-Western Area branch would reel back with a hostess after a night at a Shirley Bassey cabaret. The wife would be propping up the cocktail bar alone in the lounge of her ranch-style home in a select suburb of Walsall.

What we remember is what we become. What we have forgotten is more kindly and disturbs only our dreams. We become resemblances of our past. So Sam Beckett appears as an ancient bird, like the one in the Apocryphal Book of Tobit, who dropped a good large mess in the eye of those who dared to look upwards to heaven. Perhaps it was the onset of a new pattern of daily constraints and fresh habits, but the events that took place after we moved into the Love-Nest remain with me very clearly.

We had only just begun to test the novelty when Tony Richardson rang me early one evening from Lower Mall. He sounded openly distressed, a most unusual concession to plain dealing. He was also, just as rarely, almost incoherent. What became evident was that he and Goestschius, the American sociologist and genial guru with whom he shared a flat overlooking the river, had just had a violent clash of wills. I knew that he was most unlikely to confide any of the details, but I was relieved and flattered that he had been constrained to ask for my practical assistance.

Did I know of anywhere he could stay? 'I mean immediately, now, this moment!' His insistence was so urgent and as he was such a profligate spirit, I wondered why he didn't take the most obvious course and book into a hotel. I hesitated. The Walsall executive's love-nest would surely make Tony's lip curl up like a goosed caterpillar. Yet the sudden helplessness of his appeal was so insistent. 'Well, there *is* a spare room here, but it's tiny and I don't think you'd care for it. It's pretty tawdry.' 'That sounds absolutely marvellous. I'll be half an hour.' And he was. I had a drink ready for him from our own cocktail cabinet, a huge, glistening affair like a mini cinema organ. He was seemingly unaware of the hideousness of the room. He didn't confide in me any further and went around the corner to Woodfall's offices.

During the days that followed, Penelope and I scarcely saw Tony for more than a few minutes, although we would hear him return late at night and crash into the bed in the room beside our own. He was always an early riser and usually left in the morning before we were awake. I expected him to move on soon, for both room and bed were very small and scarcely comfortable. However, he continued to come and go mysteriously. One Wednesday, after Penelope's last midweek film screening – most probably a compelling study of peasant passion in pre-revolutionary Slovenia – we decided to brave the draughts, noise and discomforts imposed by the builders and spend a long weekend at the Old Water Mill, this time without the company of Anthony and his new-found Fleet Street admirers.

When we returned early on Monday morning, in time for Penelope's next weekly offerings from the Art of Film, the morose porter was waiting at Hertford Street. 'Oh, Mr Osborne, I must ask you to accompany me upstairs to your flat.' He sounded like a police inspector going through the official proceedings before making an arrest. 'And *Mrs* Osborne, of course.' He knew full well that she wasn't. We followed him into the lift and ascended the three flights to our perch, where the front door was open and the housekeeper was waiting with buckets, mops and an assortment of cleaning equipment.

'Mr and Mrs Osborne have returned,' the porter boomed. 'I should like you to take a look at your flat . . . before witnesses.' We went in. The reason for all this gravity and preamble was plain. There was undeniable evidence of concerted damage of a rather haphazard nature, obviously not executed with the vindictive fury of a frustrated burglar.

'Allow me to show you,' he said, pointing a finger in the direction of the debris. A pane had been smashed in the French windows; a length of curtain was hanging loosely as if a chimpanzee had gone for a swing. The ugly iron-framed glass dining-table was chipped and cushions were scattered everywhere, some stained with a murky coffee-like substance. There were cigarette burns on the uncut-moquette of the drab three-piece suite, and a G-plan coffee-table had collapsed. Bottles of Cutty Sark and Moët et Chandon were strewn around, some of them half-full. In the kitchen there was similar chaos. The porter ushered us solemnly into the small bedroom. It looked as if it had been serviced by a tribe of Sumo wrestlers. Our own room was quite untouched.

He finally pointed to his prize exhibit, several piles of juicy dog-shit. 'Well, Mr Osborne?' 'We've been away since Wednesday.' 'I know, I know.' 'Burglars?' 'Burglars! Burglars with *small* dogs?' As a professional dog-walker, he doubtless knew about this kind of thing. 'I tell you, Mr Osborne. This is an inside job.' He was beginning to grow slightly hysterical. 'There has been an orgy in this flat. Most definitely an orgy.' He pronounced the word with a hard 'g', which for some reason made it seem very funny.

I decided that polite sympathy, some indignation and a small bribe were necessary or he would detain us all day. I made puzzled noises, offered – naturally – to pay for the damage, and slipped him £20. Penelope went off to her movie and I began to clear up the wreckage. Going into Tony's bedroom, I noticed that all over the sheets and scattered among the pillows was a large quantity of hairpins. Tony's favourite brand of whisky was Cutty Sark, but he never smoked. The flat had indeed become a love-nest, and a very soiled one. And what about the little dog?

Later that morning, I called in at Curzon Street. Oscar Lewenstein was bleating anxiously about my tardiness in delivering the full *Tom Jones* script and Tony's foot was wagging furiously behind his desk. It had quite a punch. I decided to ask no questions. But I was still intrigued about the hairpins. In Acapulco, Tony had shared a room with Diane Cilento. He had been greatly taken with her for a long time, insisting on a general deference to her. I very much liked her broken-glass Aussie coarseness, but she didn't strike me as a girl who'd bother with hairpins. As I sat there, listening to Oscar's strictures and watching Tony's foot pumping perilously near the pretty Georgian window, the penny finally dropped from the very heaven of incongruity.

Vanessa Redgrave, hereinafter known as Big Van, had just made her debut as Rosalind. It had been received with a tumult of rapture. I had first come across her in the 1959 Stratford season, when she had played alongside Mary in Peter Hall's Hamley's-window-display production of *A Midsummer Night's Dream*. Her hoydenish-netball capering was no worse than Mary's tinny-toylike Titania in this resolutely un-magicked evening. Her Tory innocence and pro-Suez passions had afforded the rest of the company some amusement, and Tony especially.

The following year I caught Vanessa in a collector's item for hard-hearted dealers in theatrical folklore. It was a delightfully fatuous piece called *Look on Tempests*. She played a young bride who discovers that her husband is homosexual. It was the work of a Lady Playwright in joined-up writing, and it was common knowledge, even outside the profession, that the innocent bride's wilful naïvety exactly matched Big Van's perception of her own father, Sir Michael. Art was rapidly imitating life all right.

Later the same year, I went with Jocelyn R. to see her in Robert Bolt's *The Tiger and the Horse*. Jocelyn, in one of her opinionated pitches for inspired speculation, turned to me and said, 'Mark me, that girl is going to be a very, very big star.' I wasn't sure whether I was appalled by her forecast or troubled by her descent into feeble-mindedness. But then, if I had been asked to take a flier on the future of Coca-Cola, I would have probably have been the single vote against it.

Later on, with great difficulty and faint hope of changing my mind about the rising star's sorcery, I hustled a couple of lowly seats for *As You Like It*. I spotted Tony a few rows in front of us. He was on his own. The evening was exactly as I had expected. Afterwards, Penelope hurtled us into the basilica of Big Van's dressing-room. Robert Bolt was seated by her dressing-table, like a presiding elder, leaning on it almost in an attitude of contemplation, as if he had been there all evening.

I scarcely knew Robert but, like many, or some, of the people who live by the same trade as myself, I had always felt a kind of arm's-length affectionate regard for him. I had a feeling that, even if one would never become close friends or enjoy the clash of personal disagreement, one's isolation would never be quite total while he and others existed at the same time in the same world, however uncontacted and even remote.

Tony glared round the door. Two men face to face: one whom I knew so well and understood so little and the other known hardly at all but perhaps more understood. Robert rose politely, 'I'm Robert Bolt,' he said, looking like a prosperous farmer from the Dales. At least they're both Yorkshiremen, I thought. 'I know,' said Tony. There was a silence which Tony could sustain for ever. 'Taking Vanessa out for supper then?' Bolt could almost have been a Victorian father sounding out a young whipper-snapper and his intentions towards his daughter. Tony ignored this and looked at me, as if I should do something. Robert continued in his alderman's plain manner: 'I understand – people tell me – that you don't care overmuch for my work.' It was expressed as a matter of reportage. He could just as well have said, 'I understand you've just come up on the train from Brighton.'

When Big Van appeared, Penelope looked set to gush for two, if not even for England. But Rosalind was still trailing clouds upon clouds of Arden. She let out one of her breathy, deflating sounds like the slumbrous yawn of some waking beast, a kind of mooing acknowledgement. She embraced Tony and stared above my head, perhaps at some departing dreaming lyricism. Penelope shifted into overdrive.

Tony had a tight vice on Vanessa's arm and was swivelling her firmly towards the door. It was only then that I realized that Vanessa's attention had switched to a shivering bundle at her breast, a beribboned miniature Yorkshire terrier, no bigger than an animated pen-wiper. Soon all three of them disappeared. If she was wearing pins, they were firmly fixed in her upswept hair.

A few days after the pillage of Hertford Street, Tony invited us to join them both for supper. It was a disarming gesture, quite out of keeping with his customary methods of manipulating his friends and isolating them from each other. Perhaps he wanted openly to declare his new obsession for all the world to see. The following day he summoned me to Woodfall and suggested that the four of us leave that 'horrible little place of yours' and move into a cute little house he had leased in Eaton Mews North. I suggested that he and Vanessa might be happier alone together, but, with his usual tortuous powers of persuasion, he presented the move as a huge adventure, one that Penelope and I would be very dowdy not to join in.

They were a bizarre couple. Similar in some tangled physical way, they seemed to compound a piranha-toothed androgynous power within each other. The prospect of sharing a small mews house with them sounded less an adventure than a punishing military exercise. But Penelope was most eager, and I didn't want to jeopardize my friendship with Tony by allowing him to expose my true feelings about his weird trophy. With luck, it might be re-awarded before long.

The reality was worse than muddle-headed melancholy could have envis-aged. The house was small enough for two, normal-sized, co-ordinated people. Life shared within its walls was not easy. In the use of the one-minute bathroom, Tony and Vanessa both had the marauding skills of German tourists bagging early-morning deck-chairs. They could sprint to it in a quarter of a second, barricade themselves in for hours and emerge leaving a sodden wreckage of uncapped toothpaste tubes, every item of toiletry dripping, dropped to the floor or lying in moist clusters among a slimy compost of towelling. Both bath and basin would be overflowing with grey, tepid water.

I resigned myself to bathless days on my trips to London, which became less frequent. Sloane Square was only a ten-minute walk away and I could shave and clean my teeth at the Royal Court Hotel. Penelope chose to regard it all as the prerogative of the godlike and gifted. To me it seemed like middle-class dedication to good old Number One.

They had assumed the whole bag of flailing adolescent romance – all whirlwind love, locked eyeball-to-eyeball overfond gazing, kissing, fondling, fumbling – and all played out in a full-frontal, embarrassingly athletic public show. It was as sentimental as the doggerel on a Christmas card.

Worse was their determination to perform a comic double act. They had decided that they were the real-life counterparts of the characters in the recent Truffaut film *Jules et Jim*, a pair of Gallic, custard-pie, cerebral comics. Tony Laurel and Vanessa Hardy. One evening, Penelope and I arrived late and they insisted on giving us the full cabaret. In the course of it, they piled up a trail of damage very similar to the one in Hertford Street.

A few weeks later, long after I had decided that the builders' trannies and day-long rock music in Sussex were preferable to life among the godlike and gifted, Tony met me at the Woodfall office with an indignant solicitor's letter. Our landlady, who was rather grand and a figure at Court (Buckingham Palace, not Sloane Square), had visited her house and been outraged at its condition and the breakages, which included her most cherished Coronation chair – a splendid memento of the crowning of George VI, which she claimed was beyond repair – and an entire floor of fitted carpet which had been sprayed indelicately by the Yorkshire pen-wiper.

'I mean, don't you think it's a disgrace?' 'No, I don't. The damage you've done to her little house would sound impossible to achieve. You've had a right old orgy.' I pronounced it with a hard 'g'. 'And you must pay up.' 'What do you mean – Augie!' 'I mean, my dear friend, that you and Vanessa should live together in a brick underground shelter with wall-to-wall rubber sheeting.' He looked astonished and angry. We had a frosty script conference.

I was prepared to dissemble shamelessly over my feelings for Big Van after their marriage the following year, determined that a wedge of such banality would not come between Tony and myself. Newly married women sometimes conduct a scorched-earth policy on their spouse's past, and previous wives, lovers and male friendships are the first targets for annihilation, especially if there is the merest hint of sexual ambiguity. I knew that Tony's acute perception of his friends' weaknesses might also allow him to accept their feigned complaisance at its face value.

Shortly after their first child, Natasha, was born, he invited Penelope and me to dinner at the marital home in St Peter's Square, a lofty house in a row built for Wellington's officers returning from Waterloo. It was elegant and spacious, but inhabited by Tony, Big Van, Natasha, a ferocious toucan, South American parakeets, bush babies and an assortment of lizards, it was even more in need of wall-to-wall rubber sheeting than Eaton Mews North.

Two of Tony's pre-set explosive devices had been primed to enliven the evening. Staying with the Richardsons was the Broadway actress Kim Stanley, who had worked with Tony in New York. From the battery of coded glares I was receiving from my host, it was clear that I was being instructed to fawn on her. She was in some state of apparent distress, and I refused to be bullied into accepting responsibility for it. I had no idea what had driven her to such fondness for the hard stuff – in American panic-speak, her alcohol 'problem' – but I wasn't going to be snared into a conspiracy of collective guilt for her condition. Brendan Behan, Wilfred Lawson, Trevor Howard, all so-called 'hell-raisers', might become tedious during the course of a long and entertaining evening, but they had the redeeming grace of charm.

Before the meal had ended, Tony pushed his first button. Big Van undid her shirt and clamped the young Natasha to her bosom. 'I shouldn't do that in front of Johnny, Vanessa. I mean, he's very *peculiar* about that kind of thing.' Indeed I was, and didn't deny it. Momentarily wrenched from permanent self-absorption, she glanced at me pityingly, gathered up the hungry infant and left the room. Game and set uncontestably to Richardson *père*.

Penelope, who would never have subjected herself to what she regarded as the ignominy and female subjection of breast-feeding, looked on in embarrassment at old Muddle-Head's crude prejudice. I was probably the only one present who found the idea of non-evangelistic suckling quite erotic. Conducted in private, that is.

Tony's next fuse looked set to activate itself prematurely as Miss Stanley prowled around the room whenever the conversation at table veered away from her own preoccupations. She was one of those women I was rarely to meet who set up an instant wave of magnetic, mutual dislike between themselves and me. She turned up an Edith Piaf record to full volume and began dancing to it, like Blanche du Bois gripped in a bad fit of the Isadoras, wailing in a whisky baritone, '*This* is the real me! This is *my* life!' Resistant to the plight of the famous Parisian sparrow, I was encouraged to shout above the noise, 'You're dead right.'

Tony's prepared booby-trap might well blow up in ugly melodrama. With some relish, I noticed that he was looking rather alarmed. The pinched fear on Penelope's face was stimulating, too. I prepared to pick up the grenade and lob it back at him, but he intervened swiftly, grasped the stumbling star in his arms and bore her away, protesting, upstairs. When he returned, his mouth was tight and reproachful, his anger, for once, unsimulated: 'The trouble with you, Johnny, is that you will never understand the rawness and sensitivity of a creature like Kim.' 'You're right,' I said, 'I won't.' And we left.

When the Richardsons' second daughter, Joely, was born, Tony took a villa for the summer outside St Tropez. Ostensibly it was a recompense for the trials his wife had suffered during the birth. In fact, it was another annual diversion, an auditorium where his friends could be put through their paces like so many performing dogs. Penelope and I were among the early contestants.

We were met at the airport by Jan, Woodfall's driver and Tony's personal valet, nanny and hit-man. He was Polish, an ex-prisoner of war to the Germans, bearer of hideous personal suffering, great-hearted, sweet-natured and a dedicated lecher. His dedication to Tony's needs was passionate and his loyalty total. Less ardent but indisputable was his affection for myself. In Los Angeles he went to great trouble to entertain me with blue movies he had 'borrowed' from the Police Department. In London he would take me along to his Polish club in South Kensington, introduce me to his friends and charge me with the endless sweet and potent liqueurs of his native land.

However, his sweeping affections were by no means undiscriminating and he could nose out suspect enemies and anyone inimical to our well-being. No one ever demonstrated so eloquently the invocation of the Prayer Book's Second Collect of the Day: 'To serve is perfect freedom.' On the journey from the airport, he made his allegiance clear. 'Oh, Mister Osborne, is so good you are here. Mister Richardson, he so unhappy. I never seen him like it before. He need you so badly, but he never bring himself to tell you. He loves you, but he can't say that. Mister Osborne, please help him, is only you can do it.' He was on the edge of tears and hesitated in the darkening track leading to the house. 'That woman, she is a bitch, Mister Osborne, she is not a kind person and she makes Mister Richardson so unhappy.'

He had not exaggerated. The atmosphere in the pre-war bungalow was poisonous and Tony was unmistakably in the grip of it as he went through an abstracted mime of semi-relieved welcome. Big Van smiled vaguely à la Giaconda at the Alpes Maritimes somewhere above our heads. Once again, I cursed myself for letting myself be gulled. 'I mean, it'll be such *fun*, all of us together.'

We went out for dinner that evening because Vanessa was 'so tired'. Jan drove, the Richardsons beside him, the Osbornes in the back. No one spoke. As Jan took us down the rocky path towards St Tropez I settled into a numb apprehension which was broken by Tony and Big Van punching each other at close quarters. Jan crouched beside the wheel as the protagonists ejected themselves from the car. The three of us sat in silence while the Oscar-winning lad from Shipley and his adulated wife slugged it out. They returned without a word, and Jan drove on.

The following morning, Tony cornered me. 'You've *got* to talk to Vanessa.' 'Why?' 'She thinks you don't like her.' I couldn't believe he thought I might be taken in by such a disingenuous appeal, but he did. So, for days, I tried to talk to her, to arouse her curiosity or vanity, to engage her in any way. It was no use. I cast not a shadow on her awareness of the world outside herself.

A stream of visitors descended. We left our enseamed, unchanged sheets to be inherited by Jock and Pamela Addison. Three months later I was helping Pamela across the north-west corner of Sloane Square. 'You know I'm pregnant again,' she said. No, I didn't. They already had five children, which seemed enough. 'It's all your fault,' she went on. '*Your* sheets. Tony and Vanessa were so beastly to us we stayed in that bed all day simply to get away from it all.'

Life at Hellingly took on a pattern which I had not expected, but then I had not given it much thought. I had assumed that, having moved in, Penelope and I would spend most of our time there. She had given me the impression that her job as film critic of the *Observer* was more or less a part-time commitment which could easily be adapted to accommodate the principal thrust of her life, which included me. It wasn't so. At first, she went up to London for the first two days of the week, returning early on Tuesday evening. That seemed reasonable enough. But the reality turned out to be something else; another central-European peasant passion would be scheduled for Wednesday afternoon. Her working life in London became permanently extended.

She was understandably tired and also abstracted. Thursday was referred to as '*Observer* Day'. At eight in the morning she would take a pot of coffee over to the granary and stay there until almost midnight to finish her 'piece'. On Friday morning she delivered it to Polegate Station. It would be put on the train for Victoria, where it would be collected by an *Observer* messenger. On Friday afternoon her proofs arrived by the same system in reverse.

The next twenty-four hours would be taken up, as I had discovered in Folkestone, with editorial telephone calls, queries, arguments with the libel lawyers and so on until the paper was finally put to bed. But on Saturday evening she would still fret about what she might have omitted. The shadow of this anxiety often persisted well into Sunday, when she would go over her own piece repeatedly and then spend hours poring over the efforts of others.

In other words, it was effectively a seven-day week, with little time or inclination to divert to other pleasures or relaxation. I tried to point out that it seemed an inordinate amount of time and effort to expend on a thousand-word review to be read by a few thousand film addicts and forgotten almost at once. She was immovable and denied, in the face of the week's passing, that a two-and-a-half-day job had become a seven-day obsession. She was the grotesque adult embodiment of that properly despised schoolboy creature of fretful, incontinent ambition, a swot.

Wherever we went, the albatross typewriter followed. Every fresh absorption was concentrated on something like a script, uncommissioned, of a film which would never be made, or a dashed-off novel which should, and could, have been worked on without hurry. For someone who insisted that work was so important, it seemed a strangely unserious approach.

Penelope shared the public's illusion that writing is something that you sit down and do at prescribed sittings, and not that it is something that must be lived daily amid preoccupations that have nothing to do with putting together sentences – ordinary activities like cooking, going to the races, walking the dogs, seeing a bad movie and *not* writing about it, reading only for pleasure, going to pubs, the seaside, church. Not for her: an embassy supper was obligatory, the church fête a tiresome frivolity.

She was to become increasingly obsessed with fripperies and titles. She insisted on writing 'FRSL' after her name, a negligible bauble which she wore like a banner. She took to calling herself 'Professor Gilliatt' when she answered the telephone or replied to letters. She told me she had received an honourary doctorate from Oxford. In Debrett's *People of Today* she awards herself an exhaustive bunch of unperformed plays and operas. All this was yet to come. But muddle-headed Johnny, with his primitive talents, would clearly provide only a limited diversion for her questing spirit.

When our daughter was born, she was rather eccentrically christened Nolan, after the wild captain who delivered the fatal order to Lords Lucan and Cardigan at the head of the Light Brigade. When the child was older, her mother told her that she had been named after a character in an essay by James Joyce. There's intellect for you.

27. *All the Day Long*

Deliver me from blood-gatherers, O God,
Thou art the God of my health.
The sacrifice of God is a troubled spirit;
A broken and contrite heart, O God, shalt Thou not despise.

'A Commination', Book of Common Prayer

Why do sinners' ways prosper? and why must
Disappointment all I endeavour end?

Gerard Manley Hopkins, 'Thou Art Indeed Just, Lord'

1962

17 FEBRUARY, HELLINGLY: Well, Osborne, where is your lustre now? I am increasingly alone. These whole Thursday *Observer* days. Penelope beavering lather in the granary, pints of coffee and whisky and nothing else, all for 900 words about a biblical epic, another western or some pharisaical French tosh. Despite it all, *Plays for England* are done: *Blood of the Bambergs* and *Under Plain Cover*.

Bambergs is simply a broadly satiric account of one of the permanent fixtures in English life, a Royal Wedding. It's quite affectionately based on Anthony Hope's superb invention of Ruritania and the familiar plot of *The Prisoner of Zenda*. It seems a good idea to match the shuffling pantomime of contemporary royal fantasy with the real, romantic thing. *Under Plain Cover* is equally circumspect, a light *cadenza* on the clash of public prurience and private innocence.

No one will want them, but they'll be better than anything else on offer. One must be allowed – no, encouraged – to indulge these sportive fancies. Penelope *not* keen on *Plays for England*. Thinks I should do something more *ambitious*. ('You're got it *in* you, darling.') She wants experiment . . . 'But don't go *too* far, darling.'

1 APRIL, ROYAL COURT: *Plays for England*. John Dexter will do *Bambergs*. But he's terrified of *UPC*. Which is OK. Heterosexual sex scares the shit out of him. Jonathan Miller agrees to do *UPC*. No one else wants it. It might still be fun. You never know.

George bemused by St James's Palace lack of response to the repetition of 'knickers' some forty-five times in less than an hour. Penelope is impressed by Dr Miller. London's Intellectual Life. She's not much time for Dexter, Derby's son, although he's infinitely cleverer and, in rehearsal, it shows.

18 JULY, ROYAL COURT: *Plays for England*. Dress rehearsal. Not brilliant but it will do. Not much of a lark for anyone. *UPC*: I'm glad I've kept away from J. Miller. No chance of much contact there. The striving fluency of the Hampstead nanny's boy is deceptive and occasionally plausible. With its cultural allusions and cross-references to other disciplines, it is the gab-gift of someone to whom English is an adoptive tongue. Intellect does terrible things to the mind. As a director, he's an Armenian carpet-seller, although the cast is decent enough – Anton Rogers in particular, and little Annie Beach.

Bambergs: John Dexter *has* provided a few larks, though the actors are afraid of him. As George says, a born NCO. *Not* officer material. Oh, well, it'll soon be over.

I am already fired up into the future with *Inadmissible Evidence* and, maybe, *A Patriot for Me*. (I *am* good at titles, if little else.)

Inadmissible: I read a letter in a newspaper from a woman who was distraught at the spectacle of her husband, a man she admired and respected, being slowly isolated by the dislike and suspicion he aroused in other people. For all his tangible good and honour, she watched others recoil from his presence, until it overcame their children and, finally, even herself. Bill Maitland was born. It was an overpowering image of desolation.

Working away for hours in the Mill on *Inadmissible* was technically absorbing, but left me feeling so permanently despoiled that, at the end of a day, it called out for respite, some consuming recompense of fire. I found it at once in *Patriot*, which, by now, was like an old friend, and even an acquaintance to others, like Christopher Isherwood, to whom over the years I had confided its future.

Where *Inadmissible* was a banged up, irreversible journey, *Patriot* was a grand, operatic venture, all aria, history, sweep and grandeur. One made the other bearable. Alfred Redl and Bill Maitland demanded to be born across the half century of the terrible, Old Testament perils of the time. Anyway, it made sense to me, and that's how I did it.

19 JULY, ROYAL COURT: *Plays for England*. Well, we opened. They didn't like it. Princess Melanie (Vivian Pickles) was magnificent as the Bride in *Bambergs*

when she said, 'I'm so bored'; Alan Bennett, too, as the Archbishop. Jocelyn R. shrieked, maddeningly, at all my Australian jokes.

1 NOVEMBER: Mary sues for divorce.

14 DECEMBER: She *gets* it. Names poor Francine, Jocelyn, and Penelope. Admitted own adultery (who *dates* wins!). Brave smiles all round. Costs to me. Beuselinck: 'Got off lightly there, son.' Fancy! How lawyers and accountants gloat over the defeats of the likes of myself.

1963

8 MAY: Max Miller, the great priapic God of Flashness dies. 'There'll never be another.' As old John Betjeman says, an English genius as pure gold as Dickens or Shakespeare – or Betjeman, come to that. Max's last words: 'Oh, Mum,' to his wife. There is so much to dread.

25 MAY, HELLINGLY: Penelope and I are married. Tony is best man (again). Penelope's sister, Angela, another witness. The Addisons come and Pamela complains about the dog-shit on the lawn. George arrives, Jocelyn H., too. Big Van sends a typical telegram: 'I wish I could write an epithalamium for you.' Bet she thought I wouldn't know what that was. Oh, but Penelope would. She did.

1964

4 JANUARY, 'DAILY CINEMA': *Tom Jones* longest running picture at London Pavilion. Over six months. Grossed record-shattering £100,000 plus. In thirteenth New York week broke all-time house record.

5 JANUARY, HELLINGLY: Nellie Beatrice's birthday. Why does Penelope pretend to *like* her? To irritate me? Surely not. What made me take her to Venice (merry St Marks!) of all earth's wonders? Let alone New York. Barbados, now she liked that. Well, she would. One day, the cunning and the unteachable, like N.B., will run the show and give no quarter.

27 FEBRUARY: *Tom Jones* nominated for ten Oscars.

16 MARCH, QUEEN'S THEATRE: The English Stage Company's West End season, in conjunction with Binkie, opens with *The Seagull*. Everyone is moved

by George's performance as Dorn. In his white suit and hat, he looks almost dapper – well, jaunty at least. During his speech about what he'd like to say to Konstantin about his play, to *tell* him that he liked it, my eyes felt like pincushions at the beautiful autobiography of it.

And then, when he is left to bring down the curtain. 'How distraught they all are! How distraught! And what a quantity of love about. It's the magic lake. [*Tenderly*] But what can I do, my child? Tell me, what can I do? What?'

He was *really* asking a question. As always. And daring for an answer.

20 MARCH: Dear Brendan Behan dead. I remember him banging on our door at the Algonquin. 'Is there anyone at home in this fuckin' cat house?' Strangely *un*cruel for an Irishman (IRA, at that).

24 MARCH, HELLINGLY: All hell's been going on at the Queen's Theatre. Big Van is in the club and the season of *The Seagull* and *St Joan of the Stockyards* has been put on especially for her! Binkie insists she have an abortion. T.R. quite lost control. Siobhan McKenna might take over from her. Lindsay Anderson brought in to deal with the hysteria. *He* can't cope either. Up to George now. I think Binkie's right!

7 APRIL, HELLINGLY: *Inadmissible Evidence.* I am rid of Bill Maitland. Last night I dragged myself into the Mill with a bottle of champagne – later, at about 5 a.m. came back for more – and *finished* the play. Penelope full of pity for primitive man at work. Sister Angela playing Bach fugues all night – or motets, or something. She's *still* mooning on about the death of Dag Hammarskjöld.

Anyway, with *Inadmissible* I've done new language things for the first time. *No* one will notice. Still, that's not what the enterprise is about. Whole of Maitland's opening speech is a parody of Harold Wilson's at Scarborough. All that bullshit about technology . . .

(FAST FORWARD: When the play was revived in 1978, the audience laughed, as intended. By then they had seen the Wilson future and *knew* it didn't work.)

21 APRIL, INDIA: On holiday. This is the only way to avoid United Artists shipping me off in handcuffs to the Oscars ceremony. Edith [Evans] will do it for me, perfectly. The actors saved that film. Jock's music covered up some holes too . . .

Penelope glowing and in quite mischievous mood. *Suggests* getting pregnant. In India . . . ? Typewriter clattering from Bombay to Rajasthan for what . . . ? She saved my life last week after an attack by wasps in a temple. Too hot for sex – let alone work.

2 JUNE, ROYAL COURT: *Inadmissible Evidence.* Auditions. For Bill Maitland we need someone with the periscope view of an Olivier, scanning the oceanic grip of squalor from the secret, submerged depths in an echoing chamber of hollowness. All my suggestions – good actors all – a disaster.

At the end of the afternoon, Anthony [Page, the director] brings on his dark horse: Nicol Williamson. Nicol is in *costume.* He's *it.* Somehow the play rises. It takes flight. This twenty-seven-year-old, pouting, delinquent cherub produced the face to match the torment below the surface. He's much too young, but no matter. He is *old* within.

(FAST FORWARD: Addition to the John Gielgud Anthology of Dropped Bricks. During dinner in his house, he stopped in mid-flight: 'That actor – oh dear me – young, Scottish, *most* unattractive . . . He was in that long, terribly dull, boring play. Oh, dear God, of course, you wrote it.' That was *Inadmissible.*)

12 JULY, COVENT GARDEN: Crush Bar. Penelope is wearing a full-length frock made from raw silk stuff we got in Kashmir. 'Well,' she says, 'you're going to be a dad.' *No* excitement. Grandma O. on Boxing Day. In the Crush Bar. '*No one* must be told. *Only* Angela.' Brown eyes gone to black, with what – fury, disappointment? I feel sick with the contemptuous repudiation of it. There is an obdurate malignity in this? God, I hope not.

13 AUGUST, BRIGHTON: *Inadmissible Evidence.* We open at the Theatre Royal. The stage carpenter says, again: 'Not *you* again!' We have a lovely night at the pub where all the actors are staying. John Hurt shaking with lust and banging on Ann Beach's bedroom door. Can't blame him. Funny girl . . .

9 SEPTEMBER, ROYAL COURT: *Inadmissible* opens.

43, Cloth Fair, EC1

My dear old Top,

Here, in the calm of the morning, I affirm what I said last night to you – that is a tremendous play. The best thing you – yes, even you – have ever written. Apart from the sentiments in the diatribe – which I heartily endorse – it is the most heart-rending and tender study of every man who is not atrophied. We want to avoid giving pain and we want to be left in peace. Love makes us restless and we resist it. I felt increasingly that the play was about *me* and that is what all the great playwrights and poets can do for their watchers and readers.

Oh, my dear boy, I can't exactly *thank* you for such an agonizing self-analysis. I can only reverence the power and generosity in you which makes you write such a shattering and releasing piece. Once more my warmest congratulations on a mighty achievement – Oh, hell, what words are there to express myself? I feel as though I am writing to the elements.

Love from,

Bill Maitland-Betjeman

1 OCTOBER, CALIFORNIA: Chez Richardson. Fly to LA to talk to T.R. about *Patriot* and when he will be able to direct it. Neil Hartley, his assistant on *The Loved One*, meets me at the airport. He was Merrick's henchman for twenty years (an amazing testimonial to toughness and endurance) and T.R. shrewdly seduced him away during *Luther*'s run in New York.

Not, as expected, a taciturn bespoke-tailor of concrete overcoats, but a tall, handsome man from North Carolina, might have been a thirties' film star himself. Immaculate manners, good humour, diplomatic skills. Almost a parody of a Southern gent. The prospect of a new, permanent friendship.

T.R., three months into the shooting of Waugh, has set up an impregnable GHQ in a collection of Hollywood Tudor buildings recently vacated by Rex Harrison. There's the main house, surrounding the pool, and several bijou bungalows occupied by various adjutants, 'writers' and assistants in obligatory shorts and sneakers. Neil wryly assures me that the majority of staff officers have been flushed out in anticipation of my arrival. He has the impeccable gift of confiding in me without compromising his loyalty to T.R.

I am summoned to a location in a depressing street in Watts. T.R. is shooting a scene in a clapboard hovel in which Mr Joyboy, improbably played by Rod Steiger, cooks an orgiastic meal and stuffs his bullfrog, bed-ridden mother with tureens of spaghetti, meatballs, haunches of fat pork and offal. I stand at the back of the suffocating little room all the morning, feeling sick. I have never seen such a venomous, uncoordinated assault, such a crowing repudiation of the female species and distortion of its physicality.

I escape into the smoggy street and wait for the lunch break. T.R. arrives, exhilarated, bubbling with the results of the morning. Suddenly, slamming down this flow of self-excitement, he turns to the script of *Patriot*. 'I read this last night. Frankly, Johnny, I'm a bit mystified. I mean, you'll have to *explain* it to me. I mean, what's it all *about?*'

I had never thought he would put such a question to me. I handed him a letter from Penelope, which she had rightly trusted me not to open. I suspected it was some garbled rationalization of her pregnancy. He opens it and flips through it, leg stabbing virulently. He throws it aside and fixes the messenger with a hostile stare, as if I am some accosting beggar.

'I mean, *what*'s it about?' I feel even more sickened and humiliated. I can't think of anything to say. We look at each other in fixed alienation.

He begins to pour mock surprise scorn on Evelyn Waugh, who has evidently heard news of the savage mutilation of his novel. 'Don't you think he's being very *peculiar*?' The final result was to be one of the most ill-judged films ever perpetrated. He tried to appal me further with descriptions of the morgue and corpses hanging from their ears in neat plastic bags.

There is no point. I must face it: it is unarguable that he dislikes *Patriot* and won't do it. I shall have to look elsewhere. I decide to flee, before I myself die in that terrible place, suspended like a bundle at the dry cleaners.

22 OCTOBER, ROYAL COURT: *Cuckoo in the Nest.* Back on to the boards again in the blessed Ben Travers masterpiece. *He* thinks we are all marvellous! Arthur Lowe certainly is. Penelope not pleased by her exclusion from my vagabond life, once again. But absorbed in spending my money on massive renovations on the house we have bought in Chester Square, her refuge against the country, complete with copper dining-room doors and Swedish experiments in the drawing-room.

1965

1 JANUARY, SAVOY HOTEL: George, ground down by illness and the tit-swingers of Sloane Square, has decided that he will step down, after ten years, as director at the Court in September. I dread Neville Blond's annual lunch for the critics. They are prickly and oleaginous, full of pique and ill-feeling. This time, most of all, I dread George's retirement speech.

'When a man begins to feel he is part of the fixtures and fittings it is time he left. I am deeply tired. The weight of this edifice had driven me up to my neck like poor Winnie in *Happy Days*. I should have passed the job on years ago. I am getting out just in time.'

There was a vote of thanks from some nonentity, as if we had just heard the Chairman of the local Rotary Club turning it in. Chairs started to crunch. That was it then. Those ten years . . . Rage and impatience. Suddenly, we hear the voice of Lindsay Anderson: 'I cannot let this occasion go by so unrewarded.' Some honour was plucked from the shoddy moment.

5 JANUARY, HELLINGLY: Nellie Beatrice's birthday. The Lord Chamberlain gives *Patriot* the full thumbs down. No quarter. It's now clear that if the Council agrees to turn the Court into a club for the play – which *terrifies* them – they'll make *me* stump up at least half. Budget £15,000 at present. J.O.: £7,000. After all the money *I've* earned for them. This place would have closed five years ago if it wasn't for me.

12 JANUARY, CHESTER SQUARE: *Patriot*. Marge Vosper for lunch. Wonders if the Lord Chamberlain might not just be right, after all, dear. The public *will* only take *so* much and *you* have given them quite enough to be getting on with all these years. *We mustn't expect too much*. (I never do. And I never get it.) Dear old Marge. Still hasn't got over *UPC*, and all those unnecessary jokes about knickers. Ewan (her husband) hated it so much he had to go to bed. Yet he tells all those filthy jokes about Robert Burns:

> His breeks were doon,
> His airse was bare,
> His balls were swinging in the air.
> If he nae was nae fucking
> I was nae there.

Cultured Scottish gentility, I dare say.

4.30, WOODFALL OFFICES: *The Charge of the Light Brigade*. Cecil Woodham-Smith, author of *The Reason Why*, has slapped an injunction on us. Oscar Beuselinck is relishing it. How he hates people who create things. He thinks everyone steals. *I've* plagiarized no one. Only myself, in the style of G.F. Handel (never stopped, and who better to steal from?). Beuselinck declares triumphantly that it's going to cost us £12,000 to buy off Laurence Harvey, who owns Woodham-Smith's rights. I hear T.R. has already offered him 'my part' as the Russian prince.

19 JANUARY, ENGLISH STAGE COMPANY: *Patriot*. Elaine Blond more surly and charmless than ever. Blacksell, the redundant schoolteacher from Devon, drones on about 'Young People'. When *I* was Young People, they treated us like dirt. Didn't matter. Now, not to be reverential about the little bastards is regarded as a logical extension of anti-Semitism. Dear Greville Poke looks and behaves more like Ralph Lynn than ever, spats and all. Perhaps I should give him a monocle for the opening of *Patriot*. But would he wear it?

21 JANUARY, WOODFALL OFFICES: *Patriot*. We are *summonsed* by T.R. to Curzon Street. He sits there, the papal legate from Shipley. We crouch on nasty Swedish-Gilliatt-style chairs. Marge Vosper is mystified, Anthony Page is sweaty *and* shifty, Maximillian Schell is polite.

T.R., however, is in machiavellian form: 'I mean, the thing is, well, it's so embarrassing, but when Johnny [don't!] brought his play to me in Los Angeles, I had to tell him I couldn't do it – because of, ah – commitments. [Too windy, you mean.] Well, the thing is: *now*, it appears I can, after all. Do it. *That*'s the situation.'

I don't know what he expected. Old Marge didn't know what to say. Page looked like a Wykehamist about to deny he'd fiddled his New College viva by offering up his body. Max was very good, already very Colonel Redl, I thought.

T.R. was smirking at this display of full house. Bang down went my royal flush. Expressed with most circumspect, triumphant piety. I'm sorry, Tony. But while you were away in California, I've spent a great deal of time with Anthony [Page, none of it very enjoyable, spitting food all over me]. We've worked on the casting, the sets, the music. He's been down on the usual run to St James's Palace. I couldn't change horses in mid-stream.

Collapse of long, thin party. I shall cherish his leg arrested in mid-thrust, the old Shipley jaw wrenched back like a pulled-up stallion.

It will never happen again!

22 JANUARY, WELBECK STREET: Saw Dr Hemans (Penelope's gynaecologist). Too wise for that job. Saw *Divorce Me, Darling*. Blimey. It's *still* 1956. Maybe always will be.

29 JANUARY, ENGLISH STAGE COMPANY: Another meeting. Usual stuff about ladies' lavatories. Elaine seems to spend so much time in there, why doesn't she just whip out her chequebook and buy us a new ballcock. God, the rich are tight-fisted. How they *live* money.

30 JANUARY, COVENT GARDEN: *Arabella*. Now, that's more like it. Old Strauss does for ladies' voices what oats does for horses. He *invented* another human sound. I looked rather pretty in my black waistcoat, which may be why a lavendery Loamshire gent said, 'I suppose *you're* our Verdi.' [Popular? No. Vulgar and hummable, I suppose he meant.] 'No,' said his companion, 'Mozart.' That's pitching it a bit too high. Berlioz would do. Vaughan Williams really best of all.

2 FEBRUARY, ROYAL COURT: *Patriot*. Anthony does waffle on. I *do* dislike greedy people. He's at the peanuts, stuffing his face, all the time. Gluttony *really* is a sin. Lust can constrain itself. He's intent on getting a Continental lady for the Countess. Now, it's (no!) Delphine Seyrig (model) and old Swedish black-looks, Liv Ullman. I do tell him there are plenty of our own girls at hand. Jill Bennett, he suggests. Not keen. I saw her being very patronizing to her husband, Willis Hall, one night in Beoty's. We'll see.

3 FEBRUARY, PAMELA'S FLAT: 11.30 a.m. Once again, easy slide between sheets. Very cosy Tiggywinkle Kilburn basement. Bland still upon bland, but quite affectionate. Says the weekly sums she got from her piece of *Inadmissible*

have kept her going. Quite a large sum when I think of it – £200 a month at least. No, more. And then there'll be America.

16 FEBRUARY, WOODFALL: *The Charge of the Light Brigade.* T.R. is hell-bent on making an anti-war film. Oscar Lewenstein looks as glum as he did in the Acapulco brothel. I am losing heart. T.R. is tampering with history – all there in Kingslake's classic account of the battle, minute by minute. I think they should forget me and get in Charles Wood. He's not only a proper writer but a professional soldier – Seventeenth/Twenty-First Lancers. War? Loves it, abominates it.

17 FEBRUARY, OLD VIC: *Much Ado.* Zeffirelli's with Robert and Margaret Stephens. Loved all this wog nonsense. He's a clever bugger.

Penelope insists she writes it up for Friday. Proofs on Saturday. She looks thin and ghostly. Baby due on Wednesday. And no one has a clue that she's pregnant. Well, she's done it. *Not* very flattering to me. Calculated disavowal. Nolan will be born with a proof in his/her mouth.

18 FEBRUARY, CHESTER SQUARE: Went to a factory in Sevenoaks to get Penelope her harpsichord to celebrate the birth. I hope she'll be pleased. Not just to perfect her Bach, but a bit of Fats Waller, Hoagy Carmichael. I fancy not. Nicol Williamson might hot it up a bit. Or Jock Addison.

24 FEBRUARY, WELBECK STREET NURSING HOME: Nolan Kate Conner – ! – Osborne born, 9.05 a.m. Saw her at 9.15. Not at all red and nasty. Caesarean swank, I suppose. Quite pretty. By 4.00 p.m. Penelope is in a state of rage about some hooray friend of the family whose own wife was in a prolonged state of labour in the room next door and talked about the possibility of 'putting the ferrets up her'. Standard coarse upper-class joke I'd have thought.

She wants to go home *tonight*! Uncorrected Proofs. Even she conceded she couldn't make it. Perhaps she'll start eating again now.

26 FEBRUARY, ROYAL COURT: *Meals on Wheels.* Corporal Charles Wood has sent the Court a bizarre comic extravaganza of such inventiveness that nobody understands it. None of the tame resident directors will risk it, which is a disgrace. *I* don't 'understand' it either, but so what? It's clearly very good. Told George I'll direct it.

WELBECK STREET: Penelope still in a rage about the ferrets. She rails about the food (which *is* terrible). She has to be *thin*. George and Jocelyn H. bring her some fish and chips, which she pretends to enjoy. Her eyes black again with outrage, ill-use. A drop of milk splashes from her breast to her knee. She throws up. That same *obdurate malignity*. It is. Don't.

26 MARCH, ST JAMES'S PALACE: *A Patriot For Me.* The Lord Chamberlain stands firm. So, it will have to be the Club Theatre, £7,000 out of my own money, working for nothing, and the plod of policemen's feet. And all on account of this. They've sent it back, confirmed:

Cuts and alterations requested by the Lord Chamberlain

I–I	'His spine cracked in between those thighs . . . All the way up.'
I–I	This scene must not be played with the couple both in bed.
I–4	From: 'She moves over to the wall . . . ' To: ' . . . Presently he turns away and sits on the bed.'
I–5	Reference to 'clap' and 'crabs'.
I–9	Reference to 'clap'.
I–10	Omit the whole of this scene.
II–11	Ditto.
III–1	From: 'You'll never know that body like I know it . . . ' To: ' . . . you've not looked at him. You never will.'
III–1	From: 'Your turn, Stefan, . . . ' To: ' . . . than any ordinary man'.
III–2	Omit: 'You were born with a silver sabre up your whatsit.'
III–4	Omit: 'Tears of Crisst'.
III–5	Omit: the whole of this scene.

And, of course, the Drag Ball. OMIT THE WHOLE OF THIS SCENE. And put half the queens of Chelsea out of a job? Poor George. What grief I bring him.

19 APRIL, ROYAL COURT: *Meals on Wheels.* Usual dismal first reading. Comic actors are even *worse* on these occasions. At least the stage management laughed. Frank Thornton knows his stuff. Very good. That's over. I equivocated very prettily. Well, *I* thought so.

ST JAMES'S PALACE: *Meals on Wheels.*

Page 24:	'She never knew the Duke of Windsor', substitute 'She never knew Leslie Howard'.
Page 25:	'Duke of Windsor', substitute 'God Bless the Prince of Wales'.
Page 61:	'Because you looked like the Duke of Windsor', substitute 'Because you looked like him'.
Page 63:	'I can't help looking like the Duke of Windsor', substitute 'I can't help what I look like'.

There will, of course, be no attempt to impersonate the Duke of Windsor.

6 MAY, PALLADIUM: In an attempt to lift the *Meals on Wheels* cast into the higher realm of Corporal Wood's imagination, I take them to see Ken Dodd.

Once again, Betjemanesque divine genius. 'This morning I woke up with Miss Givings' . . . 'Grandad used to stand with his back to the fire. We had to have him swept.' Don't know what they made of it.

9 MAY, ROYAL COURT: *Meals on Wheels*. Despondent rehearsal. I dread facing one of the actors, Lee Montagu, first thing. He smokes a pipe at 10 o'clock. He actually *looks* for the few difficulties we *haven't* got. His wife always seems to have had an *idea* in bed the night before. I pretend to listen . . .

They keep on asking does it (whatever) mean *this* – or – that? I reply: 'I suspect . . . it's both.' They stare at me resentfully. 'We'll ask Charles when he comes up from Bristol.' He does. 'Well, Charles,' I say, feeling a shit for not protecting him, 'what does it mean?' With a fine soldier's simplicity, he replies, 'Both.'

20 MAY, ROYAL COURT: *A Patriot For Me*. 'Victory or Westminster Abbey!' First reading. George *very* grumpy. Don't blame him. It's beyond belief that Page should have made him *audition*, and twice, for the Baron. He is going to be magnificent, I know. Everyone is agog at the prospect. In his dressing-room, he tells me what 'girls have to go through for tights and mascaras'. He is fondling his wig and gloves as if they were the rarest objects. All this with legs wide *open* and a pipeful of Edgeworth blasting out into Sloane Square.

26 JUNE, ROYAL COURT: *Patriot*. Dress rehearsal. George says to me, 'I thought people *hated* Tony Richardson in this theatre – until I saw Anthony Page at work.'

30 JUNE, ROYAL COURT: *Patriot*. Opening night.

My dear Friend,
   Don't know quite how to express myself tonight. It is a great night and must be viewed as such, although it seems the end of a period and all that. But these things are what we make them. The essentials remain – and the way our friendship has grown over these years is vastly important to me.
   Love, ever.
   George

9 AUGUST, ROYAL COURT: *Patriot*. Sloane Square stifling. Theatre sweltering after matinée. George collapses with heart attack in full gear. Oh, God. Taken to St George's Hospital.

14 AUGUST, ROYAL COURT: *Patriot*. Last night. Audience told George is recovering. I suppose he is. But the thought of his spirit stifling in that dreary

ward hangs over the whole theatre. Scene after scene; his memory seems to pierce everything, the costumes, the words and, of course, the Drag Ball . . . a silk shirt, an ancient Greek ring. George, our play, our world, coming to an end. I could scarcely bear to watch it.

There am I, tears streaming from every orifice and some dumb accusing creature accosts me during the second interval. She had, she tells me smugly, been deeply hurt by the play, and found it most offensive. Her mother is one of the Sloane Square Zionists. Life *is* offensive, I say, hardly able to see for the disintegration of my own world. All those painful anti-Semitic remarks? That's how it was in 1912 Vienna, I suggest. She nods in disbelief at my insensitivity. 'You don't understand.' I do, lady, I do.

St George's Hospital, SW1

(Just been told I can feed myself. Get that for progress.)

My dear John,

I thought of you this morning when I remarked to the nurse that we hadn't had any new casualties since I came in on Saturday. 'Oh, yes, we have,' she replied rather snootily. 'There's the gentleman down the end in No. 24 who passed out watching the changing of the Queen's Guard!'

What a shock, without any warning at all, I really thought I'd had my chips that night, but about fifty miles behind my head I was obstinately hanging on, answering their questions with an angry resentful snarl. I was in an oxygen mask and my speech was distorted so when I heard one cry, 'How old is he?' 'Oh, about 57 or 58,' I lashed out 55 with great venom . . .

Above all, John, your card meant the most. I can't help thinking I made a balls of it by collapsing. I suppose I should not have gone on on Saturday night, but the thought of all the flap and Anthony Royle in *my* costume and that packed house and one's innate vanity . . . However, it was, thank goodness, no more than a pity.

Let's talk about a trip somewhere later. Would love that.

From the Baron who went too far.

1 SEPTEMBER, ROYAL COURT: George officially retires as Artistic Director. Bill [Gaskill] takes over. Well, that's Good.

13 OCTOBER, HELLINGLY: *Charge of the Light Brigade*. Finished. Hooray.

31 OCTOBER, NEW YORK: *Inadmissible*. Back to the Algonquin for the Broadway production.

9 NOVEMBER, PHILADELPHIA: *Inadmissible.* American tour begins. Anthony Page is no good at handling gangsters like David Merrick. Showdown backstage tonight with Merrick and Nicol Williamson squaring up to each other like old-time fairground pugilists. Merrick told Williamson, 'Page is fired.' Williamson replied, 'You can't fire the fucking director without telling me.' They are both quivering with fear. St Valentine's Day Massacre. Nicol discovered next morning at the Railroad Depot singing 'Mammie'. Merrick tells me to fuck off. Back to England and my Queen. Point out an unlikely welcome from either.

12 DECEMBER, HELLINGLY: My birthday. Spiffing note from John 'Maitland' Betjeman. What did Trollope say – muddle-headed Johnny? It's deep honesty that distinguishes a gentleman. *He's* got it. He knows how to *revel* in life and have no expectations – and fear death at all times.

CHRISTMAS, HELLINGLY: A meticulous fuck-up. Penelope in filthy mood. Insisted Jock and Pamela Addison come. Fine! With their five children. No. Compromise. They come for Boxing Day without their children. 'Christmas is *for* children,' Pamela admonishes. I said it's too good for them. Penelope also insists on asking Jill Bennett. 'She's lonely now that Willis has left her in that little house.' I'm sure she doesn't want to come here. Penelope gets her way.

BOXING DAY, HELLINGLY: Penelope makes everyone go off to the Devonshire Park Theatre for the pantomime. *She* stays at home with Nolan. Pamela cheers up a bit. I think J.B. *quite* enjoyed it. I loved it.

28. *Vale Nora Noel*

By the pricking of my thumbs
Something wicked this way comes.
Macbeth, III. i

The mind is its own place and in itself
Can make a heaven of hell, a hell of heaven.
John Milton, *Paradise Lost*, Book One

Keep thou my feet; I do not ask to see
The distant scene; one step enough for me.
I loved the garish day, and spite of fears
Pride ruled my will; remember not past years
And with the morn these angel faces smile
Which I have loved long since and lost awhile.
'The Pillar of Cloud', *Lead Kindly Light*, 1833

FAST FORWARD: *Notebook, 7 October 1990*: Nora Noel Jill Bennett committed suicide yesterday. Except, of course, that she didn't, merely perpetrating a final common little deceit under the delusion that it was an expression of 'style', rather than the coarse posturing of an overheated housemaid.

Reading through the glib newspaper cant of today, it appears that only I know what should have been apparent to even the most crass journalist: that she was a woman so demoniacally possessed by Avarice that she died of it. How many people have died in such a manner, of Avarice? Of pride, sloth, gluttony and, most publicly, of lust. But to die of Avarice takes driving of the will, some low, scheming ingenuity. However, there it is, she did actually contrive to polish herself off with the deadly draught. This final, fumbled gesture, after a lifetime of glad-rags borrowings, theft and plagiarism, must have been one of the few original or spontaneous gestures in her loveless life.

I don't think she would have been too pleased with her notices this morning, in spite of the corn-drivel phrases from the lady hacks, who are simply relieved to find that they're a bit more on top of their own plundering avidity. But she would have been satisfied with the poor Silly-Jilly gush spewed up by the gay faithful and hairy show-biz sob-sisters. The power of popular sentimentality does wonders with invention.

B.A. (Freddie) Young tootles on in the *Financial Times* (she deserved a rave review there – money was her undisputed reason for living): 'Petite [he can't even remember what she looked like] and charming, she was always an active outdoor woman.' He must have been at the Garrick port a little too late in the afternoon. Something's certainly fevered his muddy old remembrance. She could have tucked little Freddie under her 'glitzy, up-market armpits' (*Daily Express*).

During the nine years I lived beneath the same roof with her, she spent half the day in bed. There was a short period when she took dressage lessons, that most intensive course in aids to severe narcissism, but in an *in*door school. She *was* intermittently athletic. She could throw a weighty punch or kick, *and* sustain it for hours on end. My friends can give you a guided tour of the scars around my head.

'At the Court, she played the Russian Countess in *A Patriot for Me*, a part she adorned beyond its proper worth.' Wrong, Freddie. Petite and charming as a rattle-snake before breakfast, she got the part by default, and it was later truly 'adorned' with considerable power, grace and charm by Sheila Gish and June Ritchie in the 1983 revival. Apart from their superior gifts, they managed to speak the text without sounding like a puppy with a mouthful of lavatory paper.

During the long nights of hearing her lines, which only laziness prevented her from getting down unassisted, I did everything I could to scrub up her diction, but it never improved. Indeed, after we separated and she was consigned to lesser parts, it became even worse. During a television series in which she stooged to Maria Aitken, lamentable even by the pier-end standards of sit-com, she was quite incomprehensible and cried out for sub-titles.

Perhaps it was Tony's declaration that she was the 'worst actress in England' and Anthony Page's capitulation to little Jilly's tiresome refusal to give a reading that persuaded me to give her the Countess nod. For once, Mary McCarthy was uncommonly perceptive when she pronounced the performance 'common and strident'. It was straight from life.

More of today's 'tributes': 'Former screen sex symbol' (the *Sun*, couldn't remember who she was); 'Tempestuous, ritzy star' (*Express*, again). Star she never was, even by the saloon-bar tally of the *T.V. Times*. All those lies she fed out *ad nauseum* are here again: of J.O. having gone off with her 'best friend', who was never more than a lunchtime acquaintance; of *her* sheepdog – mine – which *I* had destroyed. I loved him and saved him from her vicious neglect. And so on – the perpetuation of this whole rotting body of lies and invention which was her crabbed little life.

At least some of them have rumbled her real age. Poor Willis had years of grilling with immigration officials infuriated by her amateurish efforts to change her birth date. As so often, the provincial papers were on to it first.

> Marguerite Vernon, 81, of Sidford in East Devon, was Jill's cousin, and closest surviving relative. 'When she became famous, contact was broken. We went to see some of her plays but were fairly coldly received. [I'll bet.] She was a good actress, but extrovert, noisy and loud.' [Come, Mrs Vernon, don't you mean 'witty and vulnerable, warm-hearted, feline, wonderfully droll and naughty, instinctive and hard to please'?] Mr Vernon is also convinced that Jill, who won best actress award in 1968 for her part in John Osborne's *Time Present*, kept a secret of her real age.
>
> Western Morning News

But what of her 'diamond sparkle which made her so irresistible and so wonderful in *Hedda Gabler*' (Patrick Procktor, painter of her portrait and a friend of twenty-five years)? Well, he didn't have to hump her through her lines. Wasn't it her 'essential quality of intelligence and lack of sentimentality which made her Hedda so remarkable' (Anthony Page)? Sentimentality she had in abundance; feeling none.

'She was eighteen years younger than my wife,' Mr Vernon continues, 'which would make her sixty-three and not fifty-nine as she claimed.' No matter, Mr Vernon. The producer Thelma Holt recalls her 'wit and larky sense of fun. Even in recent times, when her career and personal life were sometimes in the doldrums, she maintained her essential elegance and stoic brightness.' I remember the tragic actress's stoic brightness very well, Ms Holt. I remember the shit and the vomit on the sheets and calling out my friend Patrick Woodcock every other month with his little black bag. I know how carefully she knew the practical drill of suicide and how many times she rehearsed it:

ESSENTIALS Thirty or forty sleeping pills of maximum strength. 30mg Carbitol, for instance. At least half bottle of brandy. Half a loaf of moist brown bread. Most important: make sure that you will not be accidentally disturbed. An anonymous, second-rate hotel, booked in on Friday with the Do Not Disturb notice put up at once. The Cumberland at Marble Arch is ideal.

My cheap joke about calling her 'Adolf' has followed her to Putney Vale. Even those who might consider themselves her admirers took to using it.

How do I know that Adolf didn't intend to kill herself? Very simple. Her body contained hardly a trace of alcohol. She was relying on someone 'coming on her' sufficiently comatose for a good night's sleep but not enough to feel the brush of angels' wings. But her dog-walker failed to return and the millionaire stockbroker whose bed – and fortune – she coveted, was on business in Hungary and could not be summoned.

The sound of 'I left my heart in San Francisco' will waft across Putney Vale, and that distinguished film director Michael Winner will pronounce: 'She was a bit of a sexpot. One of the kindest, nicest people you could ever meet!'

Dogs home left £½m by actress

By A J McIlroy

THE ACTRESS Jill Bennett, former wife of John Osborne, the playwright, left more than £500,000 to Battersea Dogs Home in her will.

Miss Bennett, who died last October, left estate valued at £582,530 net (£596,978 gross). The will bequeathed the residue of her estate to her mother but stipulated it should go to the dogs home should her mother die before her.

There were bequests of £5,000 each to the Theatrical Ladies Guild of Charity and her long-standing secretary and companion Mrs Linda Drew. Had her mother not died the dogs home would also have received £5,000.

Jill Bennett: always had dogs around

Daily Telegraph, 27 May 1991

258

NOTEBOOK, 27 MAY 1991: Adolf has left half a million to Battersea Dogs' Home. She never bought a bar of soap in all the time she lived with me. Always she cried poverty. 'Poor Jilly, she's got no money.' All the time she was bursting with krugerrands, cast-iron stocks and bond she inherited from her wise old dad, Randle, to say nothing of the £157,000 old mother Nora left her. Ever since those days in 1947 when I used to pass her front-of-house photograph outside the Vaudeville in the Strand on my way from Benn Brothers to pick up Renee, she had been piling up the heftiest assets of any actress since Lily Langtry.

I must have been more profitably 'touched' than most, but all her gay boyfriends, clamouring for AIDS charities, can't be well pleased. She left them only her contempt. Half a million pounds. To the Dogs' Home.

It is the most perfect act of misanthropy, judged with the tawdry, kindless theatricality she strove to achieve in life. She had no love in her heart for people and only a little more for dogs. Her brand of malignity, unlike Penelope's, went beyond even the banality of ambition. It had its roots deep in a kind of bourgeois criminality. Her frigidity was almost total. She loathed men and pretended to love women, whom she hated even more. She was at ease only in the company of homosexuals, whom she also despised but whose narcissism matched her own. I never heard her say an admiring thing of anyone. Her contempt was so petty and terrible. Everything about her life had been a pernicious confection, a sham.

I have only one regret remaining now in this matter of Adolf. It is simply that I was unable to look down upon her open coffin and, like that bird in the Book of Tobit, drop a good, large mess in her eye.

29. *Philadelphia Story*

23 JANUARY 1966, *Observer*

The Pioneer at the Royal Court

In my own life, January seems to have a gratuitous trick of springing cruelty. Perhaps it is a personal illusion that life at the beginning of the year, like life at the beginning of the day, is harder to bear or contemplate. For me a year hardly begun that springs the death of George Devine is a harsh one to face. It is a bleak week in the English theatre.

I don't think many people really knew him well. I believe I did. I would like to think I had been able to get at least one foot inside that surprising and moving personality. Like many men blessed with a gift for friendship, he was not easily accessible, although he appeared to have an almost comically natural Socratic persona.

He could appear harsh to outsiders, especially know-alls, and, like most profoundly modest and self-critical people, he could seem most arrogant when he was self-denigrating and felt himself being merely realistic. If he could have dissembled with even a little jauntiness, his career might have been more apparently successful and certainly easier. But he despised flattering and wheedling, which is probably why the relations of the Royal Court with the Press were usually a trifle prickly, to say the least of it.

Brush-off

George was a natural teacher. This was because he longed to respect his pupils and learn from them. And he was always fiercely unpatronizing, except to the over-ambitious, dewy-eyed or expedient. On these occasions his contempt could be chilling. He was unfailingly watchful and suspicious of opportunism, ambition, caution and timidity.

People think of the Royal Court as having been a forcing-house for younger writers, but this was not a matter of systematic policy. George made consistent efforts from the very beginning to bring older, established writers – novelists and poets whom he admired – into what people assumed to be a charmed circle of youth. The lack of response from his own generation disturbed him. It seemed like a lordly brush-off of the art he loved.

He was incapable of sentimentality, and I think it is important to stress that this was especially true of his dealings with younger people. What was so formidable was his nose for sham in art and people. I think perhaps the friendships he prized most were with those more or less his own age – Beckett, Michel Saint-Denis, Glen Byam Shaw; only three weeks ago he made a very special effort to entertain Ionesco. It seemed to me he also had a very rare attitude among men – he genuinely and eagerly admired and respected gifted women.

In ten years as artistic director of the Royal Court, George Devine was almost solely responsible for its unique atmosphere, which anyone who knew him knew to be a reflection of his own unique temperament. Some people with their hatred of what they believe to be a self-congratulatory theatrical in-life may think that this became cosy. It never did. It was very English in its approach – empirical is a respectable word for it, I suppose – unsystematic, non-manifesto.

In the end he was worn down by the grudging, removed attitude to decent and sustained effort that is such a recurrent and depressing aspect of English life. No one can surpass the Englishman's skill of maiming with indifference. Viewed from outside his ten years in Sloane Square may have seemed wonderfully rewarding and exciting, as indeed they often were for him. But this peculiar native climate of critical attrition chilled, bit into him and wore him down. I can imagine his special, amused shrug at the crass newspaper headlines which described him last week as 'kitchen sink director'.

If I give an impression of George Devine as someone disappointed or embittered, I would be quite wrong. His disappointment was minimal, in fact, because his expectation was relentlessly pruned. This, combined with his prodigious, hopeful effort, seemed to make his stoicism heroic and generous, rather than a pinched, carping austerity. These were exactly the qualities he admired and saw in the work of personalities as different as Beckett and Brecht. Perhaps it was a kind of reticence. Strength, gaunt lines and simplicity always excited him. During an earlier illness he used to enjoy making furniture and it always expressed this passion in a very touching way.

Thanks Due

The sort of people who were dismissive about George Devine's work were the ones who were aware of the Royal Court only when a star or a fashionable revival appeared there. In spite of that dim support he did make its name a household word. Only a tiny minority actually sampled any of its goods, but most people had at least heard of his work.

The two big subsidized companies – the National and the Royal Shakespeare – owe a debt to him that is incalculable. Their existence is directly due to him. Hundreds of writers and actors owe their present fortunes and favour to him. I am in the greatest debt of all. It seems extraordinary to have been quite so fortunate.

J.O.

FAST FORWARD: *Notebook entries 1972*: Oh, yes, after railing on about her historic performance as Hedda for yet another four hours, J.B. said:

'I was written out.' Very likely. I dare say. She's helping.

'Disliked by everyone at the Court.' – That's me again.

'Always a hopeless fuck.'

'Even the queens don't fancy me because my eyes are very Welsh and too close together.'

'Can't think *how* I earned my money' . . . Me neither.

I, the whole while being a sort of Stoneleigh Oscar Wilde again. Why did I listen? No drink. Wanted the bed. Utterly alone. Too tired. Fitzgerald's 4.00 a.m. crack-up time . . . Oh, yes, she's excited about the opening [*Hedda Gabler*] and Lufer, the sheepdog, which *I* shall have to care for and clean up after. Poor little devil. God protect me, but I can't protect you.

'You only remember the bad things.' What are the good things?

She's obsessed about getting over 40 (surely, already!). What can *I* do? She's attractive sometimes. To me, she's just a pretty scalpel.

I don't think I can last much longer. Dusty, doctoring, disapproving death. I can feel thy sting only too well at the moment. All these books to *read* and can't see the pages. I *am* like a mooching scruffy bear(!) curled up in the dirty corner of the cage he paces. No lustre, no life, only dullish dread. Drew up a list in my pacing head, sweating out the names of *all the people I no longer see* . . . What a *long* list.

Not a drink for seven days. Last night was the most difficult, surprisingly. Saw the Addisons, affectionate but, of course, undercurrent of alarm . . . Two more plays – *if* they get produced. I see no future. Not even a different one. This is over and it's a relief. Could I learn to fish? Doubt it . . . I don't think I can

262

face *managements* – even though I am so much stronger(?). This is *not* the time for God! Except in its inconsequences and wrangling squalor.

Woke at 10.30. Took too many pills: one, was it two, Carbitol. And one 10mg Valium. J.B. having one of her secretive – or secre*e*tive as she says – lunches. One of the Pouf Boswells clinging to her wit and, of course, vulnerability. I imagine pterodactyls were vulnerable but still pretty nasty till they got nature's come-uppance. J.B. is clearly going to be a great personal success as Hedda. I hope so, I do – though she says I am willing it to *fail*. Dear God . . .

Try not to be serious. I don't like guttering out much. As Lytton Strachey said on his deathbed: 'If this is it, I don't think much of it.' I look awful and that I don't care about. J.B. has brought her own strategy of ineffable emotional swindling to the play and made it possibly better than we all thought. My notes to A. Page on the acting were rather good. *She* immediately suspected conspiracy. Her own métier. Anyway, she deserves the bravos. I wouldn't know what to do with them. Some hope. Why so hurt? Perhaps that is ceasing too. Thank God, no children, no kiddies, above all no goddam *grand*children. How grisly grandparents are – all that slobbering pride.

More a.m. hours about Hedda and myself when the Carbitols haven't worked off her evening adrenalin of Ibsen. This time:
The staff hate and despise me. Mutual, on the whole.
Alan, the driver. Don't believe it.
Sonny, the housekeeper. Possibly, more like indifference. Too busy thinking up his next frock for his Shirley Bassey appearance at the Gay Ball in Grosvenor House.
My secretary. Most likely. Her office is becoming like a coven for the two of them.
The dogs. Natch.
Nolan. Partly assisted by P.G., I suppose.
Rotten actor. Not altogether true. I could have persevered.
Bad skin. True.
Taken in by 'intellectual codswallop'. – *Me*! Muddle-headed J.O.
Usual stuff about P.G.
Sex not much bother. Scarcely at all. The girls can't fancy me and I don't seem to go overmuch for them . . . After all this, I suppose I shall buy her an overpriced first-night present on Monday. Only one thing I *couldn't* dismiss. After I turned out the light, I thought she was asleep. 'Oh, yes! Even George Devine didn't like you. Do you know why? What he said about you? Because you were always being *sick*!'

2 JANUARY, OPERA HOUSE: I went to a party given for the Friends of Covent Garden. Intellectuals up from the shires and a very Penelope sort of occasion which I would normally have talked or rowed myself out of attending, but I had an incidental reason for going without argument. Robert Stephens had persuaded me to take the part of the Narrator in a crash tour of Stravinsky's *The Soldier's Tale.* He was playing the Devil, Derek Jacobi, whom I knew slightly from the National and liked, was the Soldier, and the Girl was Sally Gilpin, wife of the dancer John. The director was John Cox.

The venture consisted of three or four dates around Tyneside, ending up with a Sunday-night charity performance at the Royal Opera House. The thought of projecting up into the heavenly regions of that vast auditorium was daunting, and something most actors presently at the Court would find beyond their television-mike-trained capabilities. However, Robert's clownish gifts of persuasion won me over. Besides, it was another January and I could feel the noontime chill of midwinter casting its shadow over everything I confronted. The prospect of a.m. hours of hotel-lounge conviviality on the road again and in Robert's company was irresistible. Penelope's plain annoyance at a link with the life of my profession, which seemed to be claimed by a past no longer open to me, added conviction to my decision. It seemed worth risking my negligible reputation as a performer for the sake of a few nights of provincial touring-larks away from the sober constraints of Chester Square's intellectual life.

In the event, I did find rehearsals rather gruelling, which I decided was probably all the more effective as a chastening retort to my numb apprehensions of the Winter Blues. The conductor, an awesomely young, waspish Canadian Jew, who was administrator of the Northern Sinfonia and drove a splendid vintage Rolls, was a merciless disciplinarian. As I spluttered and stumbled, very aware of Robert's grinning relish, he would bang down his baton crossly. 'Mr Osborne, don't you recognize a *downbeat* when you see it?' 'Actually, I don't think I do. In fact, I don't. Perhaps you could give me a signal?' 'That's what I'm *doing!*'

On 17 January, I had a note from George:

6, Rossetti Studios
Flood Street

My dear boy,
Excuse the type-written letter. I was so delighted to receive a copy of

Patriot. I can't think of any better person to approach the grave with than Baron von Epp.

My best love.

On 19 January we organized a threesome train call and Robert, Jacobi and I had a merry journey up to Newcastle, where we booked in at the Station Hotel. I already wished the tour could go on for weeks. Our opening date was a late-afternoon performance at, I think, Middlesborough Town Hall, a severe Victorian building with the lofty air of a Methodist Chapel. The stage was little more than an open platform but the band made Stravinsky's harsh, hectoring music sound exciting. Robert was an ideal devil-comedian, Jacobi attractively bewildered, Mrs Gilpin performed prettily and the eager audience seemed delighted. Even Doctor Downbeat looked pleased.

We drove back happily in his Rolls to the hotel and I was more giddily and, yes, autonomously joyous than I had been for a very long time. We arranged to meet for a protracted evening of celebration, dinner and then whatever Newcastle after dark had to offer. There was a message from Mrs Gilliatt to ring her urgently. Not from Mrs Osborne. As I put the key in the door, the telephone was ringing. It was my wife, Mrs Gilliatt. 'Darling, I've been trying to get you all afternoon.' 'I've been giving my all to the burghers of Geordieland.' It was a world which excluded and even intimidated her. 'Your compatriots. They were very good, even if we weren't.' 'Darling – George is dead.'

I scarcely heard a word after that. She went on breathlessly, without pause; there was no need to respond. Presently, I became aware that her urgency was mounting as she kept reverently repeating the words *Observer* and its Arts Editor, Richard Findlater. Dragging up attention, I listened. They were *so* anxious that *I* should write George's obituary for the paper on Sunday. Could I do it? Could I? Did it matter? I couldn't write 'Wish you weren't here' on a postcard. I sensed she was becoming impatient with muddle-headed Johnny's sluggish grasp of the situation. This was the kind of professional contingency where her own critical, scalpel skills could bring some intellectual light to bear on an undoubted tragedy for the English theatre.

'Darling,' she said, like someone addressing a geriatric trundling a walking-frame, 'do you think you'll be able to manage it? I know how you must be feeling.' True, I had neither the detachment nor the skills, nor even, possibly, the grammar for the swift construction of a suitable prose tribute in a posh paper, the very phrase I had, in innocence, invented. 'I'll manage.' 'I mean, if you can't do it, everyone will understand. I'm sure Richard will.' Fuck Richard. 'But I do think it should be someone *close* and not just an outsider. Poor Georgie.' Fuck the *Observer*. Still getting no response from old muddle-brain, she persisted like a physiotherapist working on a recalcitrant limb. 'The thing is, darling ... would you like me to do it *for* you? I mean, I know it won't be the same, but George would understand.' How did she *know*? If George could point his pipe at some medium below, he would surely have chosen some other eager Madame Arcarti to interpret his 'understanding'.

'So what do you want me to do, what shall I say to them?' 'I'll do it.' 'Oh, are you really sure you can? It doesn't give you much time.' 'When do they want it?' 'About eleven at the latest. I could phone it through to the copytakers for you.' Yes, and tidy it up for the discerning *Observer* readership. 'What time does your train get in?' '8.15.' 'I'll have it ready.' 'Are you absolutely sure?' 'Yes.' 'Oh, darling. Poor, darling Georgie. Are you all right?' 'Yes.'

I ordered a bottle of whisky. It was early evening, I had about twelve hours to get my 900 words together and I needed all the aids I could get. I walked out into the night and soon found myself in darkened squares and narrow alleys. Wherever I was, it felt well above the tide and bitterly exposed to the rising sweep of icy air from the North Sea. I was wearing a thick overcoat and woolly scarf and have never felt so cold. Men were already reeling out of pubs and, caught in the light of street corners, streams of ale spewed on to the pavement. I had had no idea where I was going or what I should do next, but the streets were clearly going to become even colder and more hazardous. I remembered the days I had wandered in a daze of adolescent abandonment when Stella had left me to close the windows and turn off the electricity in Brighton. How soft and southern even that summer pain and beach breeze seemed compared to this scalding northern night.

I found myself outside a cinema, newly refurbished. It was showing *The Sound of Music* for the fifth month. In Newcastle. If only Woodfall could manage five months in a back-street picture palace. The box-office was closed but a young man and a girl were making up the evening's takings. Unable to sell me a ticket, they called a departing usherette and urged her to let me in. I don't know how I may have appeared to them but something made them act quickly and together, and all three hustled me inside. The usherette, a motherly seventeen, told me she had seen the film a hundred and twenty-three times and skilfully flashed a light on what must have been the only empty seat in the house.

For the next couple of hours I watched the trials of the unrelentingly brave Von Trapps climbing every mountain through eidelweiss and unstinting sorrow. I tried not to disturb the rapt couple beside me as I shook silently, shouting down the cry of loss with sounds alive to the tinsel of Hollywood music. My friends, to say nothing of the good readers of the *Observer*, might have been puzzled to witness England's angry not-so-young playwright sitting in a packed northern cinema watching Julie Andrews in alpine flight, blinded by tears.

I blundered out before they started the National Athem stampede, back into the night, dodging the vomit pools and broken glass. I hadn't eaten since breakfast but felt drained enough by tears and the Von Trapps to sit down with my whisky and a wedge of British Rail writing-paper and start scribbling my 'piece'. As always, a flicker of determination popped up from the flames of alcohol and that nauseous resolve that sometimes goes with it.

By eight o'clock in the morning, I had got down what I calculated in my amateurish way to be around 900 words. Fuck it – like *Luther*, or indeed anything else I had ever sweated over to the indifference of others, they were lucky to get it. So, even, was George. I began weeping again, but it was gone by the time Penelope appeared in the doorway, crabwise and concerned at about 8.30. She took in my fuddled condition at once and expectantly went through my scribbling. Whether it was more coherent than she expected I didn't know and was well past bothering. I lay on the bed and drifted into a painful sleep while she spoke to Findlater and then began the tedious process of dictating to the copytaker. It seemed to take hours and wasn't helped by her on-the-spot setting-to-rights of my personal syntax and punctuation. I thought them both superior to her own affectations, but protest in the face of dumb pedantry was beyond me. I wanted to disappear not proof-read.

With the lead given to her by the London to Newcastle timetable, Penelope was able to take over the arrangement of George's funeral. No one objected, including Jocelyn Herbert, who seemed glad to be relieved of the task of tasteful interment. As in her early days on *Vogue*, Penelope went at it as an inspirational challenge to 'creative enterprise'. Beneath the grim Golders Green towers of dispatch, it was a triumph of farce and circumstance. As Bill Gaskill said, none of us knew how to behave. Fortunately, the only decision I felt constrained to make was which suit to wear. I knew I could rely on Penelope to behave for me. Bill arrived at the crematorium with Keith Johnstone – and Sam Beckett in a taxi. All of them had forgotten the address. 'Hoop Lane', Beckett suggested.

> We waited in a dreadful little room until the door opened and a formally dressed figure beckoned us. It was Olivier, looking like an undertaker; he always knew how to transform himself. Inside we had to endure some boring piece of the *War Requiem* [Penelope's insistence], which seemed wholly inappropriate for George but it was not quite the thing to play the Modern Jazz Quartet, which we did later at a tribute on the stage of the Court. There was added tension because Sophie, George's wife, and

Jocelyn, his mistress, were both there and we felt that where we sat in the chapel was a declaration of our loyalties.

William Gaskill, *A Sense of Direction*, 1988

Three weeks later, Sophie Devine, designing a film for Polanski, was dead of cancer.

Something was most certainly over and irrecoverable, although even I was not yet aware of the bleak landscape that beckoned, or that loveless times would manifest themselves so swiftly and in such succession, and continue and consolidate for the best part of the next ten years. But I already knew that there would never be a place for me to start again. My Court days were over. It was clear enough as I walked away from the concrete and red roses of the crematorium. Yet I hung around Sloane Square, bereft of intent, for another decade or so before I was chucked out. 'Grateful as we are and mindful of your unique contribution to the theatre in general and this building in particular . . . '

On 17 February the House of Lords agreed to review one of the lesser contributors to George's death at fifty-five, the matter of stage censorship. A committee of enquiry was projected, with representatives from both Houses, to look into its application with 'regard to Law and Practice'. Along with Emile Littler, Peter Saunders, Kenneth Tynan and Peter Hall, I was invited to give evidence. The following day there was a memorial meeting, chaired by Lindsay Anderson with a skill I could not fault after his touching defence at George's farewell luncheon barely more than a year earlier. From the stage, I remember only two faces looking up from the stalls: the *Times* critic (what *could* he be doing there?) and Alec Guinness.

Ennismore Gardens Mews, sw7

Dear John Osborne,

I hope you won't feel this note an intrusion or an impertinence. I knew George fairly well for over thirty years, though of course not as intimately as you during the past decade, and I just wanted to tell you how beautifully you evoked him at the memorial meeting at the Court yesterday. All you said was riveting and pleasing and your choice of reading superb. I am sure it would have made George chuckle in that harsh voice as much as it touched many of us in the audience.

Alec Guinness

But there was committee-life after death, and on 8 April, I found myself in the cramped upstairs bar of the theatre announcing the institution of the

George Devine Award for Promising Playwrights. I managed to choke my way through that, and subsequently presented a fat cheque to some graceless recipient. Only the once.

For the past four years I had been encouraging Penelope to concentrate her creative yearnings for novel-writing and a stream of short stories and to suppress her obsession with the petty consolation of a weekly by-line. Suddenly, she agreed to take off a few weeks to write her first novel, *One by One*. I rented her a villa in Positano, from a reassuring figure in London's intellectual life; she packed her typewriter and books and was gone, leaving the departure lounge of Chester Square bare. Apart from my sporadic dalliance with J.B., which, like everything else, felt as if it were happening under water, there was little to do.

A short time passed and then, after a series of manic telephone calls, when she exploded as she had done at the Basilica in St Mark's, I decided I had better join her. When I arrived at Positano, she greeted me more effusively and more absorbed than ever. It was clear that, consumed with suspicion as she undoubtedly was, nothing could deflect her from the task of creation. The villa was comfortable and delightful, with a jolly Italian cook–maid to spare her any distracting chores and bring up the fuel to light the fire during the chilly evenings. Penelope spent all day and most of the evenings tapping at her machine. She said very little and was exceptionally secreetive over her manuscript, which she hid away at the end of each day's toil. I read, walked and listened to Dave Brubeck, which pleased her as she insisted on accepting it as a nostalgic tribute to our life together.

When it was time for me to return to London, she accompanied me on the headlong taxi-ride to Naples airport and said not a word. Her head was buried in the manuscript as she scribbled her corrections. She finished, quite literally, as we drew up at embarkation and thrust the script at me, barking simple instructions and kissing me in a kind of crippled passion. She returned to the cab and sped back to the creative eyrie over the Bay of Naples.

I don't remember the circumstances of her return to Chester Square. The summer of 1966 is all but lost to me.

At Easter in 1985, after watching *God Rot Tunbridge Wells*, an affectionate account of George Frideric Handel I had written for television, I looked at the quaintly peevish reviews of it in the Sunday papers, had a few more glasses of champagne and went into a prolonged coma. I emerged from it not cowed by the brush of the fearful angel's wing but angry and astonished at my determination not to go gentle into any good night in Tunbridge Wells or anywhere else. Unconscious in intensive care, I experienced a vivid succession of images that were comparable to the impressions I retained while more or less conscious during the summer of 1966. All I can retrieve of the cloud of events, scraps of a dream in illogical inconsequence, is the following:

Firstly: a physical, nursery brawl in Chester Square, while Penelope tried to prevent me dragging a suitcase down the staircase . . .

Escaping to the Park, finding a shady tree near the Albert Memorial and falling asleep with the suitcase as my pillow . . .

Then: rising in the early mornings, sitting alone downstairs in J.B.'s mews flat, drinking brandy from the bottle . . .

Seeing *Trelawny of the Wells* at the Old Vic, where J.B. had replaced another actress, and weeping not at her but at Pinero's lament for our calling ('What a rotten profession!') and at Robert Stephens's performance as Tom Robertson, most surely based on my own imminent degradation . . .

Lastly: having dinner at the Ivy with J.B., Svoboda, the most fashionable Czech stage-designer – all plunging staircases – Doris Lessing, who had adapted the play under discussion (Ostrovsky's *The Storm*), and Dexter, who was directing it at the peak of his energy in his early days at the National.

At some point I must have decided not to inflict on others whatever behaviour increasing oblivion was imposing on me. Knowing that the housekeeper in Sussex was away on holiday, I got myself down to Hellingly and settled in alone with my Great Dane, Western. There was plenty of tinned food in the kitchen, the house was warm and there was a wide selection of drink, although I confined myself to a hangover cocktail, recommended to me by Robin Fox, of iced Fernet Branca and *crème de menthe*. I drank it pre-emptively, obviating the in-between cause of hangover. Western curled up with me on the bed and must surely have slept for a very long time, although I know I did feed her once and she reluctantly went out for a pee.

Ringing Jocelyn R.: I must have because I saw her, beside the bed, with her new husband, looking down at me. I heard nothing. It was intensive care without wiring up.

Next: Penelope getting into bed beside me before driving me to this place, the Regent's Park Nursing Home, and kissing me on the forehead.

A very cheerful nursing sister kept giving me pills and urged me not to swallow too much water. A lanky psychiatrist, a night-club Jonathan Miller, came in now and then, palpably madder than I could be in whatever clinical extremity. He pumped Pentothal into me.

J.B. came, carefully got-up for the occasion and looking as concerned as she could manage but more honestly vexed and resentful. 'I wish *I* could afford a nervous breakdown . . . The psychiatrist thinks you should be married to a farmer's wife.' It didn't sound such a bad idea.

Tony came with the sort of book he thought might entertain a sickly blimp, *The Washing of the Spears*, a fascinating account of the Zulus' heroic resistance to the British Army, and a rather tame volume of erotic poetry. I was still in the thrall of Pentothal, Largactil and other little sweeties, and my insistent flow of chatter must have alarmed or bored him off smartly.

The day after my arrival, I suppose it was, a telegram arrived from Penelope postmarked Philadelphia. My muddle-headedness was only exacerbated by 'Philadelphia', celebrated for ever by W.C. Fields, to whom I was feeling close. The sister read it out to me in rotund Irish style:

SLEEP AND SLEEP STOP PRETEND THE NUNS ARE MEN IN DRAG STOP TAKE GREATEST CARE OF YOURSELF AND GAIN SPACE AROUND YOURSELF STOP MIKE IN HIS OWN WAY IN NEED OF MY LOVE AND SUPPORT HERE STOP WILL THINK OF YOU ALL THE TIME HOPE YOU ARE WELL AND NOT IN PANIC WITH ALL MY HEART – YOUR WIFE.

She followed Mike Nichols's pre-Broadway tour. The next prestigious date to be marked by another batch of telegrams was Boston, Mass. I can't remember the name of the play that necessitated her presence nor, indeed, if it was a palpable Broadway hit. It seems most likely. Anyway, I think that her telegrams from the real world helped my recovery and sent the neurologists packing.

In early September, Noël Coward invited – no, ordered me – to have supper, *à deux*, as he might have said. He was making his last and successful appearance in his own plays, *Suite in Three Keys*. I arrived promptly, I thought, after curtain-down. Coley opened the door. 'The Master is waiting,' he said. I was being reprimanded. Noël, however, was brisk and welcoming.

We had a simple but delicious soufflé and salad. He began to interrogate me, almost as if he knew I had been released so recently from the Bin. His second question was, 'How queer are you?' If I myself had small talent to amuse, I could at least make an effort to please. 'Oh, about twenty per cent.' 'Really! Are you? I'm ninety-five.' He went on. 'I understand you've been a very silly boy. You must never trust a woman.' 'But you've so many women friends,' I protested. More than I had. 'No matter. Never trust 'em and never, never marry them. Which you appear to do.'

His own tiredness and my weariness of such close confinement with myself for a whole summer prevented me from confiding in him. I excused myself and rose to go, feeling frail and afraid of the threatened effort of intimacy. He gave me my card of departure. 'You're *very* melancholy, aren't you?' 'Yes. Very. But I'm also sanguine when I'm able.' 'I'm glad to hear it.' He embraced me quickly and I left, grateful for his circumspection and, for once, my own.

Envoi

The prince of darkness is a gentleman . . .

> Edgar in William Shakespeare, *King Lear*, III. iv

Whatever else, I have been blessed with God's two greatest gifts: to be born English and heterosexual.

> *Notebook*, 1964

When Nolan was about six, Penelope was paying one of her rare visits to London from New York and, after a great deal of prolonged negotiation, agreed that I might come round to Chester Square and spend an hour or so in my daughter's company.

The nanny opened the door and ushered me upstairs to the airport lounge where Penelope was sprawled on the floor, much as she had been at our first unchaperoned encounters in Lowndes Square. With her was an Israeli film-director and they were going through a loud demonstration of young film-director being fired by distinguished critic-turned-writer Oscar nominee. Nolan was seated in a corner of the open-plan, L-shaped room and I tried to have some sort of conversation with her.

Penelope attempted to include me as a professional outsider privy to the problems presented by her script, which seemed to have something to do with life in England during the last war. Muttering something about only working when I was paid in advance, I felt I had endured enough crude humiliation, and took my leave.

She followed me to the front door, past the sixteen-foot-high copper doors to the dining-room which had cost me a ransom. As I said goodbye to her, her mouth slid to one side, the piercing brown of her eyes eclipsed into the black fury I had seen so often. 'Goodbye, then.' She raised her face to kiss me, drew back against the porch and contemplated me. 'You've really fucked your life up, haven't you?'

I walked past the Royal Court, down the Kings Road and back to J.B. It was hard not to agree with Penelope. There was no escaping from it. It was an irreversible judgement, the irrefutable evidence of a visible cirrhosis of my spirit.

> I will not refrain my mouth, I will speak in the anguish of my spirit, I will complain in the bitterness of my soul.
>
> Job, 7:11

I wanted to shout out and for someone to hear me. 'I am not yet dead.'

> Today I went for lunch at the Garrick. Leaning against the bar was a young man in his late twenties perhaps, not a member but a guest. He began asking me questions about myself and I made a slight effort to answer them politely. Finally, he stretched himself to his full height to follow his host-member downstairs to lunch and said very loudly, 'Of course, you *did* go through a bad patch, we know. However, I've no doubt you'll recover!'
>
> *Notebook*, 1972

Such certainty, like mediocrity, can be unbearably enviable. In particular, to a life overruled by passion.

Index

278